CATHOLIC SOCIAL TEACHING AND ECONOMIC GLOBALIZATION

THE QUEST FOR ALTERNATIVES

JOHN SNIEGOCKI

CATHOLIC SOCIAL TEACHING AND ECONOMIC GLOBALIZATION

THE QUEST FOR ALTERNATIVES

MARQUETTE
UNIVERSITY
PRESS

MARQUETTE STUDIES IN THEOLOGY
NO. 67
ANDREW TALLON, SERIES EDITOR

www.marquette.edu/mupress/

LIBRARY OF CONGRESS CATALOGING-IN-PUBLICATION DATA

Sniegocki, John, 1963-
Catholic social teaching and economic globalization : the quest for alternatives / by John Sniegocki.
p. cm. — (Marquette studies in theology ; no. 67)
Includes bibliographical references and index.
ISBN-13: 978-0-87462-744-2 (pbk. : alk. paper)
ISBN-10: 0-87462-744-3 (pbk. : alk. paper)
1. Christian ethics—Catholic authors. 2. Globalization—Religious aspects—Catholic Church. 3. Economics—Religious aspects—Catholic Church. 4. Christianity and culture. I. Title.
BJ1249.S56 2009
261.8088'282—dc22
2009031879

COVER DESIGN AND ART BY COCO CONNOLLY

∞ The paper used in this publication meets the minimum requirements of the American National Standard for Information Sciences—Permanence of Paper for Printed Library Materials, ANSI Z39.48-1992.

Association of American University Presses

MARQUETTE UNIVERSITY PRESS
MILWAUKEE

The Association of Jesuit University Presses

TABLE OF CONTENTS

LIST OF ABBREVIATIONS

CA = *Centesimus Annus*
CAFTA = Central American Free Trade Agreement
CELAM = Consejo Episcopal Latinomericano
CST = Catholic Social Teaching
CP = *The Challenge of Peace*
GS = *Gaudium et Spes*
EC = "The Ecological Crisis: A Common Responsibility"
ECLA = U.N. Economic Commission on Latin America
EJA = *Economic Justice for All*
FABC = Federation of Asian Bishops' Conferences
GATT = General Agreement on Tariffs and Trade
GDP = gross domestic product
GNP = gross national product
ILO = International Labor Organization
IMF = International Monetary Fund
ISI = import-substitution industrialization
JW = *Justice in the World*
LE = *Laborem Exercens*
MM = *Mater et Magistra*
NAFTA = North American Free Trade Agreement
NGO = non-governmental organization
NICs = newly-industrialized countries
NIEO = New International Economic Order
OA = *Octogesima Adveniens*
PP = *Populorum Progressio*
PT = *Pacem in Terris*
QA = *Quadragesimo Anno*
RN = *Rerum Novarum*
SAPs = structural adjustment policies
SRS = *Sollicitudo Rei Socialis*
TNCs = transnational corporations
UN = United Nations
UNDP = United Nations Development Programme
UNICEF = United Nations Children's Fund
UNRISD = United Nations Research Institute for Social Development
USAID = United States Agency for International Development
WTO = World Trade Organization

INTRODUCTION

> [I]f globalization is ruled merely by the laws of the market applied to suit the powerful, the consequences cannot but be negative. These are, for example, the absolutizing of the economy, unemployment, the reduction and deterioration in public services, the destruction of the environment and natural resources, the growing distance between rich and poor, unfair competition which puts the poor nations in a situation of ever increasing inferiority.[1] – Pope John Paul II

Debates concerning economic development and globalization reveal sharply different visions of our world. Proponents of current forms of globalization tend to speak in very positive terms, making bold promises about the future. They argue that dominant "neoliberal" policies of free trade, structural adjustment, and minimally regulated markets will result in high levels of economic growth throughout the world. This growth will in turn contribute to decreased levels of poverty and hunger. "A rising tide," these persons are fond of saying, "lifts all boats."[2] Critics of current forms of globalization, including Pope John Paul II, present a different perspective. They draw attention to many negative features of our global reality, such as sweatshop working conditions, the loss of land by small farmers, widespread hunger, the destruction of indigenous cultures, increased social conflicts, the growth of religious and ethnic fundamentalisms, and an array of severe ecological crises. According to these critics, current forms of economic globalization are deeply implicated in each of these problems.

This book will explore these debates over economic development and globalization. It will look at the deep roots of current policies and problems, exploring the impacts of colonialism, slavery, and the types of economic policies that were pursued after independence in

---

1 John Paul II, *Ecclesia in America*, no. 20.

2 For a detailed, critical discussion of the principles of neoliberal economics, see David Harvey, *A Brief History of Neoliberalism* (New York: Oxford University Press, 2005).

the countries of the so-called "Third World."[3] Free trade treaties and structural adjustment programs that have dominated global economic policy in the last couple decades will be examined as well. Particular attention will be given to the impacts of these policies on the poor, on women, on local cultures, and on the environment. The quest for constructive alternatives will also be explored, especially the many innovative and inspiring grassroots projects that exist throughout the world.

One very valuable resource for analyzing and responding to global justice issues is the body of thought known as "Catholic Social Teaching" (commonly abbreviated as CST). CST refers to a series of documents by Roman Catholic popes and bishops that address "social" issues such as economic justice, human rights, war and peace, and related themes.[4] The documents of the CST tradition, I will argue, provide much insight into the harmful aspects of economic development as it has been conventionally pursued. In particular, CST introduces the important idea of "integral development," which calls into question the equation of development with the maximization of economic growth. CST suggests instead that development should seek to foster the total well-being of the human person. This broader or more integral understanding of development requires that attention be given to all aspects of human life, including the social, cultural, ecological, moral and religious. Attempting simply to maximize economic growth, CST contends, may in fact undermine other central features of authentic

---

3 The term "Third World" is commonly employed to refer collectively to most of the countries of Latin America, Africa, and Asia. This term is sometimes criticized for overlooking vast diversity among the countries and for seeming to imply the inferiority of these countries within a ranked hierarchy. While sensitive to these critiques, I have not come across any alternative terminology that seems more adequate. By some persons the term "Third World" is used as a positive self-designation, as in the journal *Third World Resurgence*. It is in this positive sense that the term is employed in this book.

4 A compilation of most of the major CST documents can be found in David O'Brien and Thomas Shannon, eds., *Catholic Social Thought: The Documentary Heritage* (Maryknoll, NY: Orbis, 1992). For overviews of CST, see Donal Dorr, *Option for the Poor: A Hundred Years of Vatican Social Teaching*, rev. ed. (Maryknoll, NY: Orbis, 1992); Marvin Mich, *Catholic Social Teachings and Movements* (Mystic, CT: Twenty-Third Publications, 1998); Kenneth Himes, ed., *Modern Catholic Social Teaching: Commentaries and Interpretations* (Washington, DC: Georgetown University Press, 2005).

human flourishing. Another important contribution of CST is its emphasis on the problem of systemic injustice. CST strongly critiques existing concentrations of economic power and political power and highlights the many ways that these concentrations of power hinder the creation of more just alternatives.

OVERVIEW OF THE CONTEMPORARY GLOBAL CONTEXT: LIFE STORIES

There are many statistics that can be cited to illustrate the profound inequalities and injustices that characterize life for much of the world's population. It is estimated, for example, that approximately 1.4 billion people, over 20% of the world's population, live in the most extreme forms of poverty, on incomes of under $1.25/day. Approximately 2.6 billion people, nearly 40% of the world's population, live on under $2/day. These persons generally lack one or more vital necessities such as adequate nutrition, decent housing, proper sanitation, clean drinking water, basic education, or basic health care. This widespread deprivation occurs amidst global abundance. Current food production, for example, far exceeds what is needed for all to receive adequate nutrition, yet over a billion people are chronically hungry and malnourished.[5]

Statistics like these are shocking and should be profoundly disturbing to the Christian conscience and to the consciences of all persons of good will. Such statistics will be explored in much more detail later in this introduction. Before examining this data more closely, however, it seems important to first listen to the stories and testimonies of some of the persons whose daily realities lie behind these statistics. It is the failure to be attentive to this lived experience and the decision to instead rely on economic aggregates, such as GNP, that is at the heart of many of the world's problems.

RIGOBERTA MENCHÚ

Rigoberta Menchú is an indigenous woman from Guatemala who was awarded the Nobel Peace Prize in 1992 for her work on behalf of human rights. Menchú's life and testimony offer significant insight into

5 See Shaohua Chen and Martin Ravallion, "The Developing World is Poorer Than We Thought," World Bank Policy Research Working Paper 4703 (August 2008); Javier Blas, "Number of Chronically Hungry Tops 1 Billion," *Financial Times* (March 27, 2009), <http://www.commondreams.org/headline/2009/03/27-2>.

the realities of injustice in the Third World and provide an inspiring example of courage and commitment in the face of this injustice. Menchú emphasizes strongly that her story is not simply her own. It is rather, she says, "the story of all poor Guatemalans."[6]

Rigoberta Menchú grew up in the mountains in the Quiché region of Guatemala. It was there that her family farmed a small plot of marginal land. Because they could not grow enough food to survive, however, she and her family regularly had to migrate to work as hired labor on the large coffee and cotton plantations on the southern coast of Guatemala. Menchú tells of working twelve hour days on the plantations in horrendous conditions. The workers lived in large, unfurnished shacks, with up to 500 people in one large room. They were given very little food and often the food that they did receive was rotten. Workers were routinely mistreated in the fields. Even after working for several months in these conditions the workers would receive very little pay. These brutal conditions of plantation life took a harsh toll on many. Deaths of children due to malnutrition and pesticide poisoning were common. These experiences all had a profound impact on young Rigoberta:

> From then on, I was very depressed about life because I thought, what would life be like when I grew up? I thought about my childhood and all the time that had passed. I'd often seen my mother crying, although many times she'd hide because she'd never let us see when she was grieving....I hated [the plantations] because my friend

---

6 A testimonial of Menchú's early life is found in Elisabeth Burgos-Debray, ed., *I, Rigoberta Menchú: An Indian Woman in Guatemala* (London: Verso, 1984). The account begins: "My name is Rigoberta Menchú. I am twenty three years old. This is my testimony. I didn't learn it from a book and I didn't learn it alone. I'd like to stress that it is not only *my* life, it's also the testimony of my people....The important thing is that what has happened to me has happened to many other people too: My story is the story of all poor Guatemalans." (emphasis in original). While there has been some controversy as to whether Menchú herself directly experienced every event that she describes, the life conditions and events that she recounts are representative of the well-documented experiences of the indigenous communities of Guatemala. See, for example, Jonathan Moller, ed., *Our Culture is Our Resistance: Repression, Refuge, and Healing in Guatemala* (New York: PowerHouse Books, 2004); Beatriz Manz, *Paradise in Ashes: A Guatemalan Journey of Courage, Terror, and Hope* (Berkeley: University of California Press, 2004).

> died there and two of my brothers died there....This made me very angry and I asked myself what else could we do in life? I couldn't see any way of avoiding living as everyone else did, and suffering like they did. I was very anxious.[7]

In her teens Rigoberta worked as a maid for a wealthy family in the capital. She was treated with contempt, discriminated against both as an indigenous person and as a woman. She worked from morning to bedtime and often was verbally and physically abused. She contrasts the treatment she received with that of the family dog:

> The food they gave me was a few beans with some very hard tortillas. There was a dog in the house, a pretty, white, fat dog. When I saw the maid bring out the dog's food–bits of meat, rice, things that the family ate–and they gave me a few beans and hard tortillas, that hurt me very much. The dog had a good meal and I didn't deserve as good a meal as the dog. Anyway, I ate it, I was used to it. I didn't mind not having the dog's food because at home I only ate tortillas with chile [i.e. chili peppers] or with salt or water. But I felt rejected.[8]

When persons in Guatemala have worked to change the unjust conditions that exist, they have often been met with violence. Rigoberta's father, mother, and several of her brothers all were killed for their nonviolent work in defense of human rights, in most cases being severely tortured prior to death. Entire villages in the region where Rigoberta lived were massacred by the Guatemalan military.[9] Despite threats to her own life, Rigoberta courageously chose to continue her struggle for justice. She explains the forces that motivate her:

> Through all my experiences, through everything I'd seen, through so much pain and suffering, I learned what the role of a Christian in the struggle is, and what the role of a Christian on this Earth is....That is my cause....It wasn't born out of something good, it was born out of wretchedness and bitterness. It has been radicalized by

---

7 Burgos-Debray, *Rigoberta Menchú*, 88-89.

8 Ibid., 92.

9 Over 200,000 persons have been killed in Guatemala by the military and by paramilitary death squads associated with the Guatemalan government since a U.S.-sponsored coup installed a military dictatorship in 1954. For discussion of the coup and its aftermath, see Stephen Schlesinger and Stephen Kinzer, *Bitter Fruit: The Story of the American Coup in Guatemala*, rev. ed. (Cambridge, MA: Harvard University Press, 2005).

> the poverty in which my people live. It has been radicalized by the malnutrition which I, as an Indian, have seen and experienced. And by the exploitation and discrimination which I've felt in the flesh. And by the oppression which prevents us performing our ceremonies, and shows no respect for our way of life, the way we are. At the same time, they've killed the people dearest to me....Therefore, my commitment to our struggle knows no boundaries nor limits.[10]

Rigoberta Menchú's experiences are unfortunately representative of the experiences of many of the poor throughout the Third World. Tens of millions of people, for example, work seasonally as hired labor on large plantations in conditions similar to those described by Menchú. In Guatemala, as elsewhere in the Third World, the best land is concentrated in the hands of a few while many millions are without land or have inadequate land to support their families.[11] These disparities, which have deep roots in colonialism, have been significantly exacerbated in recent decades by development policies and free trade policies that have favored large landowners at the expense of small farmers.[12] Millions of additional persons in the Third World work as poorly treated domestic servants and in other jobs with poor pay and dehumanizing working conditions. A report of the U.S. Department of Labor highlights the plight of international child domestic workers:

> Millions of children – mostly young girls – work as domestic servants in Asia, Latin America, and Africa. The girls...are often subjected to horrendous working conditions, extended working hours, and physical and sexual abuse. They often wake up at dawn and do not go to sleep until after the rest of the family has retired. They often work seven days a week with no holidays and little leisure

10 Burgos-Debray, *Rigoberta Menchú*, 247.

11 For excellent discussion of land ownership in Guatemala and of the pressing need for land redistribution, see the pastoral letter of the Catholic Bishops of Guatemala, "The Cry for Land," in *And God Saw That It Was Good: Catholic Theology and the Environment*, ed. Drew Christiansen and Walter Grazer (Washington, DC: U.S. Catholic Conference, 1996), 275-293.

12 For discussions of the ways in which dominant economic policies have undermined small farmers throughout the world, see Jerry Buckland, *Ploughing Up the Farm: Neoliberalism, Modern Technology, and the State of the World's Farmers* (London: Zed Books, 2004); Peter Rosset, *Food is Different: Why We Must Get the WTO Out of Agriculture* (London: Zed Books, 2006).

> time or rest. Many are illiterate, and most are not permitted to go to school.[13]

Violence against those seeking social change, while varying in scope and intensity, has been common as well. As we will see, the implementation of development policies has often been accompanied by governmental violence intended to prevent or suppress resistance from those hurt by these policies.[14]

The life experiences of Rigoberta Menchú thus provide a window into certain broader realities of the Third World. The experiences of Sandra Arenal, Kali, Jun, Kabula, and Don Lito, described below, are likewise shared by many. Accounts of their experiences provide further insight into the life conditions of many of the world's poor in the aftermath of over a half century of conventional development policies and increased economic globalization.

SANDRA ARENAL

Sandra Arenal is a 22 year old woman working in a factory in a free trade zone of Mexico. Within the terms of the current development model, she is considered a fortunate person, for she has formal sector employment. Most of the Third World poor work instead in the informal sector of the economy, in jobs such as street vending, domestic service, day labor, or picking through the trash for items to eat or sell. The factory that employs Sandra–like many factories in free trade zones–hires mainly young women. These young women are generally considered to be the most docile labor force. Employees in these factories are subjected to long hours and receive low pay. Working conditions are often hazardous, including exposure to toxic chemicals and the use of dangerous machinery without adequate protection. Verbal and physical abuse is common, as is sexual harassment. Workers frequently develop illnesses or infirmities from the poor working conditions and the repetitive motions required in their work. When their performance is affected, they are fired or their contract is not renewed. Sandra, having worked six years in her factory, is one of the most long-term employ-

13 U.S. Department of Labor, *By the Sweat and Toil of Children*, vol. 2 (Washington, DC: U.S. Department of Labor, 1995), 2, 147.

14 For an overview of the use of repressive violence to prevent progressive social change in the Third World in the post-WWII era, see William Blum, *Killing Hope: U.S. Military and CIA Interventions Since World War II*, rev. ed. (Monroe, ME: Common Courage Press, 2004).

ees. Her hands, however, are deformed from working every day with a hot machine and she experiences much pain. She expects soon to lose her job. Millions of persons work in similar sweatshop conditions throughout the world.[15]

KALI

Kali is a nine year old girl in India. She has been working in a silk factory since the age of six. When her father died, her mother took out a loan to pay for the funeral. Kali was the collateral. She was sold into bonded servitude and is expected to work until the loan is repaid. She leaves home at 7 a.m., returning at 9 p.m. She earns about 3 cents per hour for her work. She and her mother do not earn enough to meet their daily living expenses, much less to repay the loan. Kali is one of tens of millions of debt slaves and one of approximately 250 million children who are forced to work long hours for economic survival.[16]

JUN

Jun is a fisherman in the Philippines. Like hundreds of thousands of persons in the Philippines and elsewhere, Jun has had his livelihood undermined by the activities of corporate-owned trawlers (huge, mechanized fishing boats). These trawlers overharvest the waters, leaving little for those fishing in a traditional manner. In order to continue to support his family, Jun began fishing with the use of dynamite, exploding part of the coral reef and then catching the fish that would

---

15 Sandra Arenal, "Blood Money," in the newsletter of the Los Angeles Catholic Worker (January 1993). For additional accounts of sweatshop working conditions, see Robert Ross, *Slaves to Fashion: Poverty and Abuse in the New Sweatshops* (Ann Arbor: University of Michigan Press, 2004); Andrew Ross, *Low Pay, High Profile: The Global Push for Fair Labor* (New York: New Press, 2004).

16 It is estimated that in South Asia alone there are 20-40 million boys and girls in debt servitude. UNICEF, *State of the World's Children 2000*, 20. Overall, there are about 250 million child laborers throughout the world – working long hours on farms and plantations, in factories and workshops, in domestic labor, selling items on the street, and in prostitution. UNICEF, *State of the World's Children 2006* (New York: UNICEF, 2005), 46. In-depth discussion of child labor can be found in U.S. Department of Labor, *Sweat and Toil of Children*. For a discussion of Kali and the problem of bonded child labor in India, see Human Rights Watch, *The Small Hands of Slavery* (New York: Human Rights Watch, 1996).

be dislodged by the explosion. He was aware that such measures were destroying the reef and its vital, delicate ecosystem, but felt he had no choice. One day, the dynamite exploded in Jun's hands. Jun amazingly survived the blast but lost both of his arms.[17]

KABULA

Kabula is a peasant in Tanzania. Because of her need for cash to pay taxes and to purchase essential items, she devotes a significant portion of her land to growing cotton. Cotton has been a favored cash crop of colonial and post-colonial development planners. Unfortunately, prices for cotton, as for most Third World cash crops, have been declining. The money Kabula receives for a year's harvest is not nearly enough to meet her needs. The continual growing of cotton as the dominant crop in the region has also been a major ecological disaster, undermining the fertility of the land and leading to widespread soil erosion and desertification.[18]

DON LITO

Don Lito is a displaced peasant from El Salvador. In his home village he was a leader of a base Christian community, a small group of people who met regularly to reflect upon their lives in the light of the Bible. Most of the members of Don Lito's community have been killed, victims of the Salvadoran military and paramilitary death squads' campaigns against those working for social change. Like Rigoberta Menchú, Don Lito speaks of faith, suffering, and his determination to continue in the struggle:

> We were nourished in that Christian community where we began, and now we feed on what we carry with us from those beginnings.... But if I have to explain how I keep going I would have to talk about the reality our country is living. Our people are living a permanent Calvary, twenty-four hours a day and all year long, every year. I already explained how the people suffer during the coffee harvest. Anyone who hasn't worked the harvest doesn't know what it is to suffer, you know? And it's the same in the cotton harvest and the sugarcane harvest. Here in the city, if we went to the poorest neighborhoods, what you'd see is a lot of people dying of anemia. You'd

17 See the account of Jun in Belinda Coote, *The Trade Trap: Poverty and the Global Commodity Markets* (Oxford: Oxfam, 1992), 14-16.

18 See the account of Kabula in ibid., 1-13.

see the sidewalks converted into people's living places....When you see things like that, how could you ever stop struggling, stop being ready to help out?

No, there's no excuse for taking a step back. It's pitiful, us being campesinos and not having land to work, when we're people from the countryside. I dream of my beanfields, my cornfields, my hens....We all dream of returning to the countryside....We're going to implement the kind of life that Christ wants–sharing our bread, like Rutilio Grande said, a common table with a big tablecloth for everyone....There will be cooperatives....We're not thinking individualistically anymore–we're thinking in terms of the community. That's why we want to return to our homes, to live a completely different way of life.[19]

AN ABUNDANCE OF OTHER STORIES:

Rigoberta Menchú, Sandra Arenal, Kali, Jun, Kabula, and Don Lito are just a few of the people whose experiences lie behind the statistics concerning the world's poor. A vast number of additional stories could be told.[20] Many of these stories reveal similar patterns. In the countryside, they tell of large numbers of people who have been dispossessed of their land by violence or who have had their livelihoods undermined by the impact of conventional development policies and free trade. Some of the dispossessed remain in rural areas, working mainly for low wages as hired labor on large plantations. Most dispossessed persons migrate to urban areas, like Don Lito. There they typically join the rapidly growing numbers of persons who inhabit the large, sprawling shantytowns on the outskirts of Third World cities. Conditions in these poor urban communities are generally very un-

19 Cited in María López Vigil, *Don Lito of El Salvador* (Maryknoll, NY: Orbis, 1990), 102-103. Rutilio Grande, mentioned by Don Lito, was a Roman Catholic priest from El Salvador who was murdered for his work on behalf of the Salvadoran poor. Grande's murder is often cited as a turning point in the life of Archbishop Oscar Romero. See James Brockman, *Romero: A Life* (Maryknoll, NY: Orbis, 2005).

20 For some additional first-hand testimonies of the world's poor, see Deepa Narayan and Patti Petesch, eds., *Voices of the Poor: From Many Lands* (New York: Oxford University Press, 2002); Christine Kovic, *Mayan Voices for Human Rights* (Austin: University of Texas Press, 2005).

healthy and insecure.[21] Residents often lack access to basic services such as sanitation and clean, affordable water. These unsanitary conditions facilitate the spread of disease, which malnourished children and the elderly are often unable to resist. Problems of crime, domestic violence, alcoholism, and broken families are also common in these communities, though so too are many examples of loving solidarity in the face of adversity.

Income possibilities for the urban poor are found largely in the informal sector of the economy. The highly capital-intensive production fostered by conventional development policies produces relatively few formal sector jobs. Many poor persons therefore seek to earn their living as domestic servants, street venders, day laborers, trash pickers, or, with increasing frequency, prostitutes.[22] The "luckier" poor get jobs in factories like that of Sandra Arenal. The most desperate are forced to make heart-wrenching choices, such as that made by Kali's mother in selling Kali into bonded servitude.

Edna Orteza of the Philippines highlights movingly some of the daily realities and choices encountered by the world's poor:

> What does it mean to be poor? It means gnawing pain in the stomach after a day without meals. It means eating a boiled banana and saving the peel for the night. It means back-breaking labor to bring home a kilo of rice. It means watching your children die because you could not feed them enough.
>
> Being poor means not being able to send your children to school because they, too, have to work – exposed to the elements, weeding, planting, harvesting, tapping rubber trees or peddling cigarettes and flowers in dangerous places and at busy intersections of city streets. It means growing up in ignorance in order to survive.

---

21 Good descriptions of life in urban shantytowns in the Third World can be found in Mark Kramer, *Dispossessed: Life in Our World's Urban Slums* (Maryknoll, NY: Orbis Books, 2006); Mike Davis, *Planet of Slums* (London: Verso, 2006); Duncan Green, *Faces of Latin America*, 3rd ed. (London: Latin American Bureau, 2006), 104-116.

22 Prostitution is one of the "growth industries" in the age of economic globalization. Even children are being forced into prostitution in alarming numbers. It is estimated that about 2 million children work in the global sex industry. UNICEF, *State of the World's Children 2005*, 26. Also see Gilbert King, *Woman, Child for Sale: The New Slave Trade in the 21st Century* (New York: Chamberlain Bros., 2004).

> Being poor means living daily with the threat of eviction, of waking up one morning to find your house being bulldozed, the walls which, together, your family has painfully put up, breaking into pieces. And then you realize you have nowhere to go.
>
> Poverty alienates. It drives people to make impossible choices. It means women selling their bodies to support starving families; parents selling the 'favors' of their children...; mothers leaving their own children to care for other mothers' babies, often abroad, to earn a few dollars; fathers enduring loneliness [working overseas] to send their children to school; young people going into drugs to escape their daily realities.[23]

DATA ON POVERTY, HUNGER, AND INEQUALITY IN AN AGE OF GLOBALIZATION

The above life stories and reflections provide some insight into the enormous human tragedies of poverty, hunger, violence, and discrimination. Unfortunately, these life stories don't represent isolated examples. They are part of much larger patterns of experience. The statistics that follow provide further evidence of how widespread these conditions are.

One of the main promises that has been made by proponents of development and of economic globalization is that these processes would eliminate, or at least greatly reduce, poverty and hunger. Despite unprecedented economic growth over the past few decades, however, hunger and poverty continue on a vast scale. Approximately 1.4 billion people (over 20% of the world's population) live in "extreme" or "absolute" poverty, on an income of under \$1.25/day.[24] Approximately 2.6 billion people live on under \$2/day.[25] Over 1 billion people (more than 1/7 of the world's population) are estimated to be chronically malnourished. This number has risen by over 150 million between 2006 and 2009 and does not yet account for the full negative impacts of the current global economic crisis.[26] Approximately 1/3 of preschool age children in the Third World are malnourished. Over 10.5

23 Edna Orteza, "The Elusive Quest for Development," in *Rice in the Storm: Faith in Struggle in the Philippines*, ed. Rebecca Asedillo and B. David Williams (New York: Friendship Press, 1989), 58-59.

24 Chen and Ravallion, "Developing World," 19.

25 Ibid., 32. Also see UNDP, *Human Development Report 2007/2008*, 25.

26 Blas, "Number of Chronically Hungry."

million children under the age of five die each year (about 29,000/day or one child every three seconds), overwhelmingly from preventable causes.[27] Many other persons lack basic necessities such as clean water, decent housing, sanitation, and access to adequate health services and education. James Gustave Speth, former administrator of the United Nations Development Programme, estimates that about half of the global population lives in "deplorable" conditions in which some of these fundamental needs are unmet.[28]

During the past couple decades many persons in the Third World have in fact experienced a worsening of living conditions.[29] In sub-Saharan Africa, for example, levels of hunger and poverty have risen considerably. The number of persons chronically hungry in the region more than doubled between 1970 and 1990.[30] This problem of hunger has continued to intensify in the period from 1990 to the present, as can be seen in studies of child malnutrition undertaken by UNICEF.[31] During the 1990s the number of persons living in extreme poverty in sub-Saharan Africa rose by approximately 20%.[32] Currently nearly half of the population lives in extreme poverty, on incomes of under

---

27 UNICEF, *State of the World's Children 2006*, 20.

28 Speth's comments, made at a press conference in Geneva, are summarized in the magazine *Development and Cooperation* (July/August 1996): 33. Globally, approximately 1.1 billion people lack access to safe drinking water and 2.6 billion lack basic sanitation. UNDP, *Human Development Report 2006*, 2. Approximately 800 million people are illiterate. Two-thirds of those who are illiterate are women. UNDP, *Human Development Report 2005*, 20.

29 For discussion of increased levels of hunger, increased child mortality rates, and decreased life expectancy experienced in numerous countries during the 1990s, see UNDP, *Human Development Report 2003*, 2. "For many countries," the report states, "the 1990s were a decade of despair."

30 Bread for the World in its 1996 World Food Day report states that the number of chronically hungry people in sub-Saharan Africa increased from 103 million in the years 1969-71 to 215 million in 1990-92. As a percentage of total population, the increase was from 38% to 43%. Similar figures are given in UNDP, *Human Development Report 1998*, 50.

31 UNICEF, *Progress for Children: A Report Card on Nutrition* (New York: UNICEF, 2006), 6.

32 John Madeley, *A People's World: Alternatives to Economic Globalization* (London: Zed Books, 2003), 272.

$1/day. This number increased by over 100 million between 1990 and 2001.[33]

In Latin America the 1980s and 1990s also witnessed significant deterioration of living standards for many. Between 1980 and 1990 the total number of poor persons in Latin America increased by about 45%.[34] During the 1990s the number of persons living in extreme poverty continued to rise slightly.[35] The early 2000s saw some improvements with regard to poverty (in part due to newly elected governments that were willing to challenge dominant neoliberal economic policies), but the global economic crisis of the past few years has undermined many of these gains.[36] Much of the overall increase in poverty in the last three decades has been due to the impact of the Third World debt crisis and the imposition of structural adjustment policies on Third World nations, topics that will be discussed extensively in subsequent chapters. As we will see it has been the poor, especially poor women and children, who have suffered most.

Even within wealthy industrialized countries such as the United States problems of poverty and hunger, though less extreme than in the Third World, are widespread. 12.3% of the population of the U.S., including approximately one in six children, lived below the poverty line in 2006.[37] An estimated 35.1 million people in the U.S. (about 11% of households) are "food insecure," according to the U.S. Department of Agriculture.[38] Approximately 47 million people in the U.S.

---

33 UNDP, *Human Development Report 2005*, 34.

34 Rolph van der Hoeven and Frances Stewart, "Social Development During Periods of Structural Adjustment," in R. Buitelaar and P. van Dijck, eds., *Latin America's New Insertion in the World Economy* (New York: St. Martin's Press, 1996), 129.

35 The rise in the number of persons living in extreme poverty (on under $1/day) in Latin America in the 1990s is documented in UNDP, *Human Development Report 2003*, 5.

36 "Latin America Poverty 'May Soar,'" BBC News (February 7, 2009), <http://news.bbc.co.uk/2/hi/americas/7876169.stm

37 U.S. Census Bureau, 2007. Excellent first-hand accounts of poverty in the U.S., along with analysis, can be found in D. Stanley Eitzen and Kelly Eitzen Smith, *Experiencing Poverty: Voices from the Bottom* (Belmont, CA: Thomson Wadsworth, 2003).

38 For the latest data on hunger in the United States and thoughtful analysis, see the website of the Food Research and Action Center at <www.frac.

lack health insurance. Millions lack adequate housing.[39] Thus, even in the nation often viewed to represent the pinnacle of current development models, many basic needs go unmet.

These high levels of poverty and hunger that exist both globally and in the U.S. are not due to a lack of resources. This is a crucial point. It was highlighted earlier and will be stressed repeatedly throughout this book. With regard to food, as we have seen, global production is presently far above what is needed to provide everyone alive with an adequate diet. Even in regions with especially abundant food production, many people go hungry. Latin America, for example, according to data from the United Nations, produces approximately three times as much food as is needed for its population, but yet 15-20% of the population remains seriously malnourished.[40] Globally it is estimated that the world produces enough to provide everyone alive with several times what is needed for a healthy diet.[41] The fundamental cause of hunger is not scarcity but rather economic and political structures that deprive the poor of the ability to produce their own food or to purchase food that is for sale. Consequently, highly disproportionate amounts of food go to the world's wealthy. The wealthy are able to consume such a disproportionate share of the world's food resources mainly due to their high levels of meat consumption. In order to produce meat, massive amounts of grains, beans, and other foods are fed to livestock. This conversion of vegetable products into meat is a very inefficient process. It takes, for example, approximately 12-16 pounds of protein in the form of grain fed to cows to produce a single pound of beef protein. The remainder of the protein (over 90%) is lost to human consumption. Similar percentages of other nutrients (vitamins, minerals, etc.) are also rendered unavailable. In this manner the world's meat-eating wealthy use highly disproportionate amounts

---

org>. Also see Loretta Schwartz-Nobel, *Growing Up Empty: The Hunger Epidemic in America* (New York: HarperCollins, 2002).

39 The U.S. Census Bureau estimates that 47 million people in the United States lacked health insurance in 2006. Data on homelessness in the U.S can be found at <www.nationalhomeless.org>.

40 United Nations, *The Millennium Development Goals: A Latin American and Caribbean Perspective* (Santiago, Chile: United Nations, 2005), 71.

41 See Frances Moore Lappé, Joseph Collins, and Peter Rosset, *World Hunger: Twelve Myths*, rev. ed. (New York: Grove Press, 1998), 8-14.

of the world's agricultural resources. Meanwhile, the world's poorest persons go hungry and often die from malnutrition-related causes.[42]

Inequitable distribution of the world's food resources is but one example of the staggering inequalities that exist in our world. Many statistics documenting these disparities could be cited. The United Nations Development Programme, for example, estimates that the wealthiest 500 people in the world receive as much income each year as the poorest 416 million people added together.[43] The total wealth of the world's 225 richest people is estimated to equal the combined annual income of nearly half of the world's population.[44] And of course it is not only billionaires who are privileged in the world economy. The 20% of the global population living in the world's richest countries is responsible for a hugely disproportionate share of the world's consumption – approximately 86%, according to the United Nations. A comparable number of people living in the poorest countries account for only 1.3% of overall consumption.[45] In other words, a person in the top 20% consumes on average over 60 times as much of the world's resources as a person in the bottom 20%.

As we will see, Catholic Social Teaching views such extreme levels of inequality to be morally intolerable. Pope Paul VI put the matter very bluntly in his 1967 encyclical *Populorum Progressio*:

> It is well known how strong were the words used by the Fathers of the Church to describe the proper attitude of persons who possess anything towards persons in need. To quote St. Ambrose: "You are not making a gift of your possessions to the poor person. You are handing over to him what is his. For what has been given in com-

42 For discussion of the inefficiency of meat-based diets, along with their impacts on ecology, human health, and animal welfare, see John Robbins, *The Food Revolution: How Your Diet Can Help Save Your Life and the World* (Berkeley, CA: Conari Press, 2001). Sally Kneidel and Sara Kate Kneidel, *Veggie Revolution: Smart Choices for a Healthy Body and a Healthy Planet* (Golden, CO: Fulcrum, 2005).

43 UNDP, *Human Development Report 2005*, 4.

44 UNDP, *Human Development Report 1998*, 30. The specific figure given is that the net wealth of the richest 225 people is equal to the combined annual income of the poorest 47% of the world's population. Because many of the world's poorest have negative net wealth (i.e. they are in debt), the total wealth of the 225 richest far exceeds the total wealth of the poorest half of the world's population.

45 Ibid., 2.

> mon for the use of all, you have arrogated to yourself. The world is given to all, and not only to the rich." That is, private property does not constitute for anyone an absolute and unconditioned right. No one is justified in keeping for his exclusive use what he does not need, when others lack necessities.[46]

Connected with massive inequality as both cause and consequence of present crises are skewed global priorities. The amount of money devoted to military expenditures provides perhaps the clearest evidence of this. Even in the post-Cold War era military expenditures remain enormously high, having surpassed $1.1 trillion per year in 2005.[47] The United States now spends nearly as much on the military as do all the rest of the world's nations combined, accounting for 48% of global military spending while constituting only about 5% of the world's population.[48] Annual worldwide spending on military purposes is equivalent to more than three times the combined annual income of the world's poorest billion people.[49] It is over 13 times the amount that UNICEF estimates would be needed to meet the basic needs of all the persons in the world whose most fundamental needs (for food, clean water, sanitation, basic health care and basic education) are not now being met.[50] In other words, according to UNICEF, reducing world military spending by about 8% and transferring those funds to social spending could (if the money is spent wisely) virtually eliminate extreme poverty and hunger and lead to dramatic reductions in child mortality and illness around the world.

---

46 Pope Paul VI, *Populorum Progressio*, no. 23.

47 For the latest figures on global military spending, see the website of the Stockholm International Peace Research Institute (SIPRI) at <www.sipri.org>.

48 According to SIPRI, U.S. military spending in 2005 accounted for approximately 48% of total world military spending. No other country is responsible for over 5%. Most of the other largest spenders are U.S. allies.

49 If the poorest billion persons live on under $1/day, as UNDP figures assert, then the total annual income of these billion persons would be under $365 billion per year ($365/person maximum multiplied by a billion people). Thus, world military expenditures of over $1.1 trillion are more than three times the annual income of the poorest billion people.

50 UNICEF estimates that about $80 billion in additional funds per year could assure that the basic needs of all (or nearly all) are met. *State of the World's Children 2001*, 56-57.

The contrast between military spending and spending to meet the needs of the poor is one that is frequently made in Catholic Social Teaching documents. Pope Paul VI states: "When so many people are hungry, when so many families suffer from destitution...when so many schools, hospitals, and homes worthy of the name remain to be built, all public or private squandering of wealth...every exhausting armaments race, becomes an intolerable scandal. We are conscious of our duty to denounce it."[51] Similarly, the Second Vatican Council condemned high levels of military spending as "an utterly treacherous trap for humanity, and one that injures the poor to an intolerable degree."[52]

Comparisons with other forms of spending can also be made. UNICEF, for example, has estimated that the amount of funds needed to provide adequate nutrition, clean water, sanitation, primary education, and basic health services to all in the Third World who lack these necessities is less than the world spends annually playing golf, less than half of what is spent annually on wine, and less than a third of the amount spent each year on cigarettes.[53] A recent United Nations report states that the funds needed each year to ensure clean water and basic sanitation for every person in the world is less than the amount that Europeans spend on perfume. It is less than the amount spent each year in the United States on elective cosmetic surgeries.[54] These comparisons make clear how relatively little of the world's resources would need to be shifted to the poor for the elimination of severe forms of poverty to be accomplished. In its *Human Development Report 2005* the United Nations Development Programme estimates that a transfer of about 1.6% of the annual income of the world's wealthiest 10% of persons would be enough to eliminate extreme poverty throughout the world.[55]

The hypothetical availability of needed funds is of course not enough to assure that basic needs are met. There must also be deep political commitment to the meeting of these needs and widespread

51 Pope Paul VI, *Populorum Progressio*, no. 53.

52 Second Vatican Council, *Gaudium et Spes*, no. 81.

53 The UNICEF comparisons can be found in UNICEF, *State of the World's Children 1995*, 59.

54 The amount needed, according to the United Nations Development Programme, is about $7 billion/year. UNDP, *Human Development Report 2005*, 93.

55 Ibid., 4.

participation of the poor themselves in the design and implementation of effective projects. Nonetheless, as UNICEF asserts, to claim that the world cannot afford to meet the basic needs of all is "plainly absurd."[56] The issue, says UNICEF, is not one of possibilities but of priorities.

In addition to the continued existence of widespread poverty, hunger, and inequality, mention must also be made of the profound ecological degradation that has occurred in the past several decades in both the wealthy countries and in the Third World. This has included severe problems of deforestation, desertification, soil erosion, declining soil fertility, toxic contamination of soil, air, and water, the depletion of groundwater supplies, ozone depletion, and global warming, among others. According to some scientists, these ecological problems may call into question the future possibilities for human life on earth.[57] As we will see throughout this book, social injustice and ecological degradation are very closely intertwined phenomena, each reinforcing the other.

THE GOALS AND STRUCTURE OF THIS BOOK

The basic thesis of this book is that the widespread existence of poverty, inequality, and environmental degradation throughout the world demonstrates the need for fundamental changes in both global and domestic policies. Included in these changes will be a rethinking of what is meant by "development." Current forms of neoliberal economic globalization unfortunately serve in many ways to perpetuate rather than overcome the flaws of past development policies. Alternatives, however, are possible. These alternatives are being worked for in many inspiring and courageous ways by people at the grassroots level around the world. The tradition of Catholic Social Teaching can be a valuable resource in the quest for these alternatives. CST can also itself

---

56 UNICEF, *State of the World's Children 1995*, 60.

57 For extensive information concerning environmental issues, see the annual *State of the World* reports issued by the Worldwatch Institute. For an excellent overview of the connections between ecology and social justice, see Patrick Hossay, *Unsustainable: A Primer for Global Environmental and Social Justice* (London: Zed Books, 2006). For one prominent scientist who warns of impending catastrophe for humanity unless major changes occur, see James Lovelock, *The Revenge of Gaia: Earth's Climate Crisis and the Fate of Humanity* (New York: Basic Books, 2006).

be further enriched through dialogue with others who are pursuing constructive alternative paths.

This book consists of seven chapters. Chapter One provides a brief overview of economic development theory and policy in the post-WWII era. It examines some of the major schools of thought in development studies and identifies some key development debates. Chapter Two takes a more in-depth look at Third World history, with particular attention to Latin America and Sub-Saharan Africa. This chapter seeks to discern some of the major factors responsible for the problems that Third World countries currently face. Chapter Three presents Catholic Social Teaching on development issues, situating CST within the context of broader development discussions. Chapter Four explores neoconservative and radical critiques of CST. These critiques focus especially on issues of structural injustice and social analysis. Neoconservatives argue that the emphasis placed upon structural injustice in CST is fundamentally misguided. Radicals in contrast assert that this emphasis is very insightful, but contend that awareness of structural injustice in CST is inconsistently applied. I argue that the radical critiques of CST contain crucial insights and suggest several ways that CST could be further strengthened by integrating these insights into its own analysis. Chapter Five presents the views of a growing number of grassroots critics of development, with special attention to the writings of Indian social theorist and activist Vandana Shiva.[58] As in the previous chapter, I suggest ways that CST could be further strengthened through dialogue with these critics. I also suggest ways that these critics of development overcome some weaknesses present in the radical perspective. Chapter Six examines some of the main components of possible alternatives to present development/globalization policies, drawing especially upon the insights of the radical political economists and grassroots activists highlighted in the preceding two chapters. Finally, Chapter Seven takes a deeper look at some of the fundamental ethical and theological themes of CST. While earlier chapters include suggestions for the enhancement of CST, it is in this

58 Among Vandana Shiva's numerous works are *Earth Democracy: Justice, Sustainability, and Peace* (Cambridge, MA: South End Press, 2005); *Stolen Harvest: The Hijacking of the Global Food Supply* (London: Zed Books, 2001); *Monocultures of the Mind: Perspectives on Biodiversity and Biotechnology* (Penang, Malaysia: Third World Network, 1993); *Staying Alive: Women, Ecology, and Development* (London: Zed Books, 1989).

chapter that these ideas are explored most systematically. In particular, I suggest the need for deeper structural analysis of capitalism, greater attention to the role of women in economic development and in the formulation of CST, deeper attention to ecological and cultural issues, and heightened awareness of the importance of grassroots social action in the implementation of CST and in the creation of development/globalization alternatives. The book then concludes with exploration of practical ways that each of us can contribute to this quest for alternatives, followed by some theological reflections on the nature of Christian discipleship in our suffering world.

CHAPTER I

DEVELOPMENT THEORY AND PRACTICE: AN OVERVIEW

The past sixty years have rightly been called "the age of development."[1] For the richer countries development has been viewed as a goal already achieved. For the poorer nations it has been held out as a future promise. This chapter provides a brief history of development thought and practice in the period since World War II. An awareness of this background history will be helpful in understanding and appreciating the views of Catholic Social Teaching on development issues that will be explored in subsequent chapters.

ORIGINS OF THE CONCEPT OF DEVELOPMENT

The contemporary notion of development has deep roots in 18th and 19th century discussions of "progress." The idea of progress, originating mainly in Europe and North America, provided a framework in which the highly disruptive social transformations being brought about by capitalism, industrialization, and urbanization could be interpreted in a positive light.[2] Grand claims in fact were made about where these changes were leading. The influential philosopher Condorcet, for example, promised that the transformations that were underway would lead ultimately to "the destruction of inequality...and finally, the real perfecting of mankind."[3] For many persons devotion to progress took on quasi-religious characteristics, becoming a type

---

1 Wolfgang Sachs, Introduction to *The Development Dictionary: A Guide to Knowledge as Power,* ed. Wolfgang Sachs (London: Zed Books, 1992), 1.

2 For an historical overview of the concept of progress in western thought, see Robert Nisbet, *History of the Idea of Progress* (New Brunswick, NJ: Transaction Publishers, 1994).

3 Marquis de Condorcet, "An Historical Picture of the Progress of the Human Mind," in *The Idea of Progress: A Collection of Readings,* ed. F. Teggart (Berkeley: University of California Press, 1949), 337.

of secularized faith.[4] Even critics of the impact of capitalism such as Karl Marx accepted the positive role that innovations in science and technology and the spread of capitalist markets were playing, viewing them as necessary steps (albeit containing some very regrettable components) on the path to yet further progress through a transition to socialism.

The inaugural speech of U.S. President Harry Truman on January 20, 1949 was a pivotal event in the rise to prominence of "development" language in public discourse. In this speech the links between development and the older notion of progress are clear. Truman spoke of the need for "a bold new program for making the benefits of our scientific advances and industrial progress available for the improvement and growth of underdeveloped areas....What we envisage is a program of development...."[5] This usage of the terms "underdeveloped areas" and "development," relatively unknown at the time, would thereafter become commonplace. Critics argue that these new terms served to obscure the cultural richness of the world's poorer countries. "All the treasure trove of diverse human cultures," C. Douglas Lummis laments, was "defined as the wretched and pitiable condition of 'underdevelopment.'"[6]

The concepts of development and underdevelopment would serve many purposes in U.S. policy and intellectual life in the coming decades, shaping the lens through which most U.S. citizens would view their relationship to the majority of the world's peoples. Emphasis on development provided a comforting understanding of the United States as a nation at the top of a social evolutionary scale, a nation worthy of emulation. This prosperity-centered vision of development was also presented to the countries of the Third World as an attractive alternative to socialism. The leaders of the United States, says Wolfgang Sachs, "launched the idea of development with a call to every nation to follow in their footsteps."[7]

4 For a discussion of progress as a "distinctly modern faith", see José María Sbert, "Progress," in *Development Dictionary*, 192-205.

5 Harry S. Truman, "Inaugural Address." Cited in Gustavo Esteva, "Development," in *Development Dictionary*, 6.

6 C. Douglas Lummis, "Equality," in *Development Dictionary*, 45.

7 Sachs, Introduction to *Development Dictionary*, 1.

MODERNIZATION THEORY

The concept of development highlighted by President Truman was quickly taken up and further refined by persons in the fields of economics, sociology, and political science. From the work of these persons emerged the "modernizationist" paradigm of development. The core assertion of modernizationist theory is that development necessitates for the undeveloped nations a radical break with the past and the replacement of traditional values and forms of social organization and production with "modern" institutions, technologies, and cultural values. Among the most important of modern cultural values are greater individualism, economic initiative, and an increased desire for material goods.[8] This need for a radical break with the past is well summarized by modernizationist theorist J.L. Sadie:

> Economic development of an underdeveloped people...is not compatible with the maintenance of their traditional customs and mores. A break with the latter is a prerequisite to economic progress. What is needed is a revolution in the totality of social, cultural, and religious institutions and habits, and thus in their psychological attitude, their philosophy and way of life.

Sadie acknowledges the socially disruptive aspects of such all-encompassing change, yet he argues that it is nonetheless essential:

> What is...required amounts in reality to social disorganization. Unhappiness and discontentment in the sense of wanting more than is obtainable at any moment is to be generated. The suffering and dislocation that may be caused in the process may be regrettable, but appears to be the price that has to be paid for economic development, the condition of economic progress.[9]

Similar views were expressed by many others, often without any expression of regret at the disruption caused. Modernizationist theorist C. E. Ayres boldly asserts:

---

8 For overviews of the modernizationist approach to development, see S.C. Dube, *Modernization and Development: The Search for Alternative Paradigms* (Tokyo: United Nations University, 1988); Alvin Y. So, *Social Change and Development: Modernization, Dependency, and World-Systems Theories* (Newbury Park, CA: Sage, 1990).

9 J.L. Sadie, "The Social Anthropology of Economic Underdevelopment," *The Economist Journal* 70 (1960): 302.

> The arbitrary authority and irrational values of pre-scientific, pre-industrial cultures are doomed....Industrial society is the most successful way of life mankind has ever known....At the height of the technological revolution we are now living in a golden age of scientific enlightenment and artistic achievement.[10]

Among economists, the person who had the most significant impact on development thinking and U.S. development policy in the early postwar period was Walt W. Rostow. Rostow's best-known book, *The Stages of Economic Growth: A Non-Communist Manifesto,* set forth a broad alternative to Marxist visions of history.[11] Rejecting the dialectical views of Marx, Rostow presented an understanding of the development of societies as a linear progression through a series of stages, beginning with "traditional" forms of society and subsistence economies and culminating in what Rostow terms the "age of high mass consumption." In this process modern political institutions and capitalist economic institutions would be put into place and the most "advanced" First World technologies would be adopted. For Rostow and other modernizationist economists, the central goal of development was the achievement of high levels of economic growth. This growth, it was assumed, would over time benefit all members of society, though it was understood that in the short-run increased inequality might be required to facilitate the accumulation of funds by the wealthy for investment.[12] These modernizationist economists envisioned the state as having a central role to play in the development process. Among its important responsibilities were development planning, the creation of incentives for investment, the undertaking of major infrastructural projects, and the provision of education and training.

---

10 C.E. Ayres, *The Theory of Economic Progress* (New York: Schocken Books, 1962), xxiv-xxv.

11 Walt W. Rostow, *The Stages of Economic Growth: A Non-Communist Manifesto* (Cambridge: Cambridge University Press, 1960).

12 Such views are often expressed by appeal to the "Kuznets hypothesis." Kuznets argued that in the process of economic growth there has been an historical tendency for inequality first to rise, then to level off, and ultimately to decrease. See Simon Kuznets, "Economic Growth and Income Inequality," *American Economic Review* 45, no. 1 (March 1955): 1-28.

MODERNIZATION THEORY AND U.S. AID POLICY

During the 1950s and 1960s the United States was by far the major supplier of international development aid, both directly and through multilateral institutions such as the World Bank. Influenced by modernizationist views, this aid was concentrated largely on capital-intensive industrialization projects, large-scale infrastructure projects such as highways and dams, technical training, the education of Third World elites in the First World, and the creation of a modern bureaucratic state and capitalist economic institutions.[13] The approach to development was very top-down, with little or no participation in the design of projects by those who would be affected by them.

In the wake of the Cuban Revolution in 1959, changes in U.S. policy took place. Increased emphasis began to be placed on military aid and training along with encouragement of limited social reform, both intended to avert revolutionary upheavals. These dual emphases are clearly seen in U.S. policy toward Latin America in the 1960s. Economic aid provided through the Alliance for Progress program initiated by President Kennedy in 1961 was accompanied by escalating U.S. involvement in equipping and training Latin American military forces. The reform aspects of the policy, however, were rather short-lived. As social tensions continued to increase, in part due to the very limited nature of the reforms deemed acceptable by the U.S. government and by local elites, the military dimensions of U.S. policy came to predominate. By the late 1960s, states development historian Jan Knippers Black, "social reform as an objective ceased to enjoy even rhetorical currency" in official U.S. circles. Aid was increased shifted to military and security support and general budgetary assistance to bolster friendly regimes.[14] Increasingly, the U.S. became actively involved in supporting military governments known for massive human rights violations, often taking a central role in overthrowing democratically elected reformist governments and installing repressive military regimes in their place (as in Brazil in 1964 and Chile in 1973) or intervening militarily on behalf of repressive regimes to prevent their ouster (as in the Dominican Republic in 1965 and in South Vietnam

---

13 For a good history of U.S. aid policy, see Jan Knippers Black, *Development in Theory and Practice: Bridging the Gap* (Boulder: Westview Press, 1991).

14 Black, *Development in Theory and Practice*, 51.

throughout the 1960s). At the same time, the nature of economic aid changed as loans increasingly replaced grants and funds that were provided were tied ever more tightly to strategic considerations or to measures benefitting U.S. corporations, such as requirements that the funds be used to purchase U.S. products or services.[15]

THE IMPACT OF MODERNIZATIONIST DEVELOPMENT

By the mid-1960s it was becoming increasingly apparent that development as it had been pursued was causing significantly increased hardship for poor majorities in the Third World.[16] Benefits of the large-scale infrastructural projects went largely to local elites and foreign corporations, while the poor were often displaced by them. Highly capital-intensive methods of industrial production created relatively few jobs, while often putting large numbers of local artisans out of business. Efforts to modernize agriculture, such as the Green Revolution with its emphasis on the importation of the latest First World technologies, led to increased concentration of rural landholdings, less need for labor, and dispossession and displacement of the rural poor.[17] Often land was taken over by multinational agribusiness corporations. Not only were the poor majorities becoming worse off in relative terms compared to tiny wealthy minorities (which modernizationist theorists argued might be necessary), but in fact they were often becoming worse off even in absolute terms. The report of a 1969 U.N.-sponsored meeting highlighted the urgent need for concern: "The fact that development either leaves behind, or in some ways even creates, large areas of poverty, stagnation, marginality, and actual exclusion

---

15 Ibid., 52.

16 For discussion of the impacts of conventional development policies, see Patrick Hossay, *Unsustainable: A Primer for Global Environmental and Social Justice* (London: Zed Books, 2006); John Cavanagh and Jerry Mander, eds., *Alternatives to Economic Globalization: A Better World is Possible*, 2nd ed. (San Francisco: Berrett-Koehler, 2004); David Korten, *When Corporations Rule the World*, 2nd ed. (San Francisco: Berrett-Koehler, 2001); The Ecologist, *Whose Common Future? Reclaiming the Commons* (Philadelphia: New Society Publishers, 1993); Vandana Shiva, *Staying Alive: Women, Ecology, and Development* (London: Zed Books, 1989).

17 For discussion of the impact of the Green Revolution, see Frances Moore Lappé, Joseph Collins, and Peter Rosset, *World Hunger: Twelve Myths*, 2nd ed. (New York: Grove Press, 1998), 58-84.

from social and economic progress is too obvious and too urgent to be overlooked."[18]

A series of important studies served to confirm the negative impacts of the modernizationist development policies that were being pursued. The most well-known are the studies made of income shares in 43 non-communist Third World countries in the 1950s and 1960s conducted by Irma Adelman and Cynthia Taft Morris.[19] Adelman and Morris found that as economic growth proceeded in these countries (and most countries did experience significant levels of aggregate growth during this time), the share of income going to the bottom 60% of the population consistently decreased. Even more disturbing, they found that not only the share of income but also the very amount of real income of the bottom 40-60% generally decreased as well. Thus, they reached the conclusion that many of the poor were being further impoverished rather than achieving greater economic security as a consequence of conventional capitalist development processes. "The results of our analyses came as a shock to us," Adelman and Morris stated, for they had previously accepted standard economic wisdom about the trickle-down benefits of economic growth.[20] This study by Adelman and Morris is frequently cited as a landmark work in the development literature.[21]

Additional studies subsequently supported Adelman and Morris' basic findings. Summarizing in a 1978 article in *World Development* the results of a series of studies which they undertook in Asia, Keith Griffin and Azizur Rahman Khan state:

> Development of the type experienced by the majority of Third World countries in the last quarter century has meant, for very large numbers of people, increased impoverishment....Certainly there is no evidence that growth as such has succeeded in reducing the incidence of poverty....Indeed, the evidence from the case studies points to an even stronger conclusion. In almost every

18 United Nations, "Report of the 1969 Meeting of Experts on Social Policy and Planning." Quoted in Esteva, "Development," 13.

19 Irma Adelman and Cynthia Taft Morris, *Economic Growth and Social Equity in Developing Countries* (Stanford: Stanford University Press, 1973).

20 Ibid., viii.

21 See for example the comments of Charles Oman and Ganeshan Wignaraja, *The Postwar Evolution of Development Thinking* (New York: St. Martin's Press, 1991), 113.

> case a significant portion of low-income households experienced an absolute decline in their real income....[22]

In light of these realities of deepening poverty and increased human rights abuses, prevailing modernizationist development policies began to be the target of strong criticisms. The most prominent of the critics were those persons espousing views that came to be known as "structuralism" and "dependency theory."

STRUCTURALIST ECONOMIC THEORIES

The structuralist school of economic thought came into existence in Latin America in the late 1940s and 1950s under the leadership of Raul Prebisch and other persons associated with the United Nations Economic Commission for Latin America (ECLA).[23] The fundamental cause of the lack of development in poorer countries, according to the structuralists, is that the economies of these "peripheral" nations were shaped by colonialism to be oriented to the provision of low cost products for export to the First World ("center") nations, rather than being oriented to meeting domestic needs and fostering processes of internally generated economic growth. In order to facilitate development, structuralists argued that fundamental structural changes were required in peripheral economies, particularly greater industrialization and a greater focus on production to meet local needs.

With respect to the necessity of industrialization, structuralist views largely coincided with the modernizationist theories discussed above. In their inward-oriented economic focus and views on trade, however, the structuralists sharply differed from the modernizationists. Whereas modernizationists like Rostow generally accepted classical economic arguments concerning the benefits of free trade (i.e. the claim that all countries benefit from maximizing trade between nations), the structuralists argued that the benefits of trade in conditions of significant inequality go disproportionately to the stronger nations.

22 Keith Griffin and Azizur Rahman Khan, "Ugly Facts and Fancy Models: Poverty in the Third World," *World Development* 6:3 (1978): 295-304. Reprinted in abridged form in *Poverty Amidst Plenty*, ed. Edward Weisband (Boulder: Westview, 1989). The quotation can be found on page 64 of the Weisband volume.

23 For overviews of structuralist thought, see Hunt, *Economic Theories of Development*, chapter 5; Oman and Wignaraja, *Postwar Evolution of Development Thinking*, chapter 5.

In their policy proposals, they placed great emphasis on the strategic use of tariffs to protect domestic industries and to lessen demand for goods imported from the center.[24] Instead, local demand would be met mainly by local production.

DEPENDENCY THEORIES

Structuralist notions such as the distinction of center and periphery played an important role in various dependency theories that originated in the mid-1960s. Dependency theorists, however, were sharply critical of other aspects of structuralist thought. This included the structuralists' rather benign view of capitalism and their rather optimistic views concerning the ability and willingness of local elites to challenge First World economic interests by implementing nationalist development strategies that would benefit local poor majorities.

While there existed a diversity of views among dependency theorists (especially concerning the necessity of violent revolution), these theorists shared much in common[25] All agreed, for example, that the modernizationist approach to development was fundamentally flawed in analysis and prescription. "Attempts to analyze backwardness as a failure to assimilate more advanced models of production or to modernize," asserts Theotonio Dos Santos, "are nothing more than ideology disguised as science."[26] Third World nations, dependency theorists argued, were not in a "primitive" state of *un*development waiting to develop in a process similar to that of the already industrialized capitalist economies. Instead, they were in a state of *under*development caused precisely by their structural interactions with the already developed economies. Dos Santos states:

---

24 Among peripheral nations themselves, greater regional integration and less restricted trade were seen as goals to be pursued. Regional integration was seen as a way of being better able to take advantage of economies of scale in industrial production, contributing to greater specialization and efficiency.

25 For overviews of dependency thought, see Hunt, *Economic Theories of Development*, chapter 7; Oman and Wignaraja, *Postwar Evolution of Development Thinking*, chapter 5.

26 Theotonio Dos Santos, "The Structure of Dependence," in *The Theoretical Evolution of International Political Economy: A Reader*, ed. G. Crane and A. Amawi (Oxford: Oxford University Press, 1991), 151.

> We see that the alleged backwardness of these economies is not due to a lack of integration with capitalism but that, on the contrary, the most powerful obstacles to their full development come from the way in which they are joined to this international system and its laws of development.[27]

Dependency theorists highlighted numerous mechanisms by which underdevelopment was said to be perpetuated. These included unequal terms of trade (e.g. declining prices for Third World commodities such as coffee, sugar, bananas, cotton, etc. in relation to First World industrial goods), interest payments on foreign debt, profit repatriation by foreign businesses, and the control exercised by multinational corporations over technology, shipping, and marketing.

In addition to being critical of modernizationist views, dependency theorists were also highly critical of the economic policies that were pursued in Latin America during the 1950s and 1960s under the influence of the structuralists. These policies are generally referred to as "import substitution industrialization" (ISI). The dependency theorists argue that these ISI policies, while well-intentioned, served in practice to cater to the interests of local elites. Only the elites could afford to purchase significant amounts of industrial goods, and thus local industry became oriented to meeting their demand for luxury products rather than producing basic goods needed by the poor. The dependency theorists stressed that an ISI strategy could only have broadly beneficial results if it was accompanied by a fundamental redistribution of wealth and the adoption of more labor-intensive methods of production. Among the policies favored by dependency theorists were substantive land reform, increased taxation of the wealthy, greater local control over the activities of multinational firms, and increased technological autonomy that would be fostered by state investment. Increased regional cooperation and solidarity was also emphasized as a way to counter the economic and military power of the First World, particularly the United States. Changes in the international economic order, such as higher prices for Third World products, were called for by many dependency theorists as well, though more radical dependency theorists stressed the need for socialist revolution and delinking from the international capitalist system.

27 Ibid.

BASIC NEEDS APPROACH

Dependency theory helped to publicize the increased levels of poverty and inequality that were being experienced throughout most of the Third World. This awareness gave rise to new perspectives on development among some of the more mainstream members of the development community as well. The most prominent of these perspectives was the "basic needs" approach.

Basic needs theorists rejected excessive reliance on trickle-down approaches to development. Instead of waiting for the rising tide to lift all boats, they argued that major investments should be made by the state to directly and immediately improve the lives of the poor. This investment should be concentrated in areas such as nutrition, education, safe water, sanitation, and housing. While the heart of the basic needs approach is ethical, i.e. the claim that society has a moral obligation to meet the basic needs of its members, proponents have also sought to make their case in terms of economic efficiency.[28] Arguing against the conventional economic wisdom which claims that a necessary trade-off exists between equity and economic growth, basic needs proponents assert that meeting basic needs in fact has a growth-enhancing effect. This is the case because better educated and healthier workers are more productive, because an emphasis on basic needs creates increased demand for locally-produced, labor-intensive products (thus stimulating the local economy), and because an emphasis on grassroots participation entails the active mobilization of previously underutilized human and natural resources.[29] It is argued also that

28 Helpful overviews of basic needs approaches can be found in Hunt, *Economic Theories of Development*, chapter 9; Oman and Wignaraja, *Postwar Evolution of Development Thinking*, chapter 4. Countries that are often highlighted for their efforts to implement basic needs strategies include China, Cuba, Tanzania, and Sri Lanka, as well as the Indian state of Kerala.

29 The claim that increased equity necessarily entails slower economic growth is based on the assumption that the wealthy have a greater propensity to productively invest their resources than do the poor. This assumption is challenged by basic needs proponents who point out that the wealthy often spend their money on luxury goods, deposit it in accounts overseas (capital flight), or engage in speculative rather than productive investment. They also highlight the fact that when small-scale credit is made available to the poor, it is generally employed in productive ways.

the meeting of basic needs would help to lower excessive population growth rates, with positive economic and social consequences.[30]

NEW INTERNATIONAL ECONOMIC ORDER

Along with this emphasis on basic needs, a movement also arose in the early 1970s calling for a New International Economic Order (NIEO). Originating within the nonaligned movement of Third World nations, the NIEO proposal was formally adopted as a non-binding framework for action by the Sixth Special Session of the UN General Assembly in 1974 and was incorporated into the UN Charter of Economic Rights and Duties of States later that same year.[31] Included in the proposed reforms were measures to stabilize and increase prices for Third World commodities. Also included were calls for increased levels of development aid, reductions in foreign debt, the adoption of an international code of conduct for multinational corporations, and increased voting rights for Third World nations in multilateral institutions such as the International Monetary Fund and the World Bank.

After the NIEO was adopted by the UN General Assembly, negotiating processes were established with the goal of reaching binding agreements on the specifics of reform and on the procedures of implementation. During the negotiations, the First World nations (especially the United States[32]) refused to agree to substantive reforms. By the early 1980s, with the rise of the debt crisis and a significantly weakened and less unified Third World, the issue largely disappeared from discussion.

30 This assertion is based on the view that key factors contributing to high birth rates are economic insecurity and the inferior social status of women. As basic needs are met and social guarantees put in place, and as women become educated and more willing to assert their rights, birth rates tend to fall substantially. For more information, see Lappé, Collins, and Rosset, *World Hunger*, chapter 3.

31 For discussions of the NIEO, see Björn Hettne, *Development Theory and the Three Worlds: Towards an International Political Economy of Development*, 2nd ed. (New York: Wiley, 1995), 119-120; Oman and Wignaraja, *Postwar Evolution of Development Thinking*, 110-111.

32 For a discussion of United States opposition to the NIEO, see Hettne, *Development Theory*, 119.

ALTERNATIVE DEVELOPMENT

In addition to reform efforts centered on basic needs and the NIEO, the 1970s also saw calls for a more fundamental rethinking of the nature of development. Among the distinguishing features of this "alternative development" approach are a positive appreciation of traditional cultures, a recognition of the importance of non-material dimensions of life (e.g. community, spirituality), strong emphasis on ecology, and a view of participation that extends to participation in discernment concerning the very nature of the development to be pursued. In this approach the industrialized west is not viewed as a model to be emulated, nor is the industrialized east. Rather, each society must be free to pursue development based on its own resources, traditions, and values. Much emphasis in placed on the need for "appropriate technology." Sufficiency for all is stressed, rather than the pursuit of maximum economic growth. Important figures influencing this strand of thought include Gandhi and his views concerning village-based development in India, as well as E.F. Schumacher's views on Buddhist economics and appropriate technology as set forth in his 1973 book *Small is Beautiful: Economics as if People Mattered.*[33] This approach, as we will see, shares much in common with Catholic Social Teaching.

THE IMPACT OF REFORMIST THOUGHT ON DEVELOPMENT POLICY

The ideas of the basic needs, NIEO, and alternative development approaches had a significant impact on debates about development. They had only limited impact, however, on actual development policy. While the language of basic needs, for example, came to be adopted in the late 1970s by the World Bank, studies reveal that the Bank's policies in this period were not substantively different from earlier modernizationist policies.[34] With regard to development aid provided by the United States government, reformist ideas also had some im-

33 E.F. Schumacher, *Small is Beautiful: Economics as if People Mattered* (New York: Harper and Row, 1973). An overview of thinking on alternative development can be found in Hettne, *Development Theory,* 160-206.

34 Extensive discussion of World Bank projects can be found in Michael Goldman, *Imperial Nature: The World Bank and Struggles for Social Justice in the Age of Globalization* (New Haven, CT: Yale University Press, 2005); Catherine Caufield, *Masters of Illusion: The World Bank and the Poverty of Nations* (New York: Henry Holt and Co., 1996); Bruce Rich, *Mortgaging*

pact in the 1970s, though again more on stated policy than on actual practice.[35] In 1973, in reaction to the increased militarization of U.S. aid that prevailed in the late 1960s and in response to the new reformist thought, Congress passed several "New Directions" amendments. These amendments were intended to reorient U.S. aid toward meeting basic human needs. While some funding was shifted to these purposes, however, the overall impact was minimal. The "new directions" called for by the amendments, argues Jan Knippers Black in her history of U.S. aid policy, "were never more than marginal" to the aid policies implemented.[36]

NEOLIBERAL RESURGENCE AND STRUCTURAL ADJUSTMENT POLICIES

The 1980s witnessed a resurgence of neoliberal economic thought.[37] Fundamental principles of neoliberalism include the primacy of markets and stress on the benefits to be gained from free trade. Intervention by the state in economic policy (in the form of development planning, the operation of state-owned enterprises, the use of protective tariffs, and similar measures) is rejected as economically inefficient. These neoliberal principles were embraced especially by the Reagan administration, the IMF, and the World Bank. Using the leverage provided by the Third World debt crisis, the IMF and the World Bank began to require the implementation of "structural adjustment policies" (SAPs) in Third World countries. Among the required policies

---

the Earth: The World Bank, Environmental Impoverishment, and the Crisis of Development (Boston: Beacon Press, 1994).

35 One notable exception has been the work of the Inter-American Foundation, a U.S. government agency which began operations in 1972. This small agency, independent of the State Department, has provided small loans and grants to organizations representing the poor and has "consistently pursued a course that might be called liberational, or empowering." Black, *Development in Theory and Practice*, 190. A sister organization, the Inter-African Development Foundation, was established by Congress in 1980 and began operations in 1984. Only a tiny percentage of U.S. aid funds, however, are channeled through these two organizations.

36 Black, *Development in Theory and Practice*, 55.

37 For an overview of the neoliberal (or "neoclassical") paradigm, see John Toye, *Dilemmas of Development: Reflections on the Counter-Revolution in Development Economics*, 2nd ed. (Oxford: Blackwell, 1993), especially chapters 3 and 4.

were a prioritization of exports, the reduction or elimination of tariffs, decreased social spending by the state, cutbacks in government employment, the elimination of subsidies and price controls (including those pertaining to public transportation and to basic foods for the poor), privatization of government-owned enterprises, and decreased regulation of transnational corporations.

These structural adjustment policies, critics claim, have had devastating consequences on the Third World poor, causing significant increases in hunger and poverty. According to UNICEF, they have contributed to the deaths of millions of children.[38] Widespread opposition to SAPs has arisen at the grassroots level and among nongovernmental organizations that work with the poor. Many of the social tensions that now exist in Third World nations are centered on the impacts of these policies. Various alternatives to SAPs have been proposed. Some alternatives have begun to be implemented, especially in several Latin American countries. All of these issues will be discussed in much more detail in the next chapter.

CURRENT DEBATES IN DEVELOPMENT STUDIES

The resurgence of neoliberal thought, the reality of increasing economic globalization, and the demise of state socialism in Eastern Europe have all played key roles in precipitating a crisis within conventional development theory.[39] The root of the crisis lies in the perception that there currently exists very little room for national governments to implement independent policies, due to their utter dependence on global capital. Colin Leys states:

> The era of national economies and national economic strategies is past – for the time being, at least. With capital free to move where

38 For excellent discussion of the impact of SAPs, see Structural Adjustment Participatory Review International Network (SAPRIN), *Structural Adjustment: The Policy Roots of Economic Crisis, Poverty, and Inequality* (London: Zed, 2004).

39 This sense of crisis is reflected in the titles of some recent works in the development field, such as Colin Leys, *The Rise and Fall of Development Theory* (Bloomington, IN: Indiana University, 1996). Since the early 2000s, however, increased hope has arisen that alternatives to neoliberalism are indeed possible. See, for example, Gary Dmyski and Silvana de Paula, eds., *Reimagining Growth: Towards a Renewal of Development Theory* (London: Zed Books, 2005).

> it wishes, no state (and least of all a small poor one) can pursue any economic policy that the owners of capital seriously dislike. Economic planning, welfare systems, and fiscal and monetary policies all became subject to control, in effect, by the capital markets, signalled, in the case of Third World countries, by the conditions attached to IMF/World Bank lending....It is hardly too much to say that by the end of the 1980s the only development policy that was approved was not to have one – to leave it to the market.[40]

In addition to confronting these powerful constraints on policy, development analysts have come to a greater appreciation of the complexity of issues involved in development, and for this reason have generally abandoned the idea that any single theory can have conceptual adequacy. Increasing emphasis has been placed on the notion of "development studies" as opposed to "development theory" in recognition of this complexity.

Despite these increasingly eclectic approaches to development, however, certain broad schools of thought can still be identified. There is the neoliberal approach, which continues to dominate official policy. There is also a reformist approach centered upon basic needs, represented for example in the publications of UNICEF and the United Nations Development Programme (UNDP).[41] In the Latin American context there has emerged a school of thought known as neostructuralism, which seeks to build upon past structuralist insights while avoiding some its weaknesses.[42] Among more radical perspectives, a prominent position is occupied by "world-systems" analysis, which incorporates some of the insights of dependency theory. These analysts argue that global capitalism in its current form has reached a crisis state. In the course of the next 50-100 years a new international system

---

40 Leys, *Rise and Fall of Development Theory*, 23.

41 See UNICEF's annual *State of the World's Children* and the United Nations Development Programme's annual *Human Development Report*. Also see Giovanni Andrea Cornia, ed., *Inequality, Growth, and Poverty in an Era of Liberalization and Globalization* (New York: Oxford University Press, 2004).

42 See Osvaldo Sunkel, ed., *Development From Within: Toward a Neostructuralist Approach to Latin America* (Boulder: Lynne Reiner, 1993); Cristóbal Kay and Robert Gwynne, "Relevance of Structuralist and Dependency Theories in the Neoliberal Period: A Latin American Perspective," in *Critical Perspectives on Globalization and Neoliberalism in the Developing Countries*, ed. Richard Harris and Melinda Seid (Boston: Brill, 2000).

will gradually emerge, either worse or better than the present one depending upon the outcome of social struggles.[43] In a similar vein there have also arisen "neo-populist" approaches to economic development and globalization whose goal is to shape globalization processes from the bottom-up in ways that protect the rights of workers, consumers, and the environment.[44] At the grassroots level many nongovernmental organizations seek to foster alternative development strategies that are participatory, ecologically sound, and culturally sensitive.[45] At the same time, there have arisen increasingly vocal opponents of the very concept of "development," which these persons deem to be too closely associated with westernization to be salvageable as a concept even when preceded by a string of adjectives like "participatory" and "sustainable."[46] The views of these critics of development will be the focus of Chapter Five.

During the past two decades a series of important international conferences related to development issues have taken place, including the World Summit for Children (New York, 1990), U.N. Conference on Environment and Development (Rio de Janeiro, 1992 – also known as the Earth Summit), U.N. Conference on Population and Development (Cairo, 1994), U.N. World Conference on Women (Beijing, 1995), the World Food Summit (Rome, 1996), the Millennium Summit (New York, 2000), the World Summit on Sustainable Development (Johannesburg, 2002), and the 2005 World Summit (New York, a follow-up to the Millennium Summit), among others. The official declarations of these conferences have incorporated a contradic-

43 See especially the works of Emmanuel Wallerstein, including *World Systems Analysis: An Introduction* (Durham: Duke University Press, 2004). An overview of world systems theory can also be found in So, *Social Change and Development*.

44 The term "neo-populist" is used by Hettne, *Development Theory*. One work exemplifying this neo-populist perspective is Jeremy Brecher and Tim Costello, *Global Village or Global Pillage: Economic Reconstruction from the Bottom Up*, 2nd ed. (Cambridge, MA: South End Press, 1998).

45 For overviews of these grassroots efforts see Cavanagh and Mander, *Alternatives to Economic Globalization*; Tom Mertes, ed., *A Movement of Movements: Is Another World Really Possible?* (London: Verso, 2004); Paul Ekins, *A New World Order: Grassroots Movements for Global Change* (New York: Routledge, 1992); Jeremy Seabrook, *Pioneers of Change: Experiments in Creating a Humane Society* (London: Zed Books, 1993).

46 See especially Sachs, *Development Dictionary*.

tory mixture of perspectives. On the one hand, principles highlighted by proponents of alternative development are frequently affirmed, e.g. the importance of basic needs, grassroots participation, human rights, ecological sustainability, and strengthening the status of women. At the same time, the documents express support for neoliberal economic policies. The neoliberal policies, critics persuasively argue, serve to directly undermine many of the laudable goals that the conferences have rhetorically adopted. At most of these conferences only non-binding suggestions are deemed acceptable, especially by the world's most powerful nations. These suggestions are subsequently often not implemented. The 1996 World Food Summit, for example, adopted a goal of reducing the number of chronically hungry people in half by 2015. It provided no additional funding, however, and secured no firm commitments to the far-reaching reforms that would be needed to truly achieve this goal. Similarly, the U.N. Millennium Conference of 2000 adopted the very inspiring Millennium Development Goals (MDGs). Among these goals are cutting extreme poverty and hunger in half, reducing under-5 child mortality by two-thirds, achieving universal primary education, and significantly increasing access to safe drinking water by the year 2015. Much of the world, however, has fallen seriously behind in making progress toward these goals. According to the United Nations Development Programme's *Human Development Report 2005*, "the overall report card makes for depressing reading. Most countries are off track for most of the MDGs."[47] At the 2005 World Summit, convened as a follow-up to the Millennium Summit, the United States' ambassador to the United Nations, John Bolton, actually proposed eliminating all references to the Millennium Development Goals. He also repudiated promises that had been repeatedly made by the United States and other wealthy nations to increase foreign aid to 0.7% of GNP. The United States only currently gives about .16% of GNP (less than 1/4 of the promised 0.7%), vying with Italy for the lowest percentage among the donor nations. Among other suggestions made by Bolton was the removal of all references to "corporate accountability," "respect for nature," and the need for affordable AIDS medicines. U.S. economist Jeffrey Sachs, director of the U.N.

47 UNDP, *Human Development Report 2005*, 2. For an in-depth update on progress toward meeting the Millennium Development Goals, see the U.N. Millennium Project, *Investing in Development: A Practical Plan to Achieve the Millennium Development Goals* (New York: Millennium Project, 2005).

Millennium Project, expressed exasperation at the U.S. position. "The United States government," Sachs lamented, "has fought a relentless battle to dissociate itself from specific obligations regarding international development, and has tried repeatedly to quash obligations that it has taken on in the past....In the end, every specific target and timetable to help the world's poorest of the poor has come under U.S. fire." "Why the U.S. government is so dead-set against doing more to help impoverished and dying people," Sachs declares, "is one of the great mysteries of our time."[48]

Despite the limited policy changes associated with these international summits, many would argue that these meetings have nonetheless played several positive roles. First, they have succeeded in raising global consciousness concerning crucial development and globalization issues. Secondly, they have provided an important opportunity, especially in the form of unofficial parallel conferences, for the strengthening of linkages among grassroots activists and organizations from throughout the world. It is with these grassroots organizations and their ongoing growth and networking, many believe, that the best hope for positive change lies. These grassroots efforts will be discussed extensively in later chapters.

---

48 Jeffrey Sachs, "The US Fight Against the Fight Against Poverty," *Financial Times* (September 13, 2005). See <www.commondreams.org/views05/0913-21.htm>.

CHAPTER 2

THE FAILURES OF MODERNIZATIONIST DEVELOPMENT: A CLOSER LOOK

The preceding chapter provided a brief overview of the history of development thought and policy over the past 60 years. Among the theories highlighted were the modernizationist and neoliberal approaches that have dominated global economic policy since WWII. Also discussed were some of the reformist and revolutionary approaches that have arisen in response to the perceived failure of these dominant economic models. One fundamental area of disagreement between the dominant approaches and their challengers concerns the extent to which systemic injustice is responsible for the widespread poverty, inequality, and ecological degradation that exists in many Third World nations. This topic of systemic injustice will be the primary focus of the current chapter. Issues that will be discussed include the legacies of colonialism, the consequences of post-colonial development policies, the Third World debt crisis, and the impact of United States foreign policy on Third World nations. I will suggest that those analysts who have stressed the importance of structural injustice – such as the dependency theorists – provide the most insight into contemporary Third World realities.

Among those who emphasize the importance of structural injustice are the authors of Catholic Social Teaching documents. Responding to current forms of neoliberal capitalist globalization, for example, Pope John Paul II highlights the ways in which wealth for some is often built upon the poverty of others:

> [V]arious places are witnessing a resurgence of a certain capitalist neoliberalism that subordinates the human person to blind market forces....From its centers of power, such neoliberalism often places unbearable burdens on less favored countries....In the international community, we thus see a small number of countries growing exceedingly rich at the cost of the increasing impoverishment of a

> great number of other countries; as a result the wealthy grow ever wealthier, while the poor grow ever poorer.[1]

A similar theme is also addressed in John Paul II's encyclical *Sollicitudo Rei Socialis:*

> One must denounce the existence of economic, financial, and social mechanisms which...often function automatically, accentuating the situation of wealth for some and poverty for the rest. These mechanisms, which are maneuvered directly or indirectly by the more developed countries...suffocate or condition the economies of the less developed countries. (SRS 16)

John Paul referred to the structures of injustice that exist in the global economy as "structures of sin." (SRS 36) It is to a closer look at these structures that we now turn.

THE IMPACTS OF COLONIALISM AND SLAVERY

A central feature shaping the histories of most Third World nations has been the experience of colonialism. The impacts of colonialism are far-reaching, manifest in every area of life. In the case of Africa the slave trade also played a major role. In the sections that follow, I will present brief overviews of the African slave trade and of colonialism in Africa and Latin America. The effects of these processes on African and Latin American societies will be discussed, as well as the contributions that this exploitation made to the development of global capitalism.

EARLY COLONIALISM AND THE GROWTH OF EUROPEAN CAPITALISM

Colonialism in Latin America had its beginnings in the 1490s, with the arrival of Spanish explorers in the Caribbean.[2] Within the next

1 John Paul II, Homily of January 25, 1998. The homily can be found at <www.vatican.va/ holy_father/john_paul_ii/travels/documents/hf_jp-ii_hom_25011998_lahavana_en.html>.

2 For insightful discussion of colonialism in Latin America and elsewhere, see L.S. Stavrianos, *Global Rift: The Third World Comes of Age* (New York: Morrow, 1981), a massive 900 page history of the Third World. A succinct account of colonialism in Latin America can be found in Thomas Skidmore and Peter Smith, *Modern Latin America*, 6th ed. (Oxford: Oxford University Press, 2005), chapter 1.

century most of the continent would come under Spanish or Portuguese control. That century would witness a decline of about 90% in the indigenous population. The decline was due to violence, overwork, and maltreatment of the indigenous by the colonizers coupled with the spread of European-introduced diseases such as smallpox, measles, and influenza.[3] Throughout the early colonial period indigenous persons were forced to work in very brutal conditions. They labored long hours on colonial plantations, worked in silver and gold mines, and were forced to undertake various other arduous and hazardous tasks. "They laid so heavy and grievous a burden of servitude on them," said the Dominican observer Bartolomé de las Casas, "that the condition of beasts was much more tolerable."[4] When the indigenous population declined, African slaves were imported in large numbers to replace them as a source of cheap labor. The largest numbers of slaves worked in the sugar plantations of Brazil. Highly inequitable structures of land ownership were established throughout Latin America during this time, as huge tracts of land were granted by the monarchs of Spain and Portugal to members of the colonizing elite. These skewed patterns of land ownership persist to the present day throughout Latin America, giving the continent the most inequitable distribution of land of any region of the world. This inequality of land ownership is at the root of many of Latin America's acute economic, social, and ecological problems.[5]

In addition to exploiting the natural resources and labor of the conquered territories, the colonizers also utilized the territories as a captive market. Trade was initially permitted only with the colonizing nations. Local manufacturing was generally hindered or forbidden. Such measures to prevent local manufacturing characterized colonialism throughout most of its history and shaped the dependence of Third World nations on the export of primary commodities such as agricul-

3 Gary MacEoin, Introduction to *500 Years: Domination or Liberation?*, ed. Philip Wheaton (Ocean City, MD: Skipjack Press, 1992), 9.

4 Cited in Harrison, *Inside the Third World: The Anatomy of Poverty*, 3rd ed. (New York: Penguin, 1993), 42.

5 For discussion of the decisive role of inequitable land ownership in the history of Latin America, see Duncan Green, *Faces of Latin America*, 3rd ed. (London: Latin America Bureau, 2006), 89-103.

tural products.[6] This is a theme that we have seen strongly emphasized by the structuralists and dependency theorists.

The wealth gained from the colonization of Latin America and later colonization in Asia, along with the profits of the African slave trade, played important roles in providing funds for the initial industrialization of Europe. Much of the wealth gained from Latin America, for example, passed through Portugal and Spain to early industrializing nations such as England and the Netherlands. British and Dutch colonialism added to this accumulation of capital. Karl Marx, in describing the role played by imperial exploitation in the early growth of capitalism, states:

> The discovery of gold and silver in the Americas, the extirpation, enslavement, and entombment in mines of the aboriginal population, the beginning of the conquest and looting of the East Indies, the turning of Africa into a warren for the hunting of black skins, signalised the rosy dawn of the era of capitalist production. These idyllic proceedings are the chief momenta of primitive accumulation [of capital].[7]

Historians generally agree that this colonial exploitation was an important factor in capitalism's early development and expansion.[8] "Even at this early stage," states Paul Harrison is his classic account of poverty in the Third World, "the exploitation of non-western societies played a key role in the emergence of western capitalism."[9]

AFRICA AND THE SLAVE TRADE

The European slave trade had a large and devastating impact on African society. It is estimated that about 23 million persons from Africa arrived in other nations as slaves during the several centuries that the slave trade existed. Many more persons were injured or killed while

---

6 The suppression of a thriving cloth and weaving industry in India is a much discussed example of these colonial policies. See The Ecologist, *Whose Common Future? Reclaiming the Commons* (Philadelphia: New Society Publishers, 1993), 28.

7 Cited in Richard Edwards, Michael Reich, and Thomas Weisskopf, eds., *The Capitalist System* (Englewood Cliffs, NJ: Prentice-Hall, 1986), 100.

8 See for example Stavrianos, *Global Rift*; Harrison, *Inside the Third World*.

9 Harrison, *Inside the Third World*, 40.

resisting enslavement or died while being transported.[10] Along with the massive human suffering involved in slavery, the slave trade also had a variety of economic and political consequences for Africa. For example, slavery limited the population of many parts of the African continent for several centuries by removing large numbers of young men, young women, and children. Numerous analysts argue that this prevented the population pressures from developing in Africa that were important factors in stimulating the intensification of agriculture and the development of manufacturing in Europe.[11] Other consequences were political, such as the fostering of increased rivalry and warfare among Africans. This resulted especially from the fact that some Africans were enlisted as the suppliers of other Africans for the slave trade.

While wreaking havoc in Africa, the slave trade, like colonialism, contributed to the growth of capitalism in other parts of the world. "There appears no reasonable doubt," says Basil Davidson, author of a highly regarded history of the slave trade, "that the overall profits of the whole Circuit trade [of which the transport and sale of slaves was a central part] became a major factor in the accumulation of English and French capital; and secondly, that this accumulation was a large, and at certain points probably decisive, contribution to the whole process of industrialization."[12] Slavery also played an important role in the development of capitalism in the United States. By 1830 slave-grown cotton accounted for more than half of the nation's exports and served to provide abundant cheap raw material for northern manufacturing.[13] According to critics, capitalism thus had its origins in massive exploitation and brutality throughout the world.

THE DECOLONIZATION OF LATIN AMERICA AND THE COLONIZATION OF AFRICA

A major wave of decolonialization took place in Latin America in the early 1800s, achieved through both violent and nonviolent means. This new independence, however, largely consisted of the consolida-

10 For discussion of the African slave trade, see Basil Davidson, *The African Slave Trade*, rev. ed. (Boston: Little, Brown, and Co., 1980).

11 See Walter Rodney, *How Europe Underdeveloped Africa* (Washington, DC: Howard University Press, 1974), 98.

12 Davidson, *African Slave Trade*, 83.

13 Rodney, *How Europe Underdeveloped Africa*, 87.

tion of power by local oligarchies of Spanish and Portugese descent. The underlying structures of society (such as vastly unequal distributions of land, the concentration of political authority in the hands of a few, and systematic discrimination against indigenous communities) remained intact. "Latin American society," says L.S. Stavrianos, "was basically unchanged by the wars of independence."[14]

Some economic changes did begin to occur in Latin America in the latter parts of the 19th century. Again, however, these changes generally did not benefit the poor. In the mid-1800s some manufacturing began, with financing, transport, and marketing controlled primarily by British corporations. In the late 1800s major expansions of export agriculture took place, involving the further displacement of indigenous persons and other small farmers from their lands, the expansion of poorly paid farm labor, and the creation of even more inequitable distributions of land ownership.

By the start of the 20th century the United States became the major foreign power in the region and the activity of U.S. corporations spread throughout the continent. U.S. involvement was most extensive in Central America, where U.S. corporations took a major interest in direct production and came to control vast expanses of land along with extensive local infrastructure such as ports and railways. This investment paved the way for the dominant economic, political, and military role that would be played by the U.S. in Central America in the 20th century.[15]

As direct colonialism came to an end in Latin America in the mid-19th century and gave way to forms of neocolonialism, formal colonialism in Africa was only about to begin. The late 1800s saw a scramble by European powers (including England, France, Germany, Portugal, Italy, and Belgium) to claim control of the African continent. By 1914 all areas of the continent except Ethiopia and Liberia were under foreign control. The imposition of colonial rule caused much

---

14 Stavrianos, *Global Rift*, 183.

15 For good historical overviews of U.S. involvement in Central America, see John Booth,, Christine Wade, and Thomas Walker, *Understanding Central America*, 4th ed. (Boulder: Westview Press, 2005); Thomas Melville, *Through a Glass Darkly: The U.S. Holocaust in Central America* (Philadelphia: Xlibris Corporation, 2005); Walter LaFeber, *Inevitable Revolutions: The United States in Central America*, 2nd ed. (New York: W.W. Norton, 1993).

immediate suffering for Africans. It also, as in Latin America, led to the establishment of political, economic, and social structures that have contributed greatly to many problems faced by Africans since that time.

One crucial dimension of life that was strongly affected by colonialism was food availability. Prior to the start of the colonial period, and despite the impact of slavery in removing healthy young workers, Africa was largely able to feed its population. "The most striking picture of pre-colonial Africa," says Bill Rau, an expert on the history of food in Africa, "was its ability to feed itself."[16] This ability to provide adequate food supplies was based on the peasants' intimate knowledge of farming techniques adapted to the highly fragile and varied African ecosystems and on indigenous social systems that placed a high priority on communal food security.[17] When droughts and other natural disasters caused reductions in food production, various coping mechanisms such as communal grain banks, sharing among extended kinship systems, and possibilities for migration usually served to prevent widespread famine.[18]

Under colonialism, the bases of food security were undermined. Large portions of the most fertile land were taken over by the colonizers to be used for the production of export crops. Various taxes were imposed that could only be paid in cash, which forced local inhabitants to either shift some of their land to cash crops (rather than growing food for their own consumption) or required them to work in the mines and plantations of the colonizers in order to earn cash to pay the taxes. Often armed force was used to ensure an abundant supply of cheap labor for colonial projects. Treatment of the native inhabitants was often extremely brutal. In testimony to a Belgian commission of inquiry, the following account was given of the life conditions of Africans who gathered rubber for a Belgian corporation in the Belgian Congo at the start of the 20th century:

---

16 Bill Rau, *From Feast to Famine: Official Cures and Grassroots Remedies to Africa's Food Crisis* (London: Zed Books, 1991), 22.

17 Indigenous agricultural expertise included a vast knowledge of soil types, seeds, planting techniques, crop rotation, intercropping, natural fertilizers, terracing, the building of ridges for erosion control, irrigation systems, etc. Ibid.

18 While evidence of a number of devastating famines is present in the historical record, such famines seem to have been rare. Ibid., 22-28.

> It used to take ten days to get the twenty baskets of rubber. We were always in the forest, and then when we were late we were killed. We had to go further and further into the forest to find the rubber..., to go without food, and our women had to give up cultivating the fields and gardens. Then we starved....When we failed, and our rubber was short, the soldiers came up [to] our towns and shot us. Many were shot; some had their ears cut off; others were tied up with ropes round their neck and bodies and taken away. Our chiefs were hanged, and we were killed and starved and worked beyond endurance to get rubber.[19]

An official Belgian commission reported in 1919 that the population of the colony declined by half between 1885 and 1908 under these conditions of treatment.[20]

The measures taken to force native Africans into the market economy served to undermine food security in numerous ways. Much land was shifted from food crops to export crops. The labor available for farming was also reduced by the out-migration of many men who were forced by taxation, economic necessity, or violence to leave their villages for at least part of the year to work in colonial enterprises. This reduced availability of male labor in the villages led to decreased food production and resulted in increased burdens for women. It also led to some changes in the food crops that were grown, including a reduction in the variety of crops and the partial replacement of more nutritious but more labor intensive crops such as millet with less labor intensive but less nutritious crops such as cassava. Says Rau:

> Smaller areas cultivated, less food grown and consumed, new crops entering the diet and fewer foods available to overcome seasonal shortages and provide diversity–such were the effects of the colonial takeover. Malnutrition, as it is known and seen today, based on structural deprivation among producing households, only emerged in African societies during the early stages of the colonial era.[21]

Not only increased structural deprivation but also increased susceptibility to famine occurred, as traditional communal coping mechanisms such as grain banks were eliminated by the colonizers. This widespread malnutrition and increased susceptibility to famine was

---

19 Cited in ibid., 36-37.

20 Ibid., 37.

21 Ibid., 42.

accompanied by the introduction of new diseases by Europeans and an increased spread of disease resulting from the migration of dispossessed persons. This combination of factors led the early colonial period to become what many consider to be "the unhealthiest period in all African history."[22]

While harming Africans greatly, colonialism in Africa again made an important contribution to capitalist development. Says African historian Walter Rodney:

> It would be extremely simple-minded to say that colonialism in Africa or anywhere else *caused* Europe to develop....However, it would be entirely accurate to say that the colonization of Africa and other parts of the world formed an indispensable link in a chain of events which made possible the technological transformation of the base of European capitalism.[23]

British colonizer and "founder" of Rhodesia, Cecil Rhodes, highlighted the importance of colonialism for British capitalism. Said Rhodes: "We must find new lands from which we can easily obtain raw materials and at the same time exploit the cheap slave labor that is available from the natives of the colonies. The colonies would also provide a dumping ground for the surplus goods produced in our factories."[24] To assure this last point, most of the colonial regimes in Africa, as elsewhere, sought to destroy local manufacturing, such as local handicrafts and textiles. The colonial regimes also generally prevented new manufacturing from developing.[25]

An additional impact of colonialism in Africa was the undermining of traditional leadership structures and the imposition of arbitrary nation-state boundaries. The carving up of Africa into nation-states without regard for the ethnic distribution of the population did much to pave the way for conflicts among ethnic groups.[26] Colonial policies, which often favored one ethnic group at the expense of others and often deliberately set ethnic groups against each other in a divide-and-conquer strategy, intensified the potential for conflict. A massive influx

22 Ibid., 42-45.

23 Rodney, *How Europe Underdeveloped Africa*, 174.

24 Cited in Ecologist, *Whose Common Future?*, 29.

25 Ibid., 33.

26 See Basil Davidson, *The Black Man's Burden: Africa and the Curse of the Nation-State* (New York: Times Books, 1992).

of arms during the Cold War would later serve to further exacerbate the situation. All of these factors have contributed greatly to recent tragic wars and so-called "ethnic" violence in places such as Rwanda, Somalia, and Zaire/Democratic Republic of the Congo.

THE LEGACY OF COLONIALISM

Overall, colonialism had a very destructive impact on Third World societies. This legacy of colonialism still serves to shape most of these societies in fundamental ways. As Paul Harrison states, "Almost all the imbalances that now cripple the economies, societies, and politics of the Third World had their origins in colonialism."[27] Among these imbalances are highly inequitable distributions of land and power, economies geared toward providing primary commodities for the international market rather than economies focused on meeting the basic needs of local inhabitants, rule by small elites pursuing policies detrimental to the interests of the poor and the environment, technological dependence on the First World, and nation-state boundaries and structures that often serve to incite and exacerbate internal conflicts.

POST-WWII DEVELOPMENT POLICIES AND THE THIRD WORLD DEBT CRISIS

The impacts of colonialism have played a major role in shaping most nations of the contemporary Third World. Another factor that has played a central role, with roots partly in the colonial legacy, is the Third World debt crisis. As a result of the debt and the measures implemented to assure debt repayment, enormous suffering has been caused, especially in Africa and Latin America. Millions of persons, especially children, have died. Many millions more have suffered serious deterioration in their quality of life. It is to a closer look at the causes of the debt crisis that we now turn.

In Africa as in Latin America, political independence consisted largely of the transfer of power from the colonizers to small local oligarchies. Even the newly independent African countries that described themselves as "socialist" generally had very top-down, centralized modes of political organization, with little active input by the peasant majorities in the formulation of public policy. These authoritarian

27 Harrison, *Inside the Third World*, 45.

practices and the acceptance by these governments of rather conventional models of economic development (urban-based, highly capital intensive, neglectful of small farmers) contributed greatly to the failure of these "socialist" policies in the African continent.[28]

The policies pursued by post-colonial governments in Africa and Latin America typically included continued emphasis on the production of primary commodities for export. This emphasis on exports served the interests of the new ruling elite and foreign corporations, who controlled much of the production and/or marketing of these commodities. Increased emphasis on agricultural exports led to the displacement of many additional small farmers from their lands. These lands were taken over by larger farmers, foreign corporations, and/or the state. Attempts were also made to convince remaining food-producing peasants, either through coercion or enticement, to switch at least part of their land from staple crops to cash crops for export. These policies perpetuated dependence upon a very small number of export commodities such as coffee, cocoa, cotton, sugar, peanuts, tea, tropical fruits, and various minerals.[29] Historically, the prices of these commodities have been in decline, particularly in relation to industrial goods produced in the First World. By the late 1990s, for example, commodity prices were at their lowest levels in a century and a half.[30] Between 1997 and 2001 the combined commodity index fell an additional 53% in real terms.[31] This terms of trade imbalance, rooted in the colonial legacy, has provided an ongoing impetus for debt buildup.

Also contributing to debt buildup was the embrace of modernizationist development policies. Attempts to modernize were pursued in all countries, albeit in somewhat different forms depending on ideological orientation. Political modernization generally involved the creation of extensive governmental bureaucracies. Economic mod-

---

28 As Samir Amin argues, socialist regimes in Africa sought largely to play catch-up with the West in terms of economic modernization rather than attempting to implement truly alternative models of social organization that included popular participation in economic and political life. See Samir Amin, *Maldevelopment: Anatomy of a Global Failure* (London: Zed Books, 1990).

29 See Belinda Coote, *The Trade Trap: Poverty and the Global Commodity Markets* (Oxford: Oxfam, 1992).

30 UNDP, *Human Development Report 1999*, 2.

31 UNDP, *Human Development Report 2005*, 118.

ernization emphasized the importation of the most recent industrial technology. Efforts were made in most countries to industrialize agriculture, requiring the expensive importation of tractors, fertilizers, hybrid seeds, and pesticides. Very costly, large-scale infrastructural projects such as highways, dams, and nuclear power plants were also common. All of these emphases were supported by First World development agencies (and in some countries by the USSR) and all contributed to high levels of debt.

Unfortunately the Third World poor were more harmed than helped by these development approaches. Benefits of the large-scale infrastructural projects went largely to wealthier local persons and to foreign corporations, while large numbers of poor and indigenous peoples were displaced. Highly capital-intensive methods of production created relatively few jobs, while putting large numbers of local artisans out of work. Efforts to modernize agriculture led to increased concentration of rural landholdings, less need for labor, and dispossession and displacement of the rural poor. The net impact of conventional development approaches was often increased poverty and hunger, even in the midst of economic growth. Another consequence of these development projects was widespread ecological damage, including problems such as deforestation, soil erosion, desertification, and contamination of air, soil, and water.

Due to both the negative impacts of colonialism and the inappropriate development strategies implemented after WWII, some form of debt crisis in the Third World seems to have been inevitable. By the 1960s significant debt had already been accumulated. The enormous scope of the debt buildup that would eventually occur, however, and the devastating consequences of the crisis which would follow, were heavily influenced by several additional factors that emerged in the 1970s and early 1980s. One of these new factors was vastly increased Third World lending by commercial banks, due in part to an influx of OPEC deposits (resulting from large hikes in the price of oil) that the banks needed to lend out. Prior to this time the private banks had done only limited lending in the Third World, most of the loans having been made by governmental sources. With economic stagnation limiting lending opportunities in the First World, however, the banks sought to locate borrowers elsewhere. Third World governments, because of their capacity to absorb large loans, were seen as especially welcome candidates. In order to encourage borrowing, the banks offered very favorable initial interest rates. A provision was generally included, however, stating that the rates could later change (so-called "floating" interest rates).

This major push by the banks in the 1970s to make loans led to the accumulation of enormous amounts of debt by Third World nations.[32] From under $100 billion at the start of the 1970s, Third World debt grew to around $750 billion by 1981.[33] Often these loans were made without serious consideration of the ability of the borrowers to repay or the uses to which the loans were being put. As one young banker explained in an article in *Harper's* magazine: "As a loan officer you are principally in the business of making loans. It is not your job to worry about large and unwieldy abstractions" such as the larger economic and social impacts of the loan. Emphasizing that "your job performance is rated according to how many loans you make," he states that there is little incentive for those making the loans to be concerned about the risks involved or the uses of loan funds.[34] The philosophy of many of the senior bankers who sent out such purveyors of loans was articulated by Walter Wriston, chairman of Citibank. Wriston asserted that loans to Third World nations are inherently low-risk because "countries do not fail to exist."[35] A country, unlike a corporation, can't simply go bankrupt. Most bankers, as evidenced by interviews and writings in finance publications, appear to have believed that First World governments would apply pressure to guarantee maximum repayment of Third World loans. If adequate repayment were not possible, they believed that First World governments would take action themselves to bail out the banks.[36] In a context characterized by these assumed

32 For discussion of the aggressive lending tactics employed, see "The Money-Mongers," chapter 2 of Susan George, *A Fate Worse Than Debt: The World Financial Crisis and the Poor*, rev. ed. (New York: Grove Weidenfeld, 1990).

33 William Greider, *One World, Ready Or Not: The Manic Logic of Global Capitalism* (New York: Simon and Schuster, 1997), 282.

34 S.C. Gwynne, "Adventures in the Loan Trade," *Harper's* (September 1983): 22-26. For another account of the prevalence of unscrupulous lending practices, see John Perkins, *Confessions of An Economic Hit Man* (San Francisco: Berrett-Koehler, 2004).

35 Quoted in George, *Fate Worse than Debt*, 13.

36 For evidence of the bankers' views, see quotations from *Euromoney*, a major trade publication of international banking, cited in Cheryl Payer, *Lent and Lost: Foreign Credit and Third World Development* (London: Zed

guarantees and by the need to lend massive amounts of money, normal banking standards for loans were often not applied. "There is little evidence," says Karin Lissakers, who interviewed many bankers while writing a book on the debt crisis, "that bankers distinguished between good investment and bad and knew or cared which investment their money was financing."[37]

The largest Third World borrowers in the 1970s and early 1980s were predominantly military dictatorships, in places such as Brazil, Chile, Argentina, Indonesia, Zaire, and the Philippines.[38] Not surprisingly, a main usage of the loans was military spending, most often spending to strengthen the capacity of these very brutal regimes to resist the demands for change being made by their own people. Estimates of the percentage of loans used for military purposes vary, but most analysts give figures of about 20-25% for all loans made prior to the formal onset of the debt crisis in the early 1980s.[39]

Another main "use" of the loans was capital flight. In various ways well-placed Third World individuals gained access to the loan funds and redeposited them in their personal accounts in First World banks or in other First World investments. It is estimated, for example, that an amount equivalent to about 50% of the loans made to Latin American countries as of the mid-1980s had returned to the First World in this manner.[40]

A third major use of loan money was the continued financing of large-scale projects such as hydroelectric dams, nuclear plants, and highways, including very ecologically destructive highways through tropical forests. These projects, like earlier projects of a similar nature,

---

Books, 1991), 71. As Payer states, "It is clear that in the case of default, the banks expected to be saved by a government bail-out." Ibid.

37 Karin Lissakers, *Banks, Borrowers, and the Establishment* (New York: Basic Books, 1991), 51.

38 A chart listing major Third World borrowers can be found in Susan George, *The Debt Boomerang: How Third World Debt Harms Us All* (Boulder: Westview, 1992), 146.

39 George Ann Potter, *Dialogue on Debt: Alternative Analyses and Solutions* (Washington, DC: Center of Concern, 1988), 94; George, *Fate Worse than Debt*, 22.

40 Potter, *Dialogue on Debt*, 56. Such estimates, of course, have a significant margin of error, but give a good sense of the sheer magnitude of capital flight.

mainly benefitted a wealthy few while often harming the poor and the environment.[41] With regard to the building of dams, for example, millions of poor persons have lost their land and homes and have been forced to relocate due to flooding caused by the construction of the dams, and many have been killed by the water-borne diseases that the dams have fostered. As to nuclear power plants, these projects have been extremely expensive. Many nuclear plants, for technical and safety reasons, have been inoperative since construction. One example is the Bataan nuclear power plant, built in the Philippines at a cost of over $2 billion. This facility is located at the foot of an active volcano, in an earthquake zone. When the Corazon Aquino government replaced the Marcos dictatorship after the success of the 1986 "people power" revolution, the plant was shut down for safety reasons. Yet the Filipino people have continued to pay over $500,000/day in interest on the loans taken out to build this one nuclear project. Similarly, in Brazil a whole series of nuclear power plants were built and then largely unused, at a cost of over $40 billion plus ever accumulating interest payments.[42] Viable alternatives for energy generation more appropriate to local environmental and social conditions, such as the use of solar, wind, small-scale hydro, and biogas projects have generally been overlooked.[43]

In addition to military spending, capital flight, and the financing of large-scale infrastructural projects, a fourth major use of the loan funds was the making of payments on earlier loans.[44] By the mid-1980s this in fact became by far the main use of new loan money. It is estimated,

---

41 For discussion of some of the environmental impacts, see Susan George, "Debt and the Environment: Financing Ecocide", chapter 10 of *A Fate Worse than Debt*. Also see Bruce Rich, *Mortgaging the Earth: The World Bank, Environmental Impoverishment, and the Crisis of Development* (Boston: Beacon Press, 1994).

42 George, *Fate Worse Than Debt*, 18, 138.

43 For discussion of hydroelectric dams and the displacement and other negative consequences that they have caused, see Edward Goldsmith and Nicholas Hildyard, *The Social and Environmental Effects of Large Dams* (San Francisco: Sierra Club Books, 1986).

44 Other uses that played an important role in debt buildup in some countries include the financing of luxury imports and the import of oil in oil-dependent countries. Many of the countries that incurred the largest debts, however, were oil exporters, such as Mexico, Indonesia, Nigeria, and Venezuela. Payer, *Lent and Lost*, 60.

for example, that by 1983 about 79% of new loans to Latin America were being used simply to make payments on previous loans.[45]

What this brief overview of the major uses of the loan funds reveals is that the poor majorities in the borrowing countries generally did not benefit from the loans, and often were hurt by them. Rather, it is the wealthy elites who profited. As UNICEF has powerfully stated, "it is hardly too brutal an oversimplification to say that the rich got the loans and the poor got the debts."[46] In some cases portions of the loans were indeed used for constructive purposes, such as maintaining essential services or financing appropriate forms of productive investment, but such responsible spending generally accounted for only a fairly small percentage of total loan funds.

Throughout the 1970s Third World countries were generally able to keep up with loan payments, in large part by borrowing new money to make payments on old loans. In 1982, however, Mexico, one of the largest debtors, declared that it could no longer afford to make its scheduled debt payments. It is at this time that the debt buildup began to be perceived as a debt crisis in the eyes of the international financial community. It was considered a crisis primarily because if Third World countries defaulted and the banks had to consider the outstanding loans as losses, it could have precipitated at least a partial collapse of the global financial system.

The major additional factor that contributed to the debt buildup reaching a crisis state was the macroeconomic policy undertaken by the U.S. government in the early 1980s. The U.S. Federal Reserve Board placed tight restrictions on the money supply to try to lower inflation rates. At the same time, the federal government during the Reagan administration began to run huge budget deficits, caused mainly by massive increases in military spending and large tax breaks for corporations and wealthy individuals. The combination of tight monetary policy and escalated borrowing by the U.S. government led global interest rates to skyrocket to record levels.[47] Since many of the Third World loans were contracted with floating interest rates, the

---

45 Potter, *Dialogue on Debt*, 8.

46 UNICEF, *State of the World's Children 1989*, 30-31.

47 For a good discussion of economic policy during the Reagan era, see Charles Wilber and Kenneth Jameson, *Beyond Reaganomics* (Notre Dame, IN: University of Notre Dame Press, 1990).

rates on these loans rose as well. Interest rates that were typically in the 4-6% range when loans were contracted rose as high as 21-22%.[48]

The macroeconomic policies of the United States, in addition to driving up global interest rates, also helped to precipitate a worldwide recession. This recession significantly reduced demand for Third World products and caused prices for these products to drop.[49] This reduction in income further exacerbated the debt problem. At the same time commercial banks became much less willing to make new loans to the Third World. This was partially due to growing concerns about the ability of Third World nations to repay and in part due to the fact that more lucrative opportunities had opened up in the First World, such as financing the U.S. budget deficit and financing corporate mergers and takeovers. The option of borrowing ever larger amounts of money to pay past debts was therefore no longer available to Third World debtors.

As an initial response to the debt crisis, the banks agreed to reschedule many of the loans (charging large fees to do so), thereby postponing potential defaults until sometime in the future. In the meantime, as long as Third World countries could continue to make substantial interest payments, the banks would continue to reap large profits. And in fact the major First World banks in the mid-1980s experienced record profits, due in significant part to money from the Third World.[50]

As a result of these record profits and various tax breaks that the banks received from First World governments in connection with the debt, the banks were able to increase their loan loss reserves to provide protection against default. The banks also began in various ways to decrease their overall levels of exposure. Among the main methods employed were restricting new lending to the Third World (while being repaid on old loans with funds provided by multilateral institutions such as the World Bank), selling debts on the secondary market,

---

48 George, *Fate Worse than Debt*, 38; Potter, *Dialogue on Debt*, 182.

49 Between 1980 and 1986 prices for non-oil Third World commodities fell over 20%. Oil prices fell even faster. David Woodward, *Debt, Adjustment, and Poverty in Developing Countries*, vol. 1 (London: Save the Children Fund, 1992), 24. It is estimated that during the years 1980-1985 the Third World lost about $553 billion due to price declines. Coote, *Trade Trap*, 8.

50 For details concerning bank profits, see Potter, *Dialogue on Debt*, 30; George, *Fate Worse than Debt*, 206.

and engaging in debt-for-equity swaps.[51] As a result of these measures, the vulnerability of the banks decreased greatly. By the early 1990s many persons in the international financial community were in fact proclaiming the debt crisis to be over. For example, Lewis Preston, president of the World Bank, declared in 1992 that "ten years after the start of the debt crisis it is now possible to celebrate its end."[52]

Unfortunately, Preston was viewing the situation strictly from the perspective of the First World banks. In the ten years referred to by Preston the total debt owed by the Third World had in fact nearly doubled, reaching $1.5 trillion in 1993.[53] Since then it has risen to over $2.5 trillion.[54] This massive increase in debt hardly seems to provide grounds for proclaiming a successful resolution of the debt crisis. From the perspective of the First World financial community, however, the ongoing debt buildup is not a crisis. This is because there is no longer any danger of financial collapse "even if the Third World debt [were to be] entirely unpaid."[55] Despite this strengthened position of the banks (at least prior to the recent crisis precipitated by imprudent subprime mortgage lending), immense pressure continues to be exerted to assure maximum payments on the debt and the banks continue to make large profits from it. As Otto Kreye states, what financial leaders really mean when they declare the debt crisis to be over is "that the banks... [will] escape largely scot-free from the financial debacle for which they themselves bear primary responsibility."[56] For the Third World poor, however, the crisis is worse than ever.

---

51 Details of the various ways in which banks reduced their exposure can be found in George, *Debt Boomerang*, 63-92; Lissakers, *Banks, Borrowers, and the Establishment*, 114-136.

52 Quoted in Otto Kreye, "The Debt Crisis Revisited," in *The Underdevelopment of Development*, ed. S. Chew and R. Denemark (Thousand Oaks, CA: Sage Publications, 1996), 115.

53 Ibid., 120.

54 A figure of $2.45 trillion for the year 2001, based on World Bank figures, is cited in Damien Millet and Eric Toussaint, *Who Owes Who? 50 Questions About World Debt* (London: Zed Books, 2004), 32.

55 George, *Fate Worse than Debt*, 245.

56 Kreye, "The Debt Crisis Revisited," 117.

CONSEQUENCES OF THE DEBT CRISIS

As a result of the debt, Third World governments have been forced to adopt "structural adjustment policies" (SAPs). These policies have been implemented under the auspices of the International Monetary Fund and the World Bank, institutions largely controlled by the United States and a handful of the world's other largest capitalist nations.[57] The policies are aimed at assuring maximum debt repayment and the restructuring of Third World economies according to neoliberal free-market principles. Among the policies are heightened emphasis on production for export rather than production to meet domestic basic needs. Reductions in government spending are also required, which have often led to increased unemployment and to substantial cuts in the funds made available for education, health care, and other social services. "Adjustment," says UNICEF, "often entailed cuts in spending on education, health, and food subsidies that disproportionately hurt the poor. These cuts hurt poor women particularly hard since they had to step up their workload both inside and outside the home so that their families could cope."[58] Government subsidies and price controls also are generally eliminated as part of structural adjustment, leading to major increases in the prices of basic items such as food and public transportation. An emphasis is placed upon the creation of "flexible" labor markets, which translates into increased part-time and temporary work, lower wages, less benefits, and less job security for workers. Other important components of SAPs have included trade liberaliza-

57 Voting in the IMF and World Bank is roughly proportionate to overall size of economy. Thus, the United States has the largest share of votes, enough to prevent any changes to the bylaws of the institutions. The Third World nations, while representing the majority of the world's population, have a minority of votes. For this reason the IMF and World Bank are often viewed as tools of First World, especially United States, policy.

58 *State of the World's Children 2004*, 21. Extensive discussion of the impact of structural adjustment policies on health can be found in Meredith Fort, Mary Anne Mercer, and Oscar Gish, eds., *Sickness and Wealth: The Corporate Assault on Global Health* (Cambridge, MA: South End Press, 2004); Jim Yong Kim, Joyce Millen, Alec Irwin, and John Gershman, *Dying for Growth: Global Inequality and the Health of the Poor* (Monroe, ME: Common Courage, 2000).

tion, currency devaluation, increased interest rates, and the privatization of government enterprises.[59]

The implementation of SAPs has made possible enormous debt payments by Third World nations. It is estimated that during the years 1982-1990, for example, the Third World paid to the First World in debt service about $418 billion more than it received in the form of new loans, grants, and investments.[60] This $418 billion is the equivalent, adjusted for inflation, of about 6 times the cost of the Marshall Plan to rebuild Europe after World War II. Thus, far from being "aided" by the First World, financial flows overall have generally been in the opposite direction.

In the late 1980s several reports were issued by UNICEF seeking to focus world attention on the enormous social costs of debt repayment and structural adjustment policies. These reports documented increased rates of malnutrition, disease, and child mortality, and decreased levels of primary school enrollment in numerous Third World countries.[61] According to UNICEF, in every year of the debt crisis "hundreds of thousands of the developing world's children have given their lives to pay their countries' debts." "[M]any millions more," UNICEF states, "are still paying the interest with their malnourished minds and bodies."[62] In one of the most powerful and strongly worded statements ever issued by a United Nations agency, UNICEF declared:

> [Several] years ago former Tanzanian President Julius Nyerere asked the question: "*Must we starve our children to pay our debts?*" That question has now been answered in practice. And the answer has been 'Yes.'....This is why the debt crisis should not be discussed

---

59 For detailed analysis of SAPs and their impacts, see Structural Adjustment Participatory Review International Network (SAPRIN), *Structural Adjustment: The Policy Roots of Economic Crisis, Poverty, and Inequality* (London: Zed Books, 2004).

60 This figure (in 1991 dollars) is provided by Susan George, *The Debt Boomerang: How Third World Debt Harms Us All* (Boulder: Westview, 1992), xv. George also makes the comparison with the Marshall Plan. The Marshall Plan transferred $14 billion 1948 dollars to Europe, the equivalent of about $70 billion 1991 dollars.

61 See the UNICEF-sponsored report by Giovanni Andrea Cornia, Richard Jolly, and Frances Stewart, *Adjustment with a Human Face* (Oxford: Oxford University Press, 1987). Also see UNICEF's annual *State of the World's Children* reports, especially the 1989 edition.

62 UNICEF, *State of the World's Children 1989*, 30.

> too politely. For polite discussion can imply a tacit acceptance of the unacceptable. And what has happened to large areas of the developing world...is truly unacceptable.
>
> The fact that so much of today's staggering debt was irresponsibly lent and irresponsibly borrowed would matter less if the consequences of such folly were falling on its perpetrators. Yet now, when the party is over and the bills are coming in, it is the poor who are being asked to pay....
>
> In short, it is hardly too brutal an oversimplification to say that the rich got the loans and the poor got the debts. And when the impact becomes visible in rising death rates among children, rising percentages of low-birth-weight babies, falling figures for the average weight-for-height of the under-5s, and lower school enrollment ratios among the 6-11 year olds, then it is essential to strip away the niceties of economic parlance and say that what has happened is simply an outrage against a large section of humanity....Allowing world economic problems to be taken out on the growing minds and bodies of young children is the antithesis of all civilized behavior. Nothing can justify it. And it shames and diminishes us all."[63]

In addition to contributing to this devastating impact on children, structural adjustment policies have also had a strongly negative impact on poor women, adding significantly to women's daily burdens.[64] Many women have had to increase the time spent on income-generating work to seek to make ends meet financially in a context of declining incomes and rising prices, while at the same time having a variety of increased household responsibilities (such as caring for sick children) as a result of cuts in governmental social services. "What is regarded by economists as increased efficiency," says Diane Elson, "may instead be a shifting of costs from the paid economy to the unpaid economy" in which work is done largely by women, including female children.[65] Among the increased household responsibilities for women caused by

63 Ibid., 30-31.

64 Good works discussing the impact of structural adjustment on women include Mariarosa Dalla Costa and Giovanna Dalla Costa, eds., *Paying the Price: Women and the Politics of International Economic Strategy* (London: Zed Books, 1995); Pamela Sparr, ed., *Mortgaging Women's Lives: Feminist Critiques of Structural Adjustment* (London: Zed Books, 1994).

65 Diane Elson, "Male Bias in Macro-Economics: The Case of Structural Adjustment," in *Male Bias in the Development Process*, ed. D. Elson (Manchester: Manchester University Press, 1995), 178.

structural adjustment are caring for ill family members who are unable to obtain medical care (or spending more time in lines to get medical care), having to walk more since bus fares are less affordable, spending more time shopping and in food preparation in attempts to minimize costs, spending more time caring for children who are no longer able to attend school or whose school hours have been reduced, spending time tending a garden in an effort to reduce food costs, and similar measures.

In addition to suffering from increased poverty and decreased governmental services, women and children also often suffer from the emphasis on export crop production that is contained in SAPs. This production for export often diverts land and energy away from staple crops, which in the past served to provide food for local families. The income from the cash crops is generally low and is typically controlled by men, who often do not use it effectively to meet the family's needs. Much evidence demonstrates that men often reserve for themselves significant portions of household income for purposes such as alcohol consumption, cigarettes, and recreational activities.[66] In situations where the money available to purchase needed food is limited, it is generally women and children who suffer most and do not receive adequate nutrition. Similarly, when educational opportunities or health care is scarce or costly, it is most often female children who are not sent to school or do not receive needed care. When mothers have to spend more time on income-generating activities, it is generally daughters who are expected to take over many of the tasks of household maintenance, often dropping out of school or attending school less regularly to do so.

Situations of economic stress also often impact women by leading to increases in the numbers of female-headed households, due both to increased abandonment and to the practice of men migrating in search of employment, in both cases increasing the burden on women.

66 There is "considerable evidence to suggest," says Diane Elson, "that while women typically pool and share their income, especially with their children, men are more inclined to reserve part of their income for discretionary spending," such as spending on recreational activities, alcohol, cigarettes, prostitution, or consumer goods such as radios. This propensity is documented in numerous accounts and studies of life among the Third World poor. "Male Bias in the Development Process: An Overview," in *Male Bias in the Development Process*, 11.

In situations of economic stress domestic violence also often increases. Particularly common is violence that occurs when women need to ask men for more money than the men have allotted to them for meeting the family's basic needs. Summarizing the impact of structural adjustment on women in a poor community in Ecuador, Carolyn Moser states: "It is not simply a matter of income foregone...or even of extra work having to be done; it is a matter of the disintegration of people's lives."[67]

The claim made by the World Bank and the IMF, under whose direction SAPs have been adopted, is that the implementation of these policies would lead to increased economic growth that would have trickle-down benefits for all. While the rather narrow identification of development and economic growth contained in these policies is very problematic and needs to be challenged, it should also be noted that these policies have largely failed even on their own macroeconomic terms. As UNICEF states, "Adjustment also failed even on its own terms, resulting in next-to-no economic growth."[68] These macroeconomic issues will be discussed in the next two sections of this chapter, along with more detailed discussion of the human consequences of the debt crisis in Sub-Saharan Africa and Latin America.

THE IMPACT OF ECONOMIC CRISIS AND STRUCTURAL ADJUSTMENT IN SUB-SAHARAN AFRICA

As a result of debt, economic crisis, and the implementation of structural adjustment policies, Sub-Saharan Africa (SSA) in the past several decades has experienced major declines in both macroeconomic indicators and social welfare.[69] In the years 1980-1995, according to the World Bank, the region experienced an average decline in per capita GDP of 1.4%/year and an average annual decline in per capita consumption of 1.8%/year, for cumulative declines of over 20%

67 Cited in Elson, "Male Bias in Macroeconomics," 185.

68 UNICEF, *State of the World's Children 2004*, 21-22.

69 For good discussions of the impact of debt, structural adjustment, and other neoliberal policies in Africa, see Patrick Bond, *Looting Africa: The Economics of Exploitation* (London: Zed Books, 2006); James Ferguson, *Global Shadows: Africa in the Neoliberal World Order* (Durham, NC: Duke University Press, 2006).

and 25% respectively.[70] An important role in this decline was played by a sharp deterioration in commodity prices throughout the 1980s. Prices for major Third World commodities such as coffee, tea, cocoa, and cotton declined in real terms by about 50%.[71] This sharp fall in prices was related in part to the impact of global recession in the early 1980s and in part to overproduction caused by structural adjustment policies themselves. Because these policies require all countries to seek to maximize export production, excess supply and reduced prices for many commodities often result. Overall commodity prices would in fact later fall ever further, reaching new record lows in the late 1990s and then falling another 53% in real terms between 1997 and 2001.[72]

In terms of social indicators, levels of both poverty and hunger have risen substantially in SSA in the past several decades. Between 1970 and 1990 the numbers of persons going hungry more than doubled.[73] This problem of hunger continued to intensify in the period from 1990-2004, as revealed for example in studies of child malnutrition.[74] According to the United Nations, per capita food consumption in SSA by the mid-1990s was about 10% lower than in the mid-1970s,

70 This data is from the World Bank, cited in the magazine *Development and Cooperation* (July/August, 1996). For additional data, which includes somewhat higher estimates of the rate of per capita GDP decline and income decline in SSA in the 1980s, see Dharam Ghai and Cynthia Hewitt de Alcantara, "Sub-Saharan Africa and Latin America/The Caribbean," in *The IMF and The South: The Social Impact of Crisis and Adjustment*, ed. Dharam Ghai (London: Zed Books, 1991), 14.

71 UNDP, *Human Development Report 1996*, 17.

72 See *Africa Recovery* 12 (April 1999): 35; UNDP, *Human Development Report 2005*, 118. To give one example, the price of coffee fell from around $1/kg in 1998 to $.30/kg in 2003, undermining the livelihoods of approximately 20 million households. Whereas in 1990 developing countries received about 1/3 of the final consumer price of coffee, by 2005 this had dropped to around 1/13. UNDP, *Human Development Report 2005*, 139-140.

73 According to Bread for the World, the number of chronically hungry people in sub-Saharan Africa increased from 103 million in the years 1969-71 to 215 million in 1990-92. As a percentage of total population, the increase was from 38% to 43%. Bread for the World, "What Governments Can Do," Annual World Food Day Report 1996. Similar figures are given in UNDP, *Human Development Report 1998*, 50.

74 UNICEF, *Progress for Children: A Report Card on Nutrition* (New York: UNICEF, 2006), 6.

with the average person consuming only about 87% of needed calories.[75] With regard to poverty, the 1990s saw a continued decline in per capita income, while the number of people living in absolute poverty (on less than $1/day) grew from 241 million in 1990 to 315 million in 1999.[76] The United Nations estimates that this number could rise as high as 426 million by 2015.[77] Currently nearly half of all persons in SSA live in absolute poverty.[78] With regard to health and education, structural adjustment policies have led to cuts in governmental spending in these crucial areas. The United Nations "New Agenda for the Development of Africa Mid-Term Review" states:

> Africa's social sector has remained under great pressure...primarily due to major cutbacks in public expenditure on education and health under the weight of economic instability and structural adjustment. Many governments have been prompted to introduce user fees for schooling or social services previously offered free of charge, with the result that the poor often go without health care and must sacrifice their children's education.[79]

Of the money that is spent on health care, most is spent not on primary or preventive care for the poor but rather on urban hospitals that serve mainly the non-poor. In the rural health clinics and clinics for the urban poor that do exist (and even in some of the hospitals), most of the spending goes to wages, leaving little money available for maintenance, equipment, or even for basic drugs or other essential supplies. The U.N. speaks of SSA's "deteriorating health and education infrastructures."[80] It is women and children again who are most strongly affected by lack of access to adequate health care. A Sub-Saharan African woman, for example, has a 1-in-13 chance of dying as a result of complications of pregnancy and childbirth.[81]

75 John Prendergast, *Crisis and Hope in Africa* (Washington, DC: Center of Concern, 1996), 41; United Nations, "New Agenda for the Development of Africa Mid-Term Review," in *Africa Recovery* 10:2 (October 1996):18.

76 Michael Fleshman, "Africa Struggles to Attain Millennium Goals," *Africa Recovery* 17:3 (October 2003).

77 Ibid.

78 UNDP, *Human Development Report 2005*, 34. The exact figure given is 46.4%.

79 United Nations, "New Agenda," 26.

80 Ibid., 25.

81 Ibid., 26.

The past couple decades have seen the re-emergence and/or spread of serious diseases such as cholera, yellow fever, malaria, measles, diphtheria, and pertussis.[82] Recent decades have also seen a massive increase in HIV infections and AIDS, in part due to a lack of resources for efforts aimed at HIV/AIDS prevention. About 2/3 of the global total of persons with HIV live in Sub-Saharan Africa and about 70% of AIDS-related deaths occur there.[83]

With regard to education, declines in governmental funding have led to what the UN calls a "near collapse of educational infrastructure."[84] Problems in education are manifest in declining or stagnant primary enrollment rates, a lack of basic educational supplies, high rates of attrition and repetition of grades, inadequate teacher education, and increased levels of illiteracy. Nearly half of eligible children are not enrolled in primary school.[85] Inadequate education especially affects girls, about 64% of whom do not receive sufficient education to become fully literate.[86] Many children are forced to drop out of school in order to devote more time to household chores and income-producing or food-producing work.

On the positive side, despite all of the above, levels of child mortality in SSA appear to have declined, due mainly to a variety of low-cost interventions championed by UNICEF such as immunization and the practice of oral rehydration therapy to prevent deaths from diarrhea-related dehydration, one of the major killers of young children. Even with these improvements, however, nearly 1 in 5 children in SSA still die before the age of five.[87] It should also be noted that existing data on child mortality in SSA is fragmentary and often considered to be un-

82 Ibid.; Eva Jespersen, "External Shocks, Adjustment Policies, and Economic and Social Performance, in *Africa's Recovery in the 1990s*, ed. G.A. Cornia, et al. (New York: St. Martin's Press, 1992), 42.

83 UNDP, *Human Development Report 2005*, 26.

84 United Nations, "New Agenda," 23.

85 Sub-Saharan Africa has a primary school enrollment rate of about 57%. Only about 1/3 of the children who enroll complete a full primary education. UNDP, *Human Development Report 2003*, 6.

86 United Nations, "New Agenda," 27.

87 The United Nations Development Programme estimates the under-5 mortality rate in SSA as being 174 per 1000 children born. UNDP, *Human Development Report 2006*, 318.

reliable, therefore preventing any definite conclusions about improvements in child mortality to be drawn.[88]

THE IMPACT OF ECONOMIC CRISIS AND STRUCTURAL ADJUSTMENT IN LATIN AMERICA

Latin America, like Africa, has experienced significant economic and social problems as a result of the debt crisis and structural adjustment. During the 1980s, per capita income declined by about 16%.[89] The number of persons living in poverty increased by about 45%, climbing from 136 million in 1980 to approximately 196 million (46% of the total population) by 1990.[90] Per capita spending on health and education and social services generally declined during this time, with negative consequences similar to those highlighted in the discussion of Africa.

Since 1990 macroeconomic indicators have experienced some improvement. Per capita economic output, for example, has risen. In general, however, the benefits of increased economic performance have not trickled-down. "Growth," states an Oxfam report, "has largely bypassed the poor."[91] While there has been a reduction in the rate of poverty in a few countries, the overall number of poor persons rose to around 222 million by 2004. Levels of officially acknowledged unemployment also rose, from 6.9% in 1990 to 10% in 2004.[92]

---

88 See Jespersen, "External Shocks," 42-43.

89 Eliana Cardoso and Ann Helwege, *Latin America's Economy* (Cambridge, MA: MIT Press, 1992), 110. For the sake of comparison, it should be noted that per capita GDP and per capita incomes are several times higher in Latin America than in SSA.

90 Rolph van der Hoeven and Frances Stewart, "Social Development During Periods of Structural Adjustment," in *Latin America's New Insertion in the World Economy*, ed. Ruud Buitelaar and Pitou van Dijck (New York: St. Martin's Press, 1996), 129; Duncan Green, *Silent Revolution: The Rise of Market Economics in Latin America* (London: Latin America Bureau, 1995), 91.

91 Oxfam, *Structural Adjustment and Inequality in Latin America: How IMF and World Bank Policies Have Failed the Poor* (Oxford: Oxfam, 1994), 1. Quoted in Green, *Silent Revolution*, 202.

92 Economic Commission for Latin America and the Caribbean (ECLAC), *The Millennium Development Goals: A Latin American and Caribbean Perspective* (Santiago, Chile: United Nations, 2005), 291.

A look at these macroeconomic and social indicators, while important, does not fully reveal crucial aspects of the reality of the past decades in Latin America. What many analysts cite as being of most significance, even more than the increases in poverty and inequality, is a strong sense of social disintegration. This social disintegration has been manifest for example in greatly increased levels of violent crime and drug use and in increased levels of domestic violence. Some analysts see this disintegration as being fueled in significant part by increased exposure to Northern media and advertising and by rising awareness of the gaps between the vision of the "good life" portrayed in these media and the deteriorating realities of daily life experienced by the Latin American poor. Duncan Green states:

> In a cruel widening of the 'frustration gap,' the number of TVs per thousand homes rose by 40 percent in the 1980s and real wages fell by the same amount. Teenagers, out of work or out of school, or fed up with dead-end jobs, are taunted by the racy lifestyles they see on the daily diet of imported U.S. TV shows or local soap operas. They want Reeboks and Ray-Bans and on a good day they get rice and beans. Losing their jobs and status as breadwinners, men turn to alcohol and rage, while grown-up children have neither the money nor the opportunity to leave home. Houses have filled with frustrated, hungry people and the results are predictable: family breakdown, alcoholism, domestic violence, drug abuse and crime spread through the region....Crime and social disintegration have become the principal cause for public concern in many Latin American societies.[93]

The overall results of structural adjustment in Latin America, asserts Green, must be viewed as markedly negative when the human and ecological damage wreaked by these policies is taken into account. While in macroeconomic terms inflation has been brought under control and GDP growth has resumed (though other macroeconomic problems persist), this "success" has occurred in a context of increased poverty, inequality, insecurity, heightened burdens on women, increased child labor, continued dispossession of small farmers, declines in education and health, ecological devastation, and social disintegration. Says Green:

> Most coverage of the issue [of structural adjustment in Latin America] is strangely impersonal, remaining in the safe world of national

93 Green, *Silent Revolution*, 104, 203.

> economic variables....Its image is rapidly tarnished once real people are made the focus of attention....A minority of the population in each country, comprising the economic and social elite, has benefited from being drawn into the global economy through the structural adjustment process, but the costs for the majority of poor Latin Americans have been extreme.[94]

Among those who concur with Green's analysis are the bishops of the Latin American Bishops' Conference, known by its Spanish acronym CELAM. CELAM has issued numerous statements condemning the impact of structural adjustment and neoliberal economics on the Latin American poor. In their 1995 statement "Latin America: Arise and Walk," the bishops of CELAM contend that neoliberal capitalism and structural adjustment policies have caused "the impoverishment and misery of millions of Latin Americans."[95] Cardinal Oscar Andrés Rodríguez Maradiaga of Honduras, a former president of CELAM, has also spoken out strongly on this theme. "Neoliberal capitalism," he argues, "carries injustice and inequality in its genetic code....The neoliberal economic model is not the panacea promised and will not help us overcome our crisis."[96] In a document entitled "For Life and Against Neoliberalism," the Jesuit Provincials of Latin America further develop this critique. Among the harmful impacts that the Jesuit leaders highlight are:

> the immense imbalances and perturbations neoliberalism causes through the concentration of income, wealth and land ownership; the multiplication of the unemployed urban masses or those surviving in unstable and unproductive jobs; the bankruptcy of thousands of small- and medium-sized businesses; the destruction and forced displacement of indigenous and peasant populations; the expansion of drug trafficking based in rural sectors whose traditional products can no longer compete; the disappearance of food security; an increase in criminality often triggered by hunger; the destabilization of national economies by the free flow of international speculation;

94 Ibid., 200.

95 Quoted in Bill and Patty Coleman, "Latin Bishops Rebuke 'Neoliberal Bandits,'" *National Catholic Reporter* (May 19, 1995).

96 Quoted in ibid.

and maladjustments in local communities by multinational companies that do not take the residents into account.[97]

ECOLOGICAL ISSUES AND THE IMPACT OF THE DEBT CRISIS ON THE FIRST WORLD

Along with the massive transfer of wealth from the Third World to the First World that the debt crisis has precipitated and the increased levels of poverty and inequality that have accompanied it in many Third World countries, there are additional negative impacts of the debt crisis and SAPs that should be noted. For example, the environmental damage that was already occurring as a result of modernizationist policies has been further exacerbated. There has been increased exploitation of natural resources, such as tropical forests, in order to earn money to repay loans. Increased emphasis on modernized agricultural production for export has led to accelerated soil erosion and the increased toxic contamination of soil, water, and workers. The elimination or non-enforcement of environmental regulations in an effort to attract foreign corporations has also led to major pollution problems. And the Third World has increasingly been used as a dumping ground for First World toxic wastes, which some Third World countries have agreed to accept out of a desperate need for foreign exchange.[98]

It should be noted that many persons in the First World have also suffered negative consequences of the debt crisis, feeling the impact of what Susan George terms the "debt boomerang." These consequences have included a loss of jobs due to the decreased ability of the impoverished Third World to import First World products, an increased inflow of drugs (as drug sales became a main source of national revenue in highly indebted countries such as Peru and Colombia), increased greenhouse gases in the atmosphere due to the burning of tropical forests, and loss of tax revenues due to the debt-associated tax write-offs given to First World banks. As well, the immigration into North America and Europe of large numbers of impoverished Third World

97 Jesuit Provincials of Latin America, "For Life and Against Neoliberalism," in Ann Butwell, Kathy Ogle, and Scott Wright, eds., *We Make the Road by Walking: Central America, Mexico, and the Caribbean in the New Millennium* (Washington, DC: EPICA, 1998), 76.

98 For examinations of the negative environmental impacts of structural adjustment, see Rich, *Mortgaging the Earth;* Potter, *Dialogue on Debt,* chapter 5; George, *Fate Worse Than Debt,* chapter 10.

persons uprooted by the desperate conditions in their own countries has given rise in many places to an increase in social tensions and to strong discrimination against these immigrants.[99]

THE RESPONSE OF THE WORLD BANK AND IMF TO CRITICISM OF STRUCTURAL ADJUSTMENT

Throughout much of the 1980s the World Bank and IMF responded to critics of structural adjustment by either ignoring them or telling them that they were mistaken. The debt crisis, it was believed, was only a temporary problem. The implementation of SAPs would remedy this problem, creating the basis for renewed economic growth that would ultimately improve the conditions of life for the poor.

As the crisis continued and evidence of detrimental impacts on the poor began to mount, the World Bank and IMF came under increased criticism. The scathing report on the impacts of structural adjustment issued by UNICEF in 1989, following up on its 1987 call for "adjustment with a human face," led the World Bank to adopt a new approach. While still asserting that SAPs would greatly benefit the poor in the long-run, the Bank admitted that the poor may have excessively borne some of the costs of the needed transition. "We did not think that the human costs of these programs could be so great," acknowledged the World Bank's chief economist for Africa, "and the economic gains so slow in coming."[100]

While acknowledging problems in the macroeconomic realm, the World Bank has consistently asserted that inadequate and incomplete implementation of SAPs by Third World governments is the primary problem, not any fundamental flaw in the policies themselves. So rather than fundamentally change the policies, what the Bank proposed was the creation of compensatory programs to cushion some of the impacts of SAPs on the poor. The first of these programs was begun in Ghana in the early 1990 and others soon followed. These programs have not, however, been effective in improving conditions for the poor. Multiple factors have contributed to this outcome, including inadequate funding, untimely implementation, corruption, and the failure

99 For more details on these impacts of the debt crisis on the First World, see George, *Debt Boomerang*.

100 Cited in Manfred Bienefeld, "Structural Adjustment and the Prospects for Democracy in Southern Africa," in *Debating Development Discourse*, ed. David Moore and Gerald Schmitz (New York: St. Martin's, 1995), 92.

of these programs to effectively reach the poorest persons in society. "The rhetoric sounds appealing," state the authors of a study of the impact of these programs in Ghana, "but the reality does not match up."[101] In Bolivia, Duncan Green reports, the compensatory social fund "generally ended up helping the better off, while virtually ignoring the poorest rural communities."[102] Others tell of similar results.[103] Critics argue that the compensatory programs have primarily served public relations purposes, deflecting attention from the numerous ways in which SAPs were deepening the structural roots of poverty. What is needed, these critics argue, are alternatives to SAPs themselves if poverty is to be seriously addressed. "Simply bolting-on social welfare provisions to wider adjustment policies which are themselves exacerbating poverty," says Oxfam, "does not amount to a poverty reduction strategy."[104]

Interestingly, when one examines IMF and World Bank publications it becomes apparent that much of the analysis of the anticipated impact of SAPs remains largely in the realm of theory. In a major 1994 publication on Africa, for example, the World Bank asserts that in those countries seriously implementing reform "the majority of the poor are *probably* better off," claiming that these policies have "*in all likelihood*" improved the condition of the poor.[105] Bank documents tend simply to assert that their policies should be beneficial to all, given the theoretical assumptions under which the Bank operates. Based on this theory, the Bank asserts that "there is every reason to think" that the policies are having a positive impact. The poor, the Bank insists, are "almost certainly" not worse off.[106] Like the documents of the World Bank, IMF documents tend to remain largely in the realm of theory with regard to the social consequences of adjustment policies. One IMF

101 Lynne Brydon and Karen Legge, *Adjusting Society: The World Bank, the IMF, and Ghana* (New York: Tauris, 1996), 155.

102 Green, *Silent Revolution*, 6.

103 See, for example, Carlos Vilas, "Neoliberal Social Policy," *NACLA Report on the Americas* 29, no. 6 (May/June, 1996): 16-25; SAPRIN, *Structural Adjustment*.

104 Quoted in Green, *Silent Revolution*, 55.

105 World Bank, *Adjustment in Africa: Reforms, Results, and the Road Ahead* (Oxford: Oxford University Press, 1994), 7, 165. Emphasis added.

106 Ibid., 163, 7.

study of the impact of SAPs on the poor, for example, bluntly states that its conclusions are "primarily based on deductive reasoning."[107]

Those persons and organizations actively involved in the lives of the poor, however, call into question these theoretical assertions. "In virtually all cases," says Laura Renshaw of the grassroots development organization Oxfam, "the impact of structural adjustment programs on the communities and families with whom our partners work has been negative."[108] Jaime Gonçalvez, a Roman Catholic bishop in Mozambique, states that "we see, with the Structural Adjustment Plan, the poor becoming always more poor. This is a reality that the church has to deal with every day."[109] The Structural Adjustment Participatory Review International Network (SAPRIN), which undertook the most extensive study ever done of the impacts of SAPs on local populations, asserts that the overall consequences of adjustment policies have been profoundly negative. These have included

> disappointing levels of economic growth...; the misallocation of financial and other productive resources; the 'disarticulation' of national economies; the destruction of national productive capacity; and extensive environmental damage. Poverty and inequality are now far more intense and pervasive than they were 20 years ago, wealth is more highly concentrated, and opportunities are far fewer for the many who have been left behind by adjustment.[110]

In its discussion of Africa, one of the most crucial claims made by the World Bank in its theoretical argumentation is that price liberalization in the agricultural realm (i.e. the removal of price controls, especially on basic staples) will be of great benefit to the rural poor by raising their incomes.[111] Extensive evidence shows, however, that price liberalization has often had the opposite effect, harming the rural poor. "One of the reasons for the growing extent of malnutrition in

107 P.S. Heller, et al., "The Implications of Fund-Supported Adjustment Programs for Poverty," *IMF Occasional Papers* No. 58 (May, 1988). Cited in Bienefeld, "Structural Adjustment," 103.

108 Laura Renshaw, "Global Lending Policies Hurt the Poor," *Oxfam Viewpoint* (Fall 1996): 16.

109 Quoted in Carole Collins, "African Bishops Decry World Bank, IMF Policies," *National Catholic Reporter* (November 11, 1994).

110 SAPRIN, *Structural Adjustment*, 218.

111 See for example the discussions of this topic in World Bank, *Adjustment in Africa*.

sub-Saharan Africa," asserts the U.N.'s International Labour Organization (ILO), "is related to the policy of price liberalisation for agricultural commodities."[112] The ILO explains that the majority of the farmers in the region don't grow enough marketable food to benefit from the higher prices, but do have to purchase food themselves part of the year when their own supplies run out. They are thus hurt by the higher prices. The many landless laborers in rural areas who rely entirely on purchased food are hurt even more. Overall, it is primarily the better off farmers who have benefitted from price liberalization, contributing to increased levels of rural inequality. Poor farmers, lacking access to adequate amounts of land, credit and basic inputs and faced with a context of declining governmental services, are at a great disadvantage in market competition. Thus, one of the central claims of the World Bank concerning the impact of their policies on the African poor is shown to be seriously flawed. Critiques of other aspects of SAPs – such as trade liberalization, privatization, and financial sector liberalization, in the manner that these have been implemented in conventional SAPs – have also been convincingly presented.[113]

RESPONSES TO THE DEBT CRISIS

The official responses taken by creditor organizations and governments in dealing with the debt crisis have so far been quite limited in scope. Initially, these responses consisted primarily of the rescheduling of loans. Eventually the need for actual debt reduction was affirmed, and in 1996 the IMF and World Bank announced the Heavily Indebted Poor Countries (HIPC) Initiative, which was later modified at a meeting of leaders of the G-7 nations in Cologne, Germany in 1999. The HIPC initiative provided some relief to a handful of the world's

112 International Labour Organization, *African Employment Report 1988*, 33. Cited in Susan George, "Uses and Abuses of African Debt," in *Africa Within the World: Beyond Dispossession and Dependence*, ed. Adebayo Adedeji (London: Zed Books, 1993), 68.

113 See SAPRIN, *Structural Adjustment* for detailed discussion of the individual components of SAPs. It should be emphasized that some elements of SAPs can indeed be useful (e.g. efforts to control inflation), but these measures will be of maximum benefit to the poor only when placed within the context of a different overall economic plan that stresses a more equitable distribution of assets, support for small and medium-scale farmers and businesses, grassroots participation, etc., as will be discussed more below.

poorest countries, mainly in sub-Saharan Africa. It provided no relief at all, however, for the majority of indebted nations. A particularly problematic feature of the plan was that countries became eligible for reductions only after they had demonstrated a willingness to strictly adhere to structural adjustment programs for a prolonged period of time. Critics argue that these moderate amounts of debt relief for only a handful of nations and the linkage of this relief to SAPs was far from what was needed to resolve the debt problem in a just and constructive manner.

In June of 2005, the World Bank, IMF, and leaders of the world's richest countries agreed on a plan to provide more substantive debt relief to up to 42 of the world's poorest countries. (As of August 2007, 28 countries, mostly in Africa, had received relief.) This new plan includes up to 100% elimination of debt owed directly to official multilateral lenders including the IMF, the World Bank, and the African Development Bank. While this is certainly a step forward, and represents an important victory for the widespread grassroots mobilization undertaken by the international, faith-based Jubilee debt relief movement, the plan still has serious drawbacks. It applies to less than half of the countries that are in need of debt relief in order to be able to meet the Millennium Development Goals, such as cutting extreme poverty in half. Also, the debt reductions do not apply to money owed to commercial banks or to other multilateral lenders such as the Inter-American Development Bank. And debt relief is still tied to the implementation of structural adjustment policies. Only after strictly adhering to SAPs for numerous years – in effect, according to critics, giving over control of the nation's economy to the IMF and World Bank to be reshaped in the interests of First World governments and corporations – is any debt relief granted.[114]

From an ethical perspective the most striking fact about the debt crisis is that those who played the major roles in causing the debt crisis have had to bear little or none of its burden, while those with no role in creating the crisis have suffered greatly. Three main parties can be seen to bear primary responsibility for the crisis. One party is those persons in the Third World (including governmental representatives

114 For discussion of the new debt relief plan, see Jubilee USA, "First Step on a Long Journey: Putting the G-8 Deal on Debt Into Perspective" (June 2005) and "The Unfinished Agenda on International Debt" (July 2006), both available at <www.jubileeusa.org>.

and other wealthy persons) who were responsible for contracting the loans. These persons have generally not themselves suffered financially as a result of the debt crisis, as they have been able to pass the burden of adjustment onto the small middle class and the poor majorities in their countries. Their income in fact has generally increased, as they have been able to take advantage of the weakened position of labor and have profited from local currency devaluations since much of their money is held abroad in dollars. As *The Economist* magazine has stated, "stabilisation and structural adjustment have brought magnificent returns to the rich."[115]

The second main party responsible for the debt crisis is the First World banks who imprudently made massive loans to the Third World, knowing well that most of the money was being used for purposes including military repression and capital flight and was not being responsibly employed.[116] Far from having to experience any significant negative consequences as a result of their actions, however, most of the banks have reaped high profits on their Third World loans and have received debt-related tax breaks from First World governments as well.[117]

The third main party responsible for the debt crisis is the U.S. government, whose macroeconomic policies contributed greatly to the skyrocketing interest rates and global recession in the early 1980s that caused a massive increase in Third World debt. The U.S. government, along with other First World governments and intergovernmental organizations such as the World Bank, also played a leading role in fostering the failed development policies that served as a root cause of the initial debt buildup. Like the first two parties, these parties have not had to accept responsibility for the crisis.

Those who have suffered most from the crisis have clearly been the Third World poor. These persons had no part in contracting the debts and generally did not benefit from them, yet they are being forced in many cases to literally sacrifice the lives of their children to enable debt payments to continue. Reflecting upon these realities, the U.S. Catho-

115 "A Survey of Latin America," *Economist* (November 13, 1993). Cited in Green, *Silent Revolution*, 92.

116 For discussion and documentation concerning the knowledge that bankers had, see George, *Fate Worse Than Debt*, chapter 2.

117 George, *Debt Boomerang*, 85.

lic bishops have stressed that the harm being done to the poor by debt payments and SAPs cannot go unchallenged:

> Many persons, human beings created in God's image, especially the most vulnerable – women and children – are literally dying of the consequences of the debt. And that is intolerable....We cannot accept that the world's poor be required to sacrifice in order to sustain the lifestyle of the world's more affluent people.[118]

Pope John Paul II has likewise challenged the morality of requiring debt repayment when immense suffering will be the result. "It is not right to demand or expect repayment," says John Paul, "when the effect would be the imposition of political choices leading to hunger and despair for entire peoples. It cannot be expected that the debts which have been contracted should be paid at the price of unbearable sacrifice."[119] "The debt," the All Africa Council of Churches has provocatively declared, "is a new form of slavery as vicious as the slave trade."[120]

Proponents of debt relief argue that the majority of the existing debt is in fact illegitimate or "odious" debt (such as debt contracted by unelected, repressive governments) and should not be repaid. They also contend that most debt has in reality been more than fully repaid, arguing that only usurious rates of interest have prevented this from being realized. One person making such claims is Roman Catholic Cardinal Paulo Evaristo Arns of Brazil. Says Cardinal Arns:

> It's impossible to go on this way; we have already taken everything the people had to eat....These loans were contracted by the military, mostly for military ends....The people are now expected to pay off these debts in low salaries and hunger. But we have already reimbursed the debt, once or twice over, considering the interest paid. We must stop giving the blood and the misery of our people to pay the First World.[121]

Cardinal Arns and others call for more extensive debt forgiveness for a broader array of Third World nations, without harmful structural

118 U.S. Catholic Conference, *Relieving Third World Debt: A Call for Co-Responsibility, Justice, and Solidarity* (Washington, DC: USCC, 1989), no. 62, 49.

119 Pope John Paul II, *Centesimus Annus*, no. 35.

120 Quoted in Prendergast, *Crisis and Hope in Africa*, 28.

121 Quoted in George, *Fate Worse Than Debt*, 138.

adjustment conditions attached. They also encourage measures to ensure accountability with regard to how the funds freed by debt relief are used. In Uganda, for example, a fund was set up with the money saved from debt relief. This fund is overseen by a board that includes not only representatives of the national government but also persons representing a broad cross-section of civil society, including churches, unions, and other local and international organizations with strong reputations for prioritizing the well-being of the Ugandan people. The use of this type of oversight board to ensure accountability is proposed as a constructive model for other nations to follow. While debt relief for Uganda and other countries has so far been fairly limited, that which has been received has generally had a very positive impact. In Uganda, most of the money saved has been devoted to education, enabling the number of children attending primary school to more than double. In Tanzania, money saved from debt relief has enabled over 3 million additional children to enroll in school. It has also been used to feed people negatively impacted by drought. In Zambia, fees for rural health care have been abolished, enabling the poor to have greater access to desperately needed health care. Mozambique and Burkina Faso have undertaken significant efforts to combat HIV/AIDS.[122] There is thus abundant evidence that debt relief can be managed in ways that ensure constructive uses. What is needed, however, according to debt relief proponents, is the provision of relief on a much larger scale. It is for this goal of expanded debt relief that international movements such as the Jubilee campaign continue to strive.

UNITED STATES OPPOSITION TO SOCIAL CHANGE IN THE THIRD WORLD

Another structural factor that has contributed to persistent poverty and hunger in many Third World nations (in addition to the impacts of colonialism, flawed post-colonial development policies, and the Third World debt crisis) is the existence of repressive and corrupt governments, especially military dictatorships. In Latin America these regimes often came into power in the 1960s and 1970s in response to movements for social reform. In many cases these regimes were in-

122 See Jubilee USA, "Debt Relief Works" (February 2006) and "The Unfinished Agenda on International Debt" (July 2006), both available at <www.jubileeusa.org>.

stalled, financed, and/or supported by the government of the United States.[123]

The history of U.S. military involvement in the affairs of the Third World is a long one. Between 1831 and 1891, for example, the United States invaded a dozen Latin American countries a total of 31 times, mostly on behalf of U.S. business interests.[124] At the end of the 19th century the U.S. acquired the Philippines, Cuba, Puerto Rico, and Guam as colonies after defeating Spain in the Spanish-American War. When the Filipinos resisted U.S. control, a brutal military campaign was waged against them by U.S. forces. This campaign included widespread scorched earth tactics, executions, and torture. Over a half million Filipinos were killed and many Filipino villages destroyed as the U.S. military established control of the country.[125] The Manila correspondent for the *Philadelphia Ledger* described the atrocities that he had witnessed:

> Our men have been relentless, have killed to exterminate men, women, children, prisoners and captives, active insurgents and suspected people from lads of ten up, the idea prevailing that the Filipi-

---

123 Some good works discussing U.S. policies toward the Third World include Stephen Kinzer, *Overthrow: America's Century of Regime Change from Hawaii to Iraq* (New York: Times Books, 2006); William Blum, *Killing Hope: US Military and CIA Interventions Since WWII*, rev. ed. (Monroe, ME: Common Courage Press, 2004); Greg Grandin, *Empire's Workshop: Latin America, the United States, and the Rise of the New Imperialism* (New York: Metropolitan Books, 2006); Michael Parenti, *Against Empire* (San Francisco: City Lights Books, 1995) and *The Sword and the Dollar* (New York: St. Martin's Press, 1979); Penny Lernoux, *Cry of the People: United States Involvement in the Rise of Fascism, Torture, and Murder and the Persecution of the Catholic Church in Latin America* (Garden City, NY: Doubleday, 1980).

It should be noted that the former Soviet Union also often played a negative role in the Third World, especially in Africa. The Soviet Union, like the United States, frequently used African countries as proxies in the Cold War and thereby helping to perpetuate very destructive wars and civil conflicts.

124 Parenti, *Sword and the Dollar*, 94.

125 For discussion of U.S. military activities in the Philippines, including eyewitness accounts, see Parenti, *Sword and the Dollar*, 42-43; Howard Zinn, *A People's History of the United States*, rev. ed. (New York: HarperCollins, 1995), 305-313.

> no as such was little better than a dog....Our soldiers have pumped salt water into men to make them talk, and have taken prisoners people who held up their hands and peacefully surrendered, and an hour later...stood them on a bridge and shot them down one by one, to drop them into the water below and float down, as examples to those who found their bullet-loaded corpses.[126]

In the early 20th century U.S. military activities in the Third World intensified. Dozens of additional military interventions in Latin America took place. Several Central American and Caribbean countries (e.g. Cuba, Nicaragua, Haiti) were occupied by U.S. forces for years or, in some cases, decades. Before departing, the U.S. forces often helped to install military strongmen in power, as in the case of Anatasio Somoza in Nicaragua.

Major General Smedley Butler was the commander of many of the U.S. military interventions of this period. He later shared these critical reflections on his activities:

> I spent thirty-three years in the Marines, most of my time being a high-class muscleman for Big Business, for Wall Street and the bankers. In short, I was a racketeer for capitalism.
>
> I helped purify Nicaragua for the international banking house of Brown Brothers in 1910-1912. I helped make Mexico...safe for American oil interests in 1914. I brought light to the Dominican Republic for American sugar interests in 1916. I helped make Haiti and Cuba a decent place for the National City [Bank] boys to collect revenue in. I helped in the rape of a half dozen Central American republics for the benefit of Wall Street. In China in 1927 I helped to see to it that Standard Oil went its way unmolested.
>
> I had a swell racket. I was rewarded with honors, medals, promotions. I might have given Al Capone a few hints. The best he could do was to operate a racket in three city districts. We Marines operated on three continents.[127]

In the period after WWII, U.S. involvement in the affairs of Third World nations became even more extensive and institutionalized, es-

126 Cited in Zinn, *People's History*, 308. One major reported that a general had instructed him "to kill and burn, and said that the more he killed and burned the better pleased he would be; that it was no time to take prisoners, and that he was to make...a howling wilderness." Ibid.

127 Quoted in Parenti, *Sword and the Dollar*, 94-95. These comments originally were published in a magazine entitled *Common Sense* (November, 1935).

pecially with the formation of the CIA and related national security agencies. The guiding task of U.S. foreign policy in the postwar era, as described in a 1948 State Department Planning Document written by George Kennan, was to formulate the policies needed to maintain U.S. economic dominance:

> We have about 50 percent of the world's wealth, but only 6.3 percent of its population....In this situation, we cannot fail to be the object of envy and resentment. Our real task in the coming period is to devise a pattern of relationships which will permit us to maintain this position of disparity without positive detriment to our national security.[128]

This objective of "maintain[ing] this position of disparity" would come to be closely intertwined with the notion of opposing "communism." The label of communist in this era was typically applied to anyone who called into question existing disparities, regardless of whether their views were in any formal sense supportive of communist policies. Often this label of communist would be applied to progressive elements of the Catholic Church in Latin America.

In pursuit of these objectives of maintaining economic dominance, the United States in the postwar era consistently opposed governments that sought to implement substantive social reform or who were seen to be challenging the interests of U.S. corporations. Often the U.S. government was involved in organizing, funding, and supporting the overthrow of democratically elected reformist governments, as in the cases of Guatemala, Brazil, Chile, and Nicaragua.

Guatemala – In 1954 the CIA organized a military coup against the democratically elected government of Jacobo Arbenz. Arbenz had implemented policies viewed disfavorably by the U.S. government, including a policy that required the U.S.-based United Fruit Company, Guatemala's largest landowner, to sell a small portion of its landholdings to the Guatemalan government to be distributed to landless peasants. The coup against Arbenz (who considered himself to be a reformist capitalist) was followed by harsh repression and a series of military-dominated governments. Massive inequality and harsh repression in turn gave rise to a small revolutionary movement. In the

128 PPS/23, dated February 24, 1948. Cited in Jack Nelson-Pallmeyer, *School of Assassins* (Maryknoll, NY: Orbis Books, 1997), 39.

40 years following the coup over 200,000 Guatemalans were killed by government-sponsored forces. The vast majority of these persons were noncombatants. Also, over 40,000 persons were "disappeared" by the military and right-wing death squads in an effort to bring an end through terror to all movements for social change. Common targets of the death squads included union activists, health care workers, teachers, students, and, when the Catholic Church eventually began to take a strong stand on behalf of human rights, local church leaders, especially catechists. In the 1980s scorched earth military campaigns by the government destroyed over 400 indigenous villages, whose inhabitants were indiscriminately massacred. Rape and torture have been commonplace. Throughout this entire period the United States continued to provide both overt and covert support to the Guatemalan government and military.[129]

Brazil – In the early 1960s the U.S. played a central role in organizing a massive destabilization campaign in Brazil against the democratically elected reformist government of João Goulart. This campaign culminated in a military coup that overthrew Goulart in 1964. Goulart had chosen to follow a non-aligned foreign policy and had proposed to implement a moderate land reform and place limits on the amount of profits that foreign corporations could remove from Brazil, measures which earned him the enmity of the United States government and corporations. Following the coup, intense repression prevailed in Brazil for several decades (including widespread assassinations and torture), while U.S. leaders hailed Brazil as an "economic miracle" and provided ongoing economic and military support. Life in Brazil after the coup is described by William Blum:

> Congress was shut down, political opposition was reduced to virtual extinction, habeas corpus for 'political crimes' was suspended..., labor unions were taken over by government interveners, mounting protests were met by police and military firing into crowds, the use

129 For discussion of the U.S. coup in Guatemala, see Stephen Schlesinger and Stephen Kinzer, *Bitter Fruit: The Story of the American Coup in Guatemala*, rev. ed. (Cambridge, MA: Harvard University Press, 2005); Blum, *Killing Hope*, chapter 10. For discussion of the massive human rights abuses that occurred in the decades following the coup, see Human Rights Office, Archdiocese of Guatemala, *Guatemala: Never Again!* (Maryknoll, NY: Orbis Books, 1999).

> of systematic 'disappearance' as a form of repression came upon the stage of Latin America, peasants' homes were burned down, priests were brutalized...then there was the torture and the death squads, both largely undertakings of the police and the military, both underwritten by the United States.[130]

It was in Brazil that active persecution of the Catholic Church for its stand on behalf of the poor first became commonplace, persecution that would later spread to numerous other Latin American countries.[131]

Chile – The United States government played a major role in overthrowing Chile's democratically elected president Salvador Allende, who was killed during a U.S.-backed coup in 1973. Like Arbenz in Guatemala and Goulart in Brazil, Allende had sought to implement land reform and to place certain restrictions on foreign corporations. The government of Allende, with its attempt to improve living conditions for the poor, became a symbol of hope for many Latin Americans. U.S. business and political leaders, however, viewed Allende as a major threat. The U.S. ambassador to Chile, Edward Korry, publicly declared that "not a nut or bolt will be allowed to reach Chile under Allende." "Once Allende comes to power," Korry warned, "we shall do all within our power to condemn Chile and Chileans to utmost misery and deprivation."[132] As elsewhere, the U.S.-backed coup was followed by intense repression, in this case under the brutal dictatorship of Augusto Pinochet.

> [T]hey closed the country to the outside world for a week, while the tanks rolled and the soldiers broke down doors; the stadiums rang with the sounds of executions and the bodies piled up along the streets and floated in the river; the torture centers opened for business; the subversive books were thrown to the bonfires; soldiers slit the trouser legs of women, shouting that "In Chile women wear

---

130 Blum, *Killing Hope*, 170-171.

131 For discussion of the persecution of the Catholic Church, see Lernoux, *Cry of the People*. For additional information on the U.S. role in overthrowing Goulart and establishing the military dictatorship, see Ruth Leacock, *Requiem for Revolution: The United States and Brazil, 1961-1969* (Kent, OH: Kent State University Press, 1990).

132 Edward Korry, U.S. Ambassador to Chile, cited in Parenti, *Sword and the Dollar*, 57.

> dresses!"... and the men of the world in Washington and in the halls of international finance opened up their check-books.[133]

Indeed, after the coup U.S. economic aid (which had been cut off after Allende's election) was resumed and military aid increased. The World Bank, which had stopped loans under Allende, resumed lending. A year after the coup, after many Chileans had been tortured and killed, President Gerald Ford declared that what the U.S. had done in Chile was "in the best interest of the people in Chile and certainly in our own best interest."[134]

Nicaragua – After a successful revolution against the U.S.-installed and supported Somoza dictatorship in 1979, Nicaragua became a new source of hope for many of the poor of Latin America. In the years following the revolution the Sandinista government instituted an extensive and highly successful literacy campaign (mobilizing tens of thousands of volunteers) and made important improvements in the areas of health, education, and land distribution. As a result of major improvements brought about by these reforms, the government received prestigious awards from several United Nations agencies.[135] The United States government, however, viewed the revolution very differently, and soon began efforts to undermine it using an array of military and economic means. These measures included the funding of the "contras," a group organized by the CIA whose leadership consisted primarily of former Somoza National Guard officers. The major military activities of the contras included attacks on civilians, especially teachers, health care workers, and members of agricultural cooperatives, along with the destruction of schools, health clinics, and other governmental and economic infrastructure. According to the human rights organization Americas Watch, human rights abuses on the part of the contras were "so prevalent that these may be said to be their principal means of waging war."[136] Edgar Chamorro, a former contra leader, confesses that "during my four years as a contra director, it was premeditated policy to terrorize civilian noncombatants." "Civil-

133 Blum, *Killing Hope*, 214.

134 Cited in ibid. The original source of the quotation by President Ford is the *New York Times* (September 17, 1974): 22.

135 See Dianna Melrose, *Nicaragua: The Threat of a Good Example?* (Boston: Oxfam, 1985).

136 Cited in Nelson-Pallmeyer, *School of Assassins,* 67-68.

ian murders, mutilations, tortures, and rapes" were routinely committed by the contras, says Chamorro, acts "of which the contra leaders and their CIA superiors were well aware."[137]

Even after the Sandinista government was victorious by a large margin in internationally supervised elections in 1984, the U.S. government continued to wage war against it. Claims of human rights abuses by the government were presented as the central rationale for war. Some abuses did occur, including some cases of the denial of the right to free speech and assembly and in several instances forced evacuations from war areas that included acts of violence. Americas Watch and other highly respected human rights organizations such as Amnesty International strongly deny, however, that the Sandinista government ever engaged in any sustained pattern of abuses, and emphasize that major abuses such as torture or denial of the right to life were largely nonexistent. When on several isolated occasions Sandinista soldiers were responsible for the deaths of civilians, the persons responsible were quickly punished. In contrast, neighboring regimes in El Salvador and Guatemala were known for widespread systematic government-sponsored assassinations, military massacres, and torture, yet continued to receive the backing of the U.S. government. In the eyes of critics, this made a mockery of the stated concern of the U.S. government for human rights in the region.[138]

Ongoing military and economic destabilization efforts on the part of the U.S. contributed greatly to the electoral defeat of the Sandinistas in 1990. Since then most of the Sandinista reforms in areas such as health, education, land reform, and nutrition have been overturned

137 Edgar Chamorro, "Terror is the Most Effective Weapon on Nicaragua's Contras," letter to the editor of the *New York Times* (January 9, 1986).

138 With regard to Reagan administration manipulation of the issue of human rights, Americas Watch stated: "The misuse of human rights data has become pervasive in officials' statements to the press, in White House handouts on Nicaragua, in the annual *Country Report* on Nicaraguan human rights prepared by the State Department....In Nicaragua there is no systematic practice of forced disappearances, extrajudicial killings, or torture – as has been the case with the 'friendly' armed forces of El Salvador....Nor has the Government practiced elimination of cultural or ethnic groups, [as in] Guatemala, whose government the Administration consistently defends." Cited in Nelson-Pallmeyer, *War Against the Poor: Low-Intensity Conflict and Christian Faith* (Maryknoll, NY: Orbis Books, 1989), 39-40.

and very stringent structural adjustment policies put into place. Nicaragua now again vies with Haiti for the worst social indices in the hemisphere.[139]

These examples of U.S. support for repressive regimes and efforts to undermine governments that challenged U.S. economic interests are unfortunately far from being isolated cases. In Vietnam, for example, the U.S. intervened to prevent an election that would have had unfavorable results. The Geneva Agreements of 1954, which ended the Vietnamese war with the French, had temporarily partitioned the country and established plans for an election to be held within a unified Vietnam in 1956. The problem from the U.S. perspective, however, was that Ho Chi Minh, the popular nationalist leader who had led the anti-colonial struggle against the French, would easily win this election. The U.S. government, which opposed Ho Chi Minh's leftist economic policies, therefore encouraged the government in South Vietnam, which it had helped to install, to refuse to allow the election to be held. In the coming years the U.S. committed massive amounts of money and soldiers to prop up a series of dictatorial South Vietnamese regimes, regimes that were opposed by large numbers of their own people. The results of U.S. intervention in Vietnam included over 3 million deaths (mostly noncombatants), the wounding of millions more, the destruction of thousands of villages, and the devastation of much of the countryside and forests by bombings and by the widespread use of napalm and chemical defoliants. Intense animosity had also been fostered within the country by a decade of brutal conflict. This animosity would carry over into internal postwar policies in Vietnam.[140]

In addition to the above cases, the U.S. also played a key role in the post-WWII era in overthrowing reformist regimes and replacing them with dictatorships in Iran (installing the Shah), Indonesia (installing the Suharto dictatorship), Argentina, Uruguay, Bolivia, Greece, the Dominican Republic, Guyana, and Pakistan, among others. In dozens of additional cases the U.S. supplied support to repressive regimes to prevent reformist or revolutionary challenges from arising. This included

139 See Noam Chomsky, *World Orders: Old and New* (New York: Columbia University Press, 1994), 131-134.

140 Good discussion of the Vietnam War can be found in William Griffen and John Marciano, *Teaching the Vietnam War* (Montclair, NJ: Allanheld, Osmun, and Co., 1979).

support for the dictatorships of Marcos in the Philippines, Mobutu in Zaire, Duvalier in Haiti, and repressive regimes in countries such as El Salvador, Honduras, Paraguay, Peru, Colombia, Panama, Turkey, Saudi Arabia, Somalia, South Africa, Cambodia, Thailand, South Korea, and others.[141] The U.S. also provided support for counter-revolutionary forces seeking to overthrow leftist governments in countries such as Angola, Mozambique, and Afghanistan. These counterrevolutionary forces, like the contras in Nicaragua, were often noted for their extreme brutality against civilians. For example, the UNITA movement led by Jonas Savimbi, which fought to overthrow the government of Angola, was responsible for hundreds of thousands of civilian deaths through indiscriminate use of landmines, direct attacks on schools, clinics, and other civilian targets, the kidnapping of children who were forced to fight as child soldiers, and other atrocities.[142]

Several studies have shown that U.S. military and economic aid to Third World countries in the post-WWII period has generally been "positively related to terror and improvement of investment climate and negatively related to human rights."[143] In other words, when human rights improved and efforts were being made to meet the needs of the poor, as under Arbenz and other reformers, U.S. aid would consistently decrease. After the reformist regimes were overthrown, massive violations of human rights had resumed, and the "investment climate" had improved, U.S. aid would increase. Significantly, the United States was not a passive bystander in these matters, unable to control the actions of its allies, as is sometimes claimed. Rather, abundant evidence exists that the U.S. government played a key role in formulating and spreading the doctrines of the National Security State which were used to justify repressive conduct. Frequently, as in the cases discussed above, the U.S. helped to install military regimes and provided aid to keep them in power. It is also well documented that U.S. advisors have taught and participated in activities of torture and have supported (along with the CIA) the formation of death squads in various countries. Penny Lernoux, the Roman Catholic journalist whose landmark

---

141 For in-depth accounts of these and additional cases, see Blum, *Killing Hope*, and other books cited in the preceding notes.

142 See Blum, *Killing Hope*, 249-257.

143 Noam Chomsky and Edward Herman, *The Washington Connection and Third World Fascism* (Boston: South End Press, 1979), 16.

work *Cry of the People* did much to raise awareness of these issues in the United States, wrote:

> [Accounts of torture and assassinations] are not bizarre instances of cruelty but common occurrences in Latin America, endured by thousands of innocent people....So systematized is torture that it has become a way of life in many Latin American countries....The sickness that has engulfed Latin America, that endorses torture and assassination as routine in most of these countries, was to a significant extent bred in the boardrooms and military institutes of the United States."[144]

Recent declassified documents have shown that the U.S. Army School of the Americas (now known as the Western Hemisphere Institute for Security Cooperation), formerly located in Panama and now at Fort Benning, Georgia, used training manuals that taught and advocated the use of torture and assassination by its Latin American military trainees, confirming what critics have alleged for decades. A Boston Globe editorial stated upon release of these documents: "Murder, extortion, torture – those are some of the lessons the U.S. Army taught Latin American officers at the notorious School of the Americas."[145] Numerous graduates of the school have confirmed this training in torture techniques. José Valle, School of the Americas graduate and former member of the notorious Battalion 316 in Honduras, recalls that he took a course at the School of the Americas that included "a lot of videos which showed the type of interrogation and torture they used in Vietnam."[146] A report in the *Baltimore Sun* relates that Battalion 316, to which Valle belonged,

> used shock and suffocation devices in interrogations. Prisoners were often kept naked and, when no longer useful, killed and bur-

144 Lernoux, *Cry of the People*, 156-157.

145 "Lessons in Terror," *Boston Globe* (October 1, 1996). Cited in Nelson-Pallmeyer, *School of Assassins*, 32.

146 Ibid. One graduate of the School of the Americas has testified: "The school was always used as a front for other special operations, covert operations. They would bring people from the streets [of Panama City] into the base and the experts would train us on how to torture human beings. They had a medical physician, a U.S. medical physician who I remember very well, who was dressed in green fatigues, who would...show them where to torture." Cited in ibid., 31. The original interview with this graduate is included in the video *Inside the School of Assassins*.

> ied in unmarked graves. Newly declassified documents and other sources now show that the CIA and US embassy knew of numerous crimes, including torture and murder, yet continued to support Battalion 316 and collaborate with its leaders.[147]

Similar evidence exists of U.S. involvement with and support for death squads and torture in Guatemala, El Salvador, Haiti, Uruguay, Brazil, and other countries. A former Chief of Police Intelligence in Uruguay, for example, has acknowledged publicly that it was U.S. advisors who instituted torture in Uruguay as a routine practice.[148]

In reviewing this history of U.S. involvement in the Third World, it is important to note that involvement in interventions to overthrow reformist governments and support for repressive regimes both preceded the Cold War and have continued after its end. There is evidence, for example, that the U.S. played a key role in the 2004 ouster of the Aristide government in Haiti and has been involved in efforts to overthrow the reformist government of Hugo Chavez in Venezuela, including a failed military coup that took place in 2002. At the same time, the U.S. continues to support governments with very negative human rights records in the Middle East, in Central Asia, and elsewhere, now doing so in the name of the "war on terror."[149] Stephen Zunes states: "The

---

147 Gary Cohn and Ginger Thompson, "Unearthed: Fatal Secrets," *Baltimore Sun* (a series of articles that appeared June 11-18, 1995). Cited in Nelson-Pallmeyer, *School of Assassins*, 31-32. The U.S. ambassador to Honduras at that time, who is accused of having condoned this use of torture and murder, was John Negroponte. Negroponte was appointed by President Bush as U.S. ambassador to the United Nations in 2001. He later was appointed U.S. ambassador to Iraq and then Director of National Intelligence, overseeing all of the U.S. intelligence agencies.

148 Blum, *Killing Hope*, 201. Chomsky and Herman assert that "the systematic and sophisticated use of torture in Uruguay, as elsewhere, seems to have developed as one central component of the U.S. aid program. Victims have reported that Dan Mitrione [a U.S. advisor], who was involved in the escalation of torture in Uruguay, participated directly in torture sessions. There is little doubt that local torturers were trained by the US and used equipment supplied through US assistance programs with the knowledge of their US advisors." *Washington Connection*, 272.

149 See, for example, Human Rights Watch, "U.S. Military Aid After 9/11 Threatens Human Rights," available at <www.hrw.org> and Amnesty International, "U.S. Government Steps Up Military Aid for Human Rights Abusers," available at <www.amnestyusa.org>.

anti-terrorist coalition that the United States has built for its military response to the September 2001 attacks–centered around alliances with the absolute monarchy in Saudi Arabia, the military regime of Pakistan, and the crypto-Communists that rule Uzbekistan–has been labeled 'Operation Enduring Freedom.' It's an irony lost on few Middle Easterners."[150] From the perspective of the Third World, argues Noam Chomsky, the Cold War did not represent a break from normal U.S. policy, but rather "only changed the framework in which long-standing policies were executed."[151] These policies of interventions and support for repressive regimes in the Third World have been pursued by all U.S. administrations, both Republican and Democrat, though varying somewhat in degree.[152]

In the past two decades numerous Third World countries have experienced transitions from military to civilian rule, and overt human rights violations (such as torture and assassinations) have decreased in prevalence. This is especially true in Latin America. At the same time, however, overall socio-economic conditions of the poor majorities in most Third World countries have deteriorated. Chomsky and others argue that the decline in overt repression in places like Latin America is primarily due to the fact that it is no longer viewed as necessary, because hope for substantive change has greatly declined. Says Chomsky:

> Forceful interventions and military dictatorships are not as necessary as before. One reason is the success of violence in devastating popular organizations. Another is the economic catastrophe in much of the Third World. In these circumstances, it becomes possible to tolerate civilian governments, sometimes even social democrats, now that hopes for a better life have been destroyed.[153]

---

150 Stephen Zunes, *Tinderbox: U.S. Middle East Policy and the Roots of Terrorism* (Monroe, ME: Common Courage Press, 2003), 15.

151 Chomsky, *World Orders*, 68.

152 The administration of Jimmy Carter is sometimes viewed as an exception, given its stated emphasis upon human rights. While stressing human rights in some cases, however, President Carter also provided support to numerous repressive regimes, including the Somoza dictatorship in Nicaragua, the Shah of Iran, the Marcos dictatorship in the Philippines, and numerous others. See discussions of Carter's policies in Chomsky and Herman, *Washington Connection*.

153 Chomsky, *Deterring Democracy*, 60.

Manfred Bienefeld expresses similar views. He asserts that as a result of the debt crisis and the implementation of IMF/World Bank-imposed structural adjustment policies, which remove economic decision-making from local governments, democracy in the Third World has in significant ways been emptied of substance. Democracy therefore he claims has more appeal now to those powers which previously saw democracy, particularly in its populist forms, as something to be feared:

> Governments and political processes have...been emptied of political content. Governments have become executive agencies that implement predetermined policies devised by technical experts. This has made it much easier for the IFIs [international financial institutions, such as the World Bank and IMF] and the hegemonic powers [above all the U.S.] to support democracy in the developing world, since it is no great threat to give people the democratic right to elect governments that have no effective power over social or economic policy.[154]

Moves to foster "free trade" agreements such as NAFTA, CAFTA, and the creation of the World Trade Organization are viewed by critics as ways of further ensuring that governments now and in the future not be able to depart from the neoliberal economic policies favored by the U.S. and other leading capitalist powers. These treaties, critics claim, are developed without popular input, further erode democracy, and have a variety of negative social and ecological impacts, as will be discussed extensively in subsequent chapters.

What has been the overall consequence of U.S. policies in the Third World in the postwar era? Critics such as Noam Chomsky offer a profoundly negative assessment. "The major achievement of the massive terror operations of the past years organized by Washington and its local allies," asserts Chomsky, "has been to destroy hope."[155] Much evidence indeed points to a growing sense of despair and of resignation among many of the Third World poor, especially during the 1980s and 1990s, at the same time that many of the world's wealthy hailed the triumph of global capitalism. "The pursuit of structural adjustment in the 1980s and 1990s," state Susan George and Fabrizio Sabelli, "has, in many countries, entrenched poverty and despair but also a kind of exhaustion of potential opposition forces. At the end of the millen-

154 Bienefeld, "Structural Adjustment," 108.

155 Chomsky, *World Orders*, 55. Also see Blum, *Killing Hope*.

nium the 'suffering and deprivation' of [the Third World's] absolute poor no longer readily cause revolution, only deeper despair."[156]

In the past several years, however, new movements and momentum for social change have arisen, giving rise to renewed hope. This can be seen, for example, in the strong global movements focusing on debt relief, aid to Africa, and the shaping of alternatives to current forms of globalization. Adopting the motto that "another world is possible," grassroots movements around the world have become invigorated, and in some cases have succeeded in electing governments that are more sensitive to the needs of the poor and that are critical of central components of neoliberal economic orthodoxy. This has especially been the case in Latin America, where more populist governments have recently been elected in Brazil, Venezuela, Argentina, Uruguay, Ecuador, Paraguay, El Salvador, and Bolivia. Yet significant structural constraints (such as the threat of capital flight on the part of the international capitalist community) shape the context in which these new governments operate, limiting what they can accomplish and raising the danger that the grassroots movements may feel betrayed and disillusioned if widespread social change is not quickly achieved. This has already been seen, for example, in the case of the government of Ignacio 'Lula' da Silva in Brazil, a former union leader and human rights activist who was elected president with the support of grassroots movements amidst high expectations for change. Many feel that Lula has been too willing to compromise with global capitalist interests, hindering the types of improvement in the lives of the poor that had been expected from his presidency. Lula, in turn, points to accomplishments such as reduced hunger and argues that he is pursuing the type of policies that have the most realistic hope of long-term success, aware that bolder reforms could lead to capital flight and undermine the Brazilian economy. Some countries such as Venezuela and Bolivia, on the other hand, are moving forward with attempts at more far-reaching change, trying to develop a "21st century socialism." Which of two approaches will be more successful is yet to be seen, but both are viewed by many as positive signs of a growing willingness to challenge neoliberal orthodoxy.

---

156 Susan George and Fabrizio Sabelli, *Faith and Credit: The World Bank's Secular Empire* (Boulder: Westview, 1994), 56.

SUMMARY OF MAJOR STRUCTURAL INFLUENCES ON THE THIRD WORLD

This chapter has examined some of the underlying causes of the deep social problems confronting the Third World. These causes have included :

– the impact of colonialism, which shaped Third World economies to provide cheap exports to the wealthy countries, established patterns of profound economic and political inequality, and created arbitrary boundaries that have contributed to social strife.

– flawed post-colonial development policies, which have favored the interests of First World businesses and local elites at the expense of the poor majorities of Third World countries

– declining prices for Third World commodities

– the Third World debt crisis and its aftermath, which has led to the implementation of structural adjustment policies and further harm to the environment and the poor

– superpower (especially United States) interventions to prevent constructive social change.

While playing the dominant roles, these factors are of course not the only factors that have shaped current realities in the Third World. Another important factor is the corruption that exists in many countries. This corruption, it should be noted, often has its roots in the realities highlighted above, e.g. the legacy of colonizers who collaborated with corrupt local elites or superpower installation and support for corrupt regimes. While it is crucial that corruption be confronted and overcome, it is also important that the significance of the problem not be overstated, as is sometimes done by those who seek to downplay the need for systemic changes in the global economy. Even relatively non-corrupt Third World governments face fundamental obstacles. With regard to Africa, for example, a report of the U.N. Millennium Project states: "Many parts of Africa are well governed considering the income levels and the extent of poverty, yet are caught in a poverty trap."[157]

The next chapter will explore the reflections of Catholic Social Teaching on development and globalization themes. It will be suggested that CST provides much insight into the negative aspects of

157 U.N. Millennium Project, *Investing in Development: A Practical Plan to Achieve the Millennium Development Goals* (New York: Millennium Project, 2005), 32.

past policies and provides constructive suggestions for the creation of alternative approaches.

CHAPTER 3

CATHOLIC SOCIAL TEACHING AND DEVELOPMENT

This chapter provides an overview of the history of Catholic Social Teaching and its central themes. The important contributions that CST can make to discussions of economic development and globalization are especially highlighted. Among these contributions are CST's understandings of "integral development" and "economic democracy," its recognition of structural injustice, and its emphasis on the virtue of solidarity and the need for a preferential option for the poor. In later chapters CST will be brought into dialogue with some of its critics and with other persons who are seeking alternatives to current development/globalization policies. From this dialogue will emerge several suggestions for the further enhancement of CST.

CST PRIOR TO POPE JOHN XXIII

Development and other issues related to the Third World did not come to occupy a central place in Catholic Social Teaching until the social encyclicals of Pope John XXIII in the early 1960s. Since this time attention to global justice issues in CST has intensified and these themes now generally occupy a prominent place in all CST documents. In order to understand these more recent documents, however, it is important to have some familiarity with the earlier CST tradition that these writings build upon.

Rerum Novarum (1891)

The modern tradition of CST is generally viewed as having begun with Leo XIII's encyclical *Rerum Novarum* in 1891. While papal encyclicals on a variety of topics had been published in the century and a half prior to *Rerum Novarum,* Leo's document contained important new ideas and themes that would provide the foundation for the Catholic Church's approach to modern social issues.[1] As a consequence of its groundbreaking content this encyclical has received a highly exalted status within the tradition. Pope John XXIII, for example, asserts that *Rerum Novarum* "so effected for the first time an organization of principles, and, as it were, set forth singlemindedly a future course of action, that we may regard it as a summary of Catholic teaching, so far as economic and social matters are concerned."[2]

The central theme of *Rerum Novarum* is the plight of workers within modern industrial societies:

> It has come to pass that workingmen have been given over, isolated and defenseless, to the callousness of employers and the greed of unrestrained competition....A small number of very rich men have been able to lay upon the masses of the poor a yoke little better than slavery itself. (RN 2)

In response to the plight of the workers, the pope calls for measures such as limits on working hours, an end to child labor, and freedom from work on Sundays. (RN 32-33) Major emphasis is placed as well upon the notion of a "just wage," defined as a wage sufficient to enable the father of a family to "maintain himself, his wife, and his children in reasonable comfort."[3] (RN 35) The pope here rejects the notion that the laws of supply and demand and contracts alone can rightly determine wages, arguing that the mere fact that a worker agrees to a certain wage does not necessarily make the wage just. Rather, "if through necessity or fear of a worse evil, the workman accepts harder conditions because an employer or contractor will give him no better, he is the victim of force and injustice." (RN 34)

1 The modern tradition of papal encyclicals was begun by Pope Benedict XIV in 1740. For an overview of the major themes of the pre-Leonine encyclicals, see Michael Schuck, *That They Be One: The Social Teachings of the Papal Encyclicals 1740-1989* (Washington, DC: Georgetown University Press, 1991).

2 Pope John XXIII, *Mater et Magistra*, no. 15.

3 Pope Leo views the proper task of women as being work within the home."Women," he says,"are not suited to certain trades; for a woman is by nature fitted for home work, and it is that which is best adapted at once to preserve her modesty, and to promote the good bringing up of children and the well-being of the family." (RN 33). Therefore, strong emphasis is placed by Leo upon the father receiving an adequate income to support his family without any need for paid employment on the part of his wife.

A central theme of the encyclical is the importance of private property. For the pope, the ownership of property, particularly land, is viewed as a primary means by which a family can prudently provide for its economic security. (RN 4-10) He thus argues that a just wage must be high enough that a family living a frugal lifestyle could save enough money to purchase land. He also argues that the legal system "should favor ownership, and its policy should be to induce as many people as possible to become owners." (RN 35)

While rejecting aspects of existing capitalism, especially its abuse of workers, Pope Leo at the same time presents a total condemnation of socialism. He criticizes socialism especially for its rejection of private property, its hostility towards religion, and its fostering of class conflict. (RN 12-15) Significantly, the pope condemns socialism also for its emphasis on equality. (RN 14) Though he strongly defends the rights of all to have their basic needs met, Pope Leo sees inequality in income and social status above the subsistence level as proper. His views on this issue are strongly shaped by an organic view of society derived from medieval Catholicism in which hierarchy and inequality are seen as having their proper place in the overall harmonious functioning of the social body. Reflecting such a view, the pope argues that "inequality is far from being disadvantageous" because there is the need for a variety of persons with differing abilities filling a variety of social roles, all contributing to the common good. (RN 14) In his discussion of Christian charity the pope likewise makes clear his approval of social stratification, arguing that it is justified for persons to reserve for their own use not only what is needed to meet their basic needs but also whatever is needed "to keep up becomingly [their] condition in life." It is then only from what is left over that there is an obligation to share with the poor. (RN 19) Later in CST, as we will see, equality will come to play a more central role, and this teaching on charity will be significantly modified.

Connected with the organic view of society in the thought of Pope Leo is the central emphasis that the pope places on social harmony, especially "harmony and agreement" between the capitalist class and the laboring class. (RN 15) A central task of the Catholic religion, the pope says, is to teach to each class their mutual duties so that such harmony can prevail. "The great mistake...is to possess oneself of the idea that class is naturally hostile to class....There is nothing stronger than religion (of which the Church is the interpreter and guardian) in drawing rich and poor together, reminding each class of its duties to the other." (RN 15-16) Strongly condemned by the pope are "crafty agitators" who attempt to "stir up the people to sedition" by setting workers against owners. (RN 1)

Pope Leo's emphasis on harmony is evident in his lack of encouragement for efforts by workers to actively organize in defense of their rights. Instead, workers are to depend largely on the good will of the wealthy and, as will be discussed more fully below, on intervention by the state should the wealthy neglect their duty to treat workers justly. While the pope does stress the importance of "workers' associations," he has in mind not trade unions understood in an activist sense as a countervailing power to capital, but rather organizations whose central focus is "mutual help" (setting up funds to aid members in case of accident or illness, in old age, etc.) and whose activities "pay special and principal attention to piety and morality." (RN 36, 42) Rejecting existing trade unions as too secular and adversarial, the pope calls upon Catholics to form their own workers' associations. (RN 40)

For Pope Leo, personal morality and the teachings of the church are the key to solving social problems. At the same time, however, the pope is also aware that there may be situations in which the teachings of the church are not heeded. In these cases, he says, the state has a duty to intervene to protect the common good. Rejecting the laissez-faire arguments prominent at the time, Pope Leo argues that "whenever the general interest of any particular class suffers, or is threatened with, evils which can in no other way be met, the public authority must step in to meet them." (RN 28) Above all, the pope says, the state has an obligation to protect the rights of the poor and of workers:

> When there is question of protecting the rights of individuals, the poor and helpless have a claim to special consideration. The richer population have many ways of protecting themselves...; those who are badly off have no resources of their own to fall back upon, and must chiefly rely upon the assistance of the State. And it is for this reason that wage earners who are, undoubtedly, among the weak and necessitous, should be specially cared for and protected by the commonwealth. (RN 29)

It is for this strong defense of the rights of workers that *Rerum Novarum* is mostly remembered, especially coming as it did at a time of great tension between workers and capital and in a context in which laissez-faire ideology was dominant. As Donal Dorr states, Pope Leo's encyclical was "a cry of protest against the exploitation of poor workers," and its issuance "meant that the Church could not be taken to be indifferent to the injustices of the time."[4] In its defense of workers, its rejection of socialism, its critical attitude toward capitalism and individualism, its affirmation of an important (but limited) role for the state in economic life, among other contributions, *Rerum Novarum* provided key themes that would be foundational for CST and would greatly impact the tradition's later explicit reflections on the theme of development.

Quadragesimo Anno (1931)

It would be forty years until another major papal social encyclical was published. In 1931, Pope Pius XI issued *Quadragesimo Anno*, in commemoration of the 40th anniversary of *Rerum Novarum*. Like *Rerum Novarum*, *Quadragesimo Anno* mainly concerned itself with conditions in the modern industrial societies of Western Europe and North America.

Much of *Quadragesimo Anno* consists of a reaffirmation of the teachings of *Rerum Novarum*. Especially highlighted are the rights of workers, the duty of the state to protect the poor, and the serious flaws of both socialism and existing forms of capitalism.[5]

Several new or heightened emphases are also present in Pius' encyclical. While still placing strong emphasis on social harmony, Pius nonetheless affirms a stronger role for workers' associations in actively defending workers' rights. He speaks of these associations as a means "of self-protection against oppression by the more powerful." (QA 30)

Pius affirms the rights of workers to a just wage. He also makes the suggestion that worker participation in ownership and management

4 Donal Dorr, *Option for the Poor: A Hundred Years of Catholic Social Teaching*, rev. ed. (Maryknoll, NY: Orbis, 1992), 14.

5 In developing his critique of socialism, Pope Pius acknowledges that many of the reform suggestions of moderate socialists are in fact very similar to those called for by the Catholic Church. "It cannot be denied," he says, "that [moderate socialism's] programs often strikingly approach the just demands of Christian social reformers." (QA 113) Even so, Pius argues that socialism is fundamentally flawed because socialists fail to recognize the inherently social nature of human beings and the natural orientation of humans towards God. (QA 118) It is for these reasons that Pius declares that "no one can be at the same time a sincere Catholic and a true socialist." (QA 120)

should be given increased consideration: "We deem it advisable that the wage contract should, when possible, be modified somewhat by a contract of partnership" in which "the workers and executives become sharers in the ownership or management." (QA 65)

Pope Pius' critique of capitalism is even stronger than that of Leo XIII. Writing amidst the high unemployment and misery of the Great Depression, Pius argues that unrestrained capitalism has led to "economic dictatorship," creating a situation in which "immense power and despotic economic domination [is] concentrated in the hands of a few" while, at the same time, the multitudes suffer. (QA 109, 105) Unregulated competition, the pope says, "permits the survival of those only who are the strongest. This often means those who fight most relentlessly, who pay the least heed to the dictates of conscience." (QA 107) "The whole economic life," Pius asserts, "has become hard, cruel, and relentless in a ghastly measure." (QA 109)

Singled out for special criticism as a cause of current problems are modern corporations and the legal framework supporting them:

> The regulations legally enacted for corporations, with their divided responsibility and limited liability, have given occasion to abominable abuses. The greatly weakened accountability makes little impression, as is evident, upon the conscience. The worst injustices and frauds take place beneath the obscurity of the common name of a corporative firm. (QA 132)

Pope Pius suggests the need for "a frank and sincere return to the teaching of the Gospel" as a solution to social ills. (QA 136). In addition, like Pope Leo, he suggests the need for stronger governmental regulation of economic activities on behalf of the common good:

> Free competition, and especially economic domination, must be kept within definite and proper bounds, and must be brought under effective control of the public authority, in matters pertaining to the latter's competence. The public institutions of the nations should be such as to make all human society conform to the requirements of the common good, that is, the norm of social justice.[6] (QA 110)

6 Pius XI, like Leo XIII, affirms a certain level of inequality as natural and argues that persons are entitled to keep for their own use whatever portion of their income is needed to maintain their "station" in life. (QA 50) At the same time, however, Pius stresses that inequalities carried to extremes can be very detrimental to the common good and must not be tolerated. "Every sincere observer realizes," Pius asserts, "that the vast differences between

A fundamental problem of contemporary society, the pope argues, is that the state has abandoned its proper role as guarantor of the common good and has become a "slave" of the wealthy:

> The State which should be the supreme arbiter, ruling in queenly fashion far above all party contention, intent only upon justice and the common good, has become instead a slave, bound over to the service of human passion and greed. (QA 109)

Connected with this improper nature of the state, according to Pius, is a flawed view of the human person – an individualistic view of the person that has as its corollary a view of economic life as being properly a realm of unrestrained competition. Condemning "the evil of individualism" (QA 78) and rejecting unregulated competition (QA 88), Pius stresses the social nature of the human person and the social nature of economic life. At the same time he warns of the dangers of collectivism or the simple subordination of the individual to the state. (QA 46) In suggesting a way to steer clear of both the danger of individualism and of collectivism, Pope Pius develops a notion of "subsidiarity." When social functions can be performed by non-governmental individuals and groups, the pope says, it would be wrong for the government to take over these tasks:

> It is an injustice and at the same time a grave evil and a disturbance of right order to transfer to the larger and higher collectivity functions which can be performed and provided for by lesser and subordinate bodies. Inasmuch as every social activity should, by its very nature, prove a help to members of the body social, it should never absorb or destroy them. (QA 60)

This emphasis on decentralization does not, however, prevent Pope Pius from affirming a strong role for government in overseeing and regulating economic life, as we have seen. Indeed, Pius suggests that in allowing non-state parties to do that which they are capable of, the state

> will then perform with greater freedom, vigor, and effectiveness, the tasks properly belonging to it, and which it alone can accomplish, directing, supervising, encouraging, restraining, as circumstances suggest or necessity demands....All the institutions of public and social life must be imbued with the spirit of justice, and this justice

---

the few who hold excessive wealth and the many who live in destitution constitute a grave evil in modern society." (QA 58)

> must above all be truly operative. It must build up a juridical and social order able to pervade all economic activity....It is the duty of the State to safeguard effectively and to vindicate promptly this order. (QA 80, 88)

One of the functions of the state according to Pius is to specify, in accord with natural and divine law, "what is licit and what is illicit for property owners in the use of their possessions." (QA 49) According to Pius, property has both individual and social dimensions. In its social dimension it must be conducive to the common good. While the state is forbidden by natural law to eliminate entirely the right to private property, it can rightfully place certain restrictions on its use. In placing these restrictions Pius claims that the state in fact is supporting and strengthening private property properly understood:

> When civil authority adjusts ownership to meet the needs of the public good it acts not as an enemy, but as a friend of private owners; for it effectively prevents the possession of private property, intended by nature's Author in his wisdom for the sustaining of human life, from creating intolerable burden and so rushing to its own destruction. It does not therefore abolish, but protects private ownership, and far from weakening the right to private property, it gives it new strength. (QA 49)

In addition to affirming the state's right to restrict harmful uses of private property, Pope Pius also suggests that state ownership can at times be required by the common good. "It is rightly contended," he states, "that certain forms of property must be reserved to the State, since they carry with them an opportunity of domination too great to be left to private individuals without injury to the community at large." (QA 114)

The overall form of social and economic organization that Pius recommends is the division of society into what he terms "functional groups" or "vocational groups." These groups would be composed of all the persons involved in a certain sector of the economy, both employers and employees, who would join together and agree upon standards for that economic sector in light of the common good. These cooperative groupings, the pope suggests, would help to overcome divisions between workers and owners and promote social harmony. While the state would oversee and establish a broad framework for economic life, most of the decision-making would be done at the non-state level of these intermediate groups, in accord with the principle of subsidiarity. (QA 81-87)

In summary, Pius XI in *Quadragesimo Anno* thus reaffirms the general framework set forth in *Rerum Novarum,* stressing especially the rights of workers and the duty of the state to make sure that these rights are respected. He adds to this a sharper critique of capitalism, criticizing especially the individualism connected with capitalism and capitalism's tendency to concentrate wealth and power in the hands of a few. Pope Pius suggests the need for an alternative organization of society, distinct from both socialism and capitalism, and stresses that the principle of subsidiarity must play a key role in this alternative.

THE SOCIAL TEACHING OF PIUS XII

Pope Pius XII (1939-1958) did not issue any major social encyclicals. He did in several important ways, however, contribute to the development of CST. Most important was his strong affirmation of political democracy, which he reiterated on numerous occasions during and after the Second World War. In his Christmas radio message of 1944, for example, Pius affirmed that democracy (in the present world context) was most in keeping with the dignity and liberty of the human person.[7]

With regard to economic teachings, Pius XII had little new to say, mainly reaffirming some of the fundamental themes that had been expressed in *Rerum Novarum* and *Quadragesimo Anno.* Significantly, however, Pius XII did move away from the teaching of Pius XI concerning the value of vocational groups as a principal organizing vehicle for society.[8] Pius XI's advocacy of vocational groups, despite fundamental differences, had come to be equated with the now discredited corporatist vision of society that had been promoted by fascist regimes in several European countries. It also came over time to be seen as increasingly impractical. In light of post-WWII expansion and reforms in industrial capitalist economies, Pius XII seems to largely have taken the existing economic framework of these nations for granted as the

7 For a good discussion of Pius XII's views of democracy within the context of his broader social teachings, see Dorr, *Option for the Poor,* 96-111.

8 Pius XII, in order to avoid directly contradicting Pius XI, asserts that the teaching on vocational groups was appropriate in its own time, but as a result of changed historical circumstances it is no longer to be central to the church's social mission. Address of May 7, 1949, cited in ibid., 101.

starting point for economic reflection. Further reforms were understood to be needed, but not a fundamental restructuring of the very bases of economic life.

It is in the speeches of Pius XII that the notion of economic development first appears in CST. Speaking of the duties of powerful states, Pius declares that one of these duties is to "respect the rights of...smaller states to political freedom, to economic development."[9] Pius seems to envision economic development largely in modernizationist terms, as a sharing of the advanced technologies of the industrialized countries with the poorer countries.[10] At the same time, he stresses that the economic aspects of life must not be emphasized to the neglect of the spiritual to which they are properly subordinate.[11]

EARLY REFLECTIONS ON DEVELOPMENT: JOHN XXIII AND VATICAN II

While economic development is briefly mentioned by Pius XII, it is in the social encyclicals of Pope John XXIII that the focus of CST is first turned in a substantive way beyond the internal policies of the industrialized nations. Though still a secondary concern, Pope John begins to explore in some detail the global economic and political context and, in particular, begins to focus attention on the plight of Third World (or "underdeveloped") nations. The Second Vatican Council further develops these themes.

Mater et Magistra (1961)

In *Mater et Magistra,* Pope John XXIII reflects upon changes that had taken place in the world since the issuance of *Quadragesimo Anno* thirty years earlier. He focuses especially upon the industrialized nations, highlighting the rapid development of science and technology, the increased availability of consumer goods, and the creation of the social welfare state in these nations. Significantly, Pope John assesses

9 Pius XII, "Christianity and the World Crisis," Christmas message, 1941, delivered on Vatican radio, in *The Social Teachings of the Church*, ed. Anne Freemantle (New York: Mentor-Omega, 1963), 144.

10 For evidence of this modernizationist view of development, see Pius' address to the U.N. Food and Agriculture Organization on December 6, 1953, in ibid., 170-173.

11 See Pope Pius XII, "The Internal Order of States and Peoples," in ibid., 151-2.

each of these developments rather positively. He asserts, for example, that "advances in science and technology and the prosperity resulting therefrom are truly to be counted as good things and regarded as signs of the progress of civilization." (MM 246). It is proper, he says, that the church should be "solicitous for the requirements of men in their daily lives, not merely those relating to food and sustenance, but also to their comfort." (MM 3)

Concerning the welfare state, the pope contends that the increasing complexity of modern life justifies an even stronger role in economic and social life for the state than that which was generally acknowledged in preceding CST documents. While reaffirming the primacy of individual economic initiative,[12] the pope argues that "the common good requires public authorities to exercise ever greater responsibilities." (MM 117) Reflecting the rising faith in Keynesian economic ideas, Pope John asserts that "recent developments...provide additional reasons why, to a greater extent than heretofore, it is within the power of public authorities to reduce imbalances,...to keep fluctuations in the economy within bounds, and to provide effective measures for avoiding mass unemployment." (MM 54) "Where...appropriate activity of the State is lacking or defective," the pope contends, "commonwealths are apt to experience incurable disorders, and there occurs exploitation of the weak by the unscrupulous strong." (MM 58)

Pope John focuses particular attention upon the need for the state to use its tax, credit, and insurance policies and governmental services to support small and medium-sized businesses and family farms and cooperatives, reiterating the concern of CST for widespread ownership of the means of production. (MM 84-90, 115) With regard to larger enterprises, he suggests that ways be found for workers to have increased participation in decision-making within these firms. (MM 91-97) With regard to workers in general, the pope reaffirms the various rights and duties highlighted in previous encyclicals.

When Pope John turns his attention to the Third World, a major concern is to assure that the poorer nations can come to share in some of the bounty being created by modern science and technology. For

12 "At the outset it should be affirmed that in economic affairs first place is to be given to...private initiative." (MM 51) "Experience in fact shows that where private initiative of individuals is lacking, political tyranny prevails." (MM 57) "Those in authority should favor and help private enterprise in accordance with the principle of subsidiarity." (MM 152)

this to occur, he expresses a desire that "effective aid be given in developing the underdeveloped nations." (MM 80) Unlike his successors in later CST documents, John XXIII does not pursue an analysis of the ways in which the prosperity of the industrialized nations has been dependent upon colonial and neo-colonial policies toward the Third World, policies understood by many (such as structuralist and dependency theorists) to have both created and perpetuated modern forms of poverty in these nations. Nor does he examine the role of Third World elites as obstacles to social change. Instead, largely prescinding from these issues of injustice, the pope attributes the poverty present in the Third World mainly to the lack of modern technology. Conditions of widespread, dehumanizing poverty, he says, "can be traced...to the fact that in these regions modern industrial techniques have only recently been introduced or have made less than satisfactory progress." (MM 68) "For the most part," he says, "the causes [of poverty and hunger] are to be found in the primitive state of the economy." (MM 163)

In this assessment of the situation of the Third World, John XXIII's views can be seen to agree with the main features of the modernizationist understanding of economic development. This view, as discussed in Chapter One, understands First World nations to represent a superior model of societal organization, a model that Third World nations are called to emulate. The primary emphasis of modernizationist theorists is on the need for economic growth, with the main impediments to growth being seen as the traditional productive techniques and the social institutions and worldviews of Third World inhabitants. The prescription for development suggested is the abandonment of traditional techniques and values and the adoption of modern alternatives. This modernization is to occur largely through a massive influx of capital (especially in the form of industrial technology) via grants and loans from First World governments, investment by First World-based multinational corporations, and measures such as technical assistance and the training of Third World students in the First World.

In broad terms, Pope John embraced both the analysis and the concrete policy suggestions of these modernizationist development scholars. His reference to the "primitive" nature of Third World economies as being the main cause of poverty (MM 163) and his disparaging comments concerning the "primitive and obsolete" methods of farming used in these countries (MM 154) provide striking evidence of modernizationist views, as does a passage in which he explicitly commends efforts aimed at ensuring that rural life in these countries be "modernized." (MM 156) With regard to prescriptions for action, he shares with the modernizationist theorists a primary focus on economic growth and on the provision of capital, industrial technology, and modern education. "To effect a remedy," the pope asserts, "all available avenues should be explored...to instruct citizens fully in necessary skills and...to enable them to acquire the capital wherewith to promote economic growth by ways and means adapted to our times." (MM 163) He urges as well that "as many youths as possible" be given aid to enable them to "study in the great universities of the more developed countries, thus acquiring a knowledge of the arts and sciences in line with the standards of our time." (MM 165)

Like most modernizationist theorists, Pope John was generally quite optimistic about the prospects for development. He assumed that the good will of the First World needed to bring about development existed and that the path to development not only was clear but was in fact already being pursued. "We note with pleasure," he states, "that countries with advanced productive systems are lending aid to less privileged countries." (MM 160) He strongly lauds those banks and nations making loans to the Third World. "We gladly take this opportunity to give due praise to such generous activity," he says, a comment that would take on harshly ironic significance several decades later as the Third World's foreign debt crisis created immense suffering for the Third World poor while contributing to record profits for First World banks. (MM 165)

While it is clear from the above comments that Pope John was strongly influenced by the general ethos of modernizationist thought, it is crucial to note that his views also differ from the dominant modernizationist perspective in several very important ways. While sharing modernizationist understandings of the causes of underdevelopment (mainly lack of modern technology), he does not share all of the specific economic and cultural views that modernizationist theorists generally held. For example, while placing much emphasis on the need for economic growth, Pope John places even greater stress on equity, in contrast to those modernizationist economists who saw increased inequity as being necessary for a period of time in order to bring about trickle-down benefits in the long-run. "The economic prosperity of any people," the pope states, "is to be assessed not so much from the sum total of goods and wealth possessed as from the distribution of goods according to norms of justice." (MM 74) Of even more importance, Pope John suggests, is that workers always be treated with dignity. "If the organization and structure of economic life be such that the human dignity of workers is compromised...then we judge such an economic order to be unjust, even though it produces a vast amount of goods whose distribution conforms to the norms of justice and equity." (MM 83) These claims set him strongly apart from the modernizationist theorists' almost exclusive emphasis on economic growth.

A second major way that Pope John's views differ from those of leading modernizationist theorists can be seen in the stress that the pope places upon agriculture. An extensive section of the encyclical (MM 123-149) is devoted to agricultural issues, in which the pope reflects upon the need to maintain a proper balance among agriculture, industry, and services, and suggests various concrete ways that farmers need to be supported (e.g. through the provision of infrastructure, favorable tax and credit policies, crop insurance, price protection, etc.) Very often, modernizationist economists and planners stressed industry to the relative neglect of agriculture.

A third important area of difference between the pope and modernizationist theorists is found in the stress placed by Pope John on the need to respect a proper hierarchy of goods. "There is no doubt," the pope says, "that when a nation makes progress in science, technology, economic life, and the prosperity of its citizens, a great contribution is made to civilization. But all should realize that these things are not the highest goods." (MM 175) What is of ultimate importance, Pope John contends, is the fostering of spiritual and moral values. "Things pertaining to the spirit and to moral life are to be preferred to all else." (MM 210) Otherwise human ingenuity will foster destruction rather than the enhancement of human dignity. "Separated from God," the pope declares, "man becomes monstrous to himself and others." (MM 215)

This concern for the spiritual life and morality leads the pope to take a more nuanced view of traditional cultures than do most modernizationist theorists, for he recognizes that these cultures contain important moral and spiritual treasures that need to be preserved. Modernizationist theorists, by contrast, tend to view these values negatively, regarding them as primary impediments to economic growth. In response to efforts to undermine traditional moral and spiritual values, Pope John warns:

> There are not lacking grave dangers in the help provided by more affluent nations for development of the poorer ones. For among the citizens of these latter nations, there is operative a general awareness of the higher values on which moral teachings rest – an awareness derived from ancient traditional custom....Those who seek to undermine in some measure the right instincts of these people assuredly do something immoral. (MM 176-177)

When the industrial nations provide assistance to the poorer ones they must "take special care lest, in aiding these nations, they seek to impose their own way of life on them." (MM 170). The issue of to what extent a specific modern worldview and way of life is embedded in the very nature of modern technologies, and the consequent tensions that arise between the pope's calls for technical modernization and simultaneous respect for traditional cultural values, will be explored in Chapter Five.

Along with his warnings against imposing a way of life, Pope John shows awareness of the potential danger that aid could be used as a tool of political domination by the richer nations:

> Economically developed nations should take particular care lest, in giving aid to poorer countries, they endeavor to turn the prevailing political situation to their own advantage, and seek to dominate them. Should perchance such attempts be made, this clearly would be but another form of colonialism." (MM 171-172)

Later CST documents, including another written by Pope John himself, assert that some of these potential dangers that Pope John warned against (e.g. excessive materialism and neglect of the spiritual, the imposition on developing nations of First World culture, and the use of aid for political domination) had in fact come to be realities.

Pacem in Terris (1963)

The central theme of Pope John XXIII's encyclical *Pacem in Terris* (1963) is an appeal to respect an array of social, economic, political, and religious rights and corresponding obligations. These rights and obligations are viewed as the basis of world peace. Pope John's broad, holistic conception of rights, consistent with the CST tradition, sets his views apart from the western liberal tradition of human rights that has focused primarily upon political and procedural rights. While Pope John does affirm political and procedural rights (such as freedom of expression and assembly, the right to an impartial legal system, etc.), he also asserts the fundamental importance of social and economic rights, including the right to food, shelter, medical care, and necessary social services. (PT 11) All of these rights, the pope says, are grounded in the God-given dignity and social nature of the human person (PT 9, 10, 31). At the core of social/economic rights is the right to employment with decent working conditions and a just wage. (PT 20) When persons are unable to work, however, Pope John contends that the broader society and state must guarantee that the basic needs of these persons are nonetheless met. (PT 11)

Pope John expresses a strong preference for constitutional democracy with a division of powers as the preferred system of government for the protection of human rights. The "first requisite" in the organization of states, he says, "is that a charter of fundamental human rights be drawn up in clear and precise terms and that it be incorporated in its entirety in the constitution." (PT 75) He further asserts that "it is in keeping with the innate demands of human nature that the state should take a form which embodies the threefold division of powers" among the legislative, judicial, and executive branches. (PT 68) Undergirding all of Pope John's political reflections is a fundamental emphasis placed upon active citizen participation in public life (PT 75-76) and upon respect for human rights. "If any government does not acknowledge the rights of man or violates them," the pope declares, "it not only fails in its duty, but its orders completely lack juridical force." (PT 61)

A central concern of *Pacem in Terris*, as revealed in its title, is world peace. The encyclical was issued in the aftermath of the Cuban missile crisis and the escalation of Cold War tensions that accompanied it. Among the primary obstacles to world peace cited by the pope is the Cold War itself. Cold War tensions, Pope John states, foster mistrust and a spiralling arms race with excessive military expenditures, expenditures that the pope views as diverting badly needed funds from development:

> It is with deep sorrow that we note the enormous stocks of armaments that have been and still are being made in more economically developed countries....Other countries as a result are deprived of the collaboration they need in order to make economic and social progress....Justice, then, right reason, and consideration for human dignity and life urgently demand that the arms race should cease...

> that nuclear weapons be banned, and finally that all come to an agreement on a fitting program of disarmament." (PT 109, 112)

Given the realities of modern warfare, Pope John contends that "it is contrary to reason to hold that war is now a suitable way to restore rights which have been violated." (PT 127) As a central component of developing alternatives to war Pope John strongly appeals for the extablishment of an international economic/political authority, such as a strengthened United Nations, "which is in a position to operate in an effective manner on a worldwide basis." The "universal common good" and "the moral order itself," the pope declares, "demands that such a form of authority be established." (PT 137) It is through cooperation on an international level, Pope John asserts, that alternatives to war and military spending can be found and that development can be appropriately fostered. In calling for the establishment of a global authority, the pope appeals to the principle of subsidiarity, which asserts that issues should be dealt with at the most decentralized level appropriate to the issue at hand. Some problems, Pope John contends, are global in character and cannot be effectively addressed at any lesser level. "Because of the vastness, complexity, and urgency of those problems the public authorities of the individual States are not in a position to tackle them with any hope of a positive solution." (PT 140)

Also crucial for the establishment of peace is the fostering of development. In a brief section of the encyclical concerning the Third World, the pope again calls for extensive aid to be given to the Third World by the industrialized nations. He states that he is "greatly consoled to see how widely that appeal [for aid, expressed in *Mater et Magistra*] has been favorably received" and expresses confidence that in the future the development fostered by this aid "will enable every citizen to live in conditions more in keeping with human dignity." (PT 122)

At the same time, Pope John very strongly reiterates his warning against abuses of aid. "It can never be sufficiently repeated," he asserts, that aid should be given "with the greatest respect for the liberty of the countries being developed," with "respect (for) the moral and ethnic characteristics peculiar to each," and without "any intention of political domination." (PT 123, 125)

Other comments in *Pacem in Terris* of relevance to issues of development and international justice include the pope's affirmation of the rights of ethnic minorities (including respect for their language and customs, political rights, and economic well-being – PT 96), and his affirmation of the right to emigrate and immigrate for "just reasons." (PT 25, 106) Noteworthy too is the opening which the pope provided for Catholics to cooperate with socialists and other non-Christians in addressing social justice issues, an important concern in many Third World contexts. In a frequently quoted passage, Pope John distinguishes between "false philosophical teachings" and "movements" based upon them, arguing that the movements may in practice modify the original teachings and "may contain elements that are positive and deserving of approval." (PT 159) "For these reasons," he says, "it can at times happen that meetings for the attainment of some practical results which previously seemed completely useless now are either actually useful or may be looked upon as profitable for the future."[13] (PT 160)

With regard to calls for violent revolution in the Third World, Pope John expresses his opposition. "It must be borne in mind," he says, "that to proceed gradually is the law of life in all its expressions; therefore in human institutions, too, it is not possible to renovate for the better except for working from within them gradually." (PT 162)

Gaudium et Spes (1965)

In *Gaudium et Spes* the bishops gathered at the Second Vatican Council took up the task of "scrutinizing the signs of the times and of interpreting them in the light of the Gospel." (GS 4) This document shares many of the major themes of the social encyclicals of John XXIII. Areas of overlap, for example, include similar understandings of the innate dignity and social nature of the human person (GS 12, 25), the centrality of human rights (GS 26), and the important role of the state in overseeing and managing modern economic life. (GS 75) *Gaudium et Spes* also reaffirms John XXIII's critical view of war and military spending. "[T]he arms race," the Council states, "is an utterly treacherous trap for humanity, and one which injures the poor to an intolerable degree." (GS 81) The Council stresses the need to "undertake an evaluation of war with an entirely new attitude." It argues

13 While Pope John does not mention socialists by name in these paragraphs, it is generally understood that he primarily had socialists in mind. Pope Paul VI would later quote these passages as a preface to his own discussion of socialism in *Octogesima Adveniens* (OA 30).

that acts of war aimed at populated centers deserve "unequivocal and unhesitating condemnation," affirms the right to conscientious objection, and praises, with certain cautions, those who advocate nonviolent means of defending rights. (GS 78-81) Like Pope John, the Council emphasizes the urgent need for a strengthened global authority, viewed as an essential component in putting an end to war.[14] On other issues, both Pope John XXIII and *Gaudium et Spes* express a generally optimistic view of the potential for "progress" based on advances in science and technology and view development in broadly modernizationist terms.[15] At the same time, however, both warn against materialistic consumerism and against neglect of the spiritual and social dimensions of life.[16]

Some important differences between the views expressed by John XXIII and those contained in *Gaudium et Spes* also should be noted. *Gaudium et Spes*, for example, is more critical in its assessment of the international economic order than were the encyclicals of John XXIII. It is argued that "numerous reforms" of the global economy are needed, the primary purpose of which should be "to remove as quickly as possible the immense economic inequalities which now exist" between countries and between regions and groups within countries. (GS 63, 66) "In many cases," laments the Council, "these (inequalities) are worsening." (GS 66) Although the Council does not elaborate upon the specifics of the needed reforms (a point that the authors of *Gaudium et Spes* themselves acknowledge[17]), the recognition of the need for substantial reform is itself a significant shift away from the generally more benign interpretation of the international economic order that characterized the thought of John XXIII.

The heightened emphasis on equality in *Gaudium et Spes*, it is important to note, stands in contrast to earlier affirmations of inequality

14 "It is our clear duty, then, to strain every muscle as we work for the time when all war can be completely outlawed by international consent. This goal undoubtedly requires the establishment of some universal public authority...endowed with effective power to safeguard, on the behalf of all, security, regard for justice, and respect for rights." (GS 82)

15 See GS 85-87.

16 GS 63, 86.

17 "Undeniably this conciliar program is but a general one in several of its parts....[T]he program will have to be further pursued and amplified." (GS 91)

by Pope Leo XIII and others. For the Council, excessive inequality undermines social justice and fosters violence:

> The basic equality of all must receive increasingly greater recognition....For excessive economic and social differences between the members of the one human family or population groups cause scandal, and militate against social justice, equity, the dignity of the human person, as well as social and international peace. (GS 29)

The Council emphasizes that the goods of creation are intended by God to be shared equitably by all. This intended "universal destination of created goods," they state, places limits on the right to private property. While this claim concerning limits to private property is present earlier in the CST tradition (as we saw in the case of Pius XI), it is here that its implications begin to receive the most sustained attention. The Council participants assert, for example, that the principle that the goods of the earth are intended for all may require the expropriation of idle or insufficiently cultivated large agricultural estates and the redistribution of the land to landless peasants or small land-holders. (GS 71) It can also require, they declare, "various forms of public ownership" of the means of production in circumstances in which private ownership would have an impact harmful to the common good. (GS 71)

God's intention that the earth's goods be shared by all also has implications for lifestyle choices. The Council argues that all persons have a responsibility to meet the needs of the poor not only by sharing from their superfluous wealth (as affirmed in earlier CST documents, which allowed persons to retain what was needed to maintain their "station" in life), but also by sharing in ways that will require a simplification of lifestyle. Should this sharing not be forthcoming, the Council even affirms the right of the poor, in cases of extreme necessity, to take from the wealthy what is needed for survival:

> The right to have a share of earthly goods sufficient for oneself and one's family belongs to everyone. The Fathers and Doctors of the Church held this view, teaching that men are obliged to come to the relief of the poor, and to do so not merely out of their superfluous goods. If a person is in extreme necessity, he has the right to take from the riches of others what he himself needs. Since there are so many people in this world afflicted with hunger, this sacred Council urges all, both individuals and governments, to remember the say-

> ing of the Fathers: "Feed the man dying of hunger, because if you have not fed him you have killed him." (GS 69)

In addition to the above, a final important emphasis of the Council regarding development and international justice issues is its insistence on widespread popular participation in the development process, building upon the more general emphasis placed upon participation by John XXIII:

> Economic development must not be left to the sole judgement of a few men or groups possessing excessive economic power...or of certain especially powerful nations. It is proper, on the contrary, that at every level the largest possible number of people have an active share in directing that development. (GS 65)

This emphasis on participation, it should be noted, provided a sharp contrast to the generally top-down nature of conventional development programs that existed at the time of the Council.

Overall, then, the Second Vatican Council can be seen as having made several important contributions to the young tradition of magisterial thought on issues related to development. First, by largely reaffirming the views of John XXIII, the Council gave its seal of approval to the new ideas he had presented, including the importance of a stronger economic role for the state. In addition, the Council introduced a more critical assessment of the global economy, placed a heightened emphasis on equality, began a deeper exploration of the far-reaching practical implications of the principle that the goods of the earth are intended to be equitably shared by all, and brought the notion of participation even more strongly to the fore.

THE PIVOTAL CONTRIBUTIONS OF PAUL VI, THE LATIN AMERICAN BISHOPS, AND JUSTICE IN THE WORLD

The documents of Pope Paul VI are perhaps the most important in the history of CST on the topic of development. In these documents a framework for reflection is established that would fundamentally shape all subsequent CST thought on development issues. The new openings and insights provided by Paul VI are further developed by the Latin American bishops at Medellín and Puebla and by the World Synod of Bishops in its very prophetic document *Justice in the World*.

Populorum Progressio (1967)

Pope Paul VI's encyclical *Populorum Progressio* represents the first papal encyclical whose principal theme is development and the relations between richer and poorer nations. "Today the principal fact that we must all recognize," says Pope Paul, "is that the social question has become worldwide." (PP 3)

Paul contends that an examination of the global situation gives rise to a distressing realization:

> Today no one can be ignorant any longer of the fact that in whole continents countless men and women are ravaged by hunger, countless numbers of children are malnourished, so that many of them die in infancy, while the physical growth and mental development of many others are retarded and as a result whole regions are condemned to the most depressing despondency. (PP 45)

The overarching emphasis of *Populorum Progressio* is the need to discern a proper response to these realities. In formulating this response the concept of "integral development" is set forth, derived in large part from the pioneering thought of French economist L. J. Lebret.[18] In proposing integral development the pope affirms that meeting the basic material needs of all is of crucial importance. At the same time, however, he argues that development cannot be confined simply to the economic realm. "Development," the pope says, "cannot be limited to mere economic growth. In order to be authentic, it must be complete: integral, that is, it has to promote the good of every man and of the whole man." (PP 14)

Pope Paul emphasizes that the primary goal of development should be "complete humanism." (PP 42) Development, he states, is properly understood as the process of becoming "more human." Having access to adequate material goods is a necessary part of this process, but values and activities such as love, friendship, social solidarity, artistic and intellectual endeavor, prayer, and contemplation are also crucially important. (PP 19-21) This broad conception of development expressed

18 Lebret played an important role in the drafting of *Populorum Progressio*. He is directly quoted in the encyclical (a rarity for papal encyclicals, which typically only quote other popes) and is described as an "eminent specialist" on development issues. (PP 14) For a discussion of Lebret's work, see Denis Goulet, "L.J. Lebret: Pioneer of Development Ethics," in *A New Moral Order: Development Ethics and Liberation Theology* (Maryknoll, NY: Orbis Books, 1974), chapter 2.

by Pope Paul had been implicit throughout the CST tradition, but it is in this encyclical that its various components are brought together and elaborated upon in the most coherent and unified way.

Given this holistic understanding of development, Pope Paul is very sensitive to the danger that development as conventionally understood and practiced could lead to the destruction of much that is of enduring value in Third World cultures. He warns especially of the possibility of the breakdown of traditional moral and spiritual values, a loss or depreciation of Third World peoples' intellectual and artistic heritages, and the collapse of traditional social relations of kinship and mutual aid. In one important passage, the pope states:

> Every country possesses a civilization handed down by its ancestors: institutions called for by life in this world, and higher manifestations of the life of the spirit, manifestations of an artistic, intellectual, and religious character. When the latter possess true human values, it would be a grave error to sacrifice them to the former [i.e. to economic prosperity]. A people that would act in this way would thereby lose the best of its patrimony; in order to live, it would be sacrificing its reasons for living. Christ's teaching also applies to peoples: "What does it profit a man to gain the whole world if he suffers the loss of his soul?" (PP 40)

"Less well off peoples," the pope declares, "can never be sufficiently on their guard against this temptation which comes to them from wealthy nations." (PP 41)

At the same time as showing appreciation of the values inherent in traditional cultures, the pope also expresses his view that the implementation of modern industrial technologies is "a necessity for economic growth and human progress." (PP 25) And such technologies, he is aware, tend to "break down structures which do not adapt themselves to new conditions," including the social and economic structures of traditional cultures. (PP 10) Thus, the tension between an affirmation of the need for technological modernization and a concern to maintain valuable aspects of traditional cultures, seen already with regard to Pope John, is again expressed. In giving his own response to this tension, Pope Paul suggests (somewhat vaguely) that Third World nations must "know how to discriminate among those things that are held out to them," rejecting some while accepting only those which are "sound and beneficial, in order to develop them alongside their own, in accordance with their own genius." (PP 41) Clearly, discerning how to best foster integral development is not an easy task.

Along with his introduction of the notion of integral development, Pope Paul makes another major contribution to CST through his analysis of the causes of poverty and hunger in the Third World. Unlike John XXIII, Pope Paul does not simply attribute hunger and poverty to the "primitive" nature of Third World economies, which can be overcome through a modernizing process of aid already underway. Rather, Pope Paul develops an analysis that is more in accord with the views of structuralist and dependency schools of economic thought, arguing that various structural factors in the international economic system serve to perpetuate Third World poverty and serve to widen the economic gap between the richer and poorer nations. *Gaudium et Spes* mentioned this widening gap as a reason for concern. Pope Paul seeks to analyze some of its causes.

In presenting his analysis of these structural factors, Pope Paul refers especially to colonialism's creation of a system in which many Third World economies were made to depend upon the export of one or two agricultural crops or other natural resources. This dependence, combined with declining terms of trade for these products, is viewed by the pope as a key impediment to Third World economic security. (PP 7, 44, 57) As a result of these inequities "the poor nations remain ever poor," he says, "while the rich ones become still richer." (PP 57)

The underlying problem in the view of the pope is that so-called "free trade," when undertaken in contexts characterized by highly unequal distributions of economic power, does not generally have consequences in accord with the norms of justice. "[T]he rule of free trade, taken by itself," Pope Paul states, "is no longer able to govern international relations....Prices which are 'freely' set in the market can produce unfair results." (PP 58) Underlining the radical implications of this assertion, the pope adds:

> One must recognize that it is the fundamental principle of [economic] liberalism, as the rule for commercial exchange, which is questioned here....An economy of exchange can no longer be based solely on the law of free competition, a law which, in its turn, too often creates an economic dictatorship. Freedom of trade is fair only if it is subject to the demands of social justice. (PP 58-59)

Here the sharp critique of capitalism present in Pius XI's *Quadragesimo Anno* resurfaces. Elsewhere in the encyclical, Pope Paul further develops this critique:

> It is unfortunate that...a system has been constructed which considers profit as the key motive for economic progress, competition as the supreme law of economics, and private ownership of the means of production as an absolute right that has no limits and carries no corresponding social obligation. This unchecked liberalism leads to dictatorship rightly denounced by Pius XI as producing 'the international imperialism of money.' One cannot condemn such abuses too strongly....[A] type of capitalism has been the source of excessive suffering, injustices, and fratricidal conflicts whose effects still persist." (PP 26)

This type of capitalism, the pope declares, is "a woeful system." (PP 26) While Pope Paul doesn't call for an alternative to capitalism as such, he does call for far-reaching reforms. In the international arena, specific reforms that he mentions include the creation of a stronger international authority, such as the United Nations, with regulatory and planning power in economic and political matters (PP 51, 52, 78), the establishment of norms concerning just prices for Third World commodities (PP 61), protective measures for new Third World industries (PP 61), and abundant financial aid for the poorer countries to be distributed primarily through an internationally administered "World Fund" made up of resources transferred from military spending.[19] (PP 51) As in earlier CST documents, Pope Paul denounces the arms race and excessive military spending: "When so many are hungry, when so many families suffer from destitution...every exhausting armaments race becomes an intolerable scandal. We are conscious of our duty to denounce it." (PP 53)

In the Third World itself Pope Paul calls for the state to take a strong role in development planning:

> Individual initiative alone and the mere free play of competition could never assure successful development. One must avoid the risk

19 In establishing a World Fund to provide aid to the Third World, the pope hopes that the dangers of using aid for purposes of domination will be minimized. When aid is provided through a multilateral source, he says, Third World nations "would have less cause for fearing that, under the cloak of financial aid or technical assistance, there lurk certain manifestations of what has come to be called neocolonialism." (PP 52)

> of increasing still more the wealth of the rich and the dominion of the strong, while leaving the poor in their misery and adding to the servitude of the oppressed....It pertains to the public authorities to choose, even to lay down the objectives to be pursued, the ends to be achieved, and the means for attaining these, and it is for them to stimulate all the forces engaged in this common activity. (PP 33)

Pope Paul suggests the need for land redistribution and measures to reduce capital flight (PP 24), places a strong emphasis upon the provision of basic services such as education (PP 35), and encourages regional cooperation in economic and political matters with neighboring Third World countries. (PP 64) The pope also suggests the legitimacy of governmental efforts to reduce population growth, so long as no measures opposed to the "moral law" are promoted.[20] (PP 37)

With regard to private property and the world's wealthy, the pope reiterates the strong stress placed by the Vatican Council on the fact that the goods of the earth are intended for all. Like the Council, Pope Paul appeals to the teachings of the early church in making this claim:

> It is well known how strong were the words used by the Fathers of the Church to describe the proper attitude of persons who possess anything towards persons in need. To quote St. Ambrose: "You are not making a gift of your possessions to the poor person. You are handing over to him what is his. For what has been given in common for the use of all, you have arrogated to yourself. The world is given to all, and not only to the rich." That is, private property does not constitute for anyone an absolute and unconditioned right. No one is justified in keeping for his exclusive use what he does not need, when others lack necessities. (PP 23)

A striking element of the encyclical is the sense of passion and urgency that Pope Paul conveys. "The present situation," the pope says, "must be faced with courage and the injustices linked with it must be fought against and overcome. Development demands bold transformations, innovations that go deep. Urgent reforms should be under-

20 "It is true that too frequently an accelerated demographic increase adds its own difficulties to the problems of development....It is certain that public authorities can intervene, within the limits of their competence, by favoring the availability of appropriate information and by adopting suitable measures, provided that these are in conformity with the moral law." (PP 37)

taken without delay." (PP 32) "We ask you, all of you," the pope concludes, "to heed our cry of anguish, in the name of the Lord." (PP 87)

Should the necessary "bold transformations" not occur, Pope Paul warns that dire consequences may follow. While he personally discourages violent revolution, Pope Paul argues that "continued greed" on the part of world's wealthy "will certainly call down upon them the judgement of God and the wrath of the poor, with consequences no one can foretell." (PP 49) "Development," Pope Paul asserts, "is the new name for peace."[21]

Medellín Documents (1968)

The Latin American bishops held a continent-wide conference at Medellín, Colombia in 1968. This landmark gathering has played a major role in the subsequent history of the global Catholic Church and in the content of Catholic Social Teaching. At Medellín the Latin American bishops sought to apply CST to their own conditions, conditions characterized by massive inequalities and widespread political repression. While affirming and reiterating the fundamental themes of CST, the Latin American bishops also broke new ground in several crucial areas. For example, it is at Medellín that the notions of "structural injustice" and "institutionalized violence"[22] enter into the language of CST, along with the language of "liberation."[23] It is here too that

---

21 This phrase is the heading for the fourth major section of the encyclical, located between no. 75 and 76. Also, in no. 87, the pope states: "For if the new name for peace is development, who would not wish to labor for it with all his powers?"

22 "In many instances Latin America finds itself faced with a situation of injustice that can be called institutionalized violence....This situation demands all-embracing, courageous, urgent, and profoundly renovating transformations." Medellín document on "Peace," 16.

23 See the Medellín documents on "Justice," 3, 4, 13; "Poverty of the Church," 2. Significantly, the bishops stress that liberation is multi-faceted, including at its core personal conversion. ("Justice," 3) While calling for liberation, the bishops do not embrace the use of violence. Instead, they argue that only nonviolent means are acceptable in the current context: "If we consider then, the totality of the circumstances of our countries, and if we take into account the Christian preference for peace, the enormous difficulty of a civil war, the logic of violence, the atrocities it engenders, the risk of provoking foreign intervention, illegitimate as it may be, the difficulty of building a regime of justice and freedom while participating in a process of

the notion of a preferential option for the poor, stressed by liberation theology, begins to be developed, rooted in the Hebrew Scriptures and in the teachings of Jesus.[24] In terms of political-economic analysis, the bishops at Medellín, like Pope Paul, stress themes largely derived from structuralist and dependency thought.[25]

Perhaps the most crucial emphasis of Medellín is the stress placed upon active mobilization of the poor in the struggle for justice. Whereas CST traditionally had largely focused upon appeals to those with wealth and power to bring about change (though it did also encourage a certain amount of organization among members of the working class), it is at Medellín that a focus upon the agency of the poor becomes central. "The Church–the People of God–will lend its support to the downtrodden...so that they might come to know their rights and how to make use of them."[26] "Justice, and therefore peace," the bishops state, "conquer by means of a dynamic action of awakening (*concientización*) and organization of the popular sectors."[27] This task of "awakening the social conscience" or "*concientización*" is understood to be a central part of the Church's mission.[28] As an important part of these efforts, stress is placed upon the formation of "small basic communities" (*communidades de base*).[29] Each of these major innovations of Medellín would come to be incorporated into CST at the global level in subsequent decades.

---

violence, we earnestly desire that the dynamism of the awakened and organized community be put to the service of justice and peace." ("Peace," 19)

24 The documents speak for example of giving "preference to the poorest and most needy" and of the crucial importance of "solidarity with the poor." ("Poverty of the Church," 9, 10.)

25 "Peace," 8-10, for example, discusses the multiple forms of Latin America's economic and political dependency – e.g. inequitable terms of trade, capital flight, the loss of educated persons to the First World, tax evasion and the repatriation of profits by transnational corporations, foreign debt, international monopolies, and political and military intervention by outside powers.

26 "Justice," 20.

27 "Peace," 18. One of the suggestions made for the pastoral work of bishops is "to encourage and favor the efforts of the people to create and develop their own grassroots organizations for the redress and consolidation of their rights and the search for true justice." Ibid., 27.

28 "Justice," 17.

29 Ibid., 20.

Octogesima Adveniens (1971)

Pope Paul VI's second social encyclical was issued in 1971, three years after Medellín. In it, Pope Paul asserts the need for local communities to engage in social analysis and to apply the principles of CST to their own varying social conditions.[30] Most commentators have understood this as an endorsement of the Medellín conference and its pathbreaking documents.[31] The pope also begins in this encyclical to use some language reminiscent of Medellín, speaking for example of the Gospel call to "preferential respect" for the poor (OA 23) and of the need for "liberation." (OA 45)

Two foundational themes of *Octogesima Adveniens* are the importance of participation and of equality (including a qualified affirmation of equal rights for women[32]), thus continuing the heightened stress placed upon these principles in more recent CST documents. Asserting that earlier CST documents had begun to recognize the need for widescale participation in the economic realm (including a role for workers in management and ownership), Pope Paul stresses that broader and deeper participation in the political realm is crucial as well. (OA 47)

With regard to international issues, Pope Paul reiterates his call for fundamental reforms, extending the scope of his earlier suggestions.

---

30 "It is up to the Christian communities to analyze with objectivity the situation which is proper to their own country, to shed on it the light of the Gospel's unalterable words and to draw principles of reflection, norms of judgement, and directives for action from the social teaching of the Church....It is up to these Christian communities...to discern the options and commitments which are called for in order to bring about the social, political, and economic changes seen in many cases to be urgently needed." (OA 4)

31 See Dorr, *Option for the Poor*, 219.

32 Pope Paul asserts that legislation concerning the rights of women should recognize "her independence as a person, and her equal rights to participate in cultural, economic, social, and political life." At the same time, he states that he does not have in mind "that false equality which would deny the distinctions laid down by the Creator himself and which would be in contradiction with woman's proper role, which is of such capital importance, at the heart of the family as well as within society." The policy implications of this qualifying comment are not elaborated upon. (OA 13) For earlier statements in CST concerning the proper role and rights of women, see RN 33; QA 71; PT 19, 41; GS 60.

"It is necessary," he states, "to have the courage to undertake a revision of the relationships between nations, whether it is a question of the international division of production, the structure of exchanges, the control of profits, the monetary system....(OA 43) Pope Paul is especially critical of the impact of transnational corporations on global economic, political, and social life:

> We can see new economic powers emerging, the multinational enterprises... which are largely independent of the national political powers and therefore not subject to control from the point of view of the common good. By extending their activities, these private organizations can lead to a new and abusive form of economic domination on the social, cultural, and even political level. The excessive concentration of means and powers that Pope Pius XI already condemned on the fortieth anniversary of *Rerum Novarum* is taking on a new and very real image. (OA 44)

Finally, it should be noted that it is in this encyclical that ecological issues first appear as an important concern in CST. "Man is suddenly becoming aware," Pope Paul states, "that by an ill-considered exploitation of nature he risks destroying it and becoming in turn the victim of this degradation....This is a wide-ranging social problem which concerns the entire human family." (OA 21)

ASSESSING THE CONTRIBUTION OF PAUL VI

Paul VI is without doubt the central figure in the brief history of CST on development issues. By broadening the notion of development to explicitly mean "integral development" and by adopting a more critical, more structurally focused, and less optimistic analysis, Pope Paul modified in significant ways the teaching of John XXIII and Vatican II. The major themes of Paul VI with regard to development continue to be central in CST today, having been taken up, affirmed, and further developed by Pope John Paul II, as will be discussed below.

In many respects the thought of Paul VI can be seen as having been insightfully ahead of its time. When the encyclical *Populorum Progressio* was written, for example, many of the ideas expressed by the pope ran strongly counter to the development thought then current, particularly modernizationist theories stressing the maximization of economic growth. Within a decade, however, many of these same ideas (e.g. decreased emphasis on economic growth, stress on the need for structural reforms, concern for distribution, concern for prioritizing basic needs, and recognition of the importance of grassroots participation, ecological concern, and respect for Third World cultures) would all move to the center of the development debate.

In reflections written in 1978, ten years after the publication of *Populorum Progressio,* economist Barbara Ward makes the claim that Pope Paul's ideas could be understood to "represent a sort of prophetic vision, a far clearer idea of what was going to happen in our planet than the ideas contained in many of the extremely learned economic treatises written at the time – some of them, alas, written by me."[33] Each of the major analyses of *Populorum Progressio,* she contends, "have been confirmed in the past ten years."[34]

Ward notes that in the 1960s development economists had been blinded by "the euphoria of economic growth" and uncritical optimism concerning modernization and the workings of capitalism. As the reality of what had been wrought by "development" became more painfully clear, however (e.g. worsened conditions for many of the poor, social upheaval, ecological damage), more and more persons began to shift their attention to the need to pursue alternative paths. This can be seen in the rise of the basic needs approaches to development, the calls for a New International Economic Order, and in the emergence of various proponents of "alternative development." In important ways Pope Paul's encyclicals (based on the work of Lebret and others) anticipated or shared in the early stages of each of these lines of thought.[35]

Justice in the World (1971)

Many of the insights of Pope Paul and the Latin American bishops gathered at Medellín were reaffirmed in the document *Justice in the World,* produced by an international gathering of Catholic bishops in Rome in 1971. As is evidenced by its title, the document main-

33 Barbara Ward, "Looking Back on *Populorum Progressio,*" in R. McCormick and C. Curran, eds., *Readings in Moral Theology #5: Official Catholic Social Teaching* (New York: Paulist Press, 1986), 130.

34 Ibid., 136.

35 With regard to the New International Economic Order, for instance, Barbara Ward states that "many of the ideas of the New Order have such firm roots in *Populorum Progressio* that the encyclical might almost have been its founding document." Ibid., 137.

ly concerns itself with issues of social justice, including the "right to development."[36] (JW 15)

Justice in the World reaffirms and deepens the critical, structural analysis brought into the discussion of development by Pope Paul. Notions of injustice and oppression become central. The bishops speak, for example, of "the serious injustices which are building around the world a network of domination, oppression, and abuses which stifle freedom and which keep the greater part of humanity from sharing in the building up and enjoyment of a more just and fraternal world. (JW 3) Like Paul VI, the bishops highlight the inadequacy of models of development centered upon the maximization of economic growth. They criticize the detrimental impacts of these approaches on many important dimensions of human life, including spirituality and communal cohesion. The bishops also reiterate concern about the negative ecological impacts of the these growth-focused models:

> Such is the demand for resources and energy by the richer nations... and such are the effects of dumping by them in the atmosphere and the sea that irreparable damage would be done to the essential elements of life on earth...if their high rates of consumption and pollution, which are constantly on the increase, were extended to the whole of mankind. (JW 11)

The bishops emphasize that current development models have failed in the stated goal of significantly reducing hunger and poverty:

> In the last twenty-five years a hope has spread throughout the human race that economic growth would bring about such a quantity of goods that it would be possible to feed the hungry at least with the crumbs falling from the table, but this has proved a vain hope. (JW 10)

Rejecting trickle-down theories, the bishops argue that much greater stress needs to be placed on just distribution of wealth. This will involve numerous reforms. The specific reforms proposed by the bishops are very similar to those suggested by Paul VI, including a strengthened international authority, the transfer of a certain percentage of income from the richer to the poorer countries, the establishment of

36 The official English version of *Justice in the World* does not include section numbers. These have been added by Joseph Gremillion and can be found in *The Gospel of Peace and Justice: Catholic Social Teaching Since Pope John*, ed. J. Gremillion (Maryknoll, NY: Orbis, 1976).

fairer prices for Third World products, increased regulation of the activities of transnational corporations, and the elimination of barriers in the First World against Third World products. These suggestions, the bishops state, "represent first guidelines for a graduated taxation of income as well as for an economic and social plan for the entire world" – in effect an expansion of key components of the social welfare state to worldwide dimensions. (JW 65-67) Within the Third World, emphasis is placed by the bishops on the need for land reform, support for small farmers, and efforts to meet basic needs of nutrition, health, education, employment, and housing. In all development processes popular participation must be fostered. "Participation," the bishops say, "is a right which is to be applied both in the economic and in the social and political field." (JW 18, 68)

The bishops also highlight the need for the adoption of simpler lifestyles by persons in the wealthier nations:

> It is impossible to see what right the richer nations have to keep up their claim to increase their own material demands, if the consequence is either that others remain in misery or that the danger of destroying the very physical foundations of life on earth is precipitated. Those who are already rich are bound to accept a less material way of life, with less waste, in order to avoid the destruction of the heritage which they are obliged by absolute justice to share with all other members of the human race. (JW 70)

In order to combat the various forces of oppression and injustice in the world, the bishops express their support for grassroots social movements seeking structural change:

> We have noted the inmost stirring moving the world in its depths.... In associations...among peoples...there is arising a new awareness which shakes them out of their fatalistic resignation and which spurs them on to liberate themselves....Movements are seen which express hope in a better world and a will to change whatever has become intolerable....The hopes and forces which are moving the world in its very foundations are not foreign to the dynamism of the Gospel....The Church calls on all, especially the poor, the oppressed, and the afflicted, to cooperate with God to bring about liberation from every sin [including liberation from sinful social structures.] (JW 4, 5, 77)

This emphasis on social action, reminiscent of Medellín, represents a major addition to CST at the worldwide level. As mentioned above, previous CST documents had not encouraged widespread social mobilization. Rather, these documents had directed their attention primarily to political and economic elites, either appealing to the goodwill of such persons or calling for their conversion to more adequate values. *Justice in the World* asserts that moral appeals without concrete efforts to modify social structures are inadequate, emphasizing "the objective obstacles which social structures place in the way of conversion of hearts." (JW 16)

The call for action on behalf of justice set forth by the bishops is addressed to all, but is seen in a special way to be a responsibility of Christians. In one of the most quoted passages of the document the bishops state:

> Action on behalf of justice and participation in the transformation of the world fully appear to us to be a constitutive dimension of the preaching of the Gospel, or, in other words, of the Church's mission for the redemption of the human race and its liberation from every oppressive situation. (JW 6)

While affirming the need for liberation, the bishops argue against the use of violence, stressing the need for peaceful resolution of conflicts and calling for a "strategy of nonviolence" to be fostered. (JW 65)

Significantly, in this document the bishops call for the principles of CST (concerning justice, the importance of participation, due process, the need for simpler lifestyles, etc.) to be applied within the institutional life of the Church itself, an issue not given much attention in earlier CST documents:

> While the Church is bound to give witness to justice, she recognizes that anyone who ventures to speak to people about justice must first be just in their eyes. Hence we must undertake an examination of the modes of acting and of the possessions and lifestyle found within the Church herself. (JW 40)

It is asserted that "within the Church rights must be preserved," including the right to a just wage, greater participation by lay people in decision-making, increased "responsibility and participation" for women, freedom of expression, and due process in church law. (JW 40-46)

Justice in the World thus makes numerous important contributions to the development of CST. These contributions include heightened attention to a critical, structural analysis of injustice, emphasis on the centrality of justice in the Christian faith and in the institutional life of the Church, greater stress on ecological issues, and affirmation of the need for grassroots social movements that are actively committed to the cause of social justice.

Evangelii Nuntiandi (1975)

In 1975, Pope Paul VI issued a document on "Evangelization in the Modern World," following up on a 1974 synod of bishops devoted to this theme. While this document, *Evangelii Nuntiandi,* is not primarily a social encyclical, it does discuss work for social justice as a central component of the church's evangelizing task. "Evangelization," the pope declares, "involves an explicit message...about the rights and duties of every human being,...about international life, peace, justice, and development – a message especially energetic today about liberation." (EN 29)

Of special significance is the pope's widespread usage of this language of liberation. While Pope Paul had introduced the term into major papal documents with one usage in *Octogesima Adveniens,* and while it had played an important role in the international bishops' reflections in *Justice in the World,* this is the first papal document in which liberation is a central theme. The pope stresses what could be termed "integral liberation," liberation that embraces all facets of human existence. Without diminishing the importance of liberation on the economic, political, and social levels, Pope Paul places special emphasis on the spiritual, warning against any understandings of liberation that would neglect this dimension. (EN 31-38)

Also noteworthy in this encyclical are the pope's discussions of base communities and of violence. Presenting the first discussion of base communities in papal teaching, Pope Paul affirms the value and importance of these communities. At the same time, he strongly cautions that such communities must always have a firm spiritual basis, must remain in communion with the church's Magisterium, and must not become "hypercritical" or "sectarian." (EN 58)

With regard to violence as a path to liberation, Pope Paul had expressed grave cautions in *Populorum Progessio,* though in one parenthetical comment he seemed to imply to possibility of justified revolution in extreme circumstances.[37] Now violent revolution is unequivocably ruled out:

37 In an intriguing passage, Pope Paul both strongly discourages revolution and at the same time seems to acknowledge its legitimacy in extreme

> The Church cannot accept violence, especially the force of arms...as the path to liberation, because she knows that violence always provokes violence and irresistibly engenders new forms of oppression and enslavement....We exhort you not to place your trust in violence and revolution....We must say and reaffirm that violence is not in accord with the Gospel, that it is not Christian. (EN 37)

Puebla Documents (1979)

The themes of liberation highlighted by Paul VI in *Evangelii Nuntiandi* were also central to the meeting of Latin American bishops held at Puebla, Mexico in 1979, during the first year of the pontificate of John Paul II. This conference strongly affirmed the need for liberation (including major changes in social structures), highlighted the value of base communities, cautioned against neglect of the spiritual, and rejected the use of violence. The significance of the Puebla conference lies above all in its strong reaffirmation of the preferential option for the poor asserted at Medellín, despite strong efforts by conservatives within the Latin American church hierarchy to reject or greatly modify some of the core themes of the Medellín documents.[38] Other

---

circumstances. "There are certainly situations whose injustice cries to heaven....Recourse to violence, as a means to right these wrongs to human dignity, is a grave temptation. We know, however, that a revolutionary uprising – save where there is manifest, long-standing tyranny which would do great damage to fundamental personal rights and dangerous harm to the common good of the country – produces new injustices, throws more elements out of balance and brings on new disasters. A real evil should not be fought against at the cost of greater misery." (PP 30-31) The parenthetical comment in this passage is perhaps the closest that modern CST has come to accepting the possibility of a justified revolution.

38 For discussion of conservative attempts to control the outcome of the Puebla conference, see John Eagleston and Philip Scharper, eds., *Puebla and Beyond: Documentation and Commentary* (Maryknoll, NY: Orbis, 1979).

For discussion of the following issues within the final Puebla document, see the paragraphs noted:

- preferential option for the poor; 733, 1134-1165
- structural sin and economic dependency; 28-50, 66-70, 281, 1259-1267
- critique of capitalism (and Marxism); 47, 92, 495, 542
- base communities; 96-98, 640-643
- women; 126, 443, 834-849, 1135n

important contributions of Puebla include its updated analysis of the structural causes of poverty in Latin America (which the bishops claim had worsened since Medellín), its forceful denunciation of escalating human rights abuses, and its increased attention to issues relating to women, indigenous persons, and ecology.

With regard to development as it had been pursued in Latin America in the preceding decades, the bishops state: "We note that since the decade of the fifties, and despite certain achievements, the ample hopes for development have come to nothing. The marginalization of the vast majority and the exploitation of the poor has increased." (P 1260) In many countries, the bishops state, "a cold-hearted technocracy applies development models that extort a truly inhuman price from those who are poorest." (P 50)

JOHN PAUL II: THE CENTRALITY OF SOLIDARITY

The social teachings of Pope John Paul II largely involve a reaffirmation of the key themes of recent CST documents and their application to changing historical circumstances. The relative emphasis placed on some of the themes, however, is modified. For example, the notion of "solidarity," while already important in CST, comes to occupy an even more exalted place in the encyclicals of John Paul II. Conversely, the importance of applying the principles of CST to the internal life of the church receives diminished attention, with the exception of a certain amount of attention to lifestyle issues. The social teachings of John Paul II are contained in three major social encyclicals, issued in 1981, 1987, and 1991, as well as in a variety of other important speeches and writings.

Laborem Exercens (1981)

In his first social encyclical, issued in 1981, Pope John Paul II presents an extended philosophical/theological reflection on the nature of human work. Grounded in an assertion that work is foundational to

---

– indigenous persons and values; 19, 52-62, 1164

– ecology; 139, 496

– nonviolence; 486, 533-534

– liberation; 141, 480-506

– assertions that the plight of the poor has worsened since Medellín; 487, 1135, 1260

human dignity and is a sharing with God in the task of creation, the pope takes a very positive view of work.[39] He sees the issue of work and respect for the human dignity and rights of workers as being "a key, probably the essential key, to the whole social question." (LE 3)

Most fundamentally, John Paul proclaims the necessity of respecting the "subjective dimension" of work and the "priority of labor over capital," arguing that human dignity must not be degraded for the sake of power or profits. (LE 12) In these assertions he is of course reaffirming fundamental principles of CST.

From this general principle of the priority of labor John Paul derives various practical implications. For example, he reaffirms the call of CST for increased participation by workers in the management and ownership of businesses, stresses the importance of providing opportunities for initiative and creativity on the part of workers, calls for humane working conditions along with just wages and benefits for workers, suggests the need for land redistribution to provide land to landless peasants, and reaffirms the acceptability of the socialization of ownership of the means of production in certain cases in which private ownership may be contrary to the common good. (LE 12-20) In light of his concern for the dignity and rights of workers, Pope John Paul strongly critiques both the liberal capitalism of the West and the so-called socialist systems of the East. In a later encyclical he would refer to the socialist systems as being in reality forms of "state capitalism," due to their unacceptable treatment of workers.[40] According to John Paul, any system in which the worker "is treated as an instrument of production...whatever the program or name under which it occurs, should rightly be called 'capitalism.'" (LE 7)

---

39 Pope John Paul II recognizes that work includes dimensions of toil and suffering, as a consequence of human sin. Even this, however, he interprets positively, as an opportunity to share in the redemptive cross of Christ. "All work, whether manual or intellectual, is inevitably linked with toil.... By enduring the toil of work in union with Christ crucified for us, man in a way collaborates with the son of God for the redemption of humanity." (LE 27) It is important to note that the pope defines work broadly. He is not referring only to paid employment. Housework and raising children, for example, partake of the dignity of work that he asserts. Nonetheless, much of the encyclical is devoted to the rights and duties of persons in the formal economy.

40 This claim is made in CA 35.

John Paul argues that, in order to attain justice for workers, "there is a need for ever new movements of solidarity of the workers and with the workers," solidarity which will at times manifest itself in the form of an active and assertive "struggle for social justice." (LE 20) This solidarity, the pope emphasizes,

> must be present whenever it is called for by the social degrading of the subject of work, by exploitation of the workers and by the growing areas of poverty and even hunger. The church is firmly committed to this cause for she considers it her mission, her service, a proof of her fidelity to Christ, so that she can truly be the 'church of the poor.' (LE 8)

Sollicitudo Rei Socialis (1987)

Pope John Paul II's second social encyclical was issued in 1987, to commemorate the 20th anniversary of *Populorum Progressio*. In it, the pope reflects upon what has taken place in the world with regard to the quest for development in the past 20 years. Overall, like the Latin American bishops at Puebla, John Paul presents a rather negative portrait of the current situation, asserting that the plight of the world's poor had "become notably worse" during the preceding two decades. (SRS 16) He devotes much attention to exploring what has gone wrong. Why, the pope asks, have the hopes for development held by so many in the 1960s not been fulfilled?

In answering this question, John Paul highlights several main causes. One is the continued dominance of flawed models of development, which persist in placing a primary emphasis on economic growth to the neglect of many of the other crucial factors that had been highlighted by Pope Paul VI, including issues of distribution and concern for social, spiritual, and ecological well-being. (SRS 9, 15, 28-29)

John Paul II also reaffirms the critical social analysis of Pope Paul, citing structural injustice as a key factor perpetuating the misery of the world's poor:

> One must denounce the existence of economic, financial, and social mechanisms which...often function almost automatically, accentuating the situation of wealth for some and poverty for the rest. These mechanisms, which are maneuvered directly or indirectly by the more developed countries...suffocate or condition the economies of the less developed countries. (SRS 16)

These mechanisms, the pope says, are rightly viewed as "structures of sin." (SRS 36) Also denounced as a manifestation of sin is the division of the world into contending political-economic-military blocs. The policies of both East and West, John Paul argues, are characterized by the quest for power and profit. "Both of the two blocs," the pope asserts, "harbors in its own way a tendency toward imperialism, as it is usually called, or toward forms of neo-colonialism." (SRS 22) These neo-colonial policies, the social conflicts created and exacerbated by them, and the spending of massive amounts of money for military purposes are viewed by the pope as being major factors in the failure to bring about positive change for the world's poor. (SRS 22-23)

What John Paul calls for as an alternative to the quest for power and profit and the division of the world into blocs is the practice of global solidarity. Solidarity, the pope says, is the appropriate moral response to the empirical fact of growing interdependence. (SRS 26) Solidarity is defined as a virtue, manifest above all in the overcoming of personal and group selfishness and in the desire to help others. (SRS 40) "The process of development and liberation," John Paul asserts, "takes concrete shape in the exercise of solidarity, that is to say in the love and service of neighbor, especially of the poorest." (SRS 46)

John Paul stresses that both rich and poor are harmed by the current situation of wealth for a few and poverty for many:

> This then is the picture: there are some people–the few who possess much–who do not really succeed in 'being' because, through a reversal of the hierarchy of values, they are hindered by the cult of 'having'; and there are others–the many who have little or nothing–who do not succeed in realizing their basic human vocation because they are deprived of essential goods. (SRS 28)

John Paul asserts that there is a profound need for social change, which all persons can help to bring about in a nonviolent manner. "Each individual," the pope says, "is called upon to play his or her part in this peaceful campaign, a campaign to be conducted by peaceful means, in order to secure development in peace." (SRS 47)

Centesimus Annus (1991)

The final social encyclical of Pope John Paul II was issued in 1991, in commemoration of the 100th anniversary of the publication of *Rerum Novarum*. In this document, *Centesimus Annus*, John Paul reflects extensively upon the collapse of communism in Eastern Europe. He attributes this collapse to fundamental errors in the communist view of the human person, particularly its rejection of the centrality of the transcendent and its neglect of the importance of individual freedom in the economic and political realms of human life.

In the course of his critique of communism, the pope affirms certain features traditionally associated with the capitalist economic system, such as the centrality of individual initiative. "The modern business economy," the pope states, "has positive aspects. Its basis is human freedom in the economic field."[41] (CA 32) While affirming individual initiative and an important role for markets, however, John Paul emphasizes that markets must be placed within a strongly regulated framework. (CA 35, 42) He stresses the danger of "idolatry" of markets (CA 40) and asserts that there are many basic needs that the market on its own will not meet. (CA 34, 40, 42)

When John Paul comes to an assessment of existing capitalism, he is very critical. He asserts that "the human inadequacies of capitalism and the resulting domination of things over people are far from disappearing." (CA 35) In particular, John Paul highlights the reality that "many people, perhaps the majority today," live in conditions characterized by "marginalization" and "exploitation," while a wealthy minority lives in a state of equally unacceptable "superdevelopment" characterized by crass materialism, wastefulness, apathy, alienation, and lack of spiritual values. (CA 19, 33, 36, 41; SRS 28) "Vast multitudes," the pope says, "are still living in conditions of great material and moral poverty." (CA 42) "It is unacceptable," he declares, "to say that the defeat of so-called 'real socialism' leaves capitalism as the only model of economic organization." (CA 35)

Being thus very critical of existing forms of capitalism, John Paul states that "what is being proposed as an alternative is not the socialist system, which in fact turns out to be state capitalism, but rather a society of free work, of enterprise, and of participation." (CA 35) What the pope means by this phrase –"a society of free work, enterprise, and of participation"–is not specified in extensive detail in this encyclical. This is in part because John Paul does not envision CST as

41 A nuanced appreciation of private initiative, qualified by the overriding importance of the common good, has been a consistent part of CST. See for example the comments of John XXIII in *Mater et Magistra*, discussed above.

providing an exact blueprint for economic or political life, but rather as providing general guiding principles. A broad outline of his vision can nonetheless be discerned in *Centesimus Annus* and in his earlier writings, especially *Laborem Exercens*. From these writings it appears that the type of alternative that the pope envisions would consist of a strongly regulated market-based economy (rather than a centrally-planned economy or a largely unregulated market economy), one in which workers' rights are respected and workers have significant roles in the ownership and management of business enterprises. As well, it would be an economy in which subsidiarity functions as a guiding principle, and in which concern for profit is balanced by other considerations of a social, ecological, and moral nature. (CA 15-16, 34-35, 40, 42-43, 48; LE 12-20)

With regard to First World-Third World relations, Pope John Paul makes an important reference to Third World debt, calling for measures to "lighten, defer, or even cancel the debt," emphasizing that "it is not right to demand or expect payment when the effect would be the imposition of political choices leading to hunger and despair for entire peoples," as has often been the case with recent structural adjustment policies. (CA 35) More generally, the pope stresses that true development will require "sacrificing the positions of income and of power enjoyed by the more developed economies." (CA 52) Highlighting the far-reaching nature of needed reforms, John Paul asserts the necessity of "a change of lifestyles, of models of production and consumption, and of the established structures of power which today govern societies." (CA 58)

John Paul reaffirms in this encyclical the importance and validity of social struggle, a theme that was present in *Laborem Exercens* but that had been downplayed somewhat in *Sollicitudo Rei Socialis*:

> The church is well aware that in the course of history conflicts of interest between different social groups inevitably arise, and that in the face of such conflicts Christians must often take a position, honestly and decisively. The encyclical *Laborem Exercens* moreover clearly recognized the positive role of conflict when it takes the form of a 'struggle for social justice'....What is condemned...is the idea that conflict is not restrained by ethical or juridical considerations, or by respect for the dignity of others. (CA 14)

It seems likely that the transformations in Eastern Europe, which were able to remain predominantly nonviolent in nature, led the pope to express this renewed appreciation of social struggle. In the encyclical John Paul strongly praises "the nonviolent commitment of the people who, while always refusing to yield to the force of power, succeeded time after time in finding effective ways of bearing witness to the truth." The pope then adds a powerful appeal: "May people learn to fight for justice without violence, renouncing class struggle in their internal disputes, and war in international ones." (CA 23) Elsewhere in the document the pope reflects on war in light of the experience of the 1991 Persian Gulf War:

> I myself, on the occasion of the recent tragic war in the Persian Gulf, repeated the cry: 'Never again war!' No, never again war, which destroys the lives of innocent people, teaches how to kill, throws into upheaval even the lives of those who do the killing and leaves behind a trail of resentment and hatred, thus making it all the more difficult to find a just solution of the very problems which provoked the war. (CA 52)

OTHER WRITINGS AND TALKS OF JOHN PAUL II

Centesimus Annus in 1991 was Pope John Paul II's last major social encyclical. John Paul continued, however, to develop his social teaching over the next 14 years through a variety of other writings and talks. In this section we'll briefly look at some of his more recent reflections on economic globalization and on war and nonviolence.

Economic Globalization:

John Paul expresses fear that the mechanisms of systemic injustice present in the international economy are bringing about harmful forms of economic globalization. "[I]f globalization is ruled merely by the laws of the market applied to suit the powerful," he warns," then

> the consequences cannot but be negative. These are, for example, the absolutizing of the economy, unemployment, the reduction and deterioration of public services, the destruction of the environment and natural resources, the growing distance between rich and poor, unfair competition which puts the poor nations in a situation of ever increasing inferiority.[42]

As we have seen, these phenomena highlighted by the pope are viewed by many analysts to characterize accurately what has been occurring

42 John Paul II, *Ecclesia in America*, no. 20.

throughout the world over the past couple decades as a result of structural adjustment and free trade policies that prioritize the interests of capital over the interests of small farmers, workers, and the environment. Elsewhere the pope speaks of current forms of globalization as entailing "the domination of the powerful over the weak, especially in the economic sphere, and the loss of the values of local cultures in favor of a misconstrued homogenization."[43] He warns that globalization must not be a new version of colonialism.[44]

John Paul II is especially forceful in his critique of "capitalist neoliberalism," accusing it of accumulating wealth for the few at the expense of the many:

> [V]arious places are witnessing a resurgence of a certain capitalist neoliberalism that subordinates the human person to blind market forces....From its centers of power, such neoliberalism often places unbearable burdens on less favored countries....In the international community, we thus see a small number of countries growing exceedingly rich at the cost of the increasing impoverishment of a great number of other countries; as a result the wealthy grow ever wealthier, while the poor grow ever poorer.[45]

The pope expresses concern that market mechanisms can trample upon the common good and give rise to social conflict, even contributing to acts of terrorism:

> Special interests and the demands of the market frequently predominate over concern for the common good. This tends to leave the weaker members of society without adequate protection and can subject entire peoples and cultures to a formidable struggle for survival. Moreover, it is disturbing to witness a globalization that exacerbates the conditions of the needy, that does not sufficiently contribute to resolving situations of hunger, poverty, and social inequality, that fails to safeguard the natural environment. These aspects of globalization can give rise to extreme reactions, leading

---

43 Ibid., no. 55.

44 John Paul II, "The Ethical Dimensions of Globalization," Address to the Pontifical Academy for Social Sciences (April 27, 2001), no. 4. Available at <www.cjre.org/economic_injustice_viewpoints.htm>.

45 John Paul II, Homily of January 25, 1998. The homily can be found at <www.vatican.va/holy_father/john_paul_ii/travels/documents/hf_jp-ii_hom_25011998_lahavana_en.html>.

> to excessive nationalism, religious fanaticism and even acts of terrorism.[46]

To counteract these negative forms of globalization, the pope highlights the necessity of "adequate regulation" and guidance on the part of the global community, along with a greater sharing of wealth through development aid, debt relief, and other redistributive measures. Only with this regulation and more equitable distribution of resources, John Paul insists, will globalization be able to serve the common good rather than "bringing benefit merely to a privileged few."[47] Several examples that the pope gives of needed regulations include measures to ensure a just wage for all workers, substantive reforms of the international trading system to guarantee fair rules of trade, legal recognition of the right to unionize, legislation to prevent the exploitation of child labor, and strong laws to protect the environment.[48] The pope is aware that these suggestions will meet powerful opposition from those who profit from the current system. "The Holy See is fully aware of the difficulties of devising concrete mechanisms for the proper regulation of globalization," John Paul states, "not least because of the resistance that such regulation would meet in certain quarters."[49]

War and Nonviolence:

In the years after the publication of *Centesimus Annus*, John Paul II further deepened his critique of war, especially in his annual World Day of Peace messages. This critique can also be seen in his statements

46 John Paul II, "Governance of Globalization," Address to the Pontifical Academy for Social Sciences" (May 2, 2003). Available at <http://www.zenit.org/article-7158?l=english>.

47 Ibid.

48 See John Paul II, Address to Members of the Foundation for "Ethics and Economics" (May 17, 2001); SRS 43; CA 40. For additional, specific suggestions for reform of the global economy see the Vatican's "Address to the UN Panel on the Eradication of World Poverty" (July 2, 2003), "Address to the UN Conference on Trade and Development" (June 22, 2004), and "Ethical Guidelines for International Trade: Note to the Ministerial Conference of the World Trade Organization (September 10, 2003), all available at <www.zenit.org>.

49 John Paul II, "Governance of Globalization."

of opposition to the 2003 U.S. invasion of Iraq.[50] Below are excerpts from a few of these statements:

> Peace never requires violence.... Especially those who come from countries whose soil is stained with blood know well that violence constantly generates violence. War throws open the doors to the abyss of evil.... This is why war should always be considered a defeat: the defeat of reason and of humanity.... War never again! I was convinced of this in October 1986 in Assisi, when I asked people belonging to all religions to gather side by side to invoke God for peace. I am even more convinced of it today. (September 8, 2004)[51]

> When, as in Iraq in these days, war threatens the fate of humanity, it is even more urgent to proclaim with a strong and decisive voice that peace is the only path for building a society which is more just and marked by solidarity. Violence and weapons can never resolve the problems of man. (March 22, 2003)[52]

> *Nothing is resolved by war; on the contrary, everything is placed in jeopardy by war.* The results of this scourge are the suffering and death of innumerable individuals, the disintegration of human relations and the irreparable loss of an immense artistic and environmental patrimony. War worsens the sufferings of the poor; indeed, it creates new poor by destroying means of subsistence, homes and property, and by eating away at the very fabric of the social environment....After so many unnecessary massacres, it is in the final analysis of fundamental importance to recognize, once and for all, that *war never helps the human community,* that violence destroys and never builds up, that the wounds it causes remain long unhealed, and that as a result of conflicts the already grim condition of the poor deteriorates still further, and new forms of poverty appear. (Message for World Day of Peace 1993 – emphasis in original)

---

50 For a fuller exploration of the views of Pope John Paul II on the topics of war and nonviolence, see John Sniegocki, "Catholic Teaching on War, Peace, and Nonviolence Since Vatican II," in *Vatican II: Forty Years Later,* Annual of the College Theology Society, vol. 51, ed. William Madges (Maryknoll, NY: Orbis Books, 2006), 224-244.

51 John Paul II, Message for "Men and Religions" Meeting in Milan, Italy on September 8, 2004. Available online at <http://www.zenit.org/article-10972?l=english>.

52 This quote can be found on the U.S. Catholic bishops' website at <www.usccb.org/sdwp/peace/quotes.htm>. Also see "Pope Says Iraq War Threatens Humanity" at <www.cathnews.com/news/303/124.php>.

> To attain the good of peace there must be a clear and conscious acknowledgment that violence is an unacceptable evil and that it never solves problems. Violence is a lie, for it goes against the truth of our faith, the truth of our humanity. Violence destroys what it claims to defend: the dignity, the life, the freedom of other human beings. (Message for World Day of Peace 2005)

What is striking about these and many other quotes of Pope John Paul II on the issue of war is that he generally sounds like a pacifist, making bold statements against all war and violence. John Paul did not, however, consider himself a strict pacifist. For example, he left open the possibility of the use of an armed multilateral intervention force to prevent genocide, as in cases such as Rwanda. He conceptualized this, however, more as police action than as war. Instead of being rooted in pacifism, John Paul's very strong critiques of war seem to be rooted in a strict interpretation of the just war criteria. As he applied the criteria to our current context, he saw that no modern war would be likely to meet them. This accounts for his ability to make bold blanket statements against war as such.[53]

Like earlier popes, John Paul emphasized the central role that the United Nations needs to play in preventing war. He called for the strengthening of its powers, in areas such as peacemaking, economic justice, and ecological regulation, along with a general call for increased respect for international law.[54] He frequently highlighted the connections between social justice and peace, emphasizing the need for greater efforts to overcome poverty. In his discussion of responses to terrorism, for example, John Paul stresses the need for "a courageous and resolute political, diplomatic, and economic commitment to relieving situations of oppression and marginalization which facilitate the designs of terrorists."[55] John Paul also emphasized, as we saw in our discussion of *Centesimus Annus*, the power of nonviolent action as a way of responding to oppression. He praised "the nonviolent commitment of people who, while always refusing to yield to the forces of power, succeeded time after time in finding ways of bearing effective

53 For fuller documentation of this claim, see Sniegocki, "Catholic Teaching on War."

54 See John Paul II's World Day of Peace messages for 2003 and 2004.

55 John Paul II, Message for World Day of Peace 2002, no. 5. See John Paul's World Day of Peace messages from 2002 to 2005 for his reflections on the proper ways to respond to the dangers of terrorism.

witness to the truth." (CA 23) "Those who have built their lives on the value of non-violence," John Paul states, "have given us a luminous and prophetic example."[56]

THE SOCIAL ETHICS OF BENEDICT XVI

In the first couple years of his papacy Pope Benedict XVI has issued numerous short statements on Catholic Social Teaching themes, though not yet (as of May 2009) a formal social encyclical.[57] Benedict has made repeated calls for peace, especially in the Middle East, and has strongly emphasized the priority of nonviolence. Like Pope John Paul II, Pope Benedict has expressed grave doubts that any modern war could meet just war criteria. In the context of expressing his opposition to the war in Iraq in May of 2003, for example, Benedict (at that time still Cardinal Ratzinger) stated: "There were not sufficient reasons to unleash a war against Iraq. To say nothing of the fact that, given the new weapons that make possible destructions that go beyond the combatant groups, today we should be asking ourselves if it is still licit to admit the very existence of a 'just war.'"[58]

Pope Benedict has reaffirmed many of the central themes of Pope John Paul II, such as the centrality of solidarity and the need for a more equitable distribution of the world's wealth. He speaks, for example, of the need for solidarity to be lived "so that all human beings may share more equitably in the riches of our planet....The earth, in fact, can produce enough to nourish all its inhabitants, on the condition that the rich countries do not keep for themselves what belongs to all." "It is necessary," Benedict says, "not only to relieve the greatest needs but to go to their roots, proposing measures that will give social, political, and economic structures a more equitable and solidaristic configuration." With regard to globalization, Benedict states: "In the era of globalization, it is important that political policies should not be guided mainly or solely by economic considerations or by the search for higher profits or a heedless use of the planet's resources...."

56 John Paul II, Message for World Day of Peace 2000, no. 4.

57 While not a social encyclical in the formal sense, Benedict XVI's encyclical *Deus Caritas Est* includes some reflections in the second half that are relevant to CST, particularly his discussion of the relationship of charity and justice.

58 For a transcript of the interview in which Cardinal Ratzinger made these comments, see <http://www.zenit.org/article-7161?l=english>.

Like earlier popes, Benedict is especially critical of excessive military spending as a misuse of funds that should be directed to the poor. He emphasizes that a portion of "the immense sums spent worldwide on armaments would be more than sufficient to liberate the immense masses of the poor from destitution. This challenges humanity's conscience. To peoples living below the poverty line, more as a result of situations to do with international political, commercial and cultural relations than as a result of circumstances beyond anyone's control, our common commitment to truth can and must give new hope."[59]

SUMMARY OF CATHOLIC SOCIAL TEACHING ON DEVELOPMENT ISSUES

As highlighted in the discussion above, each of the following themes can be seen as central to current Catholic Social Teaching on issues of development and economic globalization:

(a) The only true development is "integral development." This development is holistic, having economic, social, cultural, spiritual, and ecological components, and consists of all that enables persons to become more fully human.

(b) Equating development simply with economic growth is unacceptable. It is unacceptable because economic growth does not necessarily imply equitable distribution or ecological sustainability, and because an overly economic focus may be destructive of important cultural, social, moral, and religious values and institutions. While it is crucial that the basic material needs of all be met, emphasis must be placed on "being more," not simply on "having more."

(c) The richer nations as well as the poorer nations are in need of integral development. In the richer nations, significant levels of poverty and marginalization still exist, which need to be overcome. Moreover, while many in these nations possess ample material goods, high levels exist of moral underdevelopment (manifest in part as apathy towards the plight of the poor), social underdevelopment (manifest in indi-

---

59 All of these statements of Pope Benedict XVI can be found in "Pope Benedict XVI Speaks About Social Justice." This document is available from Education for Justice, an organization committed to the spread of Catholic Social Teaching. See <www.educationforjustice.org>. Also see John Sniegocki, "The Social Teaching of Pope Benedict XVI," in *Catholic Identity and the Laity*, ed. Tim Muldoon, College Theology Society Annual Volume 54 (Maryknoll, NY: Orbis, 2009), 120-133.

vidualism and the breakdown of family and community relations) and religious underdevelopment (manifest in part in the idolatry of material goods).

(d) A central principle of integral development is that the goods of the earth are intended for all. This principle places significant limits on the rights of private property and on the freedom of economic markets and implies the need for significant lifestyle changes on the part of those who possess more than they truly need in a world in which others lack necessities.

(e) Attaining development will require significant structural reforms both on the international level and within nations, along with moral/religious conversion on the part of individuals. In the present context the needed structural reforms would include especially the fostering of political and economic democracy both within and among nations, requiring measures such as the establishment of a more just system of international trade and finance, relief of the Third World debt burden, land reform, support for small and medium-sized businesses and family farmers, greater worker participation in the ownership and management of businesses, the prioritization of the meeting of basic needs, and the reform and strengthening of international organizations such as the United Nations. The needed personal conversion would, in its social aspect, be manifest primarily in the virtue of "solidarity."

(f) Working for development is a religious task, for God is concerned for the integral well-being of persons.

(g) Integral development is a human right and is dependent upon respect for all other human rights (social, economic, political, religious, and ecological).[60]

(h) Fostering participation by all in the development process, to the greatest extent possible, is essential. Persons are to be subjects of development, not its objects.

(i) Stress must be placed upon the role of the poor in the development process and special attention paid to ensuring that the rights of the poor (including the right to participation) are respected and that the basic needs of the poor are met.

---

60 The inclusion of ecological issues as human rights is a relatively new development within CST. In his 1990 World Day of Peace message Pope John Paul II affirmed the "right to a safe environment," suggesting that this right should be added to the U.N. Charter of Human Rights. "The Ecological Crisis: A Common Responsibility," no. 9.

(j) Military spending and war must be recognized as two of the most significant obstacles to development, for military spending absorbs huge amounts of human and material resources that are desperately needed to foster development, while war serves to destroy the achievements of development in the nations at war.

(k) Only nonviolent means are acceptable in the quest for development.

(l) Without authentic, integral development, international and domestic peace will not be possible, for the only true basis of peace is justice.

CHAPTER 4

CATHOLIC SOCIAL TEACHING AND POLITICAL ECONOMY:

NEOCONSERVATIVE AND RADICAL CRITIQUES

The reflections of CST on development/globalization themes have given rise to a variety of critical responses. This chapter will examine the neoconservative critique of CST articulated by Michael Novak and critiques of CST from radical perspectives expressed by persons such as Mary Hobgood, Larry Rasmussen, George McCarthy, and Royal Rhodes. Particular attention will be given to issues of political economy and the debate over structural injustice. At the end of the chapter I will highlight what I perceive to be some of the major strengths and weaknesses of the neoconservative, radical, and CST positions and will suggest several ways that CST could be further enhanced through dialogue with its critics.

NEOCONSERVATIVE REFLECTIONS ON CST

From the perspective of neoconservatives, CST has developed several major flaws in the past three decades. These flaws include its emphasis on structural injustice as a cause of poverty (which is viewed by neoconservatives as mistaken), an overreliance on action by the state, and a general neglect of the factors that foster wealth creation.[1] Michael Novak, summarizing the core of his critique of (pre-*Centesimus Annus*) CST, states:

> The intellectual model for peace and justice offered by Catholic Social Teaching is at present closer to a mild form of socialism than to democratic capitalism. It has too little to say about markets and

1 For neoconservative reflections on CST, see especially the writings of Michael Novak, George Weigel, and Richard John Neuhaus. For an extensive overview of the differences between neoconservatives and the social views of Pope John Paul II, see John Sniegocki, "The Social Ethics of Pope John Paul II: A Critique of Neoconservative Interpretations," *Horizons* 33, no. 1 (Spring 2006): 7-32.

> incentives, the ethics of production, and the habits, disciplines, and organization necessary for the creation of wealth.[2]

The CST tradition, Novak contends, "proceeds as if democratic capitalism did not exist."[3] He argues that recent CST documents have made a "preferential option for the state" and have engaged in many unfounded criticisms of the capitalist system.[4] While criticizing CST, Novak praises the political and economic traditions of the United States, which he argues are "both morally superior and far more highly developed than Catholic social teaching."[5]

Neoconservatives such as Novak are especially critical of claims that the wealth of the First World has been derived in significant part from exploitation of the Third World or that actions of the First World have perpetuated poverty in the Third World. Claims of such connections between First World wealth and Third World poverty have played an important role in CST since the issuance of *Populorum Progressio* and the Medellín documents, as we have seen. This emphasis on structural injustice has been strongly reaffirmed by Popes John Paul II and Benedict XVI. According to Novak, however, there exists "not a

---

2 Michael Novak, *The Spirit of Democratic Capitalism* (New York: American Enterprise Institute, 1982), 248.

3 Ibid., 21.

4 Novak uses the phrase "preferential option for the state" in various places. For one example, see Michael Novak and William Simon, "Liberty and Justice for All," in *Private Virtue and Public Policy*, ed. James Finn (New Brunswick: Transaction Publishers, 1990), 8. In his critique of CST Novak mainly asserts that the CST documents reflect socialist or Marxist ideas, ideas that he views to be without merit. He asserts, for example, that *Populorum Progressio* reflects the "high tide of Eurosocialism," particularly in its emphasis on structural injustice, its critiques of capitalism and free trade, and its emphasis on the subordination of the right to private property to the demands of the common good. *The Catholic Ethic and the Spirit of Capitalism* (New York: The Free Press, 1993), 149. The documents of Medellín and subsequent documents influenced by Medellín Novak views as reflecting Marxist influence. *Spirit of Democratic Capitalism*, 287. He charges that the U.S. Catholic bishops have "turned toward essential economic socialism" in a "decisive way". Ibid., 253.

5 Michael Novak, "Twilight of Socialism," *Catholicism in Crisis* 1, no. 9 (August, 1983): 2.

shred of evidence" supporting these contentions.[6] Novak's discussion of these issues focuses especially on Latin America. He argues that Latin American poverty is not due primarily to structural injustice but is rather the result of cultural factors. Latin Americans, he contends, have throughout their history not valued traits such as individual initiative, inventiveness, hard work, and thrift, traits which he views as keys to the creation of wealth. North Americans have valued these traits, and this accounts for the differences in economic status that exist between North and South America. Clearly reflecting views of the modernizationist tradition, Novak states:

> Latin Americans do not value the same moral qualities North Americans do....The 'Catholic' aristocratic ethic of Latin America places more emphasis on luck, heroism, status, and *figura* than the relatively 'Protestant' ethic of North America, which values diligent work, steadfast regularity, and the responsible seizure of opportunity....Looking at Latin America, a North American is likely to attribute its backwardness to an ethos better suited to aristocrats, monks, and peasants, who lack respect for commerce and industrial life and the moral virtues on which these depend....Thus, most North Americans are likely to feel not a shred of guilt for the relative economic positions of the two continents.[7]

"Latin America," Novak bluntly asserts, "is responsible for its own condition."[8] He argues that what Latin America needs is "democratic capitalism," claiming that until recently the continent has been characterized exclusively by feudal and statist rather than capitalist social structures.[9] He highlights the East Asian NICs (newly industrialized countries, such as South Korea and Taiwan) as examples of what can

6 Novak, *Spirit of Democratic Capitalism*, 285. "We reject as false the proposition that the poverty of poor nations is caused by the wealth of richer nations," states the Lay Commission on Catholic Social Teaching and the U.S. Economy (in which Novak played a central role), *Toward the Future: Catholic Social Thought and the U.S. Economy* (New York: Lay Commission, 1984), 50.

7 Novak, *Spirit of Democratic Capitalism*, 302. Novak laments that some educated westerners, however, "feel unworthy of their own success" and "seem to relish being made to feel guilty." Ibid.

8 Novak, *Spirit of Democratic Capitalism*, 301.

9 "In Latin America today," stated Novak in 1986, "I do not see a single capitalist economy." *Will it Liberate? Questions about Liberation Theology* (New York: Paulist, 1986), 85.

be achieved through capitalist values and practices. He suggests that in recent years Latin American countries such as Chile and Mexico have moved in this direction, with positive results.[10]

Over against liberation theology, whose prominence in Latin America Novak laments, Novak asserts "creation theology."[11] By creation theology he refers not to a theology emphasizing humanity's relationship with and concern for nature, as the term is often used, but rather to a theology emphasizing the "creation" of wealth. For Novak, democratic capitalism is the creator of wealth *par excellence*. "After five millennia of blundering," says Novak, "human beings figured out how wealth may be produced in a sustained, systemic way."[12]

When Novak speaks of democratic capitalism, he has in mind a "triune" or "tripartite" system consisting of a free market economy,[13] a democratic political system, and a pluralistic moral-cultural system that cherishes freedom, creativity, initiative, and related values.[14] He sees these three systems as being largely independent and in creative tension, each system keeping the others in check. "The fundamental reason behind the capacity for self-reform in democratic capitalism," Novak states, "lies in the independence of its moral-cultural order and its political order alike. Both operate effectively upon its economic

---

10 For discussion of the NICs, see Novak, *Will it Liberate?*, 76-77. For Novak's comments on Mexico and Chile, see *Catholic Ethic*, 231.

11 See for example the discussion of creation theology in Novak, *Will it Liberate?*, 77. Also see Lay Commission, *Toward the Future*, 43.

12 Novak, *Spirit of Democratic Capitalism*, 17.

13 In his affirmation of a free market economy, Novak recognizes the need for a certain amount of governmental regulation of economic activities. In this he distinguishes himself from more radical libertarians. Nonetheless, Novak asserts that corporations are presently greatly overregulated, particularly in the United States. *Catholic Ethic*, 135. Novak argues that far from being too powerful, as CST often suggests, corporations are in fact not powerful enough: "The case that U.S. corporations are not powerful enough to secure even their own liberty to function competitively seems to be a strong one." *Spirit of Democratic Capitalism*, 178.

14 Novak's vision of democratic capitalism is discussed extensively in *Spirit of Democratic Capitalism* and *Catholic Ethic*. After being criticized for his descriptions of democratic capitalism as "triune" and for attempting to draw explicit analogies between democratic capitalism and the Trinity in *Spirit of Democratic Capitalism* (p. 329), Novak switches in his later works to the language of "tripartite."

system."[15] Novak asserts that only capitalism is truly compatible with political democracy, viewing democracy as resulting from "the natural logic" of capitalism.[16] Significantly, however, it is important to note that the term "democratic" in "democratic capitalism" does *not* refer to economic democracy, i.e. greater worker and community participation in ownership and economic decision-making. While CST strongly affirms economic democracy, Novak rejects it as being inefficient and thus harmful to the common good. "To organize industry democratically," Novak states, "would be a grave and costly error, since democratic procedures are not designed for productivity and efficiency."[17] Novak is especially critical of the idea of economic rights (such as rights to food, shelter, and other basic necessities), and criticizes the affirmation of such rights in CST. "The extensive effort to commit the church to 'economic rights,'" Novak asserts, "has the potential to become an error of classic magnitude. It might well position the Catholic Church in a 'preferential option for the state' that will more than rival that of the Constantinian period."[18]

Novak responds to many common criticisms of capitalism, attempting to show that they are without foundation. For example, he rejects the notion that capitalism fosters excessive individualism, asserting that social cooperation in various forms (ranging from teamwork within corporations to participation in various groupings of civil society) is integral to capitalism. Novak asserts that democratic capitalism "has made possible a new type of human being, neither an individualist nor a collectivist." He terms this new being "the communitarian individual."[19] As to the claim that capitalism fosters inequality, Novak argues that a certain amount of inequality is in fact essential and very positive, providing an incentive for hard work. He asserts also that inequality in the U.S. is not such that it hinders the ability of anyone to pursue and achieve the American Dream.[20] While Novak does

15 Novak, *Catholic Ethic*, 58.

16 Novak, *Spirit of Democratic Capitalism*, 15.

17 Ibid., 178. Novak suggests that economic decisions be made by persons with talent and excellence in this area, such as CEOs. Ibid., 175.

18 Michael Novak, *Three in One: Essays on Democratic Capitalism* (Lanham, MD: Rowman & Littlefield, 2001), 159.

19 Ibid., 134, 143.

20 Novak argues that inequality of rewards is essential to provide persons with an incentive to work hard and to be creative. Democratic capitalism,

acknowledge some significant problems in the U.S. (such as crime, drug abuse, divorce, and a proliferation of out of wedlock births), he does not see these problems as being related to capitalism. Rather, he blames them primarily on the cultural system (conceived of as existing largely independently from the economic system), which he views as being under the control of the "Left" or the "adversary class/culture." This adversary culture, Novak argues, is committed to moral relativism and the undermining of Christian values.[21] Novak is especially critical of feminism, multiculturalism, and the gay rights movement, all of which he views as part of the adversary culture.[22]

---

he asserts, "recognizes the social utility of permitting the top 2% or so to swing free of restraint to whatever extent the market permits." Ibid., 217.

For Novak's claim that anyone can succeed economically in the United States, see *Catholic Ethic*, 158-159. Novak was particularly upset by the claim of the U.S. bishops that poverty in the U.S. results in part from the existence of concentrated wealth and privilege. "Where is this 'concentration'?," Novak demanded. "Which American inherits 'privilege'?...This sentence is an outrage. It is wholly unsupported by evidence, because it cannot be." "The Christian Vision of Economic Life," *Catholicism in Crisis* 3:12 (December, 1985): 27.

21 "The primary flaw in our political economy," Novak asserts, "lies not so much in our political system..., and not so much in our economic system,... *but in our moral-cultural system.*" (emphasis in original) *Catholic Ethic*, 209. For Novak's discussion of the "adversary class" or "adversary culture", see "Against the Adversary Culture," chapter 8 of ibid. Novak argues that the adversary class largely controls the media, universities, and other organs of culture.

22 For Novak's discussions of feminism, see *Confessions of a Catholic*, 193-198; "Woman Church is Not Mother Church," *Catholicism in Crisis* 2:3 (February 1984): 20-21. Novak argues that men in the church have not been assertive enough in challenging feminist demands: "In the presence of feminists, most men are meek, humble, and submissive. They scrutinize feminism seriously, seeking some possible way, absurd as it seems, in which the call of God might actually be expressed in it....The rage of feminists is partly to be explained by the weakness of the males they encounter....The Catholic church will not quiet the fury of feminists through appeasement." ("Woman Church," 20-21.) For Novak's discussions of multiculturalism and homosexuality, see *Catholic Ethic*, 200, 205.

Theologically, Novak grounds his affirmation of democratic capitalism in a version of what he calls "biblical realism."[23] Aware of the reality of sin, this realism rejects any pursuit of utopian projects, such as those which Novak views liberation theologians as pursuing. He argues that the Incarnation shows that fundamental social change is not possible:

> The point of the Incarnation is to respect the world as it is, to acknowledge its limits, to recognize its weaknesses, irrationalities, and evil forces, and to disbelieve any promises that the world is now or ever will be transformed into the City of God. If Jesus could not effect that, how shall we?"[24]

The best that can be hoped for, Novak argues, is "modest progress," which he believes that democratic capitalism represents.[25] While calling his theological views "biblical" realism, it is important to note that Novak rejects the idea that the values taught in the Bible (particularly in the Gospels) could serve as the basis for economic or political life. In fact he argues that to seek to judge the world by gospel values is a major temptation that Christians have to avoid. "The single greatest temptation for Christians," Novak contends, "is to imagine that the salvation won by Jesus has altered the human condition" and therefore "to attempt to judge the present world by the standards of the gospels."[26]

Yet while often making the case for democratic capitalism in these somewhat negative terms (as the best that can be hoped for under conditions of sin), it should be noted that at other times Novak makes much bolder claims. In his *Toward A Theology of the Corporation*, for example, Novak asserts that corporations are "signs of grace" which "mirror the presence of God" in seven sacramental ways. He affirms the "redemptive" activity of corporations, and even compares the corporation to the similarly much maligned "suffering servant" of Isaiah.[27]

---

23 See Novak's discussion of theological themes at the end of *Spirit of Democratic Capitalism*, 333-360.

24 Ibid., 341.

25 Ibid., 342.

26 Ibid., 343.

27 Novak, *Toward a Theology of the Corporation*, 33, 37-43, 54. Novak argues that one task of the theologian is "to show how corporations may be agents of redemption." (p. 54) After discussing Isaiah's vision of the suffer-

In *The Catholic Ethic and the Spirit of Capitalism,* Novak asserts that while democratic capitalism is not perfect, it is nonetheless the social form that is "perhaps the most responsive to the social implications of the gospels yet developed by the human race."[28] Such an affirmation appears to alter somewhat Novak's earlier claim that the gospels are not the standard by which social systems should be judged.

Novak and numerous other neoconservatives such as George Weigel and Richard John Neuhaus have argued that their positive views of capitalism have been vindicated in CST by John Paul II's final social encyclical, *Centesimus Annus,* which they contend represents a major shift in CST in favor of free enterprise and the capitalist system. *Centesimus Annus,* Novak claims, "exploded across the Roman sky on May 1, 1991 like a sonic boom."[29] According to Novak, this encyclical calls into question many aspects of the previous tradition of CST, particularly those elements that seemed to imply an affirmation of some type of democratic socialism rather than an affirmation of capitalism. Summarizing the fundamental change that he believes *Centesimus Annus* represents, Novak provocatively asserts: "We are all capitalist now, even the Pope."[30] As a result of this encyclical, says Novak, John Paul II "may be accorded fame as 'the pope of economic enterprise.'"[31]

Clearly, some themes favored by neoconservatives, such as economic initiative, do play an important role in John Paul's encyclical. Affirmations of economic initiative, however, are not new additions to CST.[32] Nor do such affirmations imply an embrace of capitalism, since economic initiative also plays important roles in visions of democratic socialism and economic democracy. Moreover, all of the main features of CST that Novak and other neoconservatives have objected to continue to be present in *Centesimus Annus.* John Paul, as we have seen, remained extremely critical of existing forms of capitalism. "[T]he human inadequacies of capitalism and the resulting domination of

---

ing servant, Novak states: "I would like to apply these words to the modern business corporation, a much despised incarnation of God's presence in this world." (p. 33)

28 Novak, *Catholic Ethic,* 228.

29 Ibid., 114.

30 Ibid., 101.

31 Ibid., 106.

32 In *Mater et Magistra,* for example, Pope John XXIII asserted that "where private [economic] initiative is lacking, political tyranny prevails." (MM 57)

things over people," John Paul declares in *Centesimus Annus,* "are far from disappearing." (CA 33). "It is unacceptable," John Paul states, "to say that the defeat of so-called 'Real Socialism' leaves capitalism as the only model of economic organization." (CA 35). John Paul on numerous other occasions made the same point. In a talk in Mexico in 1990, for example, John Paul stated:

> The events of recent history...have been interpreted, sometimes superficially, as...the triumph of the liberal capitalist system. Particular interests would like to carry the analysis to the extreme of presenting the system they regard as the winner as the only path for our world on the basis of the experience of the setbacks suffered by contemporary socialism, and shunning the critical judgment required toward the effects liberal capitalism has produced in the countries of the so-called Third World.[33]

Several years after the publication of *Centesimus Annus,* during a trip to Latvia, John Paul further developed this critique of capitalism. "Catholic social doctrine," he stressed, " is not a surrogate for capitalism....[T]he Church, since Leo XIII's *Rerum Novarum,* has always distanced herself from capitalist ideology, holding it responsible for grave social injustices....I myself, after the historical failure of communism, did not hesitate to raise serious doubts on the validity of capitalism."[34]

John Paul expresses an especially negative critique of neoliberal forms of globalization. He expresses grave concern about the "resurgence of a certain capitalist neoliberalism that subordinates the human person to blind market forces." Such capitalism, the pope argues, results in "a small number of countries growing exceedingly rich at the cost of the increasing impoverishment of a great number of other countries; as a result the wealthy grow ever wealthier, while the poor grow ever poorer."[35]

The views of the neoconservatives thus differ greatly from those of Pope John Paul II with regard to their assessments of capitalism, the role of structural injustice in causing poverty, and the value of economic democracy and economic rights. Other fundamental differences between the Catholic neoconservatives and Pope John Paul II

33 John Paul II, "Is Liberal Capitalism the Only Path?" *Origins* 20 (May 24, 1990): 19.

34 John Paul II, "What Catholic Social Teaching Is and Is Not," *Origins* 23 (September 23, 1993): 257.

35 John Paul II, Homily of January 25, 1998.

include John Paul's strong affirmation of the need for lifestyle simplification, his emphasis on the pressing nature of current ecological problems, his stress on the importance of strengthening the United Nations, his understanding of the proper economic role of the state, and his sharply critical assessments of war, including the war in Iraq. Any claim that John Paul II adopted or was heavily influenced by neoconservative economic or political views, I would argue, is thus deeply mistaken.[36]

RADICAL REFLECTIONS ON CST

In contrast to neoconservatives who see the fundamental flaw of CST as being its emphasis on structural injustice, radical theorists (influenced by the body of thought formally known as "radical political economy") strongly affirm structural analysis as one of CST's greatest strengths.[37] These persons, however, also voice some criticisms of CST. Their main criticisms are that the structural analysis contained in CST is not sufficiently systemic and developed, that the policy suggestions that are made are sometimes inconsistent with the deeper analysis that is presented, and that the documents are weak in envisioning how the changes called for by CST are to be implemented.[38]

36 For further discussion of the social ethics of John Paul II and the fundamental differences between his views and those of the Catholic neoconservatives, see Sniegocki, "Social Ethics of Pope John Paul II"; Dorr, *Option for the Poor*, chapters 11-14; David Hollenbach, "Christian Social Ethics After the Cold War," *Theological Studies* 53 (March 1992): 75-95.

37 For introductions to the field of radical political economy, see Charles Barone, *Radical Political Economy: A Concise Introduction* (Armonk, NY: M.E. Sharpe, 2004); Michael Yates, *Naming the System: Inequality and Work in the Global Economy* (New York: Monthly Review Press, 2003); Ron Baiman, Heather Boushey, and Dawn Saunders, eds., *Political Economy and Contemporary Capitalism* (Armonk, NY: M.E. Sharpe, 2000); Victor Lippit, ed., *Radical Political Economy: Explorations in Alternative Economic Analysis* (Armonk, NY: M.E. Sharpe, 1995); Richard Edwards, Michael Reich, and Thomas Weisskopf, eds., *The Capitalist System* (Englewood Cliffs, NJ: Prentice-Hall, 1986).

38 Some works on CST influenced by the insights of radical political economy include George McCarthy and Royal Rhodes, *Eclipse of Justice: Ethics, Economics, and the Lost Traditions of American Catholicism* (Maryknoll, NY: Orbis, 1992); Mary Hobgood, *Catholic Social Teaching and Economic Theory: Paradigms in Conflict* (Philadelphia: Temple University Press,

CST is perceived by many radical theorists to be a mixture of values and insights drawn from several different, conflicting traditions. Mary Hobgood in her book *Catholic Social Teaching and Economic Theory* suggests that three main traditions of social theory are represented, which she terms "organic," "liberal," and "radical." Organic social theory, which flourished in the Middle Ages, understands society as an organism composed of various interdependent, hierarchically structured parts, all of which are to cooperate for the common good. This organic or "communitarian" worldview she finds represented in the emphases in CST upon the common good, social harmony, and (especially in the pre-Johannine encyclicals) a defense of hierarchy and inequality as necessary components of social organization.

The second tradition is the liberal tradition, which affirms individual rights, democracy, and the value of a market-based economy. The liberal tradition envisions the economic realm as being largely independent from other realms such as the political and cultural. While CST has always been highly critical of the individualism, materialism, and stress upon self-interest contained in the liberal tradition, Hobgood and others argue that is has internalized certain liberal assumptions concerning rights, markets, the separation of spheres, and the appropriateness of private ownership of the means of production.

The third tradition that CST draws upon is the radical tradition. In contrast to the liberal tradition radicals argue that the economic, political, and social realms are best understood not as independent entities but rather as one interlocking whole, which in capitalist societies is geared toward serving the owners of capital. Radical theorists stress the importance of equality and of extending democracy to all areas of life, arguing especially that political democracy without economic democracy is largely a façade. When economic democracy is lacking, they assert, those who possess concentrated economic power tend to translate that economic power into domination of the political process, at least unless effectively challenged by progressive social movements. Much emphasis is placed by radical theorists upon understanding the internal dynamics of the capitalist system and upon grassroots organization on behalf of social change.

1991); Larry Rasmussen, "The Morality of Power and the Power of Morality," in *Prophetic Visions and Economic Realities: Protestants, Jews, and Catholics Confront the Bishops' Letter on the Economy*, ed. Charles Strain (Grand Rapids: Eerdmans, 1989).

Some elements in CST that are consistent with the radical tradition include emphasis upon the structural causes of global poverty, recognition of the existence and negative impact of concentrated economic power, recognition that foreign aid is often used for neo-colonial purposes, awareness of the connections between social injustice and war, and the recognition that inequitably distributed power in the economic realm tends to subvert the political process. The strong emphasis upon grassroots social action that is present in *Justice in the World* and in the Latin American bishops' documents can also be seen as consistent with radical views.

What radical theorists assert is that the simultaneous existence of aspects of the organic, liberal, and radical traditions in CST documents leads to a certain amount of incoherence. They claim, for example, that the concrete policy and reform suggestions put forth in CST tend generally to be based on organic and liberal assumptions, such as belief in the power of moral appeal to elites to bring about reform and belief in the relative independence of the economic and political realms. Policy suggestions based on these liberal and organic assumptions are seen by radicals as being in conflict with the deeper structural analysis that the CST documents often contain, which show insights into the interconnections of economic and political power. If the structural analysis present in CST were to be taken seriously, argues Hobgood, it would "preclude the workability of [CST's] own non-structural, orthodox policy prescriptions" by pointing to the need for both more fundamental reforms and deeper social struggle than that which the CST documents generally envision.[39] Were its more radical insights taken seriously when discussing policy, CST would not call simply for reform of capitalism, but rather would stress the need to create alternatives to capitalism. This would entail a commitment to broad-based grassroots efforts aimed at constructing alternative economic, social, and political structures characterized by greater solidarity and more authentic economic and political democracy. It would also entail support for grassroots social struggle aimed at overcoming the obstacles that would prevent these alternatives from taking root.

39 Hobgood, *Catholic Social Teaching*, 7. George McCarthy and Royal Rhodes, speaking of the U.S. Catholic bishops, contend that "[t]heir communal and moral ideals and policy recommendations become utopian when measured against the reality of the existing liberal values and institutions." McCarthy and Rhodes, *Eclipse of Justice*, 106.

What radicals propose as an alternative to capitalism are versions of what has variously been termed "economic democracy," "postliberal democracy," or "democratic socialism." In referring to this alternative I will generally use the language of "economic democracy," which is a term employed in CST. Central features of economic democracy include substantive worker and community participation in both the ownership of capital and in economic decision-making. This contrasts with systems where ownership and decision-making is concentrated in the hands of a few, whether that be capitalism or centrally-planned socialism. There is an important role for markets in economic democracy, but these markets need to be well-regulated to protect the rights of workers, consumers, and the environment. Some goods, such as health care, are viewed as basic rights and are not to be subject to the vagaries of markets at all. Also, because economic democracy assigns a strong role to governments in regulating markets and in using credit, tax, and other policies to favor the dispersion of economic power, its proponents emphasize the need for effective democratic mechanisms to hold government accountable.[40]

Radical critics recognize that some of the CST documents do call for very substantive reforms. The vision of economic democracy that is contained in the last section of the U.S. Catholic bishops' pastoral letter, *Economic Justice for All,* for example, includes measures that if implemented would help to overcome the significant disparities in economic and political power that currently exist. In this case, radical criticism centers not so much upon the ultimate vision (though some of the more short-term policy recommendations contained in the document are criticized), but rather centers upon the lack of attention given to how the deeper vision of economic democracy could realistically be brought about. *Economic Justice for All* stresses the need for harmonious cooperation between capital, labor, and government

40 For some works that explore economic democracy and democratic socialism see Robin Hahnel, *Economic Justice and Democracy* (New York: Routledge, 2005); Michael Albert, *Parecon: Life After Capitalism* (London: Verso, 2003); David Korten, *The Post-Corporate World: Life After Capitalism* (San Francisco: Berrett-Koehler, 1999); James Yunker, *Economic Justice: The Market Socialist Vision* (Lanham, MD: Rowman and Littlefield, 1997); Frank Roosevelt and David Belkin, eds., *Why Market Socialism?* (Armonk, NY: M.E. Sharpe, 1994); Roy Morrison, *We Build the Road as We Travel: Mondragon, A Cooperative Social System* (Philadelphia: New Society Publishers, 1991).

in implementing the far-reaching reforms that are called for. Radical analysts view this vision of harmonious cooperation as ignoring fundamental issues of economic and political power, particularly the fact that those who benefit from the present system will fiercely oppose the type of suggestions that the bishops make. Says Rasmussen: "The bishops make a very serious error in judgment if they assume that economic democracy is the natural extension of political democracy in this society. Existing concentrations of economic power will vigorously oppose the dispersion of economic power that the 'new experiment' clearly calls for."[41] Radical theorists assert that unless power issues are addressed CST will continue to put forth policy proposals and implementation strategies that have no chance of success.[42]

What Hobgood and other radical critics stress is the need for both a more well-developed understanding of political economy within the CST documents and action suggestions more consistent with this analysis. While elements of radical analysis are present in CST, they are viewed as being insufficiently systemic. What has often been presented in CST, radicals assert, is critique of the end products of capitalism, such as inequality and social disintegration. What is missing is analysis of how these negative results flow from capitalism's inner logic. "The bishops' account," says Larry Rasmussen, referring to *Eco-*

---

41 Rasmussen, "Morality of Power," 141.

42 With regard to *Economic Justice for All,* Larry Rasmussen states: "The difficulty is that, for the bishops, a radical faith is to pursue a liberal policy agenda by using gradualist means. The prospects of success for that, *when measured by substantial change in the condition of the poor,* are nil. But that *is* the bishops' faith-grounded criterion. Otherwise said, the normative moral commitments and the strategic commitments are on different tracks. They may be reconcilable *in thought.* The pastoral's authors can *conceive* how the interests of the poor might be served in a gradualist reform of the economy, accomplished by widespread citizen participation. But they are not reconcilable *in practice,* at least not until and unless the *power issues* are faced." (emphases in original) "Going Public: The Church's Role," in *God, Goods, and the Common Good,* ed. Charles Lutz (Minneapolis: Augsburg, 1987), 41.

According to Rasmussen, the bishops in their pastoral letter attempt a "marriage" of communalism and liberalism. Unfortunately, however, they tend to "overestimate the powers of communalism to transform liberalism" and also fail to realize that "the dynamics of power are obscured in both." "Morality of Power," 138.

nomic Justice for All, "does not include a presentation of the institutionalized dynamics that generate the very results they lament. What commands the bishops' attention are *outcomes* rather than *structural causes*."[43] Likewise, McCarthy and Rhodes argue that what is missing in the bishops' letter is "structural analysis" of capitalism in both its domestic and international forms.[44]

Among the fundamental structural features of capitalism that radical critics suggest CST should take account of are the following:

THE LINKS BETWEEN CAPITALISM AND DISPARITIES IN INCOME AND WEALTH

According to radical theorists, capitalism necessarily produces high levels of income and wealth inequality. There are various reasons for this. The main reason is that in the capitalist system there is a need for ever-increasing capital accumulation by owners of capital in order to remain competitive with other owners of capital. This need creates a constant pressure to minimize costs, particularly wages, creating a downward pressure on workers' earnings. Conditions of the past 50 years in which a minority (but nonetheless significant number) of First World workers were able to attain relatively high wages are seen by these theorists as an aberration in the history of capitalism. These higher wages were the result of a "temporary truce" between capital and some sections of labor in the First World that was made possible by the exploitation of labor, resources, and markets in the Third World and by a temporary relative lack of international intercapitalist competition.[45] In the past two decades, radicals argue, this truce has

43 Rasmussen, "Morality of Power," 136.

44 McCarthy and Rhodes assert that a key flaw of *Economic Justice for All* is its "general lack of a structural analysis of American political economy" and the fact that "there is no developed theory of international political economy," "no analysis of the historical and structural mechanism by which capitalism has developed from the First to the Third World, no examination of how this social system was instituted and rationalized, and no analysis of its effects on the people who live under its direction." *Eclipse of Justice,* 107, 214-215.

45 Mary Hobgood argues that in the post-WWII period there was never true cooperation between capital and labor. Rather, "after a long and bloody struggle, capital achieved only a temporary truce in which labor was willing to abandon all other demands in return for high wages in the most profitable industries for workers who were predominantly white and male.

ended and the true nature of capitalism is again becoming clear. In the current age of globalization, with increased international competition and enhanced capital mobility, the pressure to contain or reduce wages and other costs is especially acute, contributing to what critics call a "race to the bottom." With regard to the United States, Hobgood states: "The need for capital accumulation means that capitalism must sustain inequality....[U]nder conditions of the globalization of advanced monopoly capitalism, U.S. capitalism must increase social inequality and class conflict to remain competitive."[46] The inner logic of the capitalist system, radicals assert, makes attempts to foster "ethical" capitalists largely illusory as a way of reforming the capitalist system:

> Ethically sensitive capitalists cannot alter the basic situation of the workplace because market constraints deprive them of the option to raise wages, keep out oppressive kinds of technology, operate with ecological care....If capitalists did any of these things, they would be undersold and driven from the market.[47]

CAPITALISM AND UNEMPLOYMENT

In addition to fostering low wages, undesirable workplace conditions, and ecological damage, radical theorists argue that capitalism systematically generates significant amounts of unemployment. This is mainly because unemployment plays a crucial role in the maintenance of the capitalist system by weakening workers' power. When unemployment is high, workers are less likely to risk losing their jobs through militancy, tend to work more diligently to keep their jobs, and are will-

---

Such wages...could be paid to U.S. workers only as long as capital was successfully exploiting markets and resources in the Third World" and as long as international capitalist competition was limited. *Catholic Social Teaching,* 240. The relative lack of intercapitalist competition that existed until the late 1960s or early 1970s was due in large part to the devastation of European and Asian economies in WWII, which gave the U.S. unchallenged dominance in the international economy for several decades. Also, the existence of oligopolistic structures within individual capitalist nations in key industries served to further limit competition. For good discussion of the postwar "social structure of accumulation" and its demise, see Samuel Bowles, David Gordon, and Thomas Weisskopf, *After the Waste Land: A Democratic Economics for the Year 2000* (Armonk, NY: M.E. Sharpe, 1990).

46 Hobgood, *Catholic Social Teaching,* 41.

47 Ibid., 39.

ing to work for lower wages. As a consequence of weakened wage demands, high unemployment helps to keep inflation under control, preventing the profits of capital from being eroded by inflation's impact. From a capitalist perspective a significant amount of unemployment is therefore seen as desirable. Thus, measures are regularly taken to make sure that unemployment does not decline below relatively high thresholds. In the United States, for example, the Federal Reserve tends to raise interest rates when unemployment falls and inflationary pressures begin. This increase in interest rates slows the economy and pushes the unemployment rate back up. Radical critics further assert that the inherent tendency of capitalism to replace labor with machines also serves to keep unemployment relatively high.[48] Globally, it is estimated by the International Labour Organization (ILO) that over 1 billion persons, about 1/3 of the world's workforce, are unemployed or underemployed, the highest level ever recorded. "The global employment situation is grim, and getting grimmer," reports Michel Hansenne, Director-General of the ILO.[49]

CAPITALISM, RACISM, AND SEXISM

Radical theorists argue that racism and sexism are closely connected with the capitalist system and play functional roles within it. They do not contend that only capitalist societies experience racism and sexism, but do argue that capitalism makes it difficult for these problems to be overcome. Racism, for example, is seen as perpetuating the existence of a cheap source of labor, one which in downturns in the economy can easily be let go without political ramifications. Racism is also seen as functioning to divide the working class and to deflect the anger of workers away from owners of capital toward racial or ethnic minorities who become convenient scapegoats. Recent attacks on welfare and on immigrants in the United States, radical theorists assert, can be seen in this light. They are ways of redirecting the anger of workers who are frustrated with a declining quality of life under neoliberal capitalist forms of globalization. Rather than looking at the root causes of these problems, workers are encouraged to direct hostil-

---

48 Ibid., 62.

49 Unemployment/underemployment data is from the ILO's *World Employment Report 1998-1999* (Geneva: ILO, 1998). A summary of this report, which includes the quote from Michel Hansenne, can be found at <www.ilo.org/public/english/235press/ magazine/27/crisis.htm>.

ity toward people on welfare and immigrants.[50] Racism moreover has often functioned historically as part of the justification for economic and military domination of the Third World by the First World, to the further benefit of capitalist interests.

Sexism is similarly understood by radicals to play functional roles within capitalism. It is seen, for example, as a way of justifying lower wages for women and of providing men (especially working class men) with a sense of control and power that they lack in the capitalist workplace.[51]

CAPITALISM AND THE CONCENTRATION OF ECONOMIC POWER

Another element of the inner logic of capitalism, according to radical theorists, is a tendency towards oligopoly and monopoly and the concentration of economic power in the hands of a few. This concentration follows from the need of corporations to increase capital accumulation to remain competitive and from pressure on the part of stockholders for ongoing expansion to maximize profits. Says Hobgood: "Radical theorists believe that monopoly is the internal logic of a system that has profit enhancement and growth without interference as its only rational goal."[52] This inner logic of capitalism has had ramifications in every aspect of the economy. In agriculture, for example, it has led to the rise of agribusiness and the increasing elimination of small farms. In the retail sector, it has led to the dominance of mega-stores like Wal-Mart and the rapid decline of small, locally owned businesses. Likewise, small-scale craftspeople have been nearly eliminated in the more fully developed capitalist economies. In the area of communications, this tendency to oligopoly has given rise to the creation of a handful of multinational media conglomerates. This increasing con-

50 The stigmatization of welfare, says Hobgood, "creates an outcast class, treated with contempt, in order to manage people at the bottom and channel them into menial work. It is necessary to demean the poor, especially the welfare poor, in order to exalt by contrast even the meanest labor at the meanest wages." *Catholic Social Teaching*, 62. For good discussion of welfare from a radical perspective, see Frances Fox Piven and Richard Cloward, *Regulating the Poor: The Functions of Public Welfare*, rev. ed. (NY: Vintage, 1993).

51 Hobgood, *Catholic Social Teaching*, 57. For additional discussion of the relationship of capitalism to sexism and racism, see Edwards, Reich, and Weisskopf, *Capitalist System*, chapters 7 and 8.

52 Hobgood, *Catholic Social Teaching*, 43.

centration and centralization of ownership in the capitalist economy as a whole has led to a situation in which the world's largest 300 corporations possess over one quarter of all global productive assets and the top 500 corporations control about 70% of global trade.[53] Numerous corporations have gross sales that are larger than the GNP of the majority of the world's nations.[54]

The tendency of capitalism to increasingly concentrate wealth in the hands of a few is seen as one of the primary internal contradictions within capitalism, for this concentration can give rise to situations in which there is insufficient demand for the products that the economy can produce (since workers' wages are too low), as happened in the Great Depression and in numerous recessions since.[55]

CAPITALISM AND INEQUALITY

Each of the above features of capitalism tends to create and perpetuate inequality. Radicals highlight the fact that levels of inequality within capitalist nations and between nations have been steadily increasing. They stress that even in the boom years after WWII overall levels of inequality in the U.S. did not significantly decline. In the past several decades disparities in wealth and income in the U.S. have risen to the highest levels ever recorded, according to the U.S. Census Bureau. Internationally, levels of inequality between the First World and the Third World have also consistently widened throughout the postwar era.[56]

---

53 Richard Barnet and John Cavanagh, *Global Dreams: Imperial Corporations and the New World Order* (New York: Simon and Schuster, 1994), 15. David Korten, *When Corporations Rule the World*, 2nd ed. (San Francisco: Berrett-Koehler, 2001), 126.

54 When GNP and gross sales are compared, 47 of the top 100 largest economic entities in the world are corporations. Jeremy Brecher and Tim Costello, *Global Village or Global Pillage: Economic Reconstruction from the Bottom Up* (Boston: South End Press, 1994), 18.

55 For a thoughtful analysis which views overproduction and insufficient demand as a major crisis looming on the horizon for global capitalism, see William Greider, *One World, Ready or Not: The Manic Logic of Global Capitalism* (NY: Simon and Schuster, 1997).

56 For good discussions of inequality in the U.S. and among nations, see Yates, *Naming the System*; McCarthy and Rhodes, *Eclipse of Justice*, 111-122, 230-240; Hobgood, *Catholic Social Teaching*, 38-49; Insightful discussions of the relationship between capitalism and inequality can also be

CAPITALISM AND MILITARISM

Radical theorists see militarism and high levels of military spending as being inevitable consequences of capitalism, for several reasons. One reason is that military spending provides the high levels of demand needed to sustain the economy under conditions of inequality and does so without threatening the interests of capitalists as would a more equitable distribution of wealth or many forms of more socially useful governmental spending. High military spending also creates a powerful military-industrial complex with a major ability to influence government policy and public opinion, providing an additional impetus for maintaining high military expenditures. Militarism also is viewed by radicals as being necessary in order to foster the expansion and maintenance of the capitalist system on a global scale, as evidenced for example in the history of colonialism and in the many instances of U.S. intervention in the Third World to prop up regimes favorable to U.S. economic interests and to overthrow those which have sought to foster social reform or to restrict the operations of U.S. corporations.[57]

CAPITALISM AND THE UNDERMINING OF DEMOCRACY

The concentrated economic power generated within capitalism tends to give rise, according to radical theorists, to the domination of the political process by capitalist interests. This takes place in various ways, such as through the financing of political campaigns by corporations and wealthy individuals, extensive corporate lobbying, corporate control of the media, bribery, a revolving door between government and industry, and threats by corporations to relocate if demands for certain policies or tax breaks are not met. Perhaps most fundamentally, capitalist control of the political process comes about because the health of the economy and of the nation comes to be identified with the health of the process of private capital accumulation. Consequently, tax policies, governmental subsidies, foreign policy, and other

---

found in Edwards, Reich, and Weisskopf, *Capitalist System*, chapters 3 and 6.

57 For discussions of capitalism and militarism, see Hobgood, *Catholic Social Teaching*, 44-46. Also see the essays in Edwards, Reich, and Weisskopf, *Capitalist System*, chapter 9.

aspects of governmental policy tend all to be greatly skewed to the interests of the owners of capital.[58]

Radical critics further assert that capitalism increasingly undermines the capacity for democracy by fostering individualism, consumerism, and political noninvolvement. The political noninvolvement arises in part from disillusionment at the control of politics by monied interests. Capitalism also fosters workplace structures that for the majority of workers do not provide opportunities and encouragement to develop the kinds of skills that authentic democracy requires, such as participation in decision-making and willingness to challenge authority.[59]

CAPITALISM AND THE UNDERMINING OF COMMUNITY AND TRADITIONAL SOCIAL SYSTEMS

According to radical critics, capitalism has an inherent need for ongoing expansion. This results in new geographic areas and additional dimensions of human activity being brought into the market. Historically capitalism has been associated with the widespread destruction of non-capitalist social systems and cultures. Its expansion depends upon the elimination or weakening of those aspects of culture which stress communal bonds and non-monetary interests and values. In their place capitalism fosters greater individualism, an overriding emphasis on material consumption, and an increased commodification of all aspects of life. Highlighting the negative impact of capitalism on community and on the overall well-being of the human person, McCarthy and Rhodes state:

> Self-realization within a community cannot be accomplished amid market competition, self-interest, and a materialist culture. Bellah, Lasch, Jacoby, Slater, and Habermas have traced the debris of social psychology left in the wake of capitalism, that is 'the dead end of

58 For discussion of the ways in which capitalism undermines authentic democracy, see Korten, *When Corporations Rule the World*; McCarthy and Rhodes, *Eclipse of Justice*, chapter 4; Samuel Bowles and Herbert Gintis, *Democracy and Capitalism: Property, Community, and the Contradictions of Modern Social Thought* (New York: Basic Books, 1986). For detailed discussion of the United States, see Paul Kivel, *You Call This a Democracy?* (New York: Apex Press, 2004); William Boyer, *Myth America: Democracy vs. Capitalism* (New York: Apex Press, 2003).

59 This is a central contention of Bowles and Gintis, *Democracy and Capitalism*.

> radical individualism' and the inability to move from the emptiness and loneliness of selves in a market economy to a concern for the common good within the community.[60]

Radical critics assert that if an understanding of these major aspects of the "inner logic" of capitalism were more fully developed in CST, the authors of CST would properly be led to place greater stress upon the need for grassroots organizing and popular mobilization to bring about social change. Instead of calling for grassroots mobilization, however, CST is seen as largely appealing to the goodwill of those possessing economic and political power to bring about top-down change. "The prescribed social change agents," asserts Hobgood, "are those very governments, international agencies, and business elites that the documents' own analysis has already located as a source and beneficiary of the existing economic system and the crisis it generates."[61] "To urge class collaboration and cooperation in order to achieve a just economy," she continues, "is to urge the impossible in a system that both requires and produces continuous, privately controlled capital accumulation and the social injustice necessary to sustain the process."[62] "Capitalism," Hobgood claims, "operates structurally according to a preferential option for the rich."[63] While radical theorists don't deny that individual capitalists can be converted and join in the struggle for greater justice, they do deny that these persons in their role as capitalists can bring about fundamental positive change.[64] In order for fundamental change to be possible, radical theorists point to the need for a countervailing power to be nurtured. Says Hobgood:

---

60 McCarthy and Rhodes, *Eclipse of Justice*, 123. The works referred to in this quotation include Robert Bellah, et al., *Habits of the Heart* (Berkeley: University of California Press, 1985); Christopher Lasch, *The Culture of Narcissism* (New York: Warner Books, 1979); Russell Jacoby, *Social Amnesia* (Boston: Beacon, 1975); Philip Slater, *The Pursuit of Loneliness: American Culture at the Breaking Point* (Boston: Beacon, 1970); Jürgen Habermas, *The Theory of Communicative Action* (Boston: Beacon, 1984) and *Legitimation Crisis* (Boston: Beacon, 1975).

61 Hobgood, *Catholic Social Teaching*, 235-36.

62 Ibid., 239.

63 Ibid., 242.

64 "Capitalists," asserts Hobgood, "cannot initiate structural change because of the dynamics of the system of which they are a part." Ibid., 237.

> The power of privileged elites can only be limited by organized, imaginative counterpower....The achieving of human dignity and genuine social justice will not be the result of gifts bestowed by business elites and the states they control. Rather, social justice will occur when the marginalized mobilize to exercise their own self-empowerment.[65]

Hobgood argues that a major reason that CST is weak in the area of implementation is that it still adheres to organic assumptions about the power of church teaching to impact the social order apart from sustained social struggle.[66]

Theologically, appeal is made by the radical theorists discussed here primarily to key themes of the Biblical witness such as the Exodus account, the messages of the Hebrew prophets, and the teachings of Jesus as presented in the Gospels. Central tasks of the church are understood to be prophetic critique, pioneering creativity, and deeply embodied commitment to the struggles for justice in church and society. The reign of God proclaimed by Jesus is understood to provide a broad ethical framework for Christians, one which calls into question many of the fundamental features of capitalism.[67]

EVALUATION OF NEOCONSERVATIVE, RADICAL, AND CST VIEWS

With regard to political economy and Third World development, the most debated issue between neoconservatives and radicals is whether structural injustice (specifically structural injustice associated with capitalism) is or has been a central cause of Third World poverty. Based on the evidence presented in earlier chapters of this book, I would argue that structural injustice has indeed played a major role in creating and sustaining poverty and hunger in the Third World. This injustice has been manifested in colonialism, in distorted post-colonial development policies, in the Third World debt crisis and structural adjustment, and in superpower (especially United States) interventions in the affairs of Third World nations. It is also seen in the ten-

65 Ibid., 242.

66 Ibid., 230.

67 The notions of prophetic critique and pioneering creativity are developed in Larry Rasmussen, "The Public Vocation of an Eschatological Community," *Union Seminary Quarterly Review* 42, no. 4 (1988): 25-35.

dency of transnational corporations to create sweatshop conditions for Third World workers, exploit Third World natural resources, and enjoy monopolistic control over technology and trade in the international arena.[68] As well, various forms of what has been termed "cultural imperialism" (represented by First World dominance of global communications, entertainment, and advertising) are important to note.[69]

Catholic Social Teaching is therefore very much justified in placing strong emphasis upon the reality of structural injustice. For example, Pope Paul VI's emphasis on the major role played by colonialism in creating distorted economic priorities in the Third World and his warning that policies of unregulated markets have a tendency to foster "economic dictatorship" are vitally important insights. Likewise, much wisdom is contained in the emphasis of Medellín upon "institutionalized violence," *Justice in the World*'s critique of a global network of "domination, oppression, and abuses," and John Paul II's condemnation of "structures of sin," "imperialism," and "neo-colonialism."[70]

Unfortunately, these insights, as suggested by radical commentators on CST, are often not well-developed in the CST documents, and coexist alongside policy suggestions based on more liberal and organic presuppositions. Increased attention to the various structural features of capitalism highlighted by the radical theorists would do much to strengthen CST, as will be discussed in the concluding chapter of this book. While the CST documents are not the appropriate place in which to expect a fully developed analysis of political economy, some additional attention in the documents to these structural issues, along with encouragement of Catholic (and non-Catholic) scholars and universities to further explore and educate concerning them, would be appropriate and very helpful.

To provide some specificity to this suggestion of the need for deeper and more systemic analysis in CST, it may be instructive to explore

68 See John Madeley, *Big Business: Poor Peoples: The Impact of Transnational Corporations on the World's Poor* (London: Zed Books, 1999); Korten, *When Corporations Rule the World*; Barnet and Cavanagh, *Global Dreams*.

69 See Barnet and Cavanagh, *Global Dreams*. Also see the writings of Herbert Schiller, including *Mass Communications and American Empire*, 2nd ed. (Boulder: Westview Press, 1992); George Gerbner, Hamid Mowlana, and Herbert Schiller, eds., *Invisible Crises: What Conglomerate Control of Media Means for America and the World* (Boulder: Westview, 1997).

70 See PP 7, 59; Medellín document on "Peace," 16; JW 3; SRS 22, 36.

more thoroughly the treatment contained in CST of the Third World debt crisis. For the most part in the papal documents the causes of the debt crisis are not highlighted. Rather, attention is simply given to the negative consequences that debt repayment and structural adjustment have had for the Third World poor, and appeals are made to reduce the debt.[71] In *Economic Justice for All*, however, the U.S. bishops undertake some analysis of the causes of the crisis. They highlight three main historical factors in causing the crisis – a major USSR purchase of grain from the U.S. in 1972, OPEC price rises during the 1970s, and a global recession that began in 1979. They then argue that structural adjustment policies should not include measures that hurt the poor, and they call for steps to be taken to both reduce the debt burden and to prevent a recurrence of the debt buildup. (EJA 272-77)

While the call of the bishops for debt relief and for changing those components of structural adjustment that hurt the poor is very valuable, what is missing is analysis of some of the most fundamental causes of the debt buildup. For example, the role of colonialism and flawed development policies (fostered by First World aid agencies) is not discussed. The fact that loans were made very irresponsibly, often to military dictatorships, and were used (with the knowledge of the lenders) largely for military spending, capital flight, and socially and ecologically destructive mega-projects is not discussed. The role played by U.S. macroeconomic policy in causing/exacerbating the global recession that began in 1979 is also not discussed. Instead, factors which played at most a very minimal role in the overall debt crisis, such as the USSR grain purchase in 1972, are given high prominence.

With regard to the consequences of the crisis, little detailed analysis is provided. The bishops do strongly criticize the impact of the debt on the Third World poor, even while not discussing at length what those impacts have been. They fail, however, to locate the responses to the debt crisis in a broader context, such as by exploring the role that the crisis has played in the resubordination of the Third World. As we saw in Chapter One, Third World nations during the 1970s were uniting and demanding major reforms in the international economy, encapsulated in the call for a New International Economic Order (NIEO). Many Third World nations also began placing restrictions on the activities of transnational corporations (TNCs), attempting to require the TNCs to act in ways more favorable to the host country,

71 See for example SRS 19, CA 35.

e.g. mandating that companies reinvest a certain portion of their profits in the host country, hire local managers, or purchase local inputs. The debt crisis and the imposition of SAPs have been used as vehicles for ending all talk of an NIEO and systematically eliminating restrictions on the activities of TNCs. As Walden Bello states, SAPs "have functioned as key instruments in the North's effort to roll back the [limited] gains that had been made by South from the 1950s through the 1970s."[72] From the perspective of radical political economy, the imposed reshaping of Third World economies in the interests of the First World can be seen as part of the structural imperative of capitalist interests to seek continual, unhindered expansion. When seen in this light, the rationale behind the implementation of SAPs becomes more clear. They are not, for example, simply well-intentioned policies that had unfortunate side-effects. Also clarified is the resistance that First World governments and corporations have demonstrated to papal and episcopal calls for debt reduction and reform of the global financial system. The deep concern expressed in CST for the poor, its criticisms of those dimensions of SAPs which negatively affect the poor, and its calls for debt reduction are all extremely important and highly admirable. They don't, however, when presented apart from more systemic analysis, provide adequate insight into the debt crisis itself or into the broader workings of the global capitalist economy. These insights are very much needed to effectively diagnose and respond to the problems that Third World nations confront. Without such analysis, there is a danger, for example, that the stated intentions of institutions such as the World Bank and IMF will be taken at face value, rather than examined more critically. The World Bank in particular has shown itself to be very effective in adopting the language of critics on the public relations level, while too often leaving the harmful nature of its policies unchanged.[73]

---

72 Walden Bello, "Creating a Wasteland: The Impact of Structural Adjustment on the South, 1980-1994," *Food First Action Alert* (Winter, 1993): 3. This action alert is based on Walden Bello, *Dark Victory: The United States, Structural Adjustment, and Global Poverty* (Oakland: Institute for Food and Development Policy, 1994).

73 See, for example, World Development Movement, *Denying Democracy: How the IMF and World Bank Take Power From People* (London: World Development Movement, 2005).

The relative lack of focus in CST on the structural dynamics of injustice contributes to what is perhaps CST's key weakness, inadequate attention to how the reforms suggested in CST could be brought about. When the structural causes of the debt crisis, of widespread poverty, and of other social problems are more deeply explored, the inadequacy of appeal to those forces responsible for and often benefiting from these problems becomes apparent. Similarly, the need for broad social movements seeking change becomes more clear. Those movements that currently exist and the types of alternatives that they are calling for will be the focus of discussion in subsequent chapters of this book.

Several regional/national CST documents do move in the direction of more systemic analysis and also strongly emphasize the need for grassroots movements for structural change, particularly some Latin American and Canadian bishops' documents. These documents will be discussed in more detail in Chapter Seven. It will be suggested that papal documents, as well as the daily praxis of the global church, could be enhanced by deepened attention to the insights that these bishops' documents contain.

Given the role that structural injustice in its various forms has played in bringing about the current conditions of widespread poverty and hunger in the Third World, neoconservative attempts to deny the centrality of these factors and their relationship to global capitalism constitute a major weakness of neoconservative thought. Michael Novak, for example, seeks to absolve capitalism of responsibility for Latin American poverty by claiming that Latin American economies are not in fact capitalist. What this analysis ignores, however, is that even the so-called feudal aspects of Latin American economies (such as the large haciendas) are deeply integrated into the global capitalist system, as they produce their products for sale on capitalist markets. This integration into global capitalism provides wealth for the few at the expense of the many, as local elites find it more profitable to exploit workers for very low wages and to sell their products overseas to wealthy First World consumers (via the intermediary of transnational corporations) than to pay their workers adequate wages to develop a larger domestic market for their products. Attempts to bring about land reform and other redistributive reforms in the Third World, as we have seen, have been consistently opposed by the full force of international capitalism (led by the United States), both militarily and through the denial of loans and other assistance to reformist countries. Novak expresses recognition of the need for Third World elites to "yield place to the talented millions among the poor who show greater imagination, initiative, inventiveness, and creativity,"[74] yet has been a forceful supporter of U.S. foreign policy that has been closely allied with the interests of those elites. Referring to this contradiction, Gary Dorrien states:

> [Novak] offered no consideration of what would be required to force them [the elites] to 'yield place,' nor did he criticize the American government and the American-based corporations that had subsidized, reinforced, and supported the role of Latin America's elites. His energies were devoted, rather, to condemning the one mass-based, decentralized, nonviolent movement in Latin America that actually challenged the rule of the elites [i.e. liberation theology].[75]

Novak was a strong supporter of U.S. foreign policy in Central America during the 1980s. This support for U.S. policy included praise and support for the Nicaraguan contras, who Novak referred to as "freedom fighters" and described as being "committed to democracy."[76] The war carried out by the U.S.-funded contras (which, as seen above, consisted predominantly of a campaign of terror directed against innocent civilians) Novak characterized as a "war of the people, by the people, and for the people."[77] At the same time the sanctuary movement in the United States, in which churches and synagogues broke U.S. law and risked imprisonment to offer refuge to people fleeing government-sponsored terror in Guatemala and El Salvador, persons threatened with deportation by the U.S. government and fearing for their lives, was condemned by Novak as a politically motivated "fraud."[78]

---

74 Novak, *Will It Liberate?*, 5.

75 Gary Dorrien, *The Neoconservative Mind: Politics, Culture, and the War of Ideology* (Philadelphia: Temple University Press, 1993), 243.

76 Michael Novak, "Nicaragua: Temperature Hot," *Catholicism in Crisis* 3 (April, 1985): 5.

77 Michael Novak, "Maryknoll's Miguel D'Escoto," *Catholicism in Crisis* 3 (September, 1985): 6.

78 Michael Novak, "The Fraud That Failed," *Catholicism in Crisis* 3 (December, 1985): 54. For excellent discussions of the sanctuary movement, see Penny Lernoux, "Sanctuary," chapter 9 of *People of God* (New York: Viking, 1989); John Fife, Jim Corbett, Stacey Lynn Merkt, and Philip Willis-Con-

Novak's overall historical analysis, which views Latin American poverty as primarily due to cultural factors and praises capitalism as a positive force for change, is called into question by historians of the region. Central American historian Walter LaFeber, for example, argues that Novak's analysis "has little in common with Central American history," for capitalist interests have consistently opposed rather than supported positive social change in the region. Says LaFeber:

> Novak erred in believing Central Americans bore major responsibility for their economic dilemmas. At nearly every opportunity, North American firms had tried to fix the marketplace...by controlling or eliminating political and economic competition. They often did so, moreover, with the help of the U.S. government....One cannot use force to prevent a people from controlling their own resources and political processes, then condemn that people for failing to do so.[79]

Neoconservative views of political economy are problematic in several other important ways. The claim that the economic, political, and cultural realms of society are relatively independent, central to Novak's portrayal of democratic capitalism, is undermined by substantial evidence from many countries showing that the concentrated economic power fostered by capitalism is very effectively transformed into capitalist dominance of political processes, a dominance that has greatly increased in the past several decades.[80] Furthermore, this concentrated economic power most often includes concentrated control of major vehicles of cultural formation, such as the mass media.[81] Thus, assertions of independent economic, political, and cultural sectors, as Novak asserts, do not hold up to analysis.

---

ger, "The Sanctuary Movement: Conspiracy of Compassion," in *The Rise of Christian Conscience*, ed. Jim Wallis (New York: Harper and Row, 1987).

79 Walter LaFeber, *Inevitable Revolutions: The United States in Central America*, rev. ed. (New York: W.W. Norton, 1984), 282.

80 See Korten, *When Corporations Rule the World*; Boyer, *Myth America*.

81 For discussions of the damage to democracy brought about by concentrated corporate control of the media, see Ben Bagdikian, *The New Media Monopoly* (Boston: Beacon Press, 2004); Noam Chomsky and Edward Herman, *Manufacturing Consent: The Political Economy of the Mass Media* (New York: Vintage Books, 2006); Robert McChesney, *Rich Media, Poor Democracy* (Urbana: University of Illionois Press, 1999).

Despite these fundamental weaknesses, neoconservative thought is not without its share of insights. Neoconservative critiques of the problems of top-down, state-controlled economies contain much that is helpful, and the emphasis placed by many neoconservatives on encouraging self-help among the poor (including support for measures such as small-scale credit provision) provides an opening for constructive dialogue and joint efforts with others who support similar measures, including radicals and CST proponents. What is problematic is when the insights that neoconservative thought does contain are attached to very doctrinaire free market policies and heavily economistic views of social progress, policies and views that have many negative social, ecological, and spiritual consequences. Significantly, among these consequences are the undermining of many of the goods that neoconservatives themselves affirm. For example, free trade policies are undermining small farmers and small businesses around the world, hindering the exercise of economic initiative by many. The increased concentration of wealth generated by current forms of economic globalization is undermining political democracy, as concentrated economic power gets translated into concentrated political power. Meanwhile, the "logic of the market" (as John Paul II states) is fostering consumerist mentalities, undermining local cultures and religious values, and contributing to the breakdown of communities and families. Thus, it can be strongly argued that many of the goods that neoconservatives themselves affirm, such as democracy, small businesses, stable communities and families, and vital moral and religious commitments are being undermined by the very market forces that neoconservatives champion. Discussing the views of Catholic neoconservative Richard John Neuhaus, who sharply criticizes the loss of "traditional values," Gary Dorrien comments:

> [Neuhaus] writes virtually nothing about the chief cause of the cultural retrogression that he decries....[I]t is commercial society that uproots traditional cultural values pertaining to self-sacrifice, deferred gratification, and the importance of self-transcending loyalties....It is commercial society that assiduously encourages narcissistic self-indulgence, reduces social values to commodities, and reduces the complexities of moral discernment in the public arena to the test of economic rationality....Its image of the good life is not a vision of the common good but the life of self-gratification, self-preoccupation, and material success unceasingly paraded in the

> mass media. Having aligned himself with a political movement that celebrates the superiority of capitalism over all possible alternatives, however, Neuhaus cannot bring himself to consider that the cultural situation he decries has economic causes.[82]

Similarly, Dean Brackley (one of the Jesuit priests who volunteered to replace the Jesuits who were murdered in 1989 in El Salvador) states:

> It is becoming harder to hide the spiritual and human poverty, the despair and loneliness, the violence and contempt for life which characterize much of the search for material and private happiness in the liberal societies of the north. What irony – if not cynicism – that the same neo-conservatives who champion 'traditional values' promote the neo-liberal economics which undermine them![83]

It is in this context that the tradition of CST, with its long-standing critique of the dangers inherent in capitalism, its affirmation of well-regulated markets, its stress on economic democracy, and its commitment to integral development (including equitable distribution of wealth, ecological sustainability, and the preservation of the best of local cultures) can help to point the way forward. With regard to the tradition of radical political economy, I believe that it can be seen to contain many important insights, some of which have been highlighted above. There is much that CST can learn from it. Yet it too has serious weaknesses. What has most often been lacking in the radical tradition is adequate attention to ecological, cultural, and spiritual issues. The radical tradition has in general accepted too uncritically many features of western modernity (including prevailing understandings of "development" and of "revolution,") features that need to be more critically and discernfully assessed. The next chapter, presenting the views of grassroots critics of the concept of "development," will discuss these issues. Several additional ways will be suggested in which both CST and the radical tradition could be further strengthened through dialogue with these critics of development and of current forms of economic globalization.

---

82 Gary Dorrien, *Soul in Society: The Making and Renewal of Social Christianity* (Minneapolis: Fortress, 1995), 217-18.

83 Dean Brackley, "A Radical Ethos," *Horizons* 24, no. 1 (1997): 25.

CHAPTER 5

GRASSROOTS CRITICS OF DEVELOPMENT

Throughout the world increasing numbers of people are calling into question the pursuit of development and criticizing current forms of economic globalization.[1] Many of these critics are themselves actively engaged in grassroots efforts for social change. These critics argue that past development policies have contributed to increased inequalities, severe ecological damage, and cultural destruction. A recent U.N.-commissioned study on women, ecology, and development states:

> It has become increasingly clear in recent years that development, which has been conceived as a Western project to modernize the post-colonial societies, did not bring the promised improvement in the living conditions of people in the South. Instead, the development process contributed to the growth of poverty, to an increase in economic and gender inequalities, and to the degradation of the

---

1 The past several decades have seen a very large output of literature from grassroots critics of development and neoliberal globalization. Some of the key works include Mark Engler, *How to Rule the World: The Coming Battle over the Global Economy* (New York: Nation Books, 2008); John Cavanagh and Jerry Mander, eds., *Alternatives to Economic Globalization: A Better World is Possible,* 2nd ed. (San Francisco: Berrett-Koehler, 2004); John Madeley, *A People's World: Alternatives to Economic Globalization* (London: Zed Books, 2003); David Korten, *When Corporations Rule the World,* 2nd ed. (San Francisco: Berrett Koehler, 2001); Majid Rehnema, ed., *The Post-Development Reader* (London: Zed Books, 1997); Jerry Mander and Edward Goldsmith, eds., *The Case Against the Global Economy–And For a Turn to the Local* (San Francisco: Sierra Club Books, 1996); The Ecologist, *Whose Common Future? Reclaiming the Commons* (Philadelphia: New Society Publishers, 1993); Wolfgang Sachs, ed., *The Development Dictionary* (London: Zed Books, 1992); Vandana Shiva, *Staying Alive: Women, Ecology, and Development* (London: Zed Books, 1989).

> environment which further diminishes the means of livelihood for poor people, particularly women.[2]

For critics of development, negative consequences such as these are not viewed to be the result of the improper implementation of development policies or of unfavorable circumstances. Rather, they are understood to be rooted in the very concept of development itself. This chapter will explore the views of these grassroots critics of development, with particular attention to the thought of Indian social activist and author Vandana Shiva. I will contend that the analyses that Shiva and others set forth contain vital, urgent insights. From these discussions several important implications will be drawn for the strengthening of Catholic Social Teaching. This chapter will also provide the groundwork for the chapter that follows, in which grassroots alternatives to development and to current forms of economic globalization will be considered in greater depth.

REJECTING THE QUEST FOR DEVELOPMENT

"The idea of development," argues Wolfgang Sachs, "stands like a ruin in the intellectual landscape. Delusion and disappointment, failures and crimes have been the steady companions of development and they tell a common story: it did not work." The time has therefore come, declares Sachs, "to bid farewell to the defunct idea in order to clear our minds for fresh discoveries."[3] Others make similar claims. The "dream of development", states Arturo Escobar of Colombia, "has progressively turned into a nightmare....The debt crisis, the Sahelian famine, increasing poverty, malnutrition and violence are only the most pathetic signs of the failure of forty years of development."[4]

These comments of Sachs and Escobar are typical of the views of a growing movement of development critics throughout the world. These critics contend that the notion of development is flawed at its roots, being based on several untenable and destructive premises. The most fundamental and problematic premise is belief in the superiority

2 Rosi Braidotti, et al., *Women, the Environment, and Sustainable Development* (London: Zed Books/U.N. Research and Training Institute for the Advancement of Women, 1994), 1.

3 Sachs, Introduction to *Development Dictionary*, 1. Sachs is a prominent voice among critics of development.

4 Arturo Escobar, *Encountering Development: The Making and Unmaking of the Third World* (Princeton: Princeton University Press, 1995), 4.

of the industrial nations. These industrial nations, termed "developed" or "advanced," are viewed by development proponents to provide a model that other nations can and should follow. According to critics, however, the industrial model of the First World is ecologically and socially unsustainable and should therefore not be seen as worthy of emulation. With regard to the ecological impacts of the industrial nations, Sachs provocatively asserts:

> If all countries 'successfully' followed the industrial example, five or six planets would be needed to serve as mines and waste dumps. It is thus obvious that the 'advanced' societies are no model; rather they are most likely to be seen in the end as an aberration in the course of history.[5]

Critics cite problems such as global warming, ozone depletion, deforestation, acid rain, desertification, toxic contamination of air, water, land, food, and workers, massive soil erosion, declining soil fertility, species extinction, declining fish populations, diminishing water supplies, and numerous other ecological problems as demonstrating the ecological unsustainability of the First World model of industrial capitalism and of conceptions of development that are based upon it.[6] These critics also reject the model of industrial socialism, which they view as sharing many of the same flawed presuppositions as industrial capitalism. Most of their analysis, however, concerns the impact of the currently "triumphant" capitalist system.

Critics claim that the path of industrial capitalism is not only ecologically unsustainable but is also socially and culturally destructive. They stress that high levels of economic growth have come at the expense of pre-existing social structures and communal bonds throughout the world. Proponents of modernizationist development, as we have seen, have acknowledged the need for cultural destruction and social uprooting. Critics of development argue that these modernizationist views represent a deep form of cultural imperialism. Development and progress are equated by modernizationists with the adoption of western forms of culture and western social systems. The social, ecological

5 Sachs, Introduction to *Development Dictionary*, 2.

6 For overviews of these and other ecological problems, see the annual *State of the World* reports issued by the Worldwatch Insititute. Also see Patrick Hossay, *Unsustainable: A Primer for Environmental and Social Justice* (London: Zed Books, 2006); Joel Kovel, *The Enemy of Nature: The End of Capitalism or the End of the World?* (London: Zed Books, 2002).

and spiritual wisdoms of traditional cultures are radically devalued. "The dominant paradigm of 'development,'" asserts Indian scholar Joke Schrijvers, "is rooted in a belief in the superiority of the people of the West, of Western knowledge and technology, and of Western 'civilization' as a whole." It represents, she argues, "a direct continuation of 500 years of colonial history."[7]

DEVELOPMENT AS "ENCLOSURE"

Critics contend that development can best be seen as a continuation of processes of "enclosure" that were begun during the colonial era. Enclosure is a term used to refer to the privatization and concentration of ownership of resources which formerly were under community control and to which all or most members of the community had relatively equitable access. It involves, most fundamentally, the undermining of local self-sufficiency in order to foster the interests of local elites and outsiders.[8] We have seen in the previous discussion of colonialism, for example, the various measures which were taken to destroy the self-sufficiency of indigenous communities and to force indigenous persons to participate as subordinate, exploited members of the colonial economy. Among these measures were the expropriation of communal land, enslavement, and various forms of taxation designed to force local inhabitants to sell their labor at low wages to the colonizers or to grow cash crops for cheap export to the colonizing countries. Measures were also often taken to undermine local crafts production, forcing local inhabitants to purchase manufactured imports from the colonizing countries. All of these measures undermined local self-reliance and forced indigenous persons to participate in the colonial economies in ways beneficial to the financial interests of the colonizers.

---

7 Joke Schrijvers, *The Violence of 'Development'* (New Delhi: Kali for Women, 1993), 9.

8 For in-depth discussion of colonialism, development, and economic globalization as processes of "enclosure," see Ecologist, *Whose Common Future?*; Shiva, *Staying Alive*. Two books by John Bodley, *Victims of Progress*, 4th ed. (Mountain View, CA: Mayfield Publishing, 1999) and *Tribal Peoples and Development Issues: A Global Overview* (Mountain View, CA: Mayfield, 1988) provide extensive detail concerning the impact of colonialism and development on indigenous peoples.

These processes of enclosure and the undermining of self-reliance have been further accelerated, critics argue, by many of the policies implemented in the name of development:

> Using the slogans of 'nation-building' and 'development' to justify their actions, Third World governments have employed the full panoply of powers established under colonial rule to further dismantle the commons. Millions have lost their homelands—or the lands they had made their home—to make way for dams, industrial plants, mines, military security zones, waste dumps, plantations, tourist resorts, motorways, urban redevelopment and other schemes intended to transform the South into an appendage of the North. Deals have been made with Northern interests in return for aid and military protection; debts incurred to build projects that line the pockets of local commercial interests but which drive millions into poverty; multinational companies offered land, cheap labour and tax breaks at the expense of workers, peasants and the environment; subsidies handed out to richer farmers; industries allowed to pollute; and national economies tied ever more tightly to the interests of global capital.[9]

Among the consequences of these processes of enclosure have been the increased concentration of land ownership and of overall wealth, widening the gaps between rich and poor both within and among nations. Another consequence of capitalist enclosure, critics claim, has been the ongoing commodification of nearly all aspects of life. Needs are increasingly met less through mutual aid, as communal structures have been broken down, and more through market transactions:

> As production and exchange are enclosed by the market, economic activity is cordoned off from other spheres of social life, bounded by rules that actively undermine previous networks of mutual aid....As the market eats into the fabric of local self-reliance, commons regimes begin to atrophy. Their members can no longer rely on family, friends, neighbors, community, elders, and children for support, but increasingly must go to the market, not only for food, clothing, and shelter, but also for recreation, amusement, and care of the young, the old, the sick and the handicapped. In time, not only material and service needs but even emotional needs are channeled through the market.[10]

---

9 Ecologist, *Whose Common Future?*, 39-40.

10 Ibid., 63-64.

Whereas formerly local economies were embedded within and subordinate to broader social and cultural frameworks, the market economy now has come to itself dominate and shape social relations.[11] All that does not contribute to maximization of profits within the market is increasingly seen as being without value:

> Enclosure tears people and their lands, forests, crafts, technologies and cosmologies out of the cultural framework in which they are embedded and forces them into a new framework which reflects and reinforces the values and interests of newly-dominant groups. Any pieces which will not fit into the new framework are devalued and discarded....Enclosure reorganizes society to meet the overriding demands of the market.[12]

Two examples of this reorganization of views to suit the demands of the market concern land and forests. In traditional cultures land is widely imbued with deep religious and cultural significance. Access to land is generally regulated through local communal structures, and the buying and selling of land typically does not exist. With the rise of capitalism, however, land comes to be regarded as simply another commodity (as does human labor), and ownership is legally privatized. This commodification and privatization of land paves the way for the dispossession of the poor. During the past several centuries of colonialism and capitalist expansion many persons with deeply-rooted spiritual and cultural relationships to the land have been deprived of access to land, a result both of overt violence and of the covert violence of market forces.[13]

Understandings of the nature of forests have likewise been altered during the expansion of capitalism, with similar negative results. Forests, like agricultural land, possess deep spiritual significance in many traditional cultures. Forests also frequently serve in these cultures as a commons to provide for the needs of local inhabitants in a multitude of ways—as a source of food, fuel, fodder, medicinal herbs, and other basic goods. Critics assert that under capitalism, however, the forest is viewed simply as a 'timber mine' for the state and wealthy commercial

11 For an excellent discussion of the disembedding of the economy from broader social frameworks in the context of the rise of contemporary capitalism, see Karl Polanyi's classic work *The Great Transformation* (New York: Farrar and Rinehart, 1944).

12 Ecologist, *Whose Common Future?*, 59, 62.

13 See Bodley, *Victims of Progress*.

interests. Vast numbers of people who have depended upon the forest to meet a variety of basic needs have been excluded from access.[14]

One major consequence of capitalist enclosure, critics contend, is therefore the creation of large numbers of persons who are denied usage of the resources that they formerly relied upon for survival—farmland, communal pastures, forests, streams, rivers. In this manner subsistence lifestyles are undermined and modern forms of destitution are created. "Massive poverty in the modern sense," asserts Arturo Escobar, "appeared only when the spread of the market economy broke down community ties and deprived millions of people from access to land, water and other resources."[15]

Development critics distinguish sharply between the materially simple lifestyles of subsistence cultures and the material deprivation, uprooting, and psychological insecurity that accompanies modern forms of poverty, such as in urban shantytowns. Vandana Shiva states:

> It is useful to separate a cultural conception of subsistence living as poverty from the material experience of poverty that is a result of dispossession and deprivation. Culturally perceived poverty need not be real material poverty: subsistence economies which satisfy basic needs through self-provisioning are not poor in the sense of being deprived. Yet the ideology of development declares them so because they do not participate overwhelmingly in the market economy....[Development] destroys wholesome and sustainable lifestyles and creates real material poverty, or misery, by the denial of survival needs themselves through the diversion of resources to resource intensive commodity production.[16]

Critics highlight the connections between the modern forms of destitution experienced by a vast number of people in the contemporary world and and the massive wealth possessed by others. "The Third World of shantytowns," asserts Jean Chesneaux, "is as *modern* as that of banks or campuses....The success of the developed West –including

14 For insightful discussion of the plight of the Amazon rainforest and its peoples, see John Vandermeer and Ivette Perfecto, *Breakfast of Biodiversity: The Political Economy of Rain Forest Destruction*, 2nd ed. (Oakland, CA: Food First Books, 2005).

15 Escobar, *Encountering Development*, 22.

16 Shiva, *Staying Alive*, 10.

those parts of it that lie outside the geographic West – and the disasters of the Third World are part of the same global system."[17]

Critics emphasize also that the understanding of development as enclosure applies not only to physical resources but also to resources such as knowledge and mental imagery. Particularly troubling to development critics is the success that powerful First World forces have had–through western-style education, advertising, and the entertainment media–in convincing many Third World persons of the inferiority of traditional knowledge systems, social institutions, and values and thereby reducing the potential for creative alternatives to current ecologically unsustainable and socially unjust systems to be conceived. While these analysts argue for a critical view of traditional cultures (as opposed to a non-critical romanticization), they assert that numerous fundamental insights can be gained from traditional cultures that are crucial in addressing the crises of our time. These insights include, for example, the importance of a more intimate, mutualist relationship with nature, non-consumerist views of the good life, a strong emphasis on community, and the integration of spirituality into everyday life. Unfortunately, however, these cultural resources are quickly disappearing. "Perhaps the most insidious effect of the development era," states Wolfgang Sachs, "has been this worldwide loss of alternatives.... The mental space in which people dream and act is largely occupied by western imagery."[18] Vandana Shiva refers to this standardization of mental imagery as the creation of "monocultures of the mind." Like Sachs, Shiva highlights the ways in which monocultures limit creativity and reduce options. "Monocultures of the mind," says Shiva, "make diversity disappear from perception, and consequently from the world. The disappearance of diversity is also a disappearance of alternatives – and gives rise to the TINA (there is no alternative) syndrome."[19]

---

17 Jean Chesneaux, *Brave Modern World: The Prospects for Survival* (New York: Thames and Hudson, 1992), 57.

18 Wolfgang Sachs, "The Obsolete Race: Development After the East-West Rivalry," *New Perspectives Quarterly* (Spring, 1990): 54.

19 Vandana Shiva, *Monocultures of the Mind* (London: Zed Books, 1993), 5.

VANDANA SHIVA: THE VIOLENCE OF DEVELOPMENT AND REDUCTIONIST SCIENCE

Vandana Shiva is a grassroots activist from India and is a leading spokesperson for development critics. Her professional training is as a nuclear physicist. Shiva gave up her career as a physicist, however, in order to devote herself to work for alternatives to conventional development. In her critique of development she highlights especially the need for alternatives to the underlying worldview of modern western science, which she views as being at the root of many of the serious social and ecological problems that are being experienced in India and throughout the world. Shiva critiques above all what she terms the "reductionist" nature of dominant forms of science and the alliance of this science with contemporary capitalism.

Shiva presents her critique of modern science in broad terms, challenging above all the Cartesian worldview that she argues remains predominant in scientific practice despite more recent developments in theoretical physics that challenge this way of looking at the world.[20] The fundamental problem of modern science, Shiva argues, is contained in its conception of nature. She contends that dominant strands of science that have been shaped by Descartes, Bacon, and their followers tend to view nature as consisting of inert, passive matter, whose use is subject to few if any ethical constraints. This view of nature as inert resources for human exploitation is contrasted by Shiva with traditional views held by many indigenous persons and rural dwellers throughout the world in which nature is understood as a living, vital reality whose fundamental integrity is to be respected. While humans are permitted to take from nature what is needed for survival, they are expected to do so in ways that show respect for nature and nature's processes and that recognize the interdependence of humans and rest of the natural world.

The underlying worldview of modern science Shiva describes as "mechanistic." She contrasts this mechanistic worldview with earlier "organic" conceptions of nature. In developing her critique Shiva builds upon the pioneering analyses of historian of science Carolyn

---

20 For Shiva's critique of modern science, see "The Violence of Reductionist Science," *Alternatives* 12 (1987): 243-261; *Staying Alive*, chapter 2; *Monocultures of the Mind*; *Biopiracy: The Plunder of Nature and Knowledge* (Boston: South End Press, 1997).

Merchant, who describes the shift from organic to mechanistic views of nature brought about by the Scientific Revolution as constituting the "death of nature." This shift, Merchant argues, paved the way for widespread ecological destruction:

> The image of the earth as a living organism and nurturing mother had served as a cultural constraint restricting the actions of human beings. One does not readily slay a mother, dig into her entrails for gold or mutilate her body....The removal of animistic, organic assumptions about the cosmos constituted the death of nature–the most far-reaching effect of the Scientific Revolution. Because nature was now viewed as a system of dead, inert particles moved by external rather than inherent forces, the mechanistic framework itself could legitimate the manipulation of nature.[21]

Echoing Merchant's views, Shiva states:

> The scientific revolution in Europe transformed nature from *terra mater* [mother earth] into a machine and a source of raw material; with this transformation it removed all ethical and cognitive restraints against its violation and exploitation. The industrial revolution converted economics from the prudent management of resources for sustenance and basic needs satisfaction into a process of commodity production for profit maximization. Industrialism created a limitless appetite for resource exploitation, and modern science provided the ethical and cognitive license to make such exploitation possible, acceptable–and desirable.[22]

Along with being mechanistic, Shiva argues that modern science is predominantly "atomistic." Knowledge of isolated parts of nature, studied independently, is believed to provide knowledge of the whole. The interconnectedness and interdependencies of nature, Shiva contends, are too often ignored. It is in part due to these atomistic tendencies that Shiva terms dominant forms of modern science "reductionist." The reduction of the whole to isolated parts and the neglect of interdependencies, Shiva claims, gives rise in practice to a reduction of nature's capacity for regeneration. (These negative practical consequences of modern science will be examined below with regard to the impacts of so-called "scientific agriculture" and "scientific forestry"

21 Carolyn Merchant, *The Death of Nature: Women, Ecology, and the Scientific Revolution* (New York: Harper and Row, 1980), 3, 193.

22 Shiva, *Staying Alive*, xvii.

in the Third World.) Shiva further argues that modern science is reductionist because it excludes all other knowers and ways of knowing nature. These alternative worldviews are disparagingly labeled "prescientific," "superstitious," or "backward." Through this epistemological reductionism many traditional sources of wisdom that can play an important role in addressing contemporary problems are overlooked or are contemptuously discarded.[23]

Critiques of modern science for its epistemological exclusiveness and its negative social and ecological impacts are increasingly common. They are shared in part by grassroots critics of development and by numerous feminist theorists and postmodern philosophers, among others.[24] What sets Shiva's views apart from most other analyses is that she looks not only at the philosophical underpinnings of modern science (as the more philosophically-inclined analysts do), but she also undertakes highly detailed social and ecological examinations of science-based projects in the Third World. Among the most prominent topics that she discusses are the Green Revolution in agriculture and modern methods of scientific forestry.

THE GREEN REVOLUTION

The Green Revolution and the accompanying modernization of agriculture have been central components of development policies throughout the Third World.[25] These "modern" or "scientific" methods

---

23 For an example of Shiva's discussion of reductionism, see *Staying Alive*, 21-26.

24 "In the last five years," wrote Sandra Harding in 1991, "there has been an outpouring of critical examinations of western science, technology, and epistemology from the peace and ecology movements, the left, philosophers, historians, and sociologists of science, and Third World critics, as well as from Western feminists." *Whose Science? Whose Knowledge? Thinking From Women's Lives* (Ithaca: Cornell University Press, 1991), viii. This outpouring of critical literature has continued. For examples of critical feminist reflections on science, see the writings of Harding, Carolyn Merchant, and Evelyn Fox Keller.

25 A distinction can be made between Green Revolution agriculture (which is based on the use of hybrid high-yield seeds) and the broader modernization of agriculture that involves the application of a broad array of modern industrial techniques to the agricultural realm. In practice, however, the two phenomena are closely interrelated. In the discussion which follows these terms will be used largely interchangeably.

of agriculture entail the use of tractors and other modern machinery, chemical fertilizers, pesticides and herbicides, modern systems of irrigation, and hybrid seeds. Proponents of the Green Revolution have repeatedly made bold claims for these techniques, promising that through their use hunger in the Third World would be overcome.[26] In practice, however, the Green Revolution has consistently been accompanied by serious ecological and social problems. In some cases *increases* in hunger have occurred despite increased levels of food production. The Green Revolution, Shiva suggests, provides an excellent case study of the impact of reductionist science and capitalist development processes.

Shiva and other critics highlight a wide variety of ways in which the Green Revolution has been ecologically damaging.[27] Industrial farming methods have contributed, for example, to massive soil erosion as a consequence of the impacts of mechanized plowing and the abandonment of many traditional soil conservation practices. These modern farming methods have led also to seriously declining levels of organic matter and nutrient levels in the soil due to exclusive reliance on chemical fertilizers. The widespread use of modern irrigation methods has led to serious problems of soil salinization and waterlogging. A recent U.N. study has found that in South Asia, one of the pioneer areas in Green Revolution agriculture, nearly 50% of the land has suffered "serious degradation" from soil erosion, declining soil fertility, salinization, waterlogging, and/or other ecological problems.[28]

---

26 Norman Borlaug, often termed the "father" of the Green Revolution, stated in 1970: "To millions of these unfortunates, who have long lived in despair, the Green Revolution seems like a miracle that has generated new hope for the future." Borlaug, "The Green Revolution, Peace, and Humanity," Lecture on the Occasion of the Award of the Nobel Peace Prize (December 11, 1970). Cited in Ernest Feder, *Perverse Development* (Quezon City, Philippines: Foundation for Nationalist Studies, 1983), 9.

27 For good discussions of the ecological impacts of the Green Revolution and viable alternatives, see Shiva, *Violence of the Green Revolution*; *Staying Alive*, chapter 5; Bernhard Glaeser, ed., *The Green Revolution Revisited: Critique and Alternatives* (London: Allen and Unwin, 1987); Terry Marsden and Nicholas Parrott, *The Real Green Revolution: Organic and Agroecological Farming in the South* (London: Greenpeace Environmental Trust, 2002).

28 This data is cited in *Development and Cooperation* magazine (May/June, 1996). For discussions of soil erosion and nutrient loss, see Shiva, *Violence*

Excessive water usage for irrigation by wealthier farmers, in addition to fostering waterlogging and salinization, has also lowered the water table in many areas. This has caused local wells to run dry and has had especially negative consequences for poor women who often are required to walk long distances for water. The pollution of water supplies is also a serious problem–groundwater has frequently been contaminated by nitrates from chemical fertilizers and by highly toxic chemical pesticides and herbicides. Agricultural chemicals have contributed also to the build-up of high levels of toxicity in the soil and have caused grave harm to the health of many workers exposed to the chemicals during their application. It is estimated by the World Health Organization, for example, that over a million persons worldwide suffer from pesticide poisoning each year. About 20,000 people die, while many others suffer significant long-term damage to their health.[29] Many chemicals whose use is banned in First World nations continue to be produced and exported by First World corporations to the Third World, which exacerbates toxicity problems.[30]

The Green Revolution has contributed also to a serious decline in genetic diversity. The use of hybrid seeds and the widespread practice of monocropping that accompanies the Green Revolution model have greatly reduced the variety of crops grown and the number of different cultivars within each major crop.[31] In most cases the hybrid seeds

---

of the Green Revolution, 103-120. For discussions of waterlogging and salinization, see ibid., 128-137. Information on these and other ecological problems associated with modernized agriculture is also contained in the essays in *Green Revolution Revisited,* ed. B. Glaeser.

29 This data is cited in Dan Fagin and Marianne Lavelle, *Toxic Deception: How the Chemical Industry Manipulates Science, Bends the Law and Endangers Your Health,* 2nd ed. (Monroe, ME: Common Courage Press, 1999), 10.

30 The classic text on this issue is David Weir and Mark Schapiro, *Circle of Poison: Pesticides and People in a Hungry World* (San Francisco: Institute for Food and Development Policy, 1981). Also see *U.S. Pesticide Exports and the Circle of Poison,* Hearing before the Subcommittee on Economic Policy, Trade, and Environment of the Committee on Foreign Affairs, U.S. House of Representatives, January 26, 1994.

31 For discussions of the decline in genetic diversity and its consequences, see Shiva, *Biopiracy; Violence of the Green Revolution,* chapter 2; *Stolen Harvest: The Hijacking of the World's Food Supply* (Cambridge, MA: South End Press, 2000).

are much less well adapted to specific local ecological conditions than the traditional varieties, leading to increased susceptibility to drought and to pest damage and disease. Monocropping practices and the use of pesticides have further contributed to increases in pest and disease damage, as such practices disturb ecological balances. Predator-prey equilibrium, for example, is upset by pesticides which kill off beneficial as well as harmful organisms. Escalating pesticide use also fosters the evolution of pesticide resistant "super-pests." Monocropping eliminates the varied natural habitats for predators of pests that exist in traditional mixed cropping practices and also enables the rapid spread of diseases among homogeneous plant populations.[32]

Green Revolution/modernizationist agricultural practices are thus viewed by critics as contributing to ecological damage in numerous ways–by fostering soil erosion, soil nutrient loss, waterlogging and salinization of soils, desertification, the poisoning of land, water, and workers, and by increasing the susceptibility of crops to droughts, pests and disease. Vandana Shiva argues that widespread, pervasive ecological problems such as these are rooted in the fact that "reductionist science...fails to perceive the natural balance." It thus, she claims, "also fails to anticipate and predict what will happen when that balance is disturbed."[33]

Even the short-term productivity increases that Green Revolution proponents highlight are largely based, Shiva argues, on one-dimensional analysis. Shiva acknowledges that in India total yields of Green Revolution grains–such as wheat and rice–have increased significantly. She emphasizes, however, that this increase has been accompanied by decreased production of other crops. These displaced crops have included more nutritious local grains and legumes, the latter of which traditionally have played an important role in maintaining nitrogen levels in the soil and providing proper amino acid/protein balance in local diets.[34] Increased Green Revolution grain production has also been at the expense of decreased production of other parts of the grain plants such as leaves and stalks (as Green Revolution plants are typically dwarf varieties), parts which formerly were used for ani-

32 For discussion of the ways in which modernized farming methods increase susceptibility to damage from pests and diseases, see Shiva, *Violence of the Green Revolution*, 89-98.

33 Shiva, *Violence of the Green Revolution*, 97.

34 Ibid., 83.

mal fodder and for replenishing soil fertility.[35] The Green Revolution has also entailed the destruction by herbicides of many highly nutritious "weeds" and the killing by pesticides of fish in rice paddies, each of which was formerly an important food source for many people.[36] "The high productivity of uniform and homogeneous systems," asserts Shiva, "is a contextual and theoretically constructed category, based on taking into account only one-dimensional yields and outputs."[37] Only increased grain yields are noted, while the decline in other food sources and in the availability of fodder and organic fertilizer is ignored. "If one also includes," says Shiva, "the cost to the farm ecosystem in terms of soil degradation, waterlogging, salinity and desertification, the green revolution has actually *reduced* productivity, instead of increasing it."[38] The narrow emphasis on increased grain yield and the neglect of other negative ecological and health consequences, including issues of long-term sustainability, exemplify for Shiva the problems of scientific reductionism.

Along with negative ecological impacts, the social impacts of the Green Revolution have frequently been severe and have been overlooked by Green Revolution proponents. Critics argue that the Green Revolution has been strongly biased in favor of the interests of larger, wealthier farmers (including transnational corporations) who are able to afford to purchase the machinery, fertilizer, irrigation systems, and other inputs upon which the model depends. These are also the farmers who tend to be the major beneficiaries of governmental subsidies, credit provision, and extension services. The ability of these large farmers to increase yields through the Green Revolution has contributed to reductions in the prices of crops, forcing many small farmers into debt and leading in many cases to the loss of their land. The ability of the wealthier farmers to more easily farm larger areas has also provided increased incentive for these farmers to dispossess smaller farmers through violence and intimidation and to terminate traditional sharecropping practices. More capital intensive methods of farming and food processing have also generally contributed to reductions in employment opportunities for landless or near-landless farm labor-

35 Ibid., 72-75.

36 Shiva, *Staying Alive*, 111.

37 Shiva, "Women's Indigenous Knowledge and Biodiversity Conservation," in Shiva and Mies, *Ecofeminism*, 165.

38 Shiva, *Staying Alive*, 129.

ers and other rural workers.[39] Andrew Pearse, under whose direction the United Nations Research Institute for Social Development undertook numerous case studies of Green Revolution processes, speaks very critically of the impact of the Green Revolution. Summarizing the results of over a dozen country studies, Pearse states:

> [I]n unequal societies the new technology can facilitate 'take-off' for cultivators with land and some capital but [it] institutes changes that marginalize the small cultivators without capital and land and undermine the essential and customary means of livelihood of an ever-increasing number of people....Where inequalities exist already, the green revolutionists' strategy results in the persistence and generation of poverty for the majority of the people in rural areas.[40]

The end results of the Green Revolution, critics assert, have typically included increased rural disparity, increased numbers of landless and unemployed persons, and in some cases increased levels of hunger even in the midst of significant overall increases in measured food production. "An ever-increasing proportion of the rural population," asserts Pearse, "lose the connection with the land and its potential for feeding them, and fail to obtain any alternative food entitlements."[41]

In a landmark study of the impact of the Green Revolution in Mexico, Cynthia Hewitt de Alcantara states:

> As agricultural modernization progressed, this wealth was concentrated to an increasing extent in the hands of a very small part of the rural population in Mexico....[The consequences included] an absolute worsening of the level of living of the lowest income groups in the country during the decade of greatest attention to the modernization of privileged centres of commercial farming; the concentration of poverty in the countryside and wealth in the cities;...the stagnation of yields of corn and beans, which are the staple

39 The technological displacement of rural workers has had a major impact on women. Many women who formerly were employed in the threshing and hand milling of grains, for example, have lost their work due to the introduction of more capital-intensive machinery.

40 Andrew Pearse (on behalf of UNRISD), *Seeds of Plenty, Seeds of Want: Social and Economic Implications of the Green Revolution* (Oxford: Clarendon Press, 1980), 157, 207.

41 Ibid., 219.

> diet of the majority of the country; the persistence of widespread hunger in the birthplace of the 'green revolution.'[42]

Economically, the Green Revolution has also often contributed significantly to increased external debt, due to dependence on a wide array of imported machinery and inputs provided by First World agribusiness corporations.

The various ecological and social problems associated with the Green Revolution, Shiva argues, are rooted most fundamentally in a shift of understanding concerning the very nature of farming. Increasingly, traditional holistic views of farming have been displaced by reductionist, capitalist conceptions of the agricultural process that focus only on profit:

> From seeing farming as a process of nurturing the earth to maintain her capacity to provide food, a...shift takes place which sees farming as a process of generating profits. Ecological destruction is one inevitable result of this commercial outlook. Economic deprivation is the other, because production for profits instead of needs excludes large numbers of women and peasants from food production and even larger numbers of women, children, and the poor from entitlements to food.
>
> It is from the ecological perspective, that focuses on nature and needs, that it is possible to see that what has been called scientific agriculture and the green revolution is in reality a western patriarchal anti-nature model of agriculture, which shifts the control of food systems from women and peasants to food and agribusiness multinationals and disrupts natural processes.[43]

Shiva frequently highlights the negative impact of the Green Revolution on women.[44] She sees this negative impact as taking various forms. First, she argues that the status of women is undermined. For

42 Cynthia Hewitt de Alcantara, *Modernizing Mexican Agriculture: Socioeconomic Implications of Technological Change 1940-1970* (Geneva: UNRISD, 1976), 310. The negative impacts resulting from the modernization of agriculture in Mexico are also documented in Tom Barry, *Zapata's Revenge: Free Trade and the Farm Crisis in Mexico* (Boston: South End Press, 1995).

43 Shiva, *Staying Alive*, 97.

44 For one instance of Shiva's discussion of the impact of the Green Revolution on women, see ibid., 112-120. Also see Carolyn Sachs, ed., *Gendered Fields: Rural Women, Agriculture, and Environment* (Boulder: Westview, 1996).

example, the emphasis of the Green Revolution is placed upon cash crops, which typically are under the control of men. In order to raise more cash crops there is a shift of land and labor away from the production of staple foods, typically the domain of women. This shift is often to the serious detriment of family nutrition and contributes to the increased economic marginalization of women. Also, the central role played by women in maintaining the health of the soil and ecological balance in an integrated system of agriculture-forestry-animal husbandry is diminished by Green Revolution practices (as well as by "scientific forestry" practices that will be discussed below). Traditionally, for example, women were responsible for gathering plant material from the forests or pastures and for collecting animal manure to use as sources of soil enrichment. In the Green Revolution system of chemicalized agriculture this soil-enhancing work of women is devalued and replaced with the use of purchased chemical inputs, with serious negative ecological and health consequences.

While certain aspects of women's work are eliminated by agricultural modernization, this does not mean that the overall workload for women has declined. Shiva and other analysts in fact argue the opposite. The ecological damage done by the Green Revolution and other policies implemented in the name of development often increases women's workloads. Widespread deforestation, for example, often necessitates that women walk further to gather wood for fuel or other forest products for animal fodder. Similarly, the drying up of wells and the poisoning of water supplies often requires women to walk longer distances to retrieve water for drinking, cooking, and bathing. Women moreover are often required to work extra hours in a subordinate role on their husband's cash crop land. Thus, while women's independence and social status and the ecological importance of women's work is diminished, their workload is not. Says Shiva:

> As more land is diverted to cash crops and is impoverished through the ecological impact of green revolution technologies, women have decreased space but increased burdens....With the market as the measure of all productivity, the 'value' of women's work and status falls....By splitting the agricultural economy into a cash-mediated masculinised sector, and a subsistence, food-producing feminised sector, capitalist patriarchy simultaneously increases the work burden and the marginalisation of women. The cash economy first draws men away from basic food production, thus increasing

> women's workload for producing subsistence; then, the ecological disruption caused by cash crop and green revolution farming forces them to walk longer distances for water, fodder, and fuel.[45]

Many studies support Shiva's claim that the workload of rural women in the Third World has been increasing while their social status has frequently been declining in the context of so-called rural development. Gita Sen and Caren Grown, summarizing the results of studies carried out in the 1970s and 1980s, state:

> A critical examination of the large volume of empirical evidence... as well as our own experience as researchers and activists, now lead us to challenge these assumptions [that modernizationist development will benefit rural women.] These studies show that rather than improving, the socioeconomic status of the great majority of Third World women has worsened considerably throughout the decade [i.e. the U.N. Decade for the Advancement of Women, 1975-1985]. With few exceptions, women's relative access to economic resources, income, and employment has worsened, their burdens of work have increased, and their relative and even absolute health, nutritional, and educational status has declined.[46]

Similarly, Kathy McAfee of Oxfam states: "Mainly as a result of scholarship and activism by women, it is now widely recognized that development policies and practices in recent decades have frequently marginalized women and damaged their health, social status and overall well-being."[47] As we have seen in previous chapters, policies of structural adjustment have further worsened the situation for many Third World women, both rural and urban, in the 1980s, 1990s, and 2000s.

In addition to increased rich-poor inequality, increased landlessness and rural unemployment, and the worsening of life situations for many Third World rural women and their children, another negative social impact highlighted by critics of the Green Revolution is an increase in ethnic tensions. Shiva in her work *The Violence of the Green Revolution* discusses ethnic violence in India and its roots in Green Revolution policies. Typical consequences of Green Revolution/mod-

45 Shiva, *Staying Alive*, 113-114.

46 Gita Sen and Caren Grown, *Development, Crises, and Alternative Visions: Third World's Women's Perspectives* (New York: Monthly Review Press, 1987), 16. Also see their discussion on pages 34-38.

47 Kathy McAfee, *Storm Signals: Structural Adjustment and Development Alternatives in the Caribbean* (Boston: Oxfam America, 1991), 198.

ernizationist approaches to rural development, Shiva argues, include increased rural disparities, conflicts over access to water and land, the breakdown of traditional rural structures and support networks, increased centralization of economic and political power and increased dependence on the state for access to credit, subsidized inputs, and other resources. All of these consequences, Shiva contends, increase social instability. This instability provides the conditions in which ethnic conflicts can grow, particularly when one ethnic group controls the organs of the state and discriminates against others. Shiva discusses in significant detail the case of ethnic violence in the Indian state of Punjab, the heartland of India's Green Revolution. In recent years Punjab has experienced violent conflict between Sikhs, many of whom are poor farmers, and Hindus, who control the state government. Shiva traces many roots of the violence to the Green Revolution. As a result of Green Revolution policies, claims Shiva, the Punjab region

> has been left with diseased soils, pest-infected crops, water-logged deserts, and indebted and discontented farmers. Instead of peace, Punjab has inherited conflict and violence....The Punjab crisis is in large measure the tragic outcome of a resource intensive and politically and economically centralized experiment with food production. The experiment has failed.[48]

The experience of the Punjab region, Shiva argues, is not unique. Policies of agricultural modernization and development (and related structural adjustment policies) have also greatly contributed to ethnic violence in places such as Somalia, Rwanda, and Sri Lanka.[49]

Given the very negative ecological and social consequences that have followed from Green Revolution policies, Shiva argues that it needs to be asked why these policies rather than others were pursued. She and other critics argue that many alternative ways to increase agricultural production existed which would have built upon the wisdom of traditional farming methods and the cohesion of rural community and which would have fostered increased self-reliance rather than in-

48 Shiva, *Violence of the Green Revolution*, 12. Shiva estimates that in the six years preceding the writing of her book over 15,000 people were killed in so-called "ethnic violence" in the Punjab region. For extensive discussion of the social impact of the Green Revolution in Punjab, see ibid., chapter 5.

49 For Shiva's discussion of Somalia and Rwanda, see *Biopiracy*, 115-117. With regard to Sri Lanka, see Shiva, "Masculinization of the Motherland," in Shiva and Mies, *Ecofeminism*,114.

creased dependence on imported inputs.[50] Instead, a model emphasizing the purchase of inputs from western agribusiness firms was prioritized, with major agricultural lending from the World Bank and other aid agencies available only to countries adopting this model. Highlighting the options not chosen, world hunger experts Frances Moore Lappé and Joseph Collins state:

> Historically, the Green Revolution represented a choice to breed seed varieties that produce high yields under optimum conditions [e.g. irrigation, plentiful chemical fertilizer]. It was a choice *not* to start by developing seeds better able to withstand drought or pests. It was a choice *not* to concentrate first on improving traditional methods of increasing yields, such as mixed cropping. It was a choice *not* to develop technology that was productive, labor-intensive, and independent of foreign input supply. It was a choice *not* to concentrate on reinforcing the balanced, traditional diets of grain plus legumes.[51]

Even at the time of the initial development of Green Revolution policies there were researchers who had demonstrated that alternative ways of increasing yields, building upon traditional agricultural methods, were viable. Frédérique Apffel-Marglin comments:

> Research results from the 1950s show that alternative methods of increasing plant yield through...methods used by traditional farmers could produce yield increases comparable with those obtained through genetic manipulation in the lab. These alternative methods were not pursued.[52]

Shiva argues that the underlying factors motivating First World support for Green Revolution practices have been profit and power:

50 For good discussions of the wisdom of traditional farming methods and the problems associated with modern industrialized farming, see Andrew Kimbrell, ed., *Fatal Harvest: The Tragedy of Industrial Agriculture* (Washington, DC: Island Press, 2002); Michael Ableman, *From the Good Earth* (New York: H.N. Abrams, 1993); Paul Richards, *Indigenous Agricultural Revolution: Ecology and Food Production in West Africa* (Boulder: Westview, 1987).

51 Frances Moore Lappé and Joseph Collins, *Food First: Beyond the Myth of Scarcity* (New York: Ballantine Books, 1978), 153. (emphasis in original)

52 Frédérique Apffel-Marglin, Introduction to *Decolonizing Knowledge: From Development to Dialogue*, ed. F. Apffel-Marglin and Stephen Marglin (New York: Oxford University Press, 1996), 24.

> The western model propagated by [Green Revolution proponents] was clearly not the only alternative, and it was not the best. It was power, profits, and control, not yields, that made global corporate and international aid interests opt for the 'miracle seeds' which made peasants dependent on internationally produced seeds and chemicals. Other alternatives would have left control with women and peasants, and would have kept people fed, but would not have generated profits.[53]

According to Shiva, it is again desire for profits and power that is fueling the current emphasis on biotechnology, hailed by proponents as promising a second Green Revolution. Shiva argues that, like the first Green Revolution, biotechnology will have many negative impacts, particularly since it is being developed predominantly by transnational corporations in order to serve their own profit-maximizing interests. The new era of biotechnology, Shiva predicts, will further enhance corporate control of food production, displace many additional small farmers, and have a variety of harmful ecological consequences. Biotechnology, states Shiva, promises "new political and economic control of living resources, new ecological vulnerabilities, new levels of genetic erosion, and new sources of dispossession and dislocation for women and marginal communities."[54] Shiva views biotechnology as representing a furthering of the processes of colonialism and enclosure:

> Through patents and genetic engineering, new colonies are being carved out. The land, the forests, and the atmosphere have all been colonized, eroded, and polluted. Capital now has to look for new colonies to invade and exploit for its further accumulation. These new colonies are, in my view, the interior spaces of the bodies of women, plants, and animals.[55]

SCIENTIFIC FORESTRY

As in the case of scientific agriculture, Shiva argues that scientific forestry has had serious negative consequences for the poor, for women,

53 Shiva, *Staying Alive*, 134.

54 Ibid.

55 Shiva, *Biopiracy*, 5. Other good books concerning biotechnology and its potential ecological and social impacts include Miguel Altieri, *Genetic Engineering in Agriculture: The Myths, Environmental Risks, and Alternatives*, 2nd ed. (Oakland: Food First Books, 2004); Mae-Wan Ho, *Genetic Engineering: Dream or Nightmare?*, 2nd ed. (New York: Continuum, 2000).

and for nature. Traditionally, forests have played many roles in human existence. In India forests have been central to local culture, held in high esteem as a locale of the sacred. Forests have also been central to the livelihood of millions of persons. For tribal forest-dwellers all basic needs are met by the forest. For many other people forests have provided food, fodder, medicine, organic fertilizer and fuel. Forests also contribute to processes of water and soil conservation. Shiva argues that in the modern forms of scientific forestry that are increasingly common in the Third World, the multiple, diverse functions of the forest are ignored and the emphasis is placed simply upon obtaining maximum yields of wood. "In the reductionist paradigm," says Shiva, "a forest is reduced to commercial wood, and wood is reduced to cellulose fibre for the pulp and paper industry."[56] Forests are viewed as "timber mines," resulting in massive deforestation, ecological disruption, and the displacement of tribal peoples who are generally forced to relocate when forest land is privatized or placed in government forestry projects. These policies generally result also in the undermining of the livelihoods of villagers who formerly depended upon forest products and who are now also excluded from access to them. "The tropical forests, when modeled on the factory and used as a timber mine," contends Shiva, "become a non-renewable resource. Tropical peoples also become a dispensable and historical waste."[57]

Shiva is especially critical of the monoculture eucalyptus plantations that have been a favored forestry project of the World Bank, other aid agencies, and local governments and have been planted on vast acreage throughout much of the Third World.[58] Eucalyptus is commercially highly desirable because it grows straight and fast and provides excellent pulpwood. It also, however, destroys water cycles (due primarily to its high water demand), produces leaves unfit for livestock, and causes serious harm to the soil. Says Shiva:

> 'Greening' with eucalyptus is a violence against nature and its cycles, and it is a violence against women who depend on the stability of nature's cycles to provide sustenance in the form of food and water. Eucalyptus guzzles nutrients and water and, in the specific conditions of low rainfall zones, gives nothing back but terpenes to the soil. These inhibit the growth of other plants and are toxic to soil

56 Shiva, *Staying Alive*, 24.

57 Shiva, *Monocultures of the Mind*, 19.

58 For discussion of eucalyptus projects, see Shiva, *Staying Alive*, chapter 4.

> organisms which are responsible for building soil fertility and improving soil structure....Its proponents failed to calculate the costs in terms of the destruction of life in the soil, the depletion of water resources, and the scarcity of food and fodder that eucalyptus cultivation creates....Eucalyptus as an exotic, introduced in total disregard of its ecological appropriateness, has thus become an exemplar of anti-life afforestation.[59]

One form of grassroots protest employed in India has been to illegally uproot eucalyptus seedlings and to replace them with native trees useful in providing food, fodder, and organic material for soil fertilization.[60]

OTHER EXAMPLES OF REDUCTIONIST SCIENCE

Shiva explores a variety of other areas in which scientific approaches characterized by reductionism have led to harmful consequences. For example, she highlights the drying up of water supplies in many parts of the Third World. Shiva asserts that the causes are largely human in origin, traceable to factors such as deforestation, over-irrigation, and the building of dams that interfere with replenishment of downstream groundwater:

> The drying up of India, like that of Africa, is a man-made rather than a natural disaster....The manufacture of drought and desertification is an outcome of reductionist knowledge and modes of development which violate life-cycles in rivers, in the soil, in mountains. Rivers are drying up because their catchments have been mined, deforested, or over-cultivated to generate revenue and profits. Groundwater is drying up because it has been over-exploited to feed cash crops.[61]

Other examples of the application of reductionist science discussed by Shiva include energy policies, allopathic western medicine, and the "white revolution" in dairy production. In each case numerous negative social, ecological, ethical, and/or health consequences are highlighted. For example, Shiva claims that the white revolution treats the cow merely as a "milk machine." Formerly the cow had sacred significance in India and had multiple economic and cultural functions.

59 Shiva, *Staying Alive*, 81-82.

60 Ibid., 82.

61 Ibid., 179.

Now it is simply understood as a milk factory. The white revolution has also served to concentrate dairy production in the hands of large corporations, displacing many rural women from the dairy process. This displacement has led both to reduced rural income and to increased nutritional deficiencies in rural children. The children had generally consumed various by-products of dairy production and now are deprived of them. Finally, the new hybrid cows introduced have been poorly adapted to the Indian environment. They have increased disease susceptibility, for example, and require high-quality grain as feed. Traditional cows, in contrast, could thrive on grass and on agricultural by-products and did not divert grains from the human food supply. The white revolution, Shiva contends, has thus done violence to the cow, to rural people (especially rural women and children), and to poor people generally.[62]

With regard to energy policy, Shiva and other critics highlight the negative social and ecological impacts of large dams, nuclear power plants, oil drilling, and reliance on fossil fuels. They stress the need for alternative forms of energy such as wind, solar, small-scale hydroelectric, and biogas. With regard to allopathic medicine, these critics highlight the depersonalization and reductionism that they believe modern medicine entails. They argue that allopathic medicine treats health care as a "war" and the body as a battleground, often resulting in considerable collateral damage. A recent article in the *Journal of the American Medical Association*, for example, estimates that side-effects of prescription drugs are the 4th to 6th leading cause of death in the United States, trailing with certainty only heart attacks, cancer, and strokes.[63] Critics call for health care methods that are more holistic

62 For Shiva's discussion of the white revolution, see ibid., 165-178.

63 Jason Lazarou, Bruce Pomeranz, and Paul Corey, "Incidence of Adverse Drug Reactions in Hospitalized Patients" *Journal of the American Medical Association* 279 (1998): 1200-1205. A classic in the literature critical of modern allopathic medicine is Ivan Illich, *The Medical Nemesis* (New York: Pantheon, 1976). Also see John Robbins, *Reclaiming Our Health: Exploding the Medical Myth and Embracing the Source of True Healing* (Tiburon, CA: H.J Kramer, 1996). An insightful contrast between the underlying philosophies toward healing of modern western medicine (termed "the doctor as mechanic") and traditional Chinese medicine ("the doctor as gardener") can be found in Harriet Beinfeld and Efrem Korngold, *Between Heaven and Earth: A Guide to Chinese Medicine* (New York: Ballantine Books, 1991).

and that seek to restore harmony and balance within the body, primarily through natural means.

For Shiva, all of these examples point to the inherent violence of dominant forms of western science. Much scientific research, Shiva notes, is devoted explicitly to violence, e.g. military-related research. But its violence is hardly confined to that realm. Shiva asserts that "modern science is violent even in peaceful domains such as, for example, health care and agriculture, where the professed objectives of scientific research is not violence but human welfare."[64] The problem, Shiva argues, is rooted in the very nature of modern scientific knowledge—its reductionist and atomistic tendencies, its emphasis on manipulation and control (expressed in part in violent cruelties toward research animals), and its lack of humility. The fact that these processes of knowledge creation are flawed, asserts Shiva, can be discerned from the long litany of unforseen negative consequences of projects based upon these foundations: "When antibiotics create super-infection and flood control measures accentuate floods and fertilizers rob soil of their fertility, the problem is not merely between use and misuse of technology. It is rooted in the very process of knowledge-creation in modern science."[65]

Shiva and other critics of development strongly call into question the near-sacred status given to science in contemporary culture, which they argue places it almost beyond critical analysis. "Neither God nor tradition," Sandra Harding states, "is privileged with the same credibility as scientific rationality in modern cultures....The project that science's sacredness makes taboo is the examination of science in just the ways any other institution or set of social practices can be examined."[66] Shiva and Harding stress that the class- and gender-based nature of modern science especially needs to be explored. None of these critiques, however, should be taken to imply a total rejection of modern science-based knowledge. Shiva and others contend that many insights from modern science have important roles to play within a

64 Vandana Shiva, "Reductionist Science as Epistemological Violence," in *Science, Hegemony, and Violence: A Requiem for Modernity*, ed. Ashis Nandy (Tokyo: United Nations University, 1988), 233. The essays in this volume all address the connections between modern science and violence.

65 Shiva, *Staying Alive*, 34.

66 Sandra Harding, *The Science Question in Feminism* (Ithaca, NY: Cornell University Press, 1986), 30.

different, more pluralistic, less reductionist, more humble overall approach to nature. What the critics object to above all is the frequent exclusivist claims made by modern science in the name of "rationality." One recent example of these exclusivist claims to rationality can be seen in an editorial from the *New England Journal of Medicine*. This editorial argued that the rising interest in herbal medicine and other alternative forms of medicine, which Shiva would view as being based upon centuries of traditional wisdom, represent nothing short of a "reversion to irrational approaches to medical practice."[67]

THE "VIOLENCE" OF MODERN SCIENCE

Shiva views manipulation and violence as being central to the modern western scientific method. She argues that this violence is rooted in patriarchal assumptions which are used to justify the manipulation and exploitation of both women and nature. To develop her argument Shiva examines in depth the thought of Francis Bacon. Bacon is often considered to be the "father" of the modern scientific method and the founder of the modern scientific research institute.[68]

In Francis Bacon's writings nature is consistently conceptualized as female. The scientific method for exploring nature is frequently equated (positively) with forms of torture, rape, and master-slave relationships. Nature, says Bacon in his work *The Masculine Birth of Time*, must be "bound into service" and made a "slave."[69] "The nature of things," Bacon asserts,

> betrays itself more readily under the vexation of [mechanical devices] than in its natural freedom. The discipline of scientific knowledge and the mechanical inventions it leads to, do not merely exert a gentle guidance over nature's course; they have the power to conquer and subdue her, to shake her to her very foundations.[70]

---

67 M. Angell and J.P. Kassirer, "Alternative Medicine: The Risks of Untested and Unregulated Remedies," *New England Journal of Medicine* 339, no. 12 (September 17, 1998): 839-841.

68 For a good discussion of the thought and influence of Francis Bacon, see Merchant, *Death of Nature*, chapter 7.

69 Quoted in Merchant, *Death of Nature*, 169-170. Similarly, Réné Descartes speaks of becoming "masters and possessors" of nature. See the discussion of Descartes in Rich, *Mortgaging the Earth*, chapter 8.

70 Quoted in Vandana Shiva, "Let us Survive: Women, Ecology, and Development," in *Women Healing Earth: Third World Women on Ecology, Femi-*

Says Shiva:

> In Bacon's experimental method, which was central to this masculine project, there was a dichotomising between male and female, mind and matter, objective and subjective, rational and emotional, and a conjunction of masculine and scientific dominating over nature, women, and the non-west. His was not a 'neutral,' 'objective,' 'scientific' method–it was a masculine mode of aggression against nature and domination over women. The severe testing of hypotheses through controlled manipulations of nature...are here formulated in clearly sexist metaphors. Both nature and inquiry appear conceptualized in ways modelled on rape and torture...and this modelling is advanced as a reason to value science.[71]

Shiva views it as not coincidental that the rise of modern science was accompanied by witch-hunting hysteria, in which many women (particularly those with knowledge in areas such as childbirth and herbal medicine) were tortured and put to death. She views this persecution as part of the effort of patriarchal modern science to establish hegemony by marginalizing or extinguishing other competing forms of knowledge.[72]

Far from being "neutral" or "objective," Shiva argues that modern science is in fact the creation of various class- and gender-based social forces. In making her case, Shiva appeals to pioneering reflections on the socially constructed nature of science by persons such as Carolyn Merchant, Evelyn Fox Keller, and Sandra Harding. The reductionist version of science triumphed, Shiva argues, not because it was the most adequate (the ecological and social problems that it has given rise to disprove this) but rather because it best served the needs of the powerful, particularly owners of capital. Says Shiva:

> If reductionist science has displaced non-reductionist modes of knowing, it has done so not through cognitive competition, but through political support from the state [in the service of dominant elites]....Stripped of the power the state invests it with, reduction-

---

nism, and Religion, ed. Rosemary Radford Ruether (Maryknoll, NY: Orbis Books, 1996), 68; Parts of this quotation are also cited in Shiva, *Staying Alive*, 16.

71 Shiva, *Staying Alive*, 16.

72 "The witch-hunts of Europe," asserts Shiva, "were largely a process of delegitimising and destroying the expertise of European women." Ibid., 21-22.

> ism can be seen to be cognitively weak and ineffective in responding to problems posed by nature. Reductionist forestry has destroyed tropical forests, and reductionist farming is destroying tropical farming. As a system of knowledge about nature or life reductionist science is weak and inadequate; as a system of knowledge for the market, it is powerful and profitable. Modern science, as we have noted earlier, has a worldview that both supports and is supported by the socio-political-economic system of western capitalist patriarchy which dominates and exploits nature, women, and the poor.[73]

Shiva thus contends that the overall impact of forms of development based on modern science in alliance with capitalist interests has been harm to nature, traditional cultures, and the poor, especially poor women. This harm, she contends, results from the fact that the resources upon which the poor and traditional cultures depend undergo processes of enclosure, being increasingly privatized and concentrated in ever fewer hands.[74] At the same time the treatment of nature as resources to be utilized for profit maximization leads to profound ecological damage and imbalances.

OTHER THEMES OF DEVELOPMENT CRITICS

The above discussion of "development as enclosure" and the overview of Vandana Shiva's work provides insight into some of the key themes of development critics. Prominent among these themes are criticism

73 Shiva, *Staying Alive*, 24-25. Similarly, Shiva states: "The relationship between reductionism, violence, and profits is built into the genesis of masculinist science, for its reductionist nature is an epistemic response to an economic organisation based on uncontrolled exploitation of nature for maximization of profits and capital accumulation....The reductionist worldview, the industrial revolution and the capitalist economy were the philosophical, technological, and economic components of the same process." Ibid., 23.

74 "In the market economy, the organising principle for natural resource use is the maximisation of profits and capital accumulation....The ideology of development is in large part based on a vision of bringing all natural resources into the market economy for commodity production....Since these natural resources are the basis of nature's economy and women's survival economy, their scarcity [due to commercial exploitation] is impoverishing women and marginalised peoples in an unprecedented manner. Their new impoverishment lies in the fact that resources which supported their survival were absorbed into the market economy while they themselves were excluded and displaced by it." Ibid., 9, 13.

of the increased concentration of wealth, new forms of destitution, and massive ecological damage caused by past development policies. Also of central concern are the increasing commodification of all facets of life and the equation of development with capitalist westernization, to the detriment of local cultures and traditional values (though it needs to be emphasized again that these grassroots analysts argue for a *critical* appropriation of traditional values.) These analysts see development proponents as placing primary emphasis on economic growth (measured by increases in GNP), while ignoring the social, cultural, and ecological impacts of this growth.[75] While not all development critics address the nature of modern science as directly as does Shiva, many of them do, and all share concern regarding the *hubris* of western development planners and "experts" who assume the superiority of western, industrialized ways of knowing and acting.[76] Shiva in her work highlights especially the negative impacts of development upon the rural poor, especially poor women. Other critics discuss the plight of the huge numbers of marginalized poor in urban areas.[77] Some critics focus largely on cultural issues, highlighting the negative social impacts that accompany the spread of capitalist culture. These impacts, critics claim, include rising individualism and the breakdown of communal structures, a consumerist ethos that undermines traditional spiritual and moral values, increased crime and violence, widespread alcohol and drug abuse, the commodification of women, increased ethnic tensions, and a rise in psychological problems such as depression.[78] Some critics of development highlight broad trends across different countries and cultures, while others present case studies of the impact of development on a particular culture during a par-

75 See Latouche, "Standard of Living," in *Development Dictionary*, ed. W. Sachs.

76 For additional critiques of modern science by development critics, see Nandy, *Science, Hegemony, and Violence*; Rich, *Mortgaging the Earth*; Claude Alvares, ed., *Science, Development, and Violence: The Revolt Against Modernity* (Oxford: Oxford University Press, 1992).

77 For discussions of the urban poor in the Third World, see Mark Kramer, *Dispossessed: Life in Our World's Urban Slums* (Maryknoll, NY: Orbis Books, 2006).

78 See, for example, Jeremy Seabrook, *Victims of Development: Resistance and Alternatives* (London: Verso, 1993); Helena Norberg-Hodge, *Ancient Futures: Learning from Ladakh* (San Francisco: Sierra Club Books, 1991).

ticular period of time. Of the latter, Helena Norberg-Hodge's study *Ancient Futures: Learning from Ladakh,* is particularly noteworthy.[79] Some critics focus particular attention on ecological issues, exploring both the immediate impacts of ecological degradation on people's daily lives (as Shiva does) and broader, global ecological problems such as ozone depletion and global warming whose major consequences are still to be experienced. The bulk of the negative consequences of these global ecological problems, analysts suggest, will again be experienced by the world's poor.

FURTHER ISSUES IN THE DEVELOPMENT DEBATE

There are several additional topics related to development and economic globalization that are important to explore. These include a closer look at the role of the World Bank, an examination of the currently popular notion of sustainable development, and more detailed analysis of the impacts of free trade. Following this discussion I will briefly highlight the type of alternatives that grassroots critics propose. This chapter will then conclude with reflections on the implications of the insights of development critics for radical political economy and for Catholic Social Teaching.

THE WORLD BANK

Critics view the World Bank as an institution that embodies in a concentrated form some of the fundamental problems of the modern worldview that formed the basis for conventional models of economic development. "The history of the [World] Bank," argues Bruce Rich, "is a particularly instructive case study in many of the philosophical, political, and economic assumptions and currents that have shaped the modern world–and how they have gone awry."[80]

---

79 Norberg-Hodge in her book *Ancient Futures: Learning from Ladakh,* explores in a very compelling manner the harmful impacts of development on the culture, ecology, and people of the Indian state of Ladakh. She also highlights the grassroots efforts being made to resist these impacts, and from these experiences draws lessons for the broader world. An excellent companion video, with the same title, is available. For more information, see the website of the International Society for Ecology and Culture at <www.isec.org.uk>.

80 Rich, *Mortgaging the Earth,* ix. Rich refers to the World Bank as "the quintessential institution of high mid-twentieth-century modernity." Ibid.,

We have discussed the World Bank earlier in this book in the context of Third World debt and structural adjustment. Prior to its role in enforcing structural adjustment policies, the Bank had as its main stated goal the fostering of economic development in Third World nations. This was interpreted in modernizationist terms as remaking in the Third World in the image of the industrialized West. With high levels of confidence in the superiority of western knowledge and technology, the "experts" of the World Bank supported a wide variety of programs in the Third World that resulted in very negative social and ecological consequences. Among these projects, for example, have been large hydroelectric dams that have displaced and impoverished millions of persons, destroyed huge areas of agricultural land and forest, and contributed to the spread of water-borne diseases while providing electricity primarily to foreign corporations and to wealthy local elites. Other projects with harmful impacts have included Green Revolution agriculture, the building of highways through tropical forests, very expensive and dangerous nuclear power plants, monoculture forestry projects, and cattle ranching projects involving extensive deforestation, among others.[81] The result of these projects has been the displacement of tens of millions of persons from their farmland and forests and the creation of numerous ecological and economic problems, including high levels of Third World debt. The impact of structural adjustment policies, overseen by the World Bank, has further compounded this damage. Critics of the World Bank emphasize also that the policies of the Bank have historically been highly politicized, e.g. providing funding to repressive regimes friendly to the economic and political interests of the United States while refusing to lend to governments that were seeking to implement social reforms opposed by the United States.[82]

239.

81 For details concerning past World Bank-funded projects, see Rich, *Mortgaging the Earth*; Catherine Caufield, *Masters of Illusion: The World Bank and the Poverty of Nations* (New York: Henry Holt, 1996). For the latest information, see <www.bankwatch.org>. Also see the video "In the Name of Progress", part of the Race to Save the Planet video series. This video is available for free loan from the Mennonite Central Committee at <www.mcc.org/catalog>.

82 For a discussion of World Bank lending and human rights issues, see Rich, *Mortgaging the Earth*, 99-102. The Bank refused, for example, to

According to critics, key problems contributing to these flawed Bank policies include its domination by First World governments (the quantity of votes allotted to each nation within the Bank is based roughly on the size of its economy), a very top-down management style, secretive procedures, lack of contact with local populations, lack of accountability (for it bears no negative consequences for failed projects) and, above all, unswerving faith in orthodox economic models despite widespread evidence pointing to their inadequacy.[83] According to prominent World Bank critic Bruce Rich, the Bank in its decision-making processes has typically "combined blanket paternalism with breathtaking naivete, rooted in *a priori* macro- and micro-economic assumptions, rather than in empirical understanding of local social, political, and economic realities."[84] Michael Irwin, former director of the World Bank's Health Services Department, stresses that the lack of contact between World Bank officials and the poor has had a particularly negative impact on policy:

> The Bank staff, living and working comfortably in the Washington area and venturing forth in luxury, with first-class flights and hotels, are out of touch with both the realities and the causes of poverty in the Third World. World Bank staff, who deal almost exclusively with ministers and senior civil servants on their 'missions,' are simply bureaucrats talking confidentially with autocrats....Public protestations to the contrary, poverty reduction is the last thing on most World Bank bureaucrats' minds.[85]

The highly respected grassroots development organization Oxfam stresses the harmful consequences of many past World Bank projects:

---

make loans to the reformist governments of Goulart in Brazil and Allende in Chile, but quickly resumed lending to these countries once these governments were overthrown in CIA-sponsored coups and military dictatorships favorable to U.S. economic interests were installed in their place.

83 See Rich, *Mortgaging the Earth*; Caufield, *Masters of Illusion*; World Development Movement, *Denying Democracy: How the IMF and World Bank Take Power from People* (London: World Development Movement, 2005).

84 Rich, *Mortgaging the Earth*, 73.

85 Michael Irwin, "Banking on Poverty: An Insider's Look at the World Bank," in *50 Years is Enough: The Case Against the World Bank and the International Monetary Fund*, ed. Kevin Danaher (Boston: South End Press, 1994), 160, 152.

> Since the 1960s, World Bank project interventions have, in many cases, become synonymous with the worst forms of development practice. Insensitivity to local people, indifference to economic realities, and a propensity to disinformation, have combined to produce a litany of development disasters. All too often local elites have been the main beneficiaries while the poor have seen their livelihoods undermined, and suffered displacement. Women have been adversely affected by the failure of project planners to consider the gender implications of their actions.[86]

Since the late 1980s the World Bank has undertaken various policy reforms and has added new personnel in response to growing international criticism. These measures have included, for example, an expansion of the Bank's Environment Department. Critics contend, however, that these changes have had only minimal impact on the projects that the World Bank has funded. Instead, the reforms are seen to have served primarily public relations purposes. Bruce Rich, for example, contends that the Environment Department "inhabit[s] a world of paper, publishing upbeat accounts of strengthened internal directives and producing volumes of environmental issues papers and action plans, while the lending juggernaut lumber[s] ahead on a separate planet called Operations."[87] In other words, critics claim that the Environment Department is highly marginalized within the Bank and has little impact on policy. Support for large-scale environmentally and socially destructive dams, heavily-polluting coal-fired power plants, Green Revolution export-oriented agriculture, and similar problematic projects continues largely unquestioned, as does the overarching emphasis on the maximization of economic growth as the key policy concern. Critics argue that even many of the so-called environmental projects funded by the Bank, such as those funded through the Global Environment Facility established at the Earth Summit in Rio de Janeiro in 1992, have themselves caused increased environmental damage and have often consisted of the same types of programs as previously funded (e.g. programs promoting increased logging, monoculture tree plantations, and Green Revolution-type agriculture)

---

86 Oxfam, *Embracing the Future – Avoiding the Challenge of World Poverty: Oxfam's Response to the World Bank's 'Vision' for the Bretton Woods System* (London: Oxfam, 1994), 19.

87 Rich, *Mortgaging the Earth*, 183.

now presented in "green" clothing.[88] The environmental failure of the World Bank, Bruce Rich argues, is "systemic," rooted deeply in the underlying modernizationist, economistic worldview that shapes Bank policies.[89] An example of this worldview can be seen in the internal memo of then World Bank vice-president Lawrence Summers, who argued that "the economic logic behind dumping a load of toxic waste in the lowest wage country is impeccable and we should face up to it." In making his argument, Summers relied on the economic logic that measures harms in terms of lost income potential. Thus, if a person in the poorest countries dies from toxic poisoning this counts much less than a person dying in a wealthy country. "I've always thought," said Summers, "that underpopulated countries of Africa are vastly *under-polluted*." Responding to Summers, Brazilian secretary of the environment José Lutzenberger stated: "Your reasoning is perfectly logical but totally insane....Your thoughts will be quoted in full...as a concrete example of the unbelievable alienation, reductionist thinking, social ruthlessness, and the arrogant ignorance of many conventional 'economists' concerning the nature of the world we live in."[90]

SUSTAINABLE DEVELOPMENT

The term "sustainable development" is widely employed in current development discussions. It appears regularly even in reports issued by the World Bank.[91] The term, however, has a wide array of meanings. Often these meanings are incompatible with each other.[92] For

88 For discussion of the environmental damage caused by recent World Bank-sponsored environmental projects, see Rich, "The Emperor's New Clothes," chapter 6 of *Mortgaging the Earth*; Zoe Young, *A New Green Order? The World Bank and the Politics of the Global Environment Facility* (London: Pluto Press, 2002).

89 Rich, *Mortgaging the Earth*, 154.

90 Summers' memo and Lutzenberger's response are discussed in ibid., 246-249.

91 The World Bank has a history of adopting terms popularized by grassroots critics – sustainable development, participation, good governance/democracy, etc. – but then giving them very different meanings. See the discussions of this phenomenon in David Moore and Gerald Schmitz, eds., *Debating Development Discourse* (New York: St. Martin's Press, 1995).

92 Good discussions of sustainable development can be found in Josée Johnston, Michael Gismondi, and James Goodman, eds., *Nature's Revenge: Reclaiming Sustainability in an Age of Corporate Globalization* (Orchard

some persons sustainable development refers to the need to prioritize ecological concerns, which calls for simplification of lifestyles in the world's richer nations, redistribution of wealth and of political power in order to overcome global poverty, and the setting of overall limits to economic growth. For others, however, the term sustainable development is used interchangeably with the term "sustainable growth." What is to be sustained is primarily the process of economic growth itself. Sustainable development thus understood entails finding the maximum level of exploitation of nature that is possible without environmental damage becoming so severe as to undermine further economic growth, this growth in turn being viewed as the key to overcoming global poverty. It is in this latter sense that the term is employed by the World Bank, many government officials, and many global corporate officers. In a report of the influential World Commission on Environment and Development (a commission established by the United Nations and chaired by Gro Harlem Bruntland, commonly known as the Brundtland Commission), the elimination of global poverty is seen to require a 5- to 10-fold increase in global production over the next 50 years, which the Commission claims can be accomplished in an environmentally sustainable fashion.[93]

Critics find these views of the Brundtland Commission to be very problematic. The critics assert that current levels of global production and consumption are already ecologically unsustainable. A 5- to 10-fold increase in economic activity would only rapidly accelerate the damage being done.[94] The critics also argue that the Brundtland Commission is unmindful of the negative social impacts of conventional approaches to economic growth. With regard to understandings of sustainable development similar to that of the Brundtland Commission, the editors of *The Ecologist* state: "Sustainable development – now the 'buzzword' of environmentalists, politicians, business leaders, and strategic planners alike – would appear to cloak an agenda that

---

Park, NY: Broadview Press, 2006); Wolfgang Sachs, ed., *Global Ecology: Conflicts and Contradictions* (London: Zed Books, 1993); Michael Redclift, *Sustainable Development: Exploring the Contradictions* (New York: Methuen, 1987).

93 World Commission on Environment and Development, *Our Common Future* (Oxford: Oxford University Press, 1987), 15.

94 See Paul Ekins, "Making Development Sustainable," in *Global Ecology*, ed. W. Sachs, 91-103.

is just as destructive, just as undermining of peoples' rights and livelihoods as the development agenda of old."[95]

Critics view the United Nations Conference on Environment and Development (UNCED, commonly known as the Earth Summit, which was held in Rio de Janeiro in 1992) as being representative of the flaws in dominant understandings of sustainable development. At this conference the need for high levels of economic growth remained primary, and free markets and global corporations were seen as the best agents of this sustainable growth. High levels of growth would in turn reduce poverty and poverty-caused environmental destruction. The problems of the Third World were framed by the summit in ways that cast the First World and the capitalist system as potential saviors, needed to provide investment, technology, and expertise to the Third World. Far from recognizing that capitalist growth has greatly contributed to both the perpetuation of poverty and to environmental destruction, this growth is instead presented as being the solution to these problems. "The disease," says Vandana Shiva, "is then offered as a cure: growth will solve the problems of poverty and the environmental crisis it has given rise to in the first place."[96] "Unwilling to question the desirability of economic growth, the market economy, or the development process," states *The Ecologist*, "UNCED [The Earth Summit] never had a chance of addressing the real problems of 'environment and development.'"[97] Some of these real problems, according to critics, include the unsustainability of First World lifestyles (including excessive reliance on personal automobiles, meat-based diets, etc.), the negative environmental and social impacts of free trade, the need for major debt relief for the Third World, the need for regulations and restrictions on the activities of transnational corporations, the harmful social and ecological impacts of excessive military spending,[98] the need for more ecologically and socially appropriate forms of energy and technology, and the need for land reform and other measures of economic redistribution.

---

95 Ecologist, *Whose Common Future?*, vi.

96 Shiva, "Decolonizing the North," in Shiva and Mies, *Ecofeminism*, 268.

97 Ecologist, *Whose Common Future?*, 1.

98 For a discussion of the environmental impact of the U.S. military, see Seth Shulman, *The Threat at Home: Confronting the Toxic Legacy of the U.S. Military* (Boston: Beacon, 1992).

Critics see the Earth Summit as having adopted a managerial version of ecology, in which ecology largely functions as "a technocratic effort to keep development afloat against the drift of plunder and pollution."[99] In addition to having problematic goals, critics argue that managerial ecology is doomed to failure. The seeds of this failure lie in a lack of humility, which is essential to relate to nature in a constructive way. Human *hubris,* which leads scientific experts to believe that they can reliably control nature and predict the consequences of their actions in a real-world setting, has been frequently shown to lead to highly destructive consequences. Critics highlight, for example, the problems of global warming, ozone depletion, acid rain, the negative ecological and health impacts of chemicals and hormones in agriculture and animal raising, the dangers of nuclear power, the harmful side-effects of many modern drugs, the negative health impacts on women of some forms of birth control, and the global resurgence of infectious diseases (largely in response to the overuse of antibiotics) as examples of major problems that were largely unanticipated by the scientific experts who designed the products and processes that have given rise to the problems. What is needed to respond constructively to the current ecological crises, claim critics, is not so much a new technological fix but rather a fundamental change in lifestyles and in moral values, including a different, more humble relationship with nature. Those with a managerial view of ecology, argues Wolfgang Sachs, "treat as a technical problem what in fact amounts to no less than a civilizational impasse."[100]

Regarding the notion of sustainable development, critics argue that the term is inherently self-contradictory. Development, they claim, has connotations of economic growth and the superiority of the industrialized nations built into it, implying an ecologically *unsustainable* and socially and culturally destructive path of change. The term development, these critics argue, should be viewed as a "toxic" term, one that

99 Wolfgang Sachs, "Global Ecology and the Shadow of 'Development,'" in *Global Ecology,* ed. W. Sachs, 11. For further critiques of managerial ecology see the other articles in the same volume.

100 Wolfgang Sachs, "Environment," in *Development Dictionary,* ed. W. Sachs, 36.

needs to be discarded.[101] No amount of adjectives such as "sustainable," "participatory," or "grassroots" can save it:

> The debate over the word 'development' is not merely a question of words. Whether one likes it or not, one can't make development different from what it has been. Development has been and still is the *Westernization of the world*....Words are rooted in history; they are linked to ways of seeing and entire cosmologies which very often escape the speaker's consciousness....By placing itself under the banner of development, the alternative movement dons the opposition's colours, hoping perhaps to seduce rather than combat it–but more likely to fall into the abyss itself.[102]

Later in this chapter some alternative terms used by development critics to represent the constructive social changes that they seek will be explored. These include terms such as "regeneration" and "reclaiming the commons."

FREE TRADE

Vandana Shiva divides the history of economic globalization into three broad stages – the era of colonialism, the era of development, and the present era of free trade.[103] Shiva suggests that each of these stages has intensified the dispossession of the poor from their land and other resources needed for an independent livelihood. Shiva and other critics argue that the third era of globalization–that of free trade–may cause even more damage than the preceding two. The era of free trade or "corporate colonialism," says Edward Goldsmith, "is likely to dispossess, impoverish, and marginalize more people, destroy more cultures, and cause more environmental devastation than either the colonialism of old or the development of the last fifty years."[104]

Proponents of free trade foresee a different outcome. They contend that measures of economic liberalization will lead to unprecedented

---

101 For discussion of development as a "toxic" term, see Serge Latouche, *In the Wake of the Affluent Society: An Exploration of Post-Development* (London: Zed Books, 1993), 160. Similar critiques can be found in many of the essays in *Development Dictionary*, ed. W. Sachs.

102 Latouche, *In the Wake of the Affluent Society*, 160. Emphasis in original.

103 Shiva employs this three-fold division of the history of economic globalization in her work *Biopiracy*.

104 Edward Goldsmith, "Development as Colonialism," *Ecologist* 27, no. 2 (1997): 76.

economic growth on a global scale. While they admit that there may be some short-term losers as the world adjusts to free trade regimes, these supporters argue that in the long run virtually everyone will benefit from the increased efficiency and economic growth that expansion of trade will bring about.[105]

Before further exploring this debate, it may be helpful to examine what provisions are included in free trade agreements – such as the North American Free Trade Agreement (NAFTA), the global General Agreement on Tariffs and Trade (GATT – which gave rise to the World Trade Organization), and the recently implemented Central American Free Trade Agreement (CAFTA). These treaties concern in part the rules for trade between nations. They call for the progressive reduction and/or elimination of tariffs and non-tariff barriers to trade in most sectors of the economy. The agreements concern much more than trade, however. Many provisions relate to investment and require the removal of restrictions and regulations concerning the investment activities of transnational corporations. For example, rules requiring the purchase of local inputs, the hiring of a certain percentage of local managers, the reinvestment of profits in the local economy, etc. are generally forbidden. The agreements also concern intellectual property rights (IPRs), strengthening the copyright and patent protections for the products of transnational corporations.[106] Critics argue that these free trade agreements will have very negative consequences, in multiple ways.[107] These criticisms will be explored in the sections that follow:

HARM TO SMALL FARMERS

One of the most fundamental criticisms of free trade agreements is that they threaten the livelihoods of hundreds of millions of small farmers throughout the world. These farmers, who often have been

---

105 For arguments in favor of free trade, see Martin Wolf, *Why Globalization Works* (New Haven, CT: Yale University Press, 2004); Melvyn Krauss, *How Nations Grow Rich: The Case for Free Trade* (New York: Oxford University Press, 1997).

106 For a critique of the intellectual property rights provisions of free trade treaties, see Shiva, *Biopiracy*.

107 Excellent critiques of free trade can be found in Mander and Goldsmith, *Case Against the Global Economy*; Madeley, *Hungry for Trade*; Korten, *When Corporations Rule the World*.

neglected or discriminated against in conventional development policies, are generally unable to compete with the products of First World agribusiness when these products are allowed free entry to their countries. While the products of agribusiness are often produced in environmentally destructive ways, the ecological impact of this production is not factored into the market price. Moreover, these agribusiness products often receive massive direct and indirect subsidies from First World governments that enable them to be exported artificially cheaply, often below the actual cost of production. Corn produced in the United States, for example, sells in Mexico about 25% below production costs.[108]

It is estimated that as a result of NAFTA and the policies adopted in Mexico leading up to NAFTA several million people have already been displaced from their farms, most ending up joining the huge numbers of poor living in the already overcrowded shantytowns surrounding Mexico's cities (where unemployment is pervasive) or risking their lives in the attempt to immigrate illegally into the United States.[109] Similar devastating results for small farmers are expected throughout Central America from the impact of the recently ratified Central America Free Trade Agreement (CAFTA). Provisions of WTO agreements are also harming farmers worldwide. A recent *New York Times* editorial discussed the case of the Philippines:

> Put simply, the Philippines got taken. A charter member of the World Trade Organization in 1995, the former American colony dutifully embraced globalization's free-market gospel over the last decade....Instead of making any gains, the Philippines has lost hundreds of thousands of farming jobs since joining the WTO. Its modest agricultural trade surpluses of the 1990s have turned into deficits. Filipinos...increasingly view the much-promoted globalization as a new imperialism.[110]

---

108 Tina Rosenberg, "Why Mexico's Small Corn Farmers Go Hungry," *New York Times* (March 3, 2003): A22.

109 For discussion of the impact of free trade on peasant farmers in Mexico, see George Collier with Elizabeth Lowery Quaratiello, *Basta: Land and the Zapatista Rebellion in Chiapas*, 3rd ed. (Oakland, CA: Food First Books, 2005).

110 Editorial, *New York Times* (July 20, 2003). Documentation of the negative impacts of trade liberalization on farmers worldwide can be found in Madeley, *Hungry for Trade*, 73-90; Vandana Shiva and Gitanjali Bedi,

These policies of agricultural liberalization undermine the prospects for a revitalized small farm sector, which is a crucial component of most proposals for more just, balanced, and ecologically sound economic policies for the Third World.[111] These policies also bring about cultural destruction, undermining traditional cultures that are centered upon life on the land. Elena Ixcot, an indigenous Mayan woman from Guatemala, powerfully highlights these cultural implications:

> The dream of every Maya is to have a piece of land on which to plant corn, because corn gives us spiritual enrichment; corn gives us physical resistance; corn gives us strength and health. Through corn we sing. Through corn we laugh and sigh and cry. Through corn our lives are formed and we are born. To strip us of our land for planting corn means to kill our people and our culture.[112]

HARM TO SMALL BUSINESSES

A second major critique of free trade agreements, in addition to their negative impacts on Third World farmers, is that they harm small and medium-scale local businesses and industries. These businesses are forced to compete on very unequal terms with the products of transnational corporations, disadvantaged by enormous disparities of wealth and power. Mexico, for example, has seen a significant decline in its small business/small industry sector since the implementation of NAFTA.[113]

The ability of Third World nations to regulate the activities of transnational corporations (TNCs) in ways that are beneficial to the local population has also been greatly eroded by free trade agreements and

---

eds., *Sustainable Agriculture and Food Security: The Impact of Globalisation* (Thousand Oaks, CA: Sage Publications, 2002).

111 For an excellent discussion of the importance of revitalizing small-scale, ecologically sustainable agriculture, along with detailed policy recommendations, see *Alternatives to Economic Globalization*, ed. Cavanagh and Mander, 172-187.

112 Elena Ixcot, "Our Eyes Were Opened: A Mayan Woman Speaks," in *We Make the Road by Walking: Central America, Mexico, and the Caribbean in the New Millennium*, ed. Ann Butwell, Kathy Ogle, and Scott Wright (Washington, DC: EPICA, 1998), 144.

113 See Public Citizen's Global Trade Watch, "The Ten Year Track Record of the North American Free Trade Agreement," available at <www.citizen.org/trade>.

SAPs. Measures requiring, for example, that corporations purchase inputs from local suppliers or hire local managers or reinvest a certain percentage of profits in the local economy are generally prohibited in free trade agreements as unjust interference with corporate freedom. Also prohibited are measures that restrict TNC involvement in sectors of the economy that citizens believe should be under local control, such as agriculture or banking. These provisions, critics argue, all lead to more concentrated economic power in the hands of transnational corporations.

UNEMPLOYMENT, SWEATSHOPS, AND A RACE TO THE BOTTOM

As a result of economic globalization and freer trade, many small farmers, artisans, and small businesspeople have been deprived of their livelihoods. Many more will be displaced as this form of globalization proceeds. Critics argue that those displaced generally outnumber the persons hired in new jobs that are created, such as in the industrial export sectors of Third World economies. In Mexico, for example, overall rates of unemployment and poverty have increased since the implementation of NAFTA and workers' wages have dropped around 20%.[114]

The nature of the jobs that are created as a result of freer trade are also a subject of controversy. Critics argue that these jobs are generally characterized by low pay, long work hours, dangerous working conditions, lack of job security, and the frequent sexual harassment of female employees. Unions typically are either prohibited or very actively discouraged through firings and threats. It is these conditions that have given rise to the global anti-sweatshop movement.[115] While proponents of free trade argue that the jobs created by free trade are

114 Ibid. Also see Bishop Álvaro Ramazzini, "CAFTA Likely to Hurt Poor Central Americans," *National Catholic Reporter* (November 11, 2005). Says Ramazzini: "NAFTA displaced 1.5 million Mexican peasant farmers. Many of these displaced farmers sought industrial jobs, causing Mexican wages to drop by 20 percent. Communities and families were torn asunder as those who lost their livelihoods undertook the perilous journey to the United States in hopes of finding some way to support their family." Bishop Ramazzini is president of the Bishops' Secretariat of Central America and Panama.

115 See Andrew Ross, *Low Pay, High Profile: The Global Push for Fair Labor* (New York: New Press, 2004); Robert Ross, *Slaves to Fashion: Poverty and*

better than no jobs, critics contend that these are not the only choices that countries have. They argue that alternative development strategies, including the fostering of a revitalized local economy through redistributive measures and support for small and medium-sized farms and businesses, along with an enforceable global code of conduct for transnational corporations and more equitable rules of trade, could create more humane employment possibilities.

Critics of neoliberal globalization often argue that what economic globalization is leading to is a global "race to the bottom," as corporations play off one country against another in a never-ending search for lower wages, less restrictions on investment, lower environmental and safety standards, lower taxes, and higher profits.[116] The lack of substantive, enforceable standards for wages, labor rights and environmental protection in the free trade agreements, these critics argue, contributes strongly to this downward spiral.

THE UNDERMINING OF DEMOCRACY

A fourth major critique of free trade agreements is that their provisions undermine democracy and the ability of communities to control their own destinies. Agreements such as NAFTA, GATT, and CAFTA have been negotiated in near-total secrecy, with representatives of TNCs or persons formerly associated with TNCs serving to draft most of the components of the treaties and input from labor, environmental organizations, and consumer groups largely excluded. In the United States, when the agreements were voted on by Congress, they were given "fast-track" status, with debate strictly limited and no amendments permitted. Most Congresspeople had not read the documents when they voted to approve them. Various shady political tactics have also often been used to facilitate passage. With regard to CAFTA, for example, Guatemalan Bishop Álvaro Ramazzini states: "CAFTA's U.S. passage, made possible by political threats, payoff promises and procedural manipulations, resembled the tactics employed in March to pass CAFTA in Guatemala's Congress." Ramazzi-

---

Abuse in the New Sweatshops (Ann Arbor: University of Michigan Press, 2004).

116 The theme of a global "race to the bottom" is explored extensively in Korten, *When Corporations Rule the World* and Jeremy Brecher and Tim Costello, *Global Village or Global Pillage: Economic Reconstruction from the Bottom Up*, 2nd ed. (Cambridge, MA: South End Press, 1998).

ni argues that these underhanded measures, accompanied by rhetoric of democracy, are "one of CAFTA's cruel ironies."[117] The processes by which these free trade documents were created and approved can thus be seen as highly undemocratic.[118]

Critics claim that these agreements serve to further undermine democracy through their content as well. Key provisions of the agreements allow for the overturning of local and national laws (including health, safety, and environmental regulations) that are ruled to interfere with free trade. The World Trade Organization (the enforcement mechanism created through the GATT process) has recently ruled, for example, that countries cannot prohibit the importation of dairy products produced with artificial growth hormones, thereby striking down the laws of numerous European countries which restrict the importation of these products on health grounds. Other GATT/WTO rulings have included decisions overturning part of the U.S. Clean Air Act, which was seen as discriminating against dirtier gasolines produced in certain foreign countries, and a decision that the U.S. could not prohibit the importation of tuna caught with nets that trap and kill large numbers of dolphins. Many other examples of overturned or threatened laws or programs could be cited.[119] The key point here is that these agreements have removed authority in key areas of social and environmental policy from the hands of democratically elected legislatures and placed it in the hands of trade bureaucrats who are unaccountable to democratic processes. In the case of the WTO, for example, challenges that are brought against local or national laws are adjudicated by a panel of three "trade experts," often persons with close ties to transnational corporations. The deliberations are required by the charter of the WTO to be conducted in secret and to be kept secret even after the ruling is made. There are no provisions guaranteeing any voice to nongovernmental organizations such as environmental, labor, or consumer groups in the deliberations. And there is no ex-

117 Ramazzini, "CAFTA."

118 See Ralph Nader and Lori Wallach, "GATT, NAFTA, and the Subversion of the Democratic Process," in *Case Against the Global Economy*, ed. Mander and Goldsmith, 92-107.

119 See ibid. Also see Lori Wallach and Patrick Woodall, *Whose Trade Organization? A Comprehensive Guide to the WTO* (New York: New Press, 2004).

ternal appeal allowed. If countries do not bring their laws into accord with WTO rulings, they are subject to perpetual trade sanctions.

Reflecting upon the devastating impact of these agreements on democracy, Ralph Nader and Lori Wallach state:

> Approval of these agreements has institutionalized a global economic and political situation that places every government in a virtual hostage situation, at the mercy of a global financial and commercial system run by empowered corporations. This new system is not designed to promote the health and well-being of human beings but to enhance the power of the world's largest corporations and financial institutions....The agreements promote the elimination of restrictions that protect people but increase protection for corporate interests.[120]

Similarly, Vandana Shiva states: "Free trade is not free; it protects the economic interests of the powerful transnational corporations.... Transnational corporate freedom is based on the destruction of citizens' freedom everywhere."[121]

Shiva argues that current forms of economic globalization represent the expansion of western culture and of transnational corporate control across the globe, not a more positive mutual enrichment of cultures as proponents claim:

> Globalization is not the cross-cultural interaction of diverse societies; it is the imposition of a particular culture on all the others. Nor is globalization the search for ecological balance on a planetary scale....The 'global' in the dominant discourse is the political space in which the dominant local seeks global control, freeing itself of responsibility for the limits arising from the imperatives of ecological sustainability and social justice. In this sense, the 'global' does not represent a universal human interest; it represents a particular local and parochial interest and culture that has been globalized through its reach and control, its irresponsibility and lack of reciprocity.[122]

INCREASED SOCIAL CONFLICTS

A fifth major criticism of free trade is that these policies contribute to increased social tensions and conflict. The causes of this increased

120 Ibid., 93, 95.

121 Shiva, *Biopiracy*, 113.

122 Ibid., 103.

conflict are several. In some cases persons harmed by neoliberal policies take up arms to directly protest these policies, such as the indigenous Zapatista rebels in Mexico who timed the initiation of their armed uprising to coincide with the day that NAFTA went into effect. They feared that NAFTA would cause many indigenous people to lose their land and contribute to the further destruction of Mayan culture. In other cases the connections are less direct but even more deadly. As large numbers of rural people are uprooted through processes of enclosure and move to the cities in search of scarce jobs, they are often thrown into competition with persons of other ethnic groups for scarce jobs and resources. They are also faced with challenges to their cultural/religious identity and their sense of self-worth, especially from the impact of consumer culture. Persons whose independent livelihoods are undermined also typically become more dependent upon the state (as a source of jobs, credit, basic services, etc.), which may be controlled by a dominant ethnic group that shows favoritism to its own members. In these circumstances appeals to ethnic scapegoating and religious fundamentalisms can flourish, as seen in cases such as Rwanda, Sri Lanka, and India where increased ethnic/religious tensions and violence have coincided with the increased adoption of neoliberal economic policies that have exacerbated insecurity among the poor.[123] Even the Pentagon has warned that current forms of neoliberal globalization are creating the conditions for instability and violence. In recent testimony to Congress, the director of the Pentagon's Defense Intelligence Agency emphasized that current forms of globalization tend to "leave large numbers of people seemingly worse off, exacerbate local and regional tensions, increase the prospects and capabilities for conflict and empower those who would do us harm."[124]

The alleged paradox of increased globalization and increased ethnic strife noted by various commentators is thus really not a paradox at all, according to critics. Rather, the phenomena of economic global-

---

123 See Amy Chua, *World on Fire: How Exporting Free Market Democracy Breeds Ethnic Hatred and Global Instability* (New York: Doubleday, 2003); Helena Norberg-Hodge, "Globalisation and Terror," <www.isec.org.uk/articles/terror.html>. With regard to Rwanda, see Peter Uvin, *Aiding Violence: The Development Enterprise in Rwanda* (West Hartford, CT: Kumarian Press, 1998).

124 Edward Alden, "Globalisation Cited as Threat to U.S. Security," *Financial Times* (February 11, 2003).

ization and ethnic strife represent two interrelated components of a single process. "Globalization," states Vandana Shiva, "leads to the destruction of local economies and social organization, pushing people into insecurity, fear, and civil strife. The violence against people's livelihoods builds up into the violence of war."[125]

Shiva argues that economic globalization gives rise to widespread "homelessness," both physical (through various forms of displacement) and psychological. "The cumulative displacement caused by colonialism, development, and the global marketplace," says Shiva, "have made homelessness a cultural characteristic of the late twentieth century."[126] Shiva and other critics of development and globalization put great stress upon rootedness and upon the priority of the local, seeking in various ways to "reclaim the commons" that have been usurped through processes of enclosure.[127]

RECLAIMING THE COMMONS: THE POSITIVE VISIONS OF DEVELOPMENT CRITICS

Grassroots critics of development view economic globalization and development as leading increasingly to the creation of a global monoculture, one which serves the interests of those global elites in whose hands economic and political power are being concentrated. Over against this global dominance of capitalist economics and First World consumer culture, these critics emphasize the importance of the revitalization of local economies and traditional cultures. To name this

125 Shiva, *Biopiracy*, 117.

126 Shiva, "Homeless in the 'Global Village,'" in Shiva and Mies, *Ecofeminism*, 98.

127 Rootedness is especially crucial for indigenous peoples. "The state, the government, will never understand," asserts an elder of the Krenak tribe in India, "that we do not have another place to go. The only possible place for the Krenak people to live and to re-establish our existence, to speak to our Gods, to speak to our nature, to weave our lives is where God created us." Quoted in ibid., 104. Similarly, Surendra Biruli of the movement against the Suvarnarekha dam in India states: "Our links with our ancestors are the basis of our society and of the reproduction of our society. Our children grow up playing around the stones which mark the burial sites of our ancestors. They learn the ways of our ancestors. Without relating to our ancestors, our lives lose all meaning. They talk of compensation. How can they compensate us for the loss of the very meaning of our lives?" Quoted in ibid., 101.

positive vision some speak of "reclaiming the commons."[128] Others speak of "regeneration," highlighting the need for processes of change that build upon the best in local communities and cultures, while changing those features that are harmful. Much emphasis is placed upon grassroots participation in economic and political decision-making, including participation by indigenous peoples, women, small farmers, and others who often in the past have been excluded. Emphasis is also placed upon respect for local forms of knowledge, respect for local ecology, and the meeting of needs using predominantly local or regional resources.

With regard to material goods, sufficiency rather than affluence is set forth as the goal to be achieved. Critics reject consumerism and instead focus on values such as community, solidarity, meaningful work, spiritual growth, artistic creativity, and a harmonious relationship with the rest of nature. Majid Rahmena, for example, speaks of "the ideal of a livelihood based on the age-old moral principles of simplicity, frugality, sufficiency and respect for every human being and all forms of life."[129] Stress is placed upon meeting needs whenever possible through non-market means, though an important role for well-regulated markets is affirmed. In the realm of spirituality and values, it is asserted that the contemporary world has much to learn from traditional cultures, including the importance of values such as community, respect for elders, and respect for the natural world. Similarly, it is claimed that much can be learned from the practical skills of traditional cultures, especially in fields such as agriculture, medicine, psychology, architecture, law, and conflict resolution.[130]

While these critics of development highlight many positive features of traditional cultures, it is crucial to emphasize that they are *not* calling for a return to the past or rejecting modernity in its entirety. They realize that a return to past cultural forms is neither possible nor desirable. Central features of many traditional cultures, such as

---

128 For a good discussion of the meaning of "reclaiming the commons," see Ecologist, *Whose Common Future?*, especially chapter 6.

129 Majid Rahnema, "Poverty," in *Development Dictionary*, ed. W. Sachs, 171.

130 For an excellent discussion of traditional cultures and the insights and skills that they can offer to the contemporary world, see Thierry Verhelst, *No Life Without Roots: Culture and Development* (London: Zed Books, 1990).

subordinate roles for women, need to be challenged and changed, and dialogue with modernity can be helpful in this process. In any case, contact with modernity is inevitable. What these critics of development suggest is the need for a "critical traditionalism" or the creation of "alternative forms of modernity" which are rooted in, but not identical to, traditional cultures.[131] Thierry Verhelst states:

> It is not a question of rejecting modernity *a priori* nor of returning to the past, accrediting it with unconditional value just as one had once done with Western-style progress. Rather, what is necessary... is that the cultural communities who need it work towards new, *sui generis* conceptions of modernity....Far from being some kind of folk revival, it is a question of sinking to the bottom in order to rise again and, if necessary, evolve and change. For change is often the price cultural communities must pay to remain what they are....This 'recourse to sources' is no Rousseauesque dream but a burst of life to regenerate oneself.[132]

Similarly, Denis Goulet acknowledges that traditional cultures must undergo change, but asserts that this change need not imply westernization. "Something is wrong," Goulet states, "if traditional societies can gain access to modernity only by committing value suicide. The wiser course is to view traditional wisdoms as harboring latent dynamisms capable of giving birth to new indigenous forms of modernity."[133] Ashis Nandy speaks of the need for "critical traditionalism," citing the views of Gandhi as an exemplary case. Gandhi was deeply rooted in traditional wisdom and was opposed to many central features of modernity, but he was nonetheless willing to strongly criticize aspects of his own tradition, such as the practice of untouchability. "Gandhi's frame," says Nandy, "was traditional, but he was willing to criticize some traditions violently. He was even willing to include in his frame

131 The term "critical traditionalism" is used in Ashis Nandy, "Cultural Frames for Social Transformation: A Credo," *Alternatives* 12 (1987): 125-152. For discussion of the need for "alternative forms of modernity," see Verhelst, *No Life Without Roots*, 56.

132 Verhelst, *No Life Without Roots*, 62.

133 Denis Goulet, "Economic Systems, Middle Way Theories, and Third World Realities," in *Readings in Moral Theology #5: Official Catholic Social Teaching*, ed. Richard McCormick and Charles Curran (New York: Paulist, 1986), 355.

elements of modernity as critical vectors."[134] "Some aspects of some exogenous traditions of criticism," asserts Nandy, "can be accommodated in non-Western terms within the non-Western civilizations."[135] Nandy contends also that traditional cultures generally contain numerous resources with critical potential, resources that often have been relatively unexplored. He therefore argues that to speak of the importance of traditional cultures is not to appeal to an unchanging or unchangeable entity. It is rather to appeal to certain core values and insights that are manifest in different ways in different contexts, and which are capable of being enhanced through dialogue with those outside the tradition.

While critics of development place a strong emphasis on the local and on the particularity of traditions (opposing the idea of a homogeneous global culture), they are very careful to highlight the differences between their views and the views of ethnic fundamentalists who assert the value of their own traditions in ways that lead to the harming of others through discrimination or violence. Wolfgang Sachs, for example, speaks of "cosmopolitan localism" to describe the ideal he espouses, and he and other critics stress the importance of solidarity among disparate local communities who are all engaged in similar struggles against the forces of enclosure.[136]

Critics of development recognize that their vision of "reclaiming the commons" or "regeneration" based on the insights of traditional cultures will be dismissed by proponents of westernization, development, and industrial progress as being unrealistic or anachronistic, an attempt to turn back the hands of time. Jeremy Seabrook, author of *Victims of Development: Resistance and Alternatives*, responds to this criticism. His thoughts are worth quoting at length:

> [I]n the late twentieth century, more and more people have been looking at the values of indigenous peoples, tribal communities, forest dwellers, subsistence farmers who, they feel, have something vital to say to the world....This does not mean trying to live like these peoples; such an ambition would be clearly impossible; but it involves seeing how the values they bear may be applied in our own, very different, context....

---

134 Nandy, "Cultural Frames," 116.

135 Ibid., 117.

136 For Sach's discussion of "cosmopolitan localism" see "One World," in *Development Dictionary*, ed. W. Sachs, 112.

> The desire to conserve what is good is not a question of going back to the past, least of all to a mythical one of harmony and stability. It is a questions of taking from cultures that have endured precious lessons in self-reliance and sufficiency, and bringing these back to the wasting, threatened world whose resource-base must sustain us all. The advocates of industrialism without end are the ones leading us into a mythic world, for theirs is a figment, maintained by faith that science and technology will deliver human beings from the consequences of their own actions. This is clearly a project based on faith; one that has strayed from the realm of religion. The branding of conservation as nostalgia is an attempt to clear all obstructions on the path to a development to which human purposes and values have become the real 'externalities.'
>
> Sustainability in the lexicon of the West now means sustaining Western privilege. This means preserving a form of wealth-creation that diminishes us and tears humanity apart by the monstrous inequalities it imposes, at the same time as it culls the forest and mines the oceans, guts the earth and extinguishes civilizations, destroying all value and values but those that can be measured in money....
>
> It can be seen that the victims of 'development,' and those who resist it are not merely residuals, being swept aside by the forces of progress or history or any other serviceable abstraction. They are articulating a powerful and growing, if subterranean, feeling that economics, and the 'development' that serves it, are blunt instruments with which to beat humanity into submission and silence, and to compel us into forms of 'improvement' that impoverish and disempower.
>
> A new, dynamic mix of energies is emerging....The aim...is sufficiency for all, a space for human ingenuity and creativity to find answers and to fulfil our own and each others' needs....It is an extraordinary moment. Our allies in the adventure of reclaiming human development from wealth-creation are everywhere, if we know how to recognize them and join with them in their struggles, which, in the end, are ours also.[137]

CATHOLIC SOCIAL TEACHING, THE RADICAL TRADITION, AND DEVELOPMENT CRITICS

The thought of critics of development contains numerous important insights. While these critics at times make some deliberately provoca-

137 Seabrook, *Victims of Development*, 248-250.

tive and perhaps inadequately nuanced assertions, their fundamental concerns regarding the negative impacts of current development models on human life and on ecological integrity are profound, and their criticisms of modern science and inappropriate forms of technology very challenging and compelling. Likewise, their vision of grassroots alternatives, which will be explored more fully in the next chapter, has much to offer to the quest for positive forms of social change.

There are a variety of ways in which both the radical tradition and the tradition of Catholic Social Teaching could be enhanced through dialogue with the grassroots critics of development. The radical tradition and the grassroots critics of development share much in common, such as their critiques of colonialism and imperialism and their negative assessments of current forms of economic globalization. The area in which the they most strongly differ concerns the positive vision for the future that each tradition holds. According to the grassroots critics of development, the radical tradition has too uncritically accepted the ideal of industrialism and high levels of economic growth as the goal to be achieved, ignoring many of the negative social and ecological impacts of this growth. Likewise, it has been too dismissive of the values and insights of traditional Third World cultures. Radical critiques of modernizationist views of development, such as that represented by dependency theory, have in fact largely accepted the modernizationists' views of the desired society, i.e. a highly industrialized society with material abundance for all. They have simply argued that the specific policies favored by modernizationists would lead not to this goal but would lead instead to increased inequality and dependency. The radicals have sought alternative ways of achieving these same goals, e.g. through socialism or radical populism. Cristovam Buarque states:

> These dependency theorists maintained industrial development, along the lines of that implemented in developed countries, as the prime objective. They were against the country's economic dependence but adopted a dependent stance in defining the objectives of the independent economy they propounded....They denounced poor countries' economic exploitation as the source of backwardness in Third World societies but were blind to the fact that the definition of progress (and so also of backwardness) employed in

> their analysis was formulated on the basis of the cultural dependence to which they themselves were prone.[138]

Numerous dependency theorists have come to accept the legitimacy of this critique. Andre Gunder Frank, considered to be one of the founders of dependency theory, states:

> I quarreled with these orthodoxies [i.e. the modernizationist views] more about their vision of underdevelopment than with their idea of development itself. I did not find it remarkable that all also shared an essentially similar vision of 'capital accumulation through industrial growth equals development.' So did I![139]

Another dependency theorist, Herb Addo, stresses the importance of key insights of the grassroots critics of development:

> It is the survival strategies of the people that radical discourse should have looked into from the beginning. But the belief in the desirability and feasibilities of the developmentalist route of industrialization blinded us all to this. We criticized the thoughts of the 'pioneers of development' but did not critique them. We shared in common with them their epistemological assumptions: development equals Westernization via industrialization. We did not even pause to question the desirability and the feasibility of this vulgar equation.[140]

As to the tradition of Catholic Social Teaching, there are again many areas of overlap with the views of the grassroots critics of development. There exists, for example, a shared critique of structural injustice, as well as a shared critique of overly economistic and overly

---

138 Cristovam Buarque, *The End of Economics? Ethics and the Disorder of Progress* (London: Zed Books, 1993), 47. Similarly, with regard to dependency theory, Robert Vachon states: "Certainly, we must make people aware of the structures of dependence and of the external domination exercised by multinationals and governments. But the heart of the problem will remain untouched unless we are aware of the network of internal dependence and domination exercised by modern Western culture itself." Quoted in Verhelst, *No Life Without Roots*, 18.

139 Andre Gunder Frank, "The Underdevelopment of Development," in *The Underdevelopment of Development: Essays in Honor of Andre Gunder Frank*, ed. Sing Chew and Robert Denemark (Thousand Oaks, CA: Sage, 1996), 26.

140 Herb Addo, "Developmentalism: A Eurocentric Hoax, Delusion, and Chicanery," in ibid., 142.

individualistic views of society and of the human person. The CST vision of integral development–with its stress on the social, cultural, and spiritual dimensions of the human person, its emphasis on broad grassroots participation in public life, its growing concern for ecology, and its call for simpler lifestyles in the First World–coincides well with the views of grassroots development critics. Yet there are certain ambiguities in the CST tradition, and areas in which dialogue with the critics of development could lead to a deepening of insights.

One area in which CST could be strengthened is in its reflections on the desirability of following the First World model of industrialization. There exists in CST, for example, a strand of thought that is quite sympathetic to the industrial model of development. We have seen in the earlier chapter on CST that Pope John XXIII saw the solution to Third World poverty to lie largely in the transfer of "modern industrial techniques" from the First World to the Third World in order to overcome the "primitive state" of Third World economies. (MM 68, 163) Pope John speaks very positively of "science," "technology," "prosperity," and "progress," (MM 246) terms and realities that development critics find very problematic in the forms that they have historically taken. Yet Pope John also asserts that the particular cultural traditions of Third World nations should be respected. (MM 169-170, PT 125) The pope fails to address, however, the ways in which the imposition of modern technologies and modern forms of economic and social organization serve to undermine local cultures, and largely fails to address many of the negative social and ecological impacts of the modern industrial model of development that are highlighted by grassroots development critics. Similarly, later CST documents continue to both express support for modern industrial development and to urge respect for local cultures, generally not addressing in any depth the contradictions involved. Until quite recently even the issues raised by those who criticize the inappropriate nature of much First World technology for Third World contexts were largely unaddressed in CST.

A second major area in which CST could be enhanced in dialogue with grassroots critics of development concerns its vision of ecological issues. While ecological issues have come to play a more central role in CST in the past several decades, the framework adopted has been to a large extent what development critics would characterize as a "managerial" view of ecology, with a strong emphasis on the human call from

God "to subdue, to dominate" the earth for human purposes. (LE 4) Reflections such as those of Vandana Shiva concerning the need for a fundamental moral change in the way humans relate to the rest of creation contain important insights that CST could learn from.

Reflections on the desirability of First World models of industrialization, on the nature of contemporary science, and on ecological issues are thus several major areas in which CST could be enhanced through dialogue with critics of development. Additional areas for enrichment include recognition of the crucial importance of grassroots action in bringing about social change and greater attention to the role of women in the global economy and in social change processes.

As in the case of some of the radical political economists discussed above, CST has in the last couple decades moved closer to some of the positions held by the grassroots critics of development. In several recent documents–especially John Paul II's "The Ecological Crisis: A Common Responsibility" (1990) and the U.S. Catholic Bishops' *Renewing the Earth: An Invitation to Reflection and Action on Environment in Light of Catholic Social Teaching* (1991)–an important deepening of reflection of ecological, cultural, and technological issues has occurred. Much more attention is given, for example, to the social and ecological problems caused by modern technologies, greater appeal is made to the insights of traditional cultures, and the need to respect the integrity of creation apart from its usefulness to humans is increasingly affirmed.

In the final chapter of this book the deepening of CST with regard to cultural, technological, and ecological issues will be further explored, along with additional reflections on the relationship between CST and development critics. Before continuing this discussion, however, it seems important to look more closely at the alternatives that critics of development propose. These suggested alternatives will be the topic of the next chapter.

CHAPTER 6

GRASSROOTS ACTION AND POLICY ALTERNATIVES

The preceding chapter examined some of the major critiques of development and of neoliberal globalization that are put forth by grassroots critics. The current chapter will explore the visions and activities of organizations engaged in the quest for alternatives. An overview of some of the local, national, and international policies that are needed to support the construction of these positive alternatives will also be presented.

GRASSROOTS ORGANIZATIONS IN THE THIRD WORLD: AN OVERVIEW

Throughout the Third World there are a multitude of organizations that are seeking to overcome destitution, foster respect for human rights, protect and restore local ecology, revitalize local cultures, and pursue other constructive social goals.[1] These grassroots organizations take a wide variety of forms. They include peasant associations, worker associations, religious groups, neighborhood associations, women's groups, student organizations, associations of indigenous peoples, co-

1 Good descriptions of the activities of grassroots organizations around the world can be found in Ximena de la Barra and Richard Dello Buono, *Latin America after the Neoliberal Debacle: Another Region Is Possible* (Lanham, MD: Rowman & Littlefield, 2009); Marjorie Mayo, *Global Citizens: Social Movements and the Challenge of Globalization* (London: Zed Books, 2005); Frances Moore Lappé and Anna Lappé, *Hope's Edge* (New York: Jeremy P. Tarcher, 2002); Anirudh Krishna, Norman Uphoff, and Milton Esman, eds., *Reasons for Hope: Instructive Experiences in Rural Development* (West Hartford, CT: Kumarian Press, 1997); Jeremy Seabrook, *Pioneers of Change: Experiments in Creating a Humane Society* (London: Zed Books, 1993); Ponna Wignaraja, ed., *New Social Movements in the South: Empowering the People* (London: Zed Books, 1993); Paul Ekins, *A New World Order: Grassroots Movements for Global Change* (London: Routledge, 1992); Pierre Pradervand, *Listening to Africa: Developing Africa from the Grassroots* (New York: Praeger, 1989).

operatives, human rights organizations, and others. The sections that follow will briefly explore some of these groups and their activities.

RURAL/AGRICULTURAL ORGANIZATIONS

Organizations based in the countryside are among the most common grassroots organizations in the Third World. Much effort on the part of these groups is directed at improving agricultural performance in ecologically viable ways and working to overcome the negative environmental impacts of past development policies. Activities frequently center around the rediscovery or revitalization of traditional farming methods, often enhanced by modern innovations in the practice of sustainable agriculture.[2] Other common activities include reforestation efforts, infrastructural projects, efforts to expand non-agricultural forms of rural income, health and education projects, and work for the implementation of governmental policies more favorable to the interests of small farmers.[3] Several examples of widespread, successful peasant organizations include the Naam peasant movement and the 6-S association from the Sahel region of Africa and the Sarvodaya Shramadana village-based movement in Sri Lanka.

2 Common practices include the use of natural forms of soil fertilization, intercropping, crop diversification, various forms of agroforestry, the utilization of non-chemical means of pest control, the planting of seeds adapted to local ecosystems, measures to prevent soil erosion and desertification, measures to promote water conservation and availability, and the employment of draft animals. The use of draft animals leads to increased efficiency over the exclusive use of hand tools while avoiding the economic and ecological problems often associated with tractor usage in Third World contexts, such as high equipment costs, dependence on costly and environmentally harmful fossil fuels, the unavailability of spare parts, soil compaction, exacerbation of soil erosion, and significantly decreased employment opportunities for farm laborers. For good discussions of rural movements employing these agroecological practices, see Krishna, et al., *Reasons for Hope*; Pradervand, *Listening to Africa*.

3 The quest for land reform is often central to the advocacy efforts of rural organizations. In some cases the struggle for land reform includes the occupation of idle land by landless peasants. For a discussion of the extensive land takeovers that have occurred in Brazil, see Wendy Wolford and Angus Wright, *To Inherit the Earth: The Landless Movement and the Struggle for a New Brazil* (Oakland, CA: Food First Books, 2003).

Naam and 6-S

The Naam and 6-S movements are active in numerous African countries, including Burkina Faso, Senegal, Mali, Togo, Niger, and Mauritania.[4] Naam was founded in Burkina Faso in the late 1960s as a rural self-help movement, based upon the youth associations (*naam*) of traditional village life. These groups were adapted to become what is now widely recognized as "unquestionably one of the most significant success stories of contemporary African development."[5] Respecting and building upon the strengths in traditional culture, the Naam groups have engaged in a wide range of activities including soil regeneration, soil and water conservation, reforestation, agroforestry, communal farming projects, the encouragement of local savings, construction projects (including the building of schools, maternity centers, storage facilities, communal grain banks, wells, and small dams), and various projects in the areas of health, skills development, income-generation, and literacy. In addition, the Naam groups join together in national and regional alliances to lobby for governmental policies supportive of small farmers. There were by the early 2000s over 5,000 Naam and affiliated village groups in Burkina Faso, with over 500,000 members. Throughout the Sahel there are estimated to be between 15,000 and 20,000 village peasant organizations with several million members.

B. L. Ouedraogo, the founder of the Naam movement, stresses that overcoming negative self-images among African farmers has been a key factor in the success of the Naam groups:

> When we first started organizing the farmers in a way more in line with their own traditions, the farmers felt completely lost. They were afraid of being themselves. They had been convinced that their traditional attitudes were 'bad' and that they themselves were savages....One had to convince them that their real identity as African farmers was legitimate, that it was just and good for them....The main issue is self-confidence. Earlier people had managed to con-

4 For discussion of the Naam groups, the 6-S association, and an array of other grassroots movements in Africa, see Pradervand, *Listening to Africa*. Also see Bernard Lecomte and Anirudh Krishna, "Six-S: Building Upon Traditional Social Organizations in Francophone West Africa," in *Reasons for Hope*, 75-90.

5 Pradervand, *Listening to Africa*, 21.

> vince them that their culture was worthless....We have now managed to get rid of this false self-image.[6]

Discussing the importance of the Naam groups, Pierre Pradervand states:

> The Naams represent the triumph of the idea of 'development without harming' (to use an expression dear to B. L. Ouedraogo). The Naam is a form of development adapted to local needs, created by the people themselves, which instead of destroying traditional structures from the outside, slowly, like leaven, transforms them from the inside....It starts with what people *are* (based on a true appreciation of their African identity), what they *know* (respect for traditional knowledge and values...), their *know-how* (rediscovery of traditional techniques, some of which, for example in the field of water and soil conservation, have proven invaluable), and what they *wish to achieve* (which implies meaningful grassroots participation in defining the very objectives of the development process). The implications of this experiment reach far beyond the frontiers of Africa.[7]

The 6-S organization was formed in order to provide training and funding for village groups such as the Naam.[8] The village groups are provided with "flexible funding" in the form of grants or loans to be used to meet locally determined priorities.[9] Local groups receive funding, however, only after demonstrating their capacity (with training and technical assistance from 6-S) to organize their community, generate local savings, and carry out successful grassroots development projects based on their own resources. This requirement assures that local, participatory organizational structures are in place and that the groups will be able to utilize the 6-S funding in constructive, responsible ways.

---

6 Quoted in ibid., 74.

7 Ibid., 22. Emphasis in original.

8 The formal name of the 6-S organization is "Se Servir de da Saison Sèche en Savane et au Sahel," generally translated into English as "The Association for Self-Help during the Dry Season in the Savannahs and the Sahel."

9 Funding for 6-S is provided in part by foreign, particularly Scandinavian, aid agencies. Decisions concerning the distribution and use of the funds, however, are largely the responsibility of participatory, decentralized local organizational structures.

Pierre Pradervand describes the positive impact of the 6-S and Naam movements and related community organizations:

> For the past 10 to 15 years, Africa has seen remarkable developments....New energies, new experiences, a burst of creativity, a courage defying explanation are being manifested by millions of people. In the villages, especially, a silent revolution is underway that is completely changing the continent's development landscape. In tropical Africa...literally millions of farmers have moved to take their future into their own hands and to reclaim the self-reliance that was theirs until the disruption of colonial occupation and the post-Independence era of rapid modernization. As the result of the tens of thousands of small village projects that they have initiated, these farmers are improving their own living conditions, sometimes with no outside help. In many areas, village self-help groups are joining together to create powerful organizations, which for the first time can speak out in their own interest....This book (*Listening to Africa: Developing Africa from the Grassroots*) has been written to stand as a record of this silent revolution that could be the greatest sign of hope in Africa today.[10]

Sarvodaya Shramadana

The Sarvodaya Shramadana movement has worked for five decades attempting to foster an alternative model of development in Sri Lanka.[11] Founded in 1958 by A.T. Ariyaratne, Sarvodaya (which translates as "the awakening of all" or "the uplift of all") is a grassroots, village-based development movement founded upon Buddhist and Gandhian principles seeking to bring about spiritual and social renewal. The movement is centered upon the activity of work camps (called *shramadana*) in which persons join together to share their labor for the well-being of their village. Common projects include digging wells, planting communal gardens, building latrines, and other socially useful tasks. During the work camp the participants also take part in

---

10 Pradervand, *Listening to Africa*, xiii-xiv.

11 For discussion of the Sarvodaya Shramadana movement, see George Bond, *Buddhism at Work: Community Development, Social Empowerment, and the Sarvodaya Movement* (Bloomfield, CT: Kumarian Press, 2004); George Bond, "A.T. Ariyaratne and the Sarvodaya Shramadana Movement in Sri Lanka," in *Engaged Buddhism: Buddhist Liberation Movements in Asia*, ed. Christopher Queen and Sallie King (Albany: SUNY Press, 1996), 121-146; Ekins, *New World Order*, 100-111.

sessions in which Buddhist-inspired teachings are shared.[12] Song and drama play an important role in Sarvodaya activities. The goal of the movement is a dual one of personal awakening and social uplift. "The struggle for external liberation," says Ariyaratne, "is a struggle for inner liberation from greed, hatred and ignorance at the same time."[13]

For the Sarvodaya movement, which seeks to reconstruct society based on Buddhist/Gandhian values, the western model of economic development is viewed as something to be avoided rather than pursued. "In production-centered societies," says Ariyaratne, "the total perspective of human personality and sustainable relationships between [humans] and nature is lost sight of....The higher ideals of human personality and social values are disregarded."[14] With regard to western societies, Ariyaratne states: "We don't want to reach where they are. Instead we believe in a spiritual foundation, moral relationships, small economic and political organizations in a highly decentralized but coordinated way."[15] He sets forth the ideal of a village-based society characterized by "nonviolence, sharing, smallness, decentralization, relevant technologies, production by the masses, and unity."[16]

During the 1960s and 1970s the activities of Sarvodaya spread throughout much of the Sri Lankan countryside. By 1985 it was active in over 8,000 villages (about one-third of the villages in the country), had a staff of thousands of employees and volunteers, and involved approximately 3 million people in its activities. It received international acclaim as one of the world's largest and most successful grassroots development movements. Rooted in its village organizations, and aided by funding from foreign donors, it was able to undertake

12 It is important to note that while its values are derived in part from Buddhist principles, the Sarvodaya movement makes every effort not to be sectarian. Non-Buddhist Tamils, for example, have been active participants in the movement and have occupied leadership positions. This is of crucial significance in light of the recent violent conflicts between the Buddhist Sinhalese and non-Buddhist Tamil ethnic groupings within Sri Lanka. Having members from both ethnic groups, Sarvodaya has sought to be a mediating force in the conflict.

13 A.T. Ariyaratne, *In Search of Development: The Sarvodaya's Effort to Harmonize Tradition with Change* (Sri Lanka: Sarvodaya Press, 1982), 16.

14 Quoted in Bond, "Ariyaratne and Sarvodaya," 131.

15 Ariyaratne, "Waking Everybody Up," in *Engaged Buddhist Reader*, ed. Arnold Kotler (Berekeley: Parallax Press, 1996), 93-94.

16 Quoted in Bond, "Ariyaratne and Sarvodaya," 132.

projects in "nutrition, health, education, housing, water supply and sanitation, irrigation, agriculture, communication, savings and credit, rural industries and marketing, legal aid, institutional building and spiritual-moral development. In short...an integrated rural awakening programme."[17]

In recent years, Sarvodaya has suffered various setbacks. These have included the impact of ethnic violence within Sri Lanka (rooted in part in the flawed development policies that the government has pursued),[18] attacks on the movement by the Sri Lankan government,[19] and a reduction in funding from foreign aid agencies.[20] Despite these setbacks, however, the movement continues its work seeking to foster reconciliation and alternative forms of development in its troubled country. It remains one of the most discussed and numerically strong of the world's grassroots development movements.

URBAN-BASED COMMUNITY PROJECTS

Like rural-based projects, urban-based community projects in the Third World also take a variety of forms. Among them are neighborhood efforts to obtain basic services from the government such as potable water, sanitation, and electricity; crime prevention activities; community gardening projects; communal kitchens; recreation projects; cooperative day care projects; and various projects in the areas of income-generation, health, and education. Several inspiring examples of urban community organization include the cases of Villa El Salvador in Lima, Peru and the Orangi Pilot Projects near Karachi, Pakistan.

17 This list is provided by A.T. Ariyaratne, cited in Ekins, *New World Order*, 101.

18 Ariyaratne attributes the violence largely to western-inspired development policies that have destroyed much of the social, moral, and cultural fabric of the country. For Ariyaratne's discussion of the violence, see "Waking Everybody Up," 96-7. Also Bond, "Ariyaratne and Sarvodaya," 134-142.

19 These attacks have been directed against both the movement itself and Ariyaratne personally, both being perceived as threats to the government's power and popularity. See Bond, "Ariyaratne and Sarvodaya."

20 Various factors have contributed to this reduced funding, including the fact that the official aid agencies of Sarvodaya's major donor nations (mostly Western European and Scandinavian countries) came under the influence in the 1980s of persons with more neoliberal leanings who have been less sympathetic to some of Sarvodaya's major goals. For details, see ibid.

Villa El Salvador

Villa El Salvador is a squatter community located on the outskirts of Lima, Peru. The community contains an extensive network of women's groups, neighborhood associations, and other grassroots groups. Reinforced by the support of a progressive local mayor, the residents of Villa El Salvador have engaged in an impressive array of community development projects. They have, for example, planted over a half million trees, built 26 schools and 150 day care centers, organized 300 community kitchens, and trained hundreds of door-to-door health workers. Despite extreme poverty and a growing population, illiteracy has fallen to 3% and the infant mortality rate in the community is 40% below the national average.[21]

Orangi Pilot Projects

The settlement of Orangi, located on the outskirts of Karachi, Pakistan, is one of the largest squatter communities in Asia. It has a population of around a million persons. Orangi Pilot Projects (OPP) was formed in 1980 to pursue development based upon self-help and community organization within this settlement.[22] The organization undertakes research to find low-cost solutions to problems identified by the community, and then trains and organizes community members to implement these solutions. The first major project was the provision of low-cost sanitation, financed and carried out by Orangi residents themselves. OPP has since gone on to establish other programs in the areas of low-cost housing (using traditional building materials), health, and the provision of credit for family-based enterprises. It has also established women's work centers and a schools program. Akhter Hameed Khan, one of the founders of OPP, states:

> We are all living through a period of social dislocation. There is a need to re-establish a sense of belonging, the community feeling,

---

21 For information on Villa El Salvador, see Durning, *Action at the Grassroots: Fighting Poverty and Environmental Decline* (Washington, DC: Worldwatch Institute, 1989), 23; José Tavara, "Development Strategies in Latin America: Which Way Now?," in *Creating A New World Economy*, ed. Gerald Epstein, Julie Graham, and Jessica Nembhard (Philadelphia: Temple University Press, 1993), 398-399.

22 For a discussion of the Orangi Pilot Projects, see Akhter Hameed Khan, "The Orangi Pilot Project: Uplifting a Periurban Settlement Near Karachi, Pakistan," in *Reasons for Hope*, 25-40; Ekins, *New World Order*, 188-192.

> the conventions of mutual help and cooperative action, that can be done chiefly through the creation of many kinds of organisations, social and economic. Without such organisations, chaos and confusion will prevail. On the other hand, if social and economic organisations grow and become strong, services and material conditions, like sanitation, schools, clinics, training and employment will also begin to improve.[23]

INCOME-GENERATION AND CREDIT PROJECTS

Projects focusing upon the generation of income are crucial throughout the Third World. Central to these projects are various forms of training. This training often includes literacy education, an introduction to the basics of accounting and management, and programs teaching applied skills such as animal husbandry, agriculture, small-scale manufacturing and repair, and other crafts and trades. The provision of small-scale credit plays a major role in most of these projects, as often does the formation of production, distribution, and service cooperatives. One of the most well-known organizations concerned with credit provision and income-generation is the Grameen Bank of Bangladesh.[24]

The Grameen Bank

The Grameen Bank has received widespread international attention for its work in making credit available to the poor of Bangladesh, especially poor women.[25] The Bank was begun in 1976 by Muhammad Yunus, an economics professor frustrated with the unwillingness of conventional banks to loan to persons without collateral. By 2006 the borrower-owned Bank had 2185 branches serving over 69,000 Ban-

23 Quoted in Ekins, *New World Order*, 189.

24 Some other inspiring examples of organizations focusing on income generation and credit include the Bangladeshi Rural Advancement Committee and the Working Women's Forum of India. Paul Ekins discusses both of these organizations in *New World Order*, 116-122.

25 For discussion of the Grameen Bank, see Muhammad Yunus, "The Grameen Bank Story: Rural Credit in Bangladesh," in *Reasons for Hope*, 9-24; David Bornstein, *The Price of A Dream: The Story of the Grameen Bank and the Idea That Is Helping the Poor to Change Their Lives* (New York: Simon and Schuster, 1996).

gladeshi villages with over 6 million borrowers.[26] About 90% of its clients are women. Intensive training, group discussions, and consciousness-raising precede the making of loans, and groups are encouraged to adopt a sixteen-point program for social justice, group solidarity, and women's emancipation. The loans enable borrowers to avoid exploitation by local moneylenders and to engage in a wide variety of small-scale income-generating projects.

Extensive training and assistance and a system of group support/peer pressure have led to a repayment rate of over 98%, equal to or exceeding that of most conventional banks.

Muhammad Yunus, the founder of the Grameen Bank, stresses the importance of finding models for social and economic change appropriate to local cultures and conditions. In the past, he states, development policies throughout the Third World were formulated "with borrowed eyes," based on the perspective of economists and others from the First World. The projects of the Grameen Bank, he asserts, represent an attempt to see "with our own eyes."[27]

HEALTH PROJECTS

Grassroots organizations in the Third World engage in a variety of health-related activities. These include, for example, nutrition education, training in preventative and simple curative care (which often includes the use of herbs and other traditional forms of medicine), education concerning inexpensive life-saving measures such as oral rehydration therapy, and family-planning education. Often local community members with little formal education are trained as grassroots para-professionals (often termed "barefoot doctors") and these persons in turn take responsibility for educational efforts within their

26 Data is from the Grameen Bank's website at <www.grameen-info.org/bank>. The Grameen Bank is 75% owned by its borrowers, each borrower receiving one share in the Bank. The remaining 25% of shares are owned by the government of Bangladesh.

27 These quotations from Muhammad Yunus are contained in the video *Local Heroes, Global Change*, which also discusses other grassroots movements in the Third World. The video is available for free loan from Church World Service at <www.churchworldservice.org/film>.

communities. One example of a grassroots health project is the Gonoshasthaya Kendra health organization of Bangladesh.[28]

Gonoshasthaya Kendra

Gonoshasthaya Kendra (GK – "The People's Health Center") was founded by Zafrullah Chowdhury, a Bangladeshi doctor, in 1972. It has engaged in extensive training of para-professional community health workers, mostly women, who are taught a variety of simple health measures relevant to the needs of the poor. The outreach of these workers has contributed to infant mortality rates and maternal mortality rates in GK's service area that are significantly below the national average for Bangladesh. GK has also established a factory to produce high quality essential drugs at a low cost and uses the proceeds from drug sales to help fund its social programs. GK also engages in research and education devoted to herbal and homeopathic medicines. From its original health emphasis GK has expanded into a variety of projects in the areas of education, income-generation, agricultural outreach, and credit.[29]

EDUCATIONAL PROJECTS

Grassroots organizations in the Third World are frequently engaged in an array of educational projects, as seen in the examples discussed above. Literacy and adult education programs, religious education, and training in areas as diverse as health care, employment skills, and human rights are all common. In some cases grassroots organizations have formed their own schools for children and have sought to put into place models of education more suited to local cultures and social conditions than the education provided by government-sponsored

28 Another organization that has made extensive contributions to grassroots health care in the Third World is the U.S.-based Hesperian Foundation, publisher of *Where There is No Doctor: A Village Health Care Handbook*, rev. ed. (Palo Alto, CA: Hesperian Foundation, 1992). Over 2 million copies of this training manual for grassroots rural health workers have been distributed. The book has been translated into over 40 languages and is in use in community health efforts in over 150 countries. See Ekins, *New World Order*, 168-172.

29 For additional information concerning Gonoshasthaya Kendra, see Ekins, *New World Order*, 172-174.

schools. The popular school movement in Brazil is one example of such community-based schooling.

Brazilian Popular School Movement

In the shantytowns (*favelas*) surrounding Recife, Brazil the illiteracy rate approaches 50%. Unsatisfied with the government's efforts to provide adequate schooling, over 60 local *favelas* have founded their own schools. They use local youths as teachers and provide lessons that draw upon the rich traditional Brazilian and African cultural heritages of Recife's poor. "Our culture had been taken from us–traded for rock music and Coca-Cola," states Lucia de Prazeres, a community school director, "but in the schools we took it back. We discovered that reclaiming our culture gave us back our identity and gave us back our dignity. Learning is impossible if you don't believe in yourself." The community school movement in recent years has begun spreading to other regions of Brazil.[30]

HUMAN RIGHTS ORGANIZATIONS

Many countries in the Third World have suffered under the rule of dictatorial governments. These oppressive conditions have given rise to a variety of organizations whose main purpose is to foster respect for human rights. Prominent among these are the various organizations of relatives of the "disappeared" that were formed in Latin American countries during the 1970s and 1980s, including the *Grupo de Apoyo Mutuo* of Guatemala.[31] These groups have often been joined in the struggle for human rights and democratization by broad coalitions of unions, student groups, peasant organizations, women's organizations, urban community groups, indigenous organizations, base communities, and other grassroots organizations.

---

30 For information concerning the popular school movement in Brazil, see Durning, *Action at the Grassroots*, 24-25.

31 Other examples of human rights organizations include the Latin American network of Servicio Paz y Justicia (SERPAJ) groups, and various Catholic Church-sponsored human rights offices. See Philip McManus and Gerald Schlabach, *Relentless Persistence: Nonviolent Action in Latin America* (Philadelphia: New Society Publishers, 1991).

Grupo de Apoyo Mutuo

The *Grupo de Apoyo Mutuo* (GAM) is a group made up of relatives (mostly mothers and wives) of persons who have been "disappeared" by the military and right-wing death squads in Guatemala. Despite the assassination of several of their members, the bombing of their organization's office, and repeated death threats, the members of GAM have served as the conscience of a nation. At times when many others were too fearful to speak out, they courageously engaged in public witness to make known the reality of massive human rights abuses. Currently, GAM remains at the forefront of the struggle for reform and human rights in Guatemala, refusing to let the past be forgotten.[32]

WOMEN'S ORGANIZATIONS

Numerous organizations exist in the Third World which are devoted to fostering and protecting the rights of women. These organizations engage in activities such as consciousness-raising, literacy work, employment training, health education, advocacy of legal reforms and public policy changes, and the formation of mutual support groups. Among these organizations concerned with the well-being of women is the Self-Employed Women's Association (SEWA) in India.

Self-Employed Women's Association

SEWA is an organization composed of women who work in a vast array of jobs in the informal sector of the economy in India.[33] It is estimated that over half of the employment in India's major cities is in the informal sector, and the majority of informal sector workers are women. SEWA works to help these women earn a more secure living and to lessen the exploitation, abuse, and legal and social discrimination that poor women face. Activities include consciousness-raising, public demonstrations, collective bargaining, lobbying, leadership and skills development, the provision of credit and legal assistance, the formation of artisan, vendor, and service cooperatives, and the creation of

---

32 For information concerning the *Grupo de Apoyo Mutuo*, see Michelle Tooley, *Voices of the Voiceless: Women, Justice, and Human Rights in Guatemala* (Scottdale, PA: Herald, 1997).

33 For discussions of SEWA, see Ela Bhatt, *We Are Poor But So Many: The Story of Self-Employed Women in India* (New York: Oxford University Press, 2006); Kalima Rose, *Where Women are Leaders: The SEWA Movement in India* (London: Zed Books, 1992).

child care and health cooperatives. SEWA joins with other organizations concerned with the rights of women in addressing issues such as dowry, bride-burning, domestic violence, rape, the harassment of women by police, and the selective abortion of females.

ORGANIZATIONS FOR CULTURAL PRESERVATION

Numerous organizations of indigenous peoples exist throughout the world that are committed to struggling for indigenous rights (especially the right to land) and to preserving and fostering indigenous culture. This desire to preserve indigenous culture includes not only aspects of culture such as language, crafts, songs, folktales, and religious ceremonies but also traditional forms of social and economic organization, social values, and traditional knowledge in areas such as agriculture and medicine. Examples of organizations concerned with the preservation and revitalization of traditional cultures include the Naam groups (discussed above) and the Chipko movement in India.[34]

Chipko Movement

The Chipko movement began in the 1970s in the Himalayan region of India.[35] It consists primarily of village women who are dedicated to protecting local forests from destruction while preserving traditional ways of life that depend upon the ecological integrity of the forest community. Through acts of nonviolent resistance, including the embracing or hugging of trees (from which comes the name of the movement, *chipko,* a local word meaning "embrace"), the Chipko movement and similar groups have been able to significantly reduce the extent of logging in many regions of India. These groups have also been involved in a variety of other ecological and village improvement efforts.

---

34 Discussion of organizations concerned with indigenous rights and cultural preservation can be found in Verhelst, *No Life Without Roots;* Erick Langer and Elena Muñoz, *Contemporary Indigenous Movements in Latin America* (Wilmington, DE: SR Books, 2003).

35 For details concerning the Chipko movement, see Harsh Sethi, "Survival and Democracy: Ecological Struggles in India," in *New Social Movements in the South,* ed. P. Wignaraja, 127-128; Ekins, *New World Order,* 143-144. A video entitled "In the Name of Progress," part of the Race to Save the Planet video series, contains interviews with Chipko leaders. It can be obtained for free loan from the Mennonite Central Committee at <www.mcc.org/catalog>.

ORGANIZATIONS OPPOSING DESTRUCTIVE DEVELOPMENT PROJECTS

Numerous grassroots organizations have come into existence or have undertaken activities to oppose socially and ecologically destructive projects being carried out in the name of development. These destructive projects have included large dams, cattle ranching projects, ecologically unsound logging projects, monocultural forms of forestry, road building in ecologically sensitive areas, and others. Examples of groups opposing such projects are the Chipko movement (discussed above) and the rubber tappers' movement of Brazil.

The Rubber Tappers

Over 350,000 people make their living tapping rubber trees in the Amazon rainforest. This activity represents an ecologically sustainable use of the forest, since the rubber tappers can harvest rubber without damaging the trees. Local unions of rubber tappers began to form in the late 1970s, in response to widespread destruction of the rainforest by loggers, cattle ranchers, and displaced farmers. These unions have engaged in a variety of actions, including nonviolent blockades of logging operations and consciousness-raising concerning the value of the forest.[36] These activities have been met with violence by local landowners, including thousands of murders. Among the victims of these attacks was the internationally known rubber tapper union leader Chico Mendes, who was assassinated in 1988. Through an alliance with local indigenous organizations and with international environmental and social justice groups, the rubber tappers eventually succeeded in getting the Brazilian government to declare large sections of forest as "extractive reserves" to be managed by the rubber tappers. In these areas the rubber tappers are permitted to carry out their sustainable forest-based activities indefinitely, with (at least in principle, if not always in practice) governmental protection against illegal logging or other forest-destroying activities. This case highlights the crucial importance of

---

36 Information concerning the rubber tappers' movement can be found in Rich, *Mortgaging the Earth*, 127-132; Durning, *Action at the Grassroots*, 35-36. The rubber tappers are also featured in the documentary "In the Name of Progress" (discussed above) and in the movie "The Burning Season," which is based on the life and assassination of rubber tapper leader Chico Mendes.

building coalitions among grassroots organizations, both domestically and internationally, in order to achieve positive results.

ENVIRONMENTAL ORGANIZATIONS

Environmental concerns play an important role in the work being done by many different types of grassroots organizations in the Third World. This can be seen, for example, in the descriptions above of the Naam, Chipko, and rubber tappers' organizations. For the rural poor in the Third World the integrity of the environment and access to the resources that it provides (fertile land, clean water, forests, pasture) are central issues of livelihood. Often they are matters of life and death. One important movement addressing environmental issues is the Green Belt Movement of Kenya.

Green Belt Movement

The Green Belt Movement was founded in Kenya in 1977 by Wangari Maathai and the National Council of Women in response to serious problems resulting from deforestation.[37] Within a decade this grassroots movement composed primarily of women and school-age children had planted over 2 million trees in thousands of "green belts" throughout the country. These efforts continue, with over 30 million trees planted by 2004. The objectives of the movement are multifaceted. They include:

> avoiding desertification; promoting the ideas and creating public awareness of environment and development; providing fuelwood for energy; promoting a variety of trees for human and animal use; encouraging soil conservation and land rehabilitation; creating jobs in the rural areas especially for the handicapped and rural poor; creating self-employment opportunities for young people in agriculture; giving women the positive image appropriate to their leading role in development processes; promoting sound nutrition based on traditional foodstuffs; carrying out research in conjunction with academic institutions; developing a replicable methodology for rural development.[38]

---

37 For information on the Green Belt movement, see Ekins, *New World Order*, 151-152; Wangari Maathai, *The Green Belt Movement: Sharing the Approach and the Experience*, rev. ed. (New York: Lantern Books, 2004).

38 Ekins, *New World Order*, 151-152.

In carrying out its work, the Green Belt movement also became a leading voice for democracy in Kenya, challenging the corruption of the Kenyan government. In 2004 Wangari Maathai received the Nobel Peace Prize for her work with the Green Belt movement. It was the first time that an African woman was awarded the prize. Maathai subsequently was elected to the Kenyan parliament and was appointed Assistant Minister for Environment and Natural Resources by the Kenyan president. In announcing the awarding of the Nobel Peace Prize, the Nobel Committee highlighted Maathai's ability to foster awareness of the fundamental connections between ecology, the rights of women, democracy, and peace:

> Peace on earth depends on our ability to secure our living environment. Maathai stands at the front of the fight to promote ecologically viable social, economic and cultural development in Kenya and in Africa. She has taken a holistic approach to sustainable development that embraces democracy, human rights and women's rights in particular. She thinks globally and acts locally....She represents an example and a source of inspiration for everyone in Africa fighting for sustainable development, democracy and peace.[39]

RESEARCH AND ADVOCACY ORGANIZATIONS

Numerous organizations exist which are committed to research, education, and advocacy on issues of vital concern to grassroots movements in the Third World. Prominent among these organizations is the Third World Network.

Third World Network

The Third World Network (TWN) is an international network of groups and individuals devoted to articulating the needs and rights of Third World peoples, working for a more equitable distribution of the world's resources, and seeking alternative forms of development.[40] The Network highlights the need for development that is culturally-rooted, in harmony with nature, and that prioritizes the meeting of basic human needs. Based in Malaysia, TWN has branch offices and af-

39 The statement of the Nobel Committee can be found at <www.nobelprize.org/nobel_prizes/peace/laureates/2004/press.html>.

40 Information on the Third World Network can be found at <www.twnside.org.sg>.

filiated organizations in countries throughout the world. It publishes the daily *South-North Development Monitor*, the bi-monthly magazine *Third World Economics*, and a monthly magazine *Third World Resurgence*. The Network also publishes numerous books and reports, organizes workshops and seminars, and serves to represent the perspectives of Third World grassroots movements at international fora such as United Nations conferences. Key issues that the Network addresses include the impacts of the policies of the World Bank, IMF, and the WTO and the work of grassroots organizations that are seeking to resist and find alternatives to these policies.

THE IMPACT OF GRASSROOTS ORGANIZATIONS

The above overview provides but a small glimpse of the activities of the tens of thousands of grassroots organizations in the Third World that are attempting to create more just and ecologically sustainable societies. Through these grassroots efforts much has been accomplished. Millions of persons have been enabled to survive and to lead richer lives than otherwise would have been possible amidst the very difficult and challenging circumstances that they have faced. Richard Barnet and John Cavanagh, like many others, see global grassroots movements as being of vital importance:

> Local citizens' movements and alternative institutions are springing up all over the world to meet basic economic needs, to preserve local traditions, religious life, cultural life, biological species, and other treasures of the natural world, and to struggle for human dignity. Because the global economic and political systems are out of synch, and therefore unresponsive and unaccountable, people are staking out their own living space. Exiles from the new world order, they spend their lives building the small communities that give their lives meaning, establishing links with other communities with common interests....More and more people who are bypassed by the new world order are crafting their own strategies for survival and development, and in the process are spinning their own transnational webs to embrace and connect people across the world....[A] global civil society is beginning to take shape–mostly off camera. It is the only force we see that can break the global gridlock.[41]

41 Richard Barnet and John Cavanagh, *Global Dreams: Imperial Corporations and the New World Order* (New York: Simon and Schuster, 1994), 429-430.

A crucial issue to be explored is the relationship of these nongovernmental organizations to both local and foreign governments. Frequently these governments have either directly or indirectly opposed the work and the goals of these grassroots groups. Yet without supportive policies at the national and international levels, the potential for the widespread transformations that are so desperately needed is limited. Grassroots efforts all too often end up struggling against the tide of broader economic and political forces, working primarily to mitigate the harm caused by flawed development models. Alan Durning of the Worldwatch Institute highlights the critical importance of forming grassroots-government alliances:

> Despite the heartening rise of grassroots action, humanity is losing the struggle for sustainable development....The largest challenge in reversing global deterioration is to forge an alliance between local groups and national governments. Only governments have the resources and authority to create the conditions for full-scale grassroots mobilization....The difficulty in forging an alliance between powerful, often rigid institutions and the world's millions of enthusiastic but fragile community action groups can scarcely be underestimated, yet neither can its importance.[42]

Efforts to bring into existence governments supportive of alternative development approaches and efforts to hold governments accountable to the people are among the fundamental tasks of grassroots organizations and grassroots mobilization in the Third World. In those rare cases in which grassroots-government alliances in the Third World have occurred, significant accomplishments have followed. These accomplishments have included, for example, an ambitious anti-hunger program and reductions in child labor in Brazil, reductions in child mortality and increased school enrollment in Bangladesh, substantial improvements in child health and reduced child mortality in Tanzania, major improvements in literacy and health in the early years of the Sandinista government in Nicaragua, and a wide variety of positive social reforms in the Indian state of Kerala.[43]

---

42 Durning, *Action at the Grassroots*, 7, 50-51.

43 For information on Brazil's anti-hunger program undertaken after grassroots movements helped to elect the reformist Ignacio "Lula" da Silva as president, see <www.fao.org/english/newsroom/news/2003/13320-en.html>. For discussion of reductions in child labor in Brazil, see UNICEF, *State of the World's Children 2005*, 34. For discussion of Bangladesh, includ-

The case of Kerala is particularly instructive. Despite very low income levels, Kerala has some of the highest statistical indicators in the Third World in the areas of health, education, and social justice.[44] These accomplishments have resulted from the efforts of very active and vibrant grassroots organizations in alliance with supportive local governments, particularly communist-led coalition governments. This alliance has given rise to an array of social reforms and constructive governmental policies in areas such as land reform, food security, education (especially the education of women), sanitation, water provision, health care, and the abolition of untouchability. While many problems remain, impressive results have been achieved. As of the mid-1990s, Kerala had a per capita GDP of only $200, lower than the national average in India. Yet infant mortality (children dying by age one) was only 17 per 1,000 live births compared to a national average of 83; 87% of women were literate compared to a national average of only 34%; women's life expectancy was 74 years, compared to a national average of only 59 years; and the average number of births per woman was 1.9 compared to a national average of 4.0.[45] Statistics from the early 2000s show that Kerala's mortality rate for children under the age of five is 19 per thousand, in contrast to the average rate of 95 for India as a whole.[46]

---

ing the role of grassroots organizations, see UNDP, *Human Development Report 2005*, 46. For Tanzania, see Anirudh Krishna with Urban Jonsson and Wilbald Lorri, "The Iringa Nutrition Project: Child Survival and Development in Tanzania," in *Reasons for Hope*, 216-227. Good discussions of Nicaragua can be found in Dianna Melrose, *Nicaragua: The Threat of a Good Example?* (Boston: Oxfam, 1985); John Donahue, *The Nicaraguan Revolution in Health: From Somoza to the Sandinistas* (South Hadley, MA: Bergin and Garvey, 1986).

44 For information concerning Kerala, see Richard Franke and Barbara Chasin, *Kerala: Radical Reform as Development in an Indian State* (San Francisco: Institute for Food and Development Policy, 1989); V.K. Ramachandran, "On Kerala's Development Achievements," in *Indian Development*, ed. Jean Drèze and Amartya Sen (Delhi: Oxford University Press, 1997), 205-356.

45 The statistical data concerning Kerala is provided by UNICEF in its *State of the World's Children 1995*, 49. The final statistic concerning birth rates is often cited to support the claim that greater social justice a central element needed to constructively address high rates of population growth.

46 UNDP, *Human Development Report 2005*, 31.

In addition to supportive governmental policies at the local and national levels, a supportive international context is also crucial for the success of grassroots social change efforts. Currently, trends in the global economy (e.g. increased liberalization of trade, investment, and financial systems, Third World debt and structural adjustment policies, declining terms of trade for Third World products) threaten to undermine grassroots accomplishments. The impact of grassroots efforts, Alan Durning asserts, "is swamped by the global economic tide running against the poor....Over the long term, grassroots efforts will have to influence these broader forces if they are to do anything more than struggle against the tide."[47] Similarly, Kathy McAfee of Oxfam states:

> The economic success of individual cooperatives or micro-enterprises cannot provide a formula for development in the context of the continuing and deepening impoverishment of the South as a whole. Only far-reaching and fundamental structural changes can reverse the net outflow of human and natural resources from impoverished populations and indebted nations.[48]

DEVELOPMENT POLICIES: FOLLOW THE NIC MODEL?

If governmental policies supportive of grassroots efforts to create alternatives are needed, the question arises as to what these alternative policies would be. During the past two decades many persons have appealed to the example of the East Asian NICs (newly-industrialized countries, such as South Korea and Taiwan) as a development example for other Third World nations to follow. This appeal has been made both by neoliberals, who have sought to portray the NICs as a neoliberal success story, and by other more centrist or progressive theorists who have put forth the NICs as a positive alternative to neoliberalism. At the same time, there have been persons who have expressed strong criticism of the claim that the NICs do in fact represent a desirable development model. These critics highlight numerous negative features

47 Durning, *Action at the Grassroots*, 32.

48 Kathy McAfee, *Storm Signals: Structural Adjustment and Development Alternatives in the Caribbean* (Boston: Oxfam America, 1991), 244.

of the NIC experiences. They also challenge the claim that the NIC model can be successfully replicated by other Third World nations.[49]

Central to the claims of success for the NICs have been very high rates of economic growth. This growth has been based largely on strategies of export-oriented industrialization and it has been accompanied in most cases by significant reductions in poverty and by somewhat less severe rich-poor disparities than are prevalent in other parts of the Third World. Neoliberal theorists have argued that the NICs provide evidence of the value of open economies and economic liberalization, while demonstrating the folly of more inward-oriented development strategies such as import-substitution industrialization (ISI). Analysts have generally come to recognize, however, that the neoliberal interpretation of the NIC experience is highly flawed.[50] For example, neoliberals stress a very limited economic role for the state and highlight the importance of free trade. In most of the NICs, however, such as South Korea and Taiwan, the state played a central role and trade was highly regulated. The role of the state included shaping and directing investment decisions and instituting various measures to protect local industries from foreign competition. This protection from foreign competition was particularly important in the periods of inward-focused ISI which were essential in building the structural capacity for the later switch to a primary focus on industrial exports. The state also invested heavily in areas such as public education and health. In contrast, neoliberal structural adjustment and free trade policies prohibit most protection for local industries and have frequently led to reductions in spending on education, health, and other social services. As the United Nations Development Programme has stated, "The current WTO regime [with its emphasis on free trade] outlaws many of the policies that helped East Asian countries make rapid advances."[51] Redistributive measures that are opposed by neo-

49 For critiques of the NICs, see especially Walden Bello and Stephanie Rosenfeld, *Dragons in Distress: Asia's Miracle Economies in Crisis* (San Francisco: Institute for Food and Development Policy, 1990); Walden Bello, "The End of the Asian Miracle," *Nation* (January 12/19, 1998): 16-21.

50 For works which challenge the neoliberal interpretation and appropriation of the NIC experience, see Bello and Rosenfeld, *Dragons in Distress*; Haggard, *Pathways from the Periphery* (Ithaca, NY: Cornell University Press, 1990); Green, *Silent Revolution*, 178-188.

51 UNDP, *Human Development Report 2005*, 10.

liberals also played important roles in the NIC experiences. Extensive land reform in the 1950s in South Korea and Taiwan was particularly significant. These land reform measures reduced inequalities, lessened the economic and political power of local rural elites, and helped to build a strong domestic market as the initial engine of economic growth.

The evidence thus clearly seems to support a non-neoliberal interpretation of the NIC experiences. What remains highly disputed, however, are whether other nations can successfully follow the NIC model and whether it would be desirable for them to attempt to do so. With regard to the replicability of the NIC economic successes, some analysts (both those sympathetic to and those critical of the NICs) argue that unique features of the NIC experiences greatly diminish the likelihood that other nations could follow their example. These analysts stress, for instance, that the major NICs such as South Korea and Taiwan received huge quantities of economic aid from the United States as a result of their strategic importance in the anti-communist struggle. Such high levels of aid are no longer available. Analysts highlight also that the initial period of major growth of the NICs coincided with the Vietnam War, which created huge demand for goods within the East Asian region. Later policies in the United States (such as those which contributed to massive U.S. trade deficits during the 1980s) continued to stimulate large demand for NIC products. In contrast, however, the present international climate is characterized by stagnation in international demand for key NIC products and by increased competition for export markets on the part of countries such as China. These factors seriously diminish the potential for the success of export-oriented industrialization strategies. Analysts assert also that any nation that would attempt in the current international context to implement the non-neoliberal policies followed by the NICs would be ostracized by the IMF, the World Bank, and by the broader capitalist financial community, further undermining the potential of these nations for economic success.[52]

For all of the above reasons, the likelihood of new NICs is slim. Even if it were possible to follow the NIC model for economic growth,

52 With regard to the unlikelihood of new NICs arising, see Robin Broad and John Cavanagh, "No More NICs," *Foreign Policy* 72 (Fall 1988): 81-103. This essay is reprinted in *Creating a New World Economy*, ed. Epstein, et al., chapter 20.

however, many critics claim that it would not be desirable to do so. They argue that the economic growth of the NICs has come at a high social and ecological price. These critics highlight a history of severe repression of labor, widespread ecological damage,[53] the demise of small farmers,[54] the erosion of traditional cultures, and the authoritarian nature of most NIC governments as negative features of the NIC experiences. These critics have also argued that the economic successes of the NICs are themselves not sustainable, an argument that has been strengthened by the major economic crises that most of the East Asian NICs experienced in the late 1990s and early 2000s. This included major contraction in many NIC economies and significantly increased rates of unemployment, poverty, and hunger. Among the factors giving rise to the crises were the implementation of financial liberalization measures (part of the overall free trade agenda) which allowed huge amounts of unstable speculative capital to flow into the NICs. When the countries began to experience economic problems this capital was rapidly withdrawn, wreaking havoc on the NIC economies.[55]

ALTERNATIVE DEVELOPMENT POLICIES

If the policies of structural adjustment and the policies of the NICs are both problematic for the many reasons highlighted above, do feasible alternatives exist? Some grassroots critics of development refrain in principle from suggesting detailed policy changes. They express concern that an emphasis on policy tends to foster reliance on policymakers rather than on grassroots actors as the primary agents of social change. Nonetheless, even these critics do ultimately acknowledge the importance of policy changes. Their hesitancy to make policy suggestions, state the editors of *The Ecologist*, does not imply

> that one can ignore policy-makers or policy-making. The depredations of transnational corporations, international bureaucracies and national governments cannot be allowed to go unchallenged. But

53 For discussion of the ecological experiences of the NICs, see Bello and Rosenfeld, *Dragons in Distress*, 95-112, 195-214.

54 While NICs such as Taiwan and South Korea implemented policies very favorable to small farmers in the 1950s, including extensive land reform, policies since then have been increasingly harmful. See Bello and Rosenfeld, *Dragons in Distress*, 77-94, 183-194.

55 For insightful analysis of the economic crisis of the NICs, see Bello, "End of the Asian Miracle."

> the environmental [and social justice] movement has a responsibility to ensure that in seeking solutions, it does not remove the initiative from those who are defending their commons or attempting to regenerate commons regimes.[56]

While remaining cognizant of the primacy of grassroots efforts, the next section of this chapter will outline a general framework for alternative domestic and international policies. This section will draw on the work of researchers associated with institutions such as UNICEF, Oxfam, the Institute for Food and Development Policy, Third World Network, Development Alternatives with Women for a New Era (DAWN), and the International Forum on Globalization. Although these analysts differ in some of the particulars of their recommendations, they share many overall emphases.[57]

AN INWARD-ORIENTED ECONOMIC STRATEGY

In contrast to the structural adjustment and NIC approaches that have placed primacy on export production, alternative development approaches generally stress production to meet local needs. The expansion of the domestic market through land reform and other measures of economic redistribution plays a central role in these strategies. This approach, it should be noted, differs from the inward-oriented import substitution industrialization (ISI) model followed by some Third World nations in the past. For example, the ISI approach was generally conducted in the absence of redistributionist measures and therefore floundered upon inadequate levels of domestic demand.

56 Ecologist, *Whose Common Future?*, 197.

57 Some good books that explore suggested alternative policies at the international and domestic levels include Engler, *How to Rule the World*; Duncan Green, *From Poverty to Power: How Active Citizens and Effective States Can Change the World* (Oxford: Oxfam International, 2008); James Gustave Speth, *The Bridge at the Edge of the World: Capitalism, the Environment, and Crossing from Crisis to Sustainability* (New Haven, CT: Yale, 2008); John Cavanagh and Jerry Mander, eds., *Alternatives to Economic Globalization: A Better World is Possible*, 2nd ed. (San Francisco: Berrett-Koehler, 2004); Walden Bello, *Deglobalization: Ideas for a New World Economy* (London: Zed Books, 2002); David Korten, *When Corporations Rule the World*, 2nd ed. (San Francisco: Berrett-Koehler, 2001); Martin Khor, *Rethinking Globalization: Critical Issues and Policy Choices* (London: Zed Books, 2001); Gerald Epstein, Julie Graham, and Jessica Nembhard, eds., *Creating a New World Economy* (Philadelphia: Temple University Press, 1993).

Also, the alternative approach being described here emphasizes building upon local knowledge, skills, and resources. It calls for forms of technology appropriate to local conditions rather than efforts to mimic First World industrial patterns as ISI approaches generally did.

AGRICULTURE

Central to alternative development strategies are policies aimed at achieving increased self-reliance in the area of basic food production.[58] Policy suggestions include land redistribution[59] and the provision of credit, extension services[60], rural infrastructure,[61] appropriate technology,[62] and marketing assistance to small and medium-sized farmers, including those who farm communally. Subsidies or guaranteed minimal prices for specific agricultural products may also be helpful. Particular attention should be given to support for women farmers, who play a major role in Third World food production but

58 For an excellent discussion of the importance of revitalizing small-scale, ecologically sustainable agriculture, along with detailed policy recommendations, see Cavanagh and Mander, eds., *Alternatives to Economic Globalization*, 172-187.

59 Analysts suggest that land for redistribution could be obtained in a variety of ways, including redistribution of state-owned lands, high taxation of uncultivated private land and of landholdings over a certain size (in order to make possession of this land economically unviable), the removal of subsidies on agricultural inputs for large landowners, and the imposition of ceilings on land ownership.

60 It is important that agricultural research be directed more to staple foods produced by the poor and to farming conditions most commonly faced by the poor, e.g. non-irrigated agriculture. Extension workers also need to be trained in ecologically sustainable methods of agricultural production and need to develop more participatory processes of interaction with local farmers.

61 Important aspects of rural infrastructure include adequate storage, transportation, and communications capacities. The infrastructure of many Third World nations has been so strongly shaped by colonial and neo-colonial policies favoring exports that it is often easier and cheaper to import food from abroad than it is to store and transport food from rural to urban areas within the same country.

62 For discussions of appropriate technology, see Barrett Hazeltine and Christopher Bull, eds., *Field Guide to Appropriate Technology* (Boston: Academic, 2003). Additional resources can be found at <villageearth.org/atnetwork/atsourcebook/index.htm>.

who often have been neglected by governmental policies.[63] Peasant-centered agricultural measures such as the above would serve to increase food production, increase rural employment, and lead to higher rural incomes. Higher rural incomes would in turn create increased demand for farm inputs and for other basic consumer goods and services that could be produced or provided locally, further strengthening the domestic economy. As mentioned above, rural-led economic strategies similar to these played an important role in the early post-WWII experience of countries such as South Korea and Taiwan.

A major challenge to agriculture in the Third World is to address severe problems of ecological degradation. Support for ecologically sustainable farming methods, building upon traditional farming wisdom, is crucial. Crucial too are efforts to restore already degraded lands. Measures such as reforestation, agroforestry, intercropping, soil erosion prevention, organic soil fertilization, natural means of pest and weed control, small-scale irrigation and water conservation projects all have important roles to play in the establishment of ecologically viable agricultural systems.[64] As we have seen, many grassroots organizations are working to address these issues. Governmental policies supportive of the efforts of these organizations are needed.

While the primary agricultural emphasis in this alternative development strategy would be placed upon production of food for local consumption, a secondary emphasis on agricultural exports would be maintained (particularly processed or semi-processed exports, along with non-traditional export commodities) in order to obtain needed foreign exchange. In many cases staple crops and export crops can be grown by farmers in complementary mixtures.

An emphasis on a peasant-based strategy of food self-reliance would have many positive consequences. Along with decreased hunger, these include a decreased need to import food or to receive food aid, decreased vulnerability to international market volatility, and decreased susceptibility to political pressures arising from a nation's position of

63 See Carolyn Sachs, *Gendered Fields: Rural Women, Agriculture, and Environment* (Boulder: Westview, 1996).

64 For good discussions of ecologically sustainable agriculture in the Third World, see Nicholas Parrott and Terry Marsden, *The Real Green Revolution: Organic and Agroecological Farming in the South* (London: Greenpeace Environmental Trust, 2002); Bernhard Glaeser, *Environment, Development, Agriculture* (Armonk, NY: M.E. Sharpe, 1995).

food dependency. In order to prevent local farmers from being undersold by highly subsidized agricultural products imported from the First World, measures would need to be implemented to limit the quantities or types of food imports.

Food self-reliance in turn is part of a broader economic and political strategy of self-reliance. Adebayo Adedji, formerly the executive director of the United Nations' Economic Commission on Africa (ECA) and one of Africa's most prominent economists, states:

> Self-reliance, pronounced dead many times but reborn as a necessity just as often, has to raise its head again. Self-reliance is not to be understood as debilitating autarky or self- sufficiency, nor as a categorical rejection of interacting with the world, but, quite to the contrary, as a concentration on the inner condition in order to have the necessary autonomy to interact with others in a mutually beneficial, non-exploitative, and sustained manner.[65]

The greatest threat to food self-reliance and sustainable agriculture, many analysts assert, comes from neoliberal economic policies. Tom Barry states:

> Neoliberal policies that prioritize the free flow of trade and investment over human and environmental considerations run contrary to the logic of sustainable agriculture. The main components of sustainable agriculture–reduced dependence on traded inputs, decreased time and distance between production and consumption, increased local and national control of production and consumption patterns, the importance of food security and the satisfaction of basic needs, the revival of rural communities, an expanded governmental role in promoting the stability of the small farm, and conserving natural resources–are all undermined by policies that encourage the international market and international capital to take command of our agriculture and food systems.[66]

INDUSTRY AND SERVICES

Alternative development proponents stress support for small- and medium-scale producers and providers of services, including persons in the vast informal sectors of Third World economies. In the realm

65 Adebayo Adedeji, Introduction to *Africa Within the World: Beyond Dispossession and Dependence*, ed. A. Adedeji (London: Zed Books, 1993), 10.

66 Barry, *Zapata's Revenge: Free Trade and the Farm Crisis in Mexico*, 201.

of industrial production, emphasis is placed upon the use of "appropriate" forms of technology (e.g. labor-intensive and environmentally sensitive technologies), with production to meet local needs receiving the highest priority. Particular attention is given to the development of industries with linkages to the agricultural realm, including the manufacturing of tools and other farm inputs and small- and medium-scale food processing operations. Many of these industries (along with other forms of craft production and resource-based industries) could be located in rural areas, strengthening the rural economy and diminishing rural to urban migration patterns which have exacerbated many social problems throughout the Third World. The provision of credit, training, and various support services by governments have an important role to play in this industrial strategy. As in the agricultural realm, a secondary emphasis would be placed upon industrial production for export, with particular attention to the export of labor-intensive products that maximize employment opportunities. Selective measures to protect infant industries would be essential. Regional cooperation in planning allowing different countries to specialize in different products (which would allow for economies of scale and avoid inefficiency and redundancy) would also have a role to play. In the realm of services and the informal sector, the provision of credit to the poor, especially poor women, along with various support services and favorable licensing regulations would all be important.[67]

EDUCATION, HEALTH, AND OTHER BASIC NEEDS

Of fundamental importance in alternative development strategies is governmental investment in areas such as primary health care, nutrition and food security, education, the provision of safe drinking water, and sanitation.[68] These services both have inherent value, meeting human needs, and also have economic value in that an educated and

67 For discussions of industry within alternative development approaches, see Giovanni Andrea Cornia, Rolph van der Hoeven, and Thandika Mkandawire, "Overview of an Alternative Long-Term Development Strategy," in *Africa's Recovery in the 1990s* (New York: St. Martin's Press, 1992), 159-91; McAfee, *Storm Signals*, chapter 12; South Commission, *The Challenge to the South* (Oxford: Oxford University Press, 1990), chapter 3.

68 For good discussion of the social investment that is needed, see UNICEF's annual *State of the World's Children* reports. For examples of successful implementation of some of these policies, see Francke and Chasin, *Kerala*.

healthy population tends to be more productive than an uneducated and unhealthy one. Particular stress needs to be placed upon the provision of these basic services to women. The education of women, for example, is a key factor in enhancing the social status of women, increasing life choices for women, and decreasing population growth.[69]

GRASSROOTS PARTICIPATION, DEMOCRACY, AND RESPECT FOR HUMAN RIGHTS

Underlying all alternative development strategies is a rejection of top-down models of social change. Instead, grassroots participation in economic, political, and social decision-making and in project implementation is crucial. David Korten emphasizes that in his analysis of development projects he has consistently found that

> externally imposed 'development' was seriously disrupting human relationships and community life and causing significant hardship for the very people it claimed to benefit. By contrast, when people found the freedom and self-confidence to develop themselves, they demonstrated enormous potential to create a better world....Development depends on the ability of people to gain control of and use effectively the real resources of their localities–land, labor, technology, and human ingenuity and motivation–to meet their own needs. Yet most development interventions transfer control of local resources to ever larger and more centralized institutions that are unaccountable to local people and unresponsive to their needs.[70]

"The poor remain poor," states UNICEF, "principally because they are underrepresented in political and economic decisions, because their voice is not sufficiently loud in the selections of society's priorities."[71]

The creation of appropriate structures to foster optimal participation in varying tasks and contexts is a complex matter.[72] Of utmost importance in the process of developing these structures is respect for a holistic conception of human rights. These rights would include both civil-political rights, such as freedom of speech and assembly, as well as

---

69 See Frances Moore Lappé and Rachel Schurman, *Taking Population Seriously* (San Francisco: Institute for Food and Development Policy, 1990).

70 Korten, *When Corporations Rule the World*, 14-15.

71 UNICEF, *State of the World's Children 1995*, 47.

72 For a good discussion of the topic of participation in development, see Denis Goulet, *Development Ethics* (New York: Apex Press, 1995), chapter 8.

social-economic rights, such as the right to adequate food, shelter, and health care, along with corresponding obligations.

REGIONAL COOPERATION

Cooperation among neighboring countries also has an important role to play in alternative development strategies. This includes cooperation in areas such as conflict resolution, economic policy, education, appropriate technology development, and the sharing of successful approaches to social and ecological problems. In the economic realm, measures such as increased emphasis on regional trade (as an alternative to excessive dependence on trade with the First World), agreements concerning economic specialization, management of the supply of export commodities, the establishment of regional food reserves and the creation of regional banks are all important matters for deliberation and joint action. Cooperation and solidarity among Third World nations is also crucial in counteracting the harmful policies that First World economic interests have enacted and continue to attempt to enact in the international arena. The South Commission, for example, states:

> The aspirations of the South will not be fulfilled without a difficult and prolonged struggle....For its own sake and for the sake of humanity, the South has to be resolute in resisting the present moves by the dominant countries of the North to redesign the system to their own advantage....South-South cooperation alone can give the developing countries a collective weight and countervailing power that cannot be ignored by the North.[73]

REGULATION OF TRANSNATIONAL CORPORATIONS

Transnational corporations (TNCs) are of fundamental importance in the current international economy. Of the 100 largest economic entities in the world (including countries), 51 are corporations.[74] The largest 200 corporations account for about 27.5% of global economic activity, though given their highly capital-intensive nature account for only about 0.78% of global employment.[75] A crucial component of

73 South Commission, *Challenge to the South*, 285.

74 See <www.corporations.org/system/top100.html>.

75 Sarah Anderson and John Cavanagh, *Top 200: The Rise of Global Corporate Power* (Washington, DC: Institute for Policy Studies, 2000), 3. Available at <www.ips-dc.org/reports/top200.htm>.

any alternative development strategy is measures to ensure that the activities of TNCs do not cause excessive harm to local populations and ecologies. Needed regulations can take a wide variety of forms, including measures related to wages and worker rights, environmental protection, the fostering of linkages with the local economy, restrictions on the nature of items being produced or services offered for sale, measures preventing the establishment of monopolies or oligopolies, restrictions on advertising (to limit the cultural impact of corporations), and measures to minimize the potential of corporations to have disproportionate influence on political processes.[76] Gita Sen and Caren Grown of the grassroots women's organization DAWN highlight some of the reasons why extensive regulation of TNC activities is needed:

> Large corporations have been instrumental in diverting resources from basic needs toward commercialization, exports, and militarization. The employment they create in the Third World tends to be small in volume and to consist of dead-end jobs. The technology they sell is often unsuited to the consumption needs of the majority, and to domestically available resources. The outflows of profits, interest, and royalties place considerable pressures on the balance of payments as well. Greater control over the activities of multinational corporations is therefore a critical ingredient for national self-reliance, which is in turn essential for equitable development.[77]

OTHER DOMESTIC MEASURES

Other measures frequently stressed by proponents of alternative development strategies include the implementation of controls on capital flows, particularly measures to prevent or limit capital flight and measures to prevent or limit potentially destabilizing forms of speculative investment. The lack of these controls, critics claim, has played a major role in bringing about both the Third World debt crisis and the economic crisis in East Asia. Lack of these controls also undermines efforts to pursue policies that prioritize the interests of workers, the poor, and the environment over the interests of profit maximization

---

76 For discussions of the activities of TNCs in the Third World and suggested regulations, see Korten, *When Corporations Rule the World*; John Madeley, *Big Business, Poor Peoples: The Impact of Transnational Corporations on the World's Poor* (London: Zed Books, 1999).

77 Sen and Grown, *Development, Crises, and Alternative Visions*, 84.

for the owners of capital. "Capital mobility," asserts economist James Crotty, "gives the wealthy classes around the globe veto power over the economic policies and priorities of every nation. No progressive, democratically controlled system of economic regulation can function effectively if it does not break that veto power through the imposition of capital controls."[78] Both the regulation of TNCs and the implementation of capital controls would be most effective if implemented on an international scale.

FINANCING ALTERNATIVE DEVELOPMENT

The alternative development strategy outlined above would require a significant amount of governmental investment in areas such as education, health care, infrastructure, employment creation, credit provision, environmental protection and restoration, and the offering of a variety of support services for small- and medium-sized farmers and businesses. Proponents suggest a variety of ways in which such expenditures could be financed. These include reductions in military spending, the establishment of more progressive taxation structures, the elimination of subsidies for large farmers and large businesses, decreased payments on the foreign debt, taxes on environmental extraction, the introduction of user fees for governmental services provided to medium- and high-income persons, measures to decrease corruption, and the wise use of any available international aid. It is also suggested that an alternative development strategy such as the above would lead to increased rural incomes and savings and increased savings among the urban poor, savings that could be used to finance some of the needed measures. Similarly, it is suggested that volunteer labor (particularly of farm laborers in the off-season) could be effectively mobilized to undertake a variety of self-help projects if local communities were truly empowered to play a central role in project formulation and design. The experiences of grassroots organizations such as the Naam groups and the Sarvodaya Shramadana movement

78 James Crotty, "The Rise and Fall of the Keynesian Revolution in the Age of the Global Marketplace," in *Creating a New World Economy*, ed. Epstein, et al., 179. Similarly, Ilene Grabel asserts: "It is self-evident that the ability of wealth holders to veto a social agenda flies in the face of the most fundamental democratic principles." "Crossing Borders: A Case for Cooperation in International Financial Markets," in ibid., 79. Both of these chapters discuss in some detail the need for capital controls and the various forms that these controls could take.

demonstrate the possibilities that exist for bringing about significant benefits at relatively low cost when communities themselves are the originating force behind and feel a sense of ownership of social and ecological improvement projects.

INTERNATIONAL REFORMS

Proponents of alternative development strategies highlight a variety of reforms at the international level that are needed in order to provide supportive conditions for development alternatives to be pursued. Among these reforms are significant reductions in Third World debt payments, resulting either from debt forgiveness or united debt repudiation; the establishment of global standards concerning minimum wages, workers' rights, and environmental protection; measures to increase the terms of trade for Third World exports; international regulation of the activities of TNCs and of capital flows; measures to enhance exchange rate stability; favorable access by Third World nations to socially and environmentally beneficial technologies; major reforms of the Bretton Woods Institutions (IMF, World Bank, WTO) or their elimination and the transferring of their responsibilities to bodies associated with the United Nations; fundamental changes in structural adjustment policies; major reform of international aid provision; and an end to First World interventions (both military and economic) aimed at preventing Third World nations from pursuing alternative development paths.

WHAT ROLE FOR INTERNATIONAL AID?

It is important to look more closely at the issue of international development aid. Many persons of good will who are concerned about the plight of the Third World poor are instinctively supportive of non-military forms of foreign aid. Critics argue persuasively, however, that much development aid provided in the past has resulted in more harm than good for the Third World poor.[79] One fundamental reason

---

79 Good discussion of foreign aid issues can be found in Jonathan Glennie, *The Trouble with Aid: Why Less Could Mean More for Africa* (London: Zed Books, 2008); David Sogge, *Give and Take: What's the Matter with Foreign Aid?* (London: Zed Books, 2002); Frances Moore Lappé, Joseph Collins, and David Kinley, *Aid As Obstacle* (San Francisco: Institute for Food and Development Policy, 1981). For examples of some positive projects funded by U.S. government aid through the Inter-American Foundation (a small government agency established by reformers in Congress), see Da-

is that the aid has often funded flawed modernizationist development projects. Another reason is that aid provision has often prioritized the foreign policy concerns and economic interests of First World nations and corporations rather than being truly responsive to the needs of the poor. The primacy of the economic and strategic purposes of aid has at times been openly acknowledged by First World political leaders. John F. Kennedy, for example, asserted that "foreign aid is a method by which the United States maintains a position of influence and control around the world."[80] Richard Nixon put the matter even more bluntly. "Let us remember," said Nixon, "that the main purpose of aid is not to help other nations but to help ourselves."[81]

Numerous studies have shown that the top recipients of U.S. aid historically have been nations deemed to be of greatest strategic significance, not the nations with the lowest income levels or with the greatest numbers of people living in extreme poverty. Often these strategic nations have been major abusers of human rights. Conversely, nations that have explicitly sought to prioritize the needs of the poor (such as the Allende government in Chile, the Sandinista government in Nicaragua, and the current government of Hugo Chavez in Venezuela) have been cut off from U.S. aid and have become the target of U.S.-funded covert operations. The U.S. has also repeatedly used its influence in organizations such as the World Bank to deny multilateral aid to governments who were seeking to implement substantive social reforms. "Aid distribution," argues Jessica Hembhard, "has less to do with need and philanthropy than it does with military strategy, political policy, and capitalist expansion."[82]

---

vid Charles Kleymeyer, ed., *Cultural Expression and Grassroots Development* (Boulder, CO: L. Rienner, 1994). Unfortunately, only a small portion of U.S. aid funding is channeled through the Inter-American Foundation and a similar agency, the African Development Foundation. The vast majority of U.S. aid flows through the U.S. Agency for International Development (USAID), a branch of the State Department, which tends to be much more highly politicized.

80 John F. Kennedy, quoted in Graham Hancock, *Lords of Poverty: The Power, Prestige, and Corruption of the International Aid Business* (New York: Atlantic Monthly Press, 1989), 71.

81 Richard Nixon, quoted in ibid.

82 Nembhard, "Foreign Aid and Dependent Development," in *Creating a New World Economy*, ed. Epstein, et al., 314.

Much of the aid that has been given in the past half century has been "tied" aid, containing requirements that a large percentage of the aid money be spent on goods and services provided by corporations from the donor nation. Moreover, even when aid was not formally tied, similar spending patterns have resulted due to the pervasiveness of the dominant model of modernizationist development. This has led to the importation of much technology inappropriate to local conditions, a reliance on foreign "experts" often inadequately acquainted with local contexts, and production patterns favorable to the interests of local elites and TNCs. "The interlocking nature of vested interests in both donor and recipient countries," states UNICEF, has resulted in

> expenditure patterns which favour the imported over the domestically produced, the capital-intensive over the employment-creating, export crops over local food production, high-cost sewage plants over locally made latrines, ...central power stations over fuel-efficient stoves, central teaching hospitals over local health centres, ...industry over agriculture, the military over social services, the prestigious over the necessary, and ultimately the better-off over the poor.[83]

Much aid from official sources for the above projects has been in the form of loans, paving the way for the Third World debt crisis and its consequences. Aid has also often been tied to requirements that Third World nations change their public policies to be more favorable to the interests of First World corporations, to the further detriment of the Third World poor.[84]

Even such seemingly benign forms of aid such as the provision of food have often had harmful results. While enabling First World (especially U.S.) farmers to get rid of surplus production, food aid has frequently been very detrimental to Third World farmers. When given in non-emergency circumstances food aid has commonly served to drive down food prices, thereby undermining the ability of local farmers to make a living and keep their land. Food aid has also served to foster a taste for non-local products (opening new markets for First World exports and contributing to Third World balance of payment

---

83 UNICEF, *State of the World's Children 1995*, 47.

84 See Lappé, Collins, and Kinley, *Aid As Obstacle*; Rich, *Mortaging the Earth*.

problems), has served to provide support for repressive Third World governments (who have been permitted to sell the donated food and to use the proceeds for regime maintenance), has enabled governments to avoid implementing needed reforms (e.g. more equitable land distribution), and has been used to create situations of food dependence that make recipient nations susceptible to outside influence over their policies. While critics acknowledge that there is a role for food aid in certain emergency situations (the majority of food aid has been given in non-emergency contexts), they contend that in these cases the food should, if possible, be purchased primarily within the region. These purchases from non-affected areas would then function to support rather than undermine Third World farmers.[85]

While official aid has often had negative consequences, the impact of aid from NGOs has been more mixed. Some NGOs implement top-down, inappropriate, and culturally-insensitive aid projects that cause harm.[86] Others, however, are committed to grassroots development/regeneration projects, foster local participation, are sensitive to ecological and cultural issues, and generally make a very positive contribution.[87]

An important role remains for aid from official sources, along with substantive debt relief. The distribution of this aid, however, must be a matter for careful discernment. In broad terms, aid should be shifted away from geostrategic concerns and from the large-scale, socially and ecologically problematic development projects that have been predominant in the past. Emphasis should be on smaller, grassroots projects, with particular attention to investment in areas such as education, primary health care, appropriate technology, sustainable agriculture, employment-generation in small-scale manufacturing and

85 Good discussion of problems relating to food aid can be found in Lappé, Collins, and Kinley, *Aid As Obstacle*, chapter 12; Pradervand, *Listening to Africa*, 50-55.

86 Among the NGOs that are most frequently criticized for insensitivity to local populations and for inappropriate projects are some Christian evangelical organizations. See Hancock, *Lords of Poverty*, chapter 1.

87 Several international aid agencies that have very positive reputations include Oxfam, Save the Children, and World Neighbors. A couple excellent smaller organizations focusing especially on Central America include Rights Action (formerly Guatemala Partners) and the Foundation for Self-Sufficiency in Central America.

services, and ecological restoration. Aid channeled through NGOs should be in moderate amounts, based on the demonstrated capacity of the NGO to employ the funds effectively. The manner in which the 6-S organization in Africa channels foreign funding to local groups could provide a valuable model.[88] Aid should not be tied to purchases of First World products or services and should allow for flexibility on the part of NGOs in responding to the expressed needs of communities, needs that may change as circumstances change. When emergency aid is needed, goods and services should be purchased within the region to the greatest extent possible.

THE ROLE OF MARKETS IN ALTERNATIVE DEVELOPMENT STRATEGIES

The above discussion gives a broad overview of the types of domestic and international reforms that proponents of alternative development believe to be necessary. One important question that has been only indirectly addressed is the view that these analysts have of "markets." On the one hand, alternative development proponents clearly favor markets over economic models based on central planning. Central planning severely restricts individual and community control over economic decision-making and undermines the type of participatory structures that alternative development proponents view as essential. At the same time, supporters of alternative development strategies generally express grave reservations about certain aspects of so-called "free" markets. They stress, for example, that markets ultimately respond to money rather than to need. This fact is what makes possible vast amounts of hunger in a world that produces more than enough food to adequately feed all of its people. It is what makes hunger a common phenomenon even in the United States. Critics argue that markets tend to lead to the increased concentration of wealth and to the increased concentration of the political power that wealth can buy.[89]

Market forces also do not adequately take into account "externalities" such as the impact of economic activity on the environment, health, community, and on non-capitalist cultural values. Increasingly, these

88 See the discussion of the 6-S organization and the Naam peasant groups earlier in this chapter.

89 For a thoughtful discussion of the value and limitations of markets, see Lappé, Collins, and Rosset, *World Hunger*, chapter 7.

critics argue, all aspects of life are being commodified, with many negative consequences. In response to these shortcomings of free markets, proponents of alternative development stress the need for adequate regulation with regard to wages, worker and consumer rights, health and safety concerns, and environmental protection. They emphasize the need for measures to lessen the influence of wealth in the political process. They stress also the importance of redistributive measures, arguing that markets function most effectively to meet need when economic power is widely dispersed. Lastly, these critics argue that certain essentials of life (such as access to food or basic health care) should be removed from total reliance on the market and be guaranteed to all. All of these suggestions, it should be noted, are congruent with the views and suggestions expressed in Catholic Social Teaching. Thus, while the proponents of development alternatives acknowledge that markets certainly have an important role to play, they stress that markets also need to have significant limits placed upon them. David Korten argues that economic globalization as it is now occurring is increasingly removing these limits. This removal of limits, he contends, is giving rise to a

> market tyranny that is extending its reach across the planet like a cancer, colonizing ever more of the planet's living spaces, destroying livelihoods, displacing people, rendering democratic institutions impotent, and feeding on life in an insatiable quest for money....The problem is not business or the market per se but a badly corrupted global economic system that is gyrating far beyond human control.[90]

DIFFERING VISIONS: ALTERNATIVE DEVELOPMENT VS. REGENERATION

Proponents of alternatives to conventional development generally share many common emphases. These include, for example, the need for a more inward-oriented economic focus (requiring redistributive measures), the prioritization of meeting basic needs, and the importance of support for small and medium-sized farms and businesses. General agreement exists also concerning the importance of grassroots participation, greater ecological concern, measures to improve the social and economic status of women, and heightened cultural sensitivity. Significant areas of divergence within the context of this general

90 Korten, *When Corporations Rule the World*, 22-23.

agreement remain, however, and need to be more closely noted. In particular, there exist important differences between those whom I have termed grassroots critics of development (such as Vandana Shiva) who seek alternatives *to* development and proponents of alternative forms *of* development (such as the economists associated with UNICEF.) The former reject the language and conceptual framework of development, preferring to speak of "regeneration" or "reclaiming the commons," while the latter continue to operate more within conventional understandings of economic development even while rejecting certain key elements of strict economic neoliberalism.[91]

The primary disagreements between these positions center upon the ultimate goal being pursued. Is the goal a more just and ecologically sensitive version of the western industrial model (as many proponents of alternative development or sustainable development assume), or is it a more far-reaching alternative grounded in diverse local cultures and practices (as sought by many grassroots critics of development)? This debate is sometimes characterized as a debate between "critical modernist" and "critical traditionalist" views.[92] Both parties are highly critical of many features of modernizationist development and critical also of numerous aspects of most traditional cultures (e.g. the subordination of women). Both groups also generally affirm that much can be gained from dialogue between traditional cultures and modernity. Nonetheless, the positions of these groups diverge in several key areas. Among these disagreements are differing views concerning agriculture, technology, economic globalization, First World lifestyles, markets, and understandings of human-nature relations. For example, critical modernists tend to propose a more equitable and ecologically sensitive version of modern, industrialized agriculture.[93] They often view sup-

91 Neither of these broad positions – that of grassroots critics who propose alternatives *to* development or that of proponents of alternative forms *of* development – should be viewed as monolithic. There exists within each position numerous variations and significant overlap. Perhaps a better way to describe the alternatives would be to speak of a continuum, of which these two positions in their stronger forms represent the end points. Also, it should be noted that some grassroots critics of development continue to employ the language of "alternative development," but seek to give the term a more radical meaning.

92 See Nandy, "Cultural Frames."

93 See the discussion of agriculture in Giovanni Andrea Cornia, Rolph van der Hoeven, and Thandika Mkandawire, eds., *Africa's Recovery in*

port for small farmers as an interim measure to be taken until jobs can be created for these persons in other sectors of the economy, at which time a fuller transition to a more centralized and "efficient" form of industrial agriculture will be appropriate. Critical traditionalists tend to view small-scale farming as an inherently valuable way of life, which should continue to play a central role indefinitely in economic and cultural life. While open to certain modern innovations in the area of appropriate technology, a strong emphasis is placed by these persons upon the maintenance and revival of central components of traditional farming and craft systems.

Critical traditionalists stress the social and ecological unsustainability of economic globalization, such as its heavy reliance on energy-intensive long-distance transport and its undermining of local citizen control over economic, political, and social policies. These persons highlight the need for increased economic localism and bioregionalism.[94] Critical modernists in contrast tend to accept the inevitability and value of economic globalization, while calling for this globalization to occur within a more just and ecologically sensitive framework.

Critical traditionalists emphasize the values of simplicity and sufficiency and set forth views of the good life that are not centered upon the accumulation of material goods. They are highly critical of First World consumerism and First World lifestyles for a combination of ecological, cultural, social, and spiritual reasons.[95] Critical modernists on the other hand generally emphasize the importance of "sustainable growth" and tend to view First World lifestyles more positively. A central goal is to raise the material standard of living of the world's poor to the highest levels that are ecologically sustainable. Strong faith in the ability of modern science and technology to greatly increase efficiency in the use of resources and diminish pollution undergirds a belief that high material standards of living are not inherently ecologically problematic.[96]

---

the 1990s: From Stagnation and Adjustment to Human Development (New York: St. Martin's Press, 1992), especially chapter 7.

94 See Mander and Goldsmith, *Case Against the Global Economy*; Cavanagh and Mander, *Alternatives to Economic Globalization*.

95 See Shiva, *Staying Alive*; Verhelst, *No Life Without Roots*; Ecologist, *Whose Common Future?*

96 A good example of this critical modernist approach to the compatibility of high levels of material consumption and ecological sustainability can be

Critical modernists tend to have a positive view of markets. They view markets as highly efficient and as fostering economic growth. At the same time, however, they recognize certain drawbacks to markets and argue for the importance of an effective but not overly intrusive regulatory framework. They also support measures to compensate for some of the negative tendencies that markets have, such as the tendency to increase the concentration of wealth. Critical traditionalists likewise favor well-regulated markets as opposed to the central economic planning of the former Eastern European model. They tend, however, to be highly critical of an over-commodification of life and thus stress the importance of meeting basic needs through non-market means (such as through family and community support, bartering, sharing, etc.) whenever possible.[97]

Finally, with regard to the relationship of humans and nature, critical modernists tend to stress the importance of a more efficient and ecologically sensitive use of resources. Critical traditionalists, however, call for a deeper, more fundamental change in the ways in which humans view and relate to nature. Vandana Shiva, for example, stresses the importance of what she terms the "feminine principle." This term refers to a way of relating to nature that involves nonviolence and respect for the integrity and creativity of the natural world. Shiva stresses that the feminine principle is actually a trans-gender principle, able to be embodied by both men and women. This principle is contrasted with the modern Cartesian/Baconian worldview that Shiva views as being based on violence and domination.[98]

Significant differences thus exist among critics of conventional development. Currently, many shared values and emphases and a common opposition to the dominance of neoliberalism serve to broadly unite the efforts of these development critics. Should the dominance

---

found in the publications of the United Nations Development Programme. See especially UNDP, *Human Development Report 1998*.

97 For discussions of markets, the overcommodification of life, and the importance of meeting needs whenever possible through non-market means, see Ecologist, *Whose Common Future?*; Mander and Goldsmith, *Case Against the Global Economy*; Howard Richards and Joanna Swanger, *The Dilemmas of Social Democracies: Overcoming Obstacles to a More Just World* (Lanham, MD: Lexington Books, 2006).

98 For Shiva's explanation of the feminine principle, see *Staying Alive*, chapters 3 and 7.

of neoliberalism be more effectively challenged, however, then the differences existing among critics would likely be more accentuated.

PROSPECTS FOR THE ADOPTION OF ALTERNATIVE POLICIES

The short-term prospects for the implementation of alternatives to neoliberal approaches to development, even the less radical alternatives as proposed by UNICEF, do not seem particularly bright. Many of the key elements of alternative development are in fact being actively undermined by the spread of free trade treaties and by the ongoing imposition of structural adjustment policies. Free trade policies and SAPs, for example, tend to increase export dependency, diminish or eliminate support for small and medium-sized farms and businesses, result in increased concentration of land ownership and wealth, reduce social spending, deregulate TNCs, forbid protection of domestic farmers and industries, and often eliminate environmental regulations and/or undermine their enforcement. They also contribute to major increases in the exploitation of natural resources in order to make debt payments and finance imports. As Oxfam's Kathy McAfee states, free trade and SAPs "weaken, or rule out entirely, the possibility of building alternate strategies."[99] Martin Khor of the Third World Network argues that neoliberal economic globalization represents "the antithesis to sustainable development."[100]

Some critics argue that the forces supporting neoliberal globalization are so powerful that only major economic, ecological, and/or social crises of a global nature (even more severe that those currently being experienced) can create the conditions in which fundamental alternatives will become possible. They stress the importance of educating and working to strengthen grassroots movements to be able to take advantage of these opportunities when they arise, building upon the small-scale alternatives that these groups have worked to create. Others hold out hope that the growth of grassroots movements could lead to fundamental political and economic changes even apart from more fundamental breakdowns of the international system and point to recent developments in countries such as Venezuela and Bolivia,

99 McAfee, *Storm Signals*, 140.

100 Martin Khor, "Globalisation is Undermining Sustainable Development," *Third World Resurgence*, No. 81/82 (May/June 1997): 26.

where reformist governments with strong grassroots support have come to power, as signs of hope. All agree, however, that the struggle will be long and arduous, and that success is not guaranteed. "[I]t is almost impossible to hope," states Martin Khor, "that the developed world will [undertake reforms] voluntarily. It will have to be forced to do so, either by a new unity of the Third World...or by the economic or physical collapse of the world economic system."[101]

The central problem, Tom Athanasiou claims, is not that viable alternatives do not exist. It is rather that the realities of concentrated economic and political power prevent these alternatives from being implemented. "Our tragedy," says Athanasiou, "lies in the richness of the available alternatives, and in the fact that so few of them are ever seriously explored."[102]

Has the point been reached when the failures of neoliberal economics and modernizationist models of development are so clear and widespread that momentum for alternatives is rising and can prevail? Are the hopeful developments in Latin America and elsewhere harbingers of a more positive future? Can the networks of progressive grassroots movements around the world that have been engaged in so many inspiring activities help to shape broader economic and social policies? There are many signs of hope, and many obstacles yet to be overcome.

In this chapter we have examined the activities of grassroots organizations from throughout the world that are seeking to create more just, participatory, ecologically sustainable, and culturally-sensitive alternatives to conventional forms of development. We have examined in broad terms the types of policies that are needed to support these alternatives and have highlighted some of the powerful obstacles that these alternatives face. Numerous analysts predict that the key conflict of the early 21st century is likely to be between forces of neoliberal economic globalization and widespread grassroots efforts that seek in the face of this globalization to preserve community, retain aspects of local autonomy, and maintain cultural identity. Richard Barnet and John Cavanagh highlight the centrality of these tensions:

---

101 Martin Khor, "The Global Economy and the Third World," in *Case Against the Global Economy*, ed. Mander and Goldsmith, 57.

102 Tom Athanasiou, *Divided Planet: The Ecology of Rich and Poor* (Boston: Little, Brown, and Co., 1996), 304, 307.

> As traditional communities disappear and ancient cultures are overwhelmed, billions of human beings are losing the sense of place and sense of self that give life meaning. The fundamental political conflict in the opening decades of the new century, we believe, will not be between nations or even between trading blocs but between the forces of economic globalization and the territorially based forces of local survival seeking to preserve and to redefine community.[103]

Often these movements of local survival and resistance will be very positive in nature, such as those described in this chapter. In other cases, however, these movements can highly problematic, such as those involved in fostering ethnic or religious violence. Both types of movements can be understood largely as responses to the economic polarization and social and ecological disruption that dominant forms of development and economic globalization have caused.[104] A key challenge for constructive grassroots movements will be to implement programs of popular education concerning the underlying causes of economic hardship and cultural and community disruption, to actively oppose attempts at scapegoating, and to join together across ethnic and religious lines in the quest for positive alternatives.

103 Barnet and Cavanagh, *Imperial Corporations*, 22.

104 For discussions of the interrelationships between neoliberal/modernizationist economic policies and ethnic strife and terrorism, see Shiva, *Violence of the Green Revolution*; Amy Chua, *World on Fire: How Exporting Free Market Democracy Breeds Ethnic Strife and Global Instability* (New York: Doubleday, 2003); Benjamin Barber, *Jihad vs. McWorld* (New York: Times Books, 1995).

CHAPTER 7

RE-ENVISIONING CATHOLIC SOCIAL TEACHING

The preceding chapters have examined debates concerning economic development and globalization and have explored the fundamental principles of Catholic Social Teaching. This chapter will explore in greater detail the potential contribution that CST can make to the quest for alternatives to dominant neoliberal/modernizationist policies. Several suggestions will also be made for the further enhancement of CST, particularly through the incorporation of insights from radical political economists and grassroots critics of development. Among the issues that will be examined are the need for a deeper structural analysis of capitalism, increased attention to the impacts of current policies on women, increased participation by women in the formulation of CST, greater recognition of the importance of grassroots movements and nonviolent social struggle in effecting social change, and heightened attention to cultural and ecological issues. After exploring these suggested enhancements of CST, the final section of this chapter will explore concrete actions that Christians (and others) can take to respond constructively to the issues that this book has addressed.

THE CONTRIBUTIONS OF CST TO THE DEVELOPMENT DEBATE

Numerous important contributions made by CST to development discussions have been highlighted throughout this book. The notion of integral development, for example, is of utmost importance. It calls into question policies that focus primarily upon economic growth. Instead, CST calls for a more holistic conception of development that affirms the importance of just distribution, the meeting of basic needs, participation, community, ecological concern, respect for diverse cultures, and the fostering of conditions conducive to spiritual growth. To the extent that dominant approaches to development either ignore or actively undermine these aspects of authentic human flourishing they are deemed by CST to be inadequate and are viewed as being in need of reform or replacement.

The emphasis in CST upon structural sin or structural injustice also highlights the need for fundamental reform. Pope John Paul II, for example, boldly asserts the necessity of "a change of lifestyles, of models of production and consumption, and of the established structures of power which today govern societies." (CA 58) Drawing upon some of the main principles of CST, John Paul has suggested guidelines to shape the required changes. "The needs of the poor," John Paul states, "take priority over the desires of the rich; the rights of workers over the maximization of profits; the preservation of the environment over uncontrolled industrial expansion; production to meet social needs over production for military purposes."[1]

These principles are of course rather general. Additional analysis is required in order to discern what specific policies should be adopted or actions taken. CST sometimes provides this additional analysis and sometimes does not. These guidelines go far, however, in sketching the overall direction of needed reforms. In our current global context, in which dominant social forces uncritically celebrate the prevailing neoliberal economic/social model, these insights and priorities contained in CST are direly needed.

ENHANCING CATHOLIC SOCIAL TEACHING

While CST provides much valuable analysis and makes many important suggestions for action, there are nonetheless several ways that CST could be further strengthened. It is to a closer look at these topics that our discussion now turns.

STRUCTURAL ANALYSIS OF CAPITALISM

Chapter Four of this book examined the structural analysis of capitalism that has been articulated by radical political economists. These economists contend that the normal operations of capitalism give rise to widening rich-poor divisions, increased control of "democratic" political processes by the wealthy, the destruction of traditional cultures,

---

1 John Paul II, "Address on Christian Unity in a Technological Age" (September 14, 1984), in *Origins* 14 (1984): 248. Also cited in the U.S. Catholic bishops' pastoral letter *Economic Justice for All*, no. 94.

the undermining of communal social structures, and the weakening of non-consumerist social values. In addition, close connections are understood to exist between capitalism and militarism and between capitalism and the perpetuation of social divisions based on race and sex.

The documents of CST repeatedly have affirmed that the unregulated operation of capitalist markets tends to result in increased inequality and the concentration of economic power and wealth in the hands of a few. "Individual initiative alone and the mere free play of competition," Pope Paul VI states, "could never assure successful development. One must avoid the risk of increasing still further the wealth of the rich and the dominion of the strong, while leaving the poor in their misery and adding to the servitude of the oppressed." (PP 33) Calling into question policies such as free trade, Pope Paul warns that "an economy of exchange can no longer be based solely on the law of free competition, a law which, in its turn, too often creates an economic dictatorship." (PP 59)[2] In developing this critique of "economic dictatorship," CST documents often warn against the increased concentration of power in the hands of large corporations. Paul VI, for example, expresses deep concern that multinational corporations "can lead to a new and abusive form of economic domination on the social, cultural, and even political level."[3] (OA 44) Also warned against in CST has been the broader phenomenon of neo-colonialism. There exists the danger, assert the authors of *Justice in the World*, that "the conditions of life created especially by colonial domination may evolve into a new form of colonialism in which the developing countries will be the victims of the interplay of international economic forces." (JW 16) Similarly, John Paul II laments the ongoing existence of "neo-colonialism" and "imperialism." (SRS 22) "One must denounce," says John Paul, "the existence of economic, financial, and social mechanisms" which "accentuat[e] the situation of wealth for some and poverty for the rest." (SRS 16) These policies John Paul condemns in theological terms as "structures of sin." (SRS 36) Speaking of neoliberal capitalism, John Paul states:

2 Similarly, Paul VI argues that "unchecked [economic] liberalism leads to dictatorship rightly denounced by Pius XI as producing 'the international imperialism' of money." (PP 26)

3 Also see the critiques of corporations expressed by Pope Pius XI in QA 132 and by Pope John Paul II in LE 17.

> More and more, in many countries of America, a system known as 'neoliberalism' prevails; based on a purely economic conception of man, this system considers profit and the law of the market as its only parameters, to the detriment of the dignity of and the respect due to individuals and peoples. At times this system has become the ideological justification for certain attitudes and behavior in the social and political spheres leading to the neglect of the weaker members of society. Indeed, the poor are becoming ever more numerous, victims of specific policies and structures which are often unjust. (EA 20)

Certain negative tendencies of capitalism are thus highlighted in CST. As John Paul II states, "The Church, since Leo XIII's *Rerum Novarum*, has always distanced herself from capitalist ideology, holding it responsible for grave social injustices."[4] Nonetheless, CST has generally expressed optimism that these negative features of capitalism can be overcome or at least significantly mitigated, at least in part by reforms voluntarily undertaken by capitalists.[5] At the same time, many of the other structural features of capitalism pointed to by radical political economists (e.g. the connections with militarism, the functional role of racism within capitalism, or the propensity of capitalism to destroy communal bonds and traditional cultural values) are generally not explored or, to the extent that the issues themselves are discussed, the systemic connections with capitalism are not clearly highlighted.[6]

4 John Paul II, "What Catholic Social Teaching Is and Is Not," speech during 1993 trip to Latvia, *Origins* 23 (September 23, 1993), 257.

5 Pope Pius, for example, states: "It is clear then that the [capitalist] system as such is not to be condemned. Surely it is not vicious of its very nature." (QA 101). The corporatist model that Pius' encyclical proposes was viewed by him to be a reformed variant of capitalism.

6 Pope John Paul II, for example, often discusses problems such as family and communal breakdown and the dangers of consumerism. The extent to which he sees these problems as being rooted in the nature of capitalism, however, is ambiguous. At times he states that these criticisms "are directed not so much against an economic system as against an ethical and cultural system." (CA 39) Yet in other contexts he asserts a deeper structural connection between capitalism, consumerist worldviews, communal breakdown, and the loss of cultural values such as simplicity and sharing. "The market as an exchange mechanism," John Paul declares, "has become the medium of a new culture." The implications, he suggests, are profoundly disturbing: "Many observers have noted the intrusive, even invasive, character of the logic of the market, which reduces more and more the area

It is also asserted by critics that the features of capitalism that are addressed in CST do not seem to be consistently taken into account when CST addresses the question of how to implement social change. For example, while there is expressed in CST an awareness that capitalism tends to lead to concentrated economic power and that concentrated economic power generally leads to concentrated political power, this has not prevented CST from appealing primarily to existing economic and political leaders (beneficiaries of this concentrated power) as the key agents of change.

CST could be strengthened, I believe, through increased attention to the structural features of capitalism as highlighted by the radical political economists, particularly the connections between capitalism and inequality, cultural destruction, militarism, and the erosion of democracy that occurs as wealth increasingly comes to dominate political processes. Also of great value would be attention to certain other structural features of capitalism that radical political economists themselves have historically too often neglected, such as the contradiction between the capitalist growth imperative and ecological sustainability.[7] Victor Lebow, a marketing consultant writing in the 1950s, summarized well the anti-ecological (and anti-spiritual) thrust of capitalism: "Our enormous productive economy...demands that we make consumption our way of life, that we convert the buying and use of goods into rituals, that we seek our spiritual satisfactions, our ego satisfactions, in consumption....We need things consumed, burned up, worn out, replaced, and discarded at an ever-increasing rate."[8] This topic of ecological sustainability is one area in which the more

---

available to the human community for voluntary and public action at every level. The market imposes its way of thinking and acting, and stamps its scale of values upon behavior." "The Ethical Dimensions of Globalization," Address to the Pontifical Academy for Social Sciences (April 27, 2001), no. 3.

7 Some radical political economists have recently begun to give significant attention to ecological issues. See, for example, Joel Kovel, *The Enemy of Nature: The End of Capitalism or the End of the World?*; John Bellamy Foster, *Ecology Against Capitalism* (New York: Monthly Review Press, 2002); James O'Connor, *Natural Causes: Essays on Ecological Marxism* (New York: Guilford Press, 1998).

8 Cited in Adam Daniel Finnerty, *No More Plastic Jesus: Global Justice and Christian Lifestyle* (Maryknoll, NY: Orbis, 1977), 36.

ecologically-sensitive works of grassroots critics of development can profoundly enhance the insights of radical political economists.

In regional and national CST documents some of the insights of radical political economists and grassroots critics of development have been incorporated more fully than in the papal documents. The Latin American bishops, for example, have played a pioneering role within CST in undertaking a structural analysis of the impact of capitalism on the Third World. They have sought in their statements from conferences held at Medellín, Puebla, and Santo Domingo to identify and to critique those structural mechanisms by which widespread poverty and injustice have been created and continue to be perpetuated in Latin American countries. Among the factors highlighted, for example, are the legacy of colonialism, flawed development policies (designed primarily to serve capitalist interests), the negative impacts of transnational corporations,[9] declining terms of trade for Third World products, First World support for repressive Third World governments, various forms of cultural imperialism,[10] the debt crisis, structural adjustment, and neoliberal policies of free trade.

At Medellín, Colombia in 1968 the Latin American bishops set out to analyze "the misery that besets large masses of human beings in all of our countries," a situation of "injustice which cries to the heavens." The principal guilt for this misery, they argue, "rests with powers, inspired by uncontrolled desire for gain, which leads to economic dictatorship and the 'international imperialism of money' condemned by Pope Pius XI in *Quadragesimo Anno* and by Pope Paul VI in *Populorum Progessio*."[11]

At Puebla, Mexico in 1979 the structural analysis begun at Medellín was further developed. In their statement approved at the Puebla meeting the bishops contend that pervasive poverty "is the product of economic, social and political situations and structures" which "create a situation on the international level where the rich get richer at the expense of the poor." (30) "The free market economy," the bishops argue,

9 Transnational corporations are criticized for exploitation of workers, monopolistic practices, excessive profit repatriation, tax evasion, cultural imperialism (through advertising and the media), appropriation of natural resources, and erosion of national sovereignty, among other negative impacts. See especially Medellín, "Peace," no. 9; Puebla, no. 66, 1264, 1277.

10 See Puebla, no. 62, 1069-1073.

11 See "Justice," no. 1; "Peace," no. 9.

"has increased the gap between the rich and the poor by giving priority to capital over labor, economics over the social realm." (47) "Fear of Marxism," the bishops lament, "keeps many from facing up to the oppressive reality of liberal capitalism..., an equally sinful system." (92) Concerning "development," the bishops argue that "the ample hopes for development have come to nothing. The marginalization of the vast majority and the exploitation of the poor has increased." (1260)[12]

At their meeting in 1993 in Santo Domingo, Dominican Republic, the Latin American bishops focused much of their attention on a strong critique of the processes of neoliberal economic globalization and modernizationist development models, arguing that these models "have brought about current environmental and social disasters." (170) "Modernization of our societies," state the bishops, "has brought the expansion of international agribusiness, increasing integration between countries, greater use of technology, and a transnational presence. Very often these trends benefit the economically strong segments, but at the cost of small producers and workers." (174) Highlighting the reality of "growing impoverishment" which "is reaching intolerable extremes of misery," the bishops argue that neoliberal policies are exacerbating the various mechanisms of structural injustice. "Policies of a neoliberal type now prevailing in Latin America and the Caribbean further deepen the negative impact of these mechanisms. The gaps in society have widened as the market has been deregulated in an indiscriminate way; major portions of labor legislation have been eliminated and workers have been fired; and the social spending that protected working-class families has been cut back." (179)[13]

More recent statements by the Latin American bishops' conference (known by its Spanish acronym CELAM) have further developed these critiques of neoliberal, capitalist forms of economic globalization. "The disastrous nature of the Washington consensus, on which neoliberal structural adjustment programs have been based," CELAM

12 For a succinct summary of the bishops' views concerning the problems facing Latin America and their underlying structural causes, see Puebla, no. 28-70, 1257-1282.

13 For the bishops' analysis of the structures of injustice prevalent in Latin America and in the global economy, see especially no. 164-203 of the Santo Domingo final document. The documents of the Santo Domingo conference can be found in *Santo Domingo and Beyond*, ed. Alfred Hennelly (Maryknoll, NY: Orbis, 1993).

states, "is clear....Economic globalization has not reduced the gap between rich and poor countries; instead, it has aggravated it, creating victims everywhere."[14]

Other bishops' conferences, such as those of the Canadian and the Asian bishops, have similarly highlighted the importance of deeper structural analysis of global capitalism and its local manifestations. The Asian bishops, for example, have repeatedly stressed the need to analyze "the dynamics of unjust structures"[15] and have consistently disputed the notion that the Asian NICs represent a positive development model. They have noted especially the exploitation and repression of workers that has been prevalent in the NICs and in other Asian nations aspiring to become NICs. The "dreams and efforts [of the Asian people] for liberation," the bishops argue,

> are being shattered by complex, mutually reinforcing powers that are often beyond the control of workers: the dominance of transnational corporations and large local companies in traditional industries and their incursion into agribusiness, taking advantage of cheap labor or appropriating the land of small landowners; the banning of strikes and trade unions and so repressing legitimate protest; the exodus of rural workers into already overcrowded urban slums as the cities' cheap labor; the lack of supportive organizations among the vast majority of urban workers, small landowners, and landless peasants; long hours of work, harassment, job insecurity and accident hazards; deterioration of health; unemployment and underemployment. Clearly, political, economic, and agricultural structures have made both urban and rural workers cogs of an anonymous productive machine....Free enterprise, or capitalism... has...degraded the working class to being a dispensable commodity.[16]

14 CELAM, *Globalization and New Evangelization in Latin America and the Caribbean: Reflections from CELAM 1999-2003* (Bogota, Colombia: Publicaciones CELAM, 2003), no. 131, 163.

15 International Congress on Mission, "The Gospel, the Kingdom of God, Liberation, and Development," in *For All the Peoples of Asia: Federation of Asian Bishops' Conferences Documents from 1970 to 1991*, ed. Gaudencio Rosales and C.G. Arévalo (Maryknoll, NY: Orbis, 1992), 147.

16 Federation of Asian Bishops' Conferences (FABC), "The Vocation and Mission of the Laity in the Church and in the World of Asia," in ibid., 187-188.

The Asian bishops also have highlighted problems such as cultural destruction, ecological damage, the exploitation of child labor, and the increasing sexual exploitation of women that have accompanied capitalist development in Asia.[17] Summarizing many of Asia's ongoing problems, the bishops state: "[E]conomic structures are characterized by dependence, exploitation of cheap labor, destruction of natural resources and the environment, unfair prices in trade. There also exists illiteracy, problems connected with migrant labor, exploitation of women, child labor, landlessness, problems of peasant farmers, poor working conditions, inadequate salaries, unemployment and underemployment."[18]

The Latin American and Asian bishops thus emphasize the need for awareness of the structural realities of capitalism. A detailed analysis of contemporary capitalism is also contained in the documents of the Canadian bishops. Highlighting the importance of "developing a critical analysis of the economic, political, and social structures that cause human suffering," the bishops take a close look at developments within the global capitalist economic system.[19] They argue that the world economy is presently emerging from a transitional stage of capitalism whose impact in the First World was relatively benign (even while its impact on the Third World was harsh) and is "entering a more rigid stage of capitalism that holds forth the prospect of a grim future" for the majority of people throughout the world, including the First

17 See FABC, "Journeying Together Toward the Third Millennium," in ibid., 276-277.

18 FABC Office of Evangelization, "Conclusions of the Theological Consultation," 336. The Asian bishops like the Latin American bishops also warn of the dangers of cultural imperialism: "The global centers of economic power manipulate the mass media in Asian countries to create artificial needs that promote the production of luxury goods. This results in a consumerism which subtly undermines the deep religious values of Asian cultures and erodes the moral fiber of the Asian peoples. This pervasive imperialism presents a formidable new challenge to the life style of people and to religious institutions of Asia today." Ibid.

19 Canadian Conference of Catholic Bishops, "Ethical Reflections on Canada's Socio-Economic Order," no. 4. This document can be found in *Do Justice: The Social Teaching of the Canadian Catholic Bishops*, ed. E.F. Sheridan (Toronto: Jesuit Centre for Social Faith and Justice, 1987).

World.[20] Specific structural features of this new stage of capitalism that the Canadian bishops highlight include:[21]

– increased capital mobility, which enables corporations to "move capital from one country or region to another, taking advantage of cheaper labour conditions, lower corporate taxes and reduced environmental standards."[22]

– increased automation, which "points to a continuing social crisis of permanent or structural unemployment."[23]

– accelerated concentration of wealth and economic power, increased income disparities, the displacement of small farmers and small businesses. The bishops express particular concern regarding "the concentration of economic power in the hands of a small number of large corporations exercising monopoly control over key sectors of the economy."[24]

– heavy reliance on military spending

– high levels of "economic dependency" (The bishops particularly highlight Canada's dependent relationship with the United States.)

– major cut-backs in social spending undertaken in order to compete in the global economy

– worsening conditions for labor, e.g. lower wages, more oppressive working conditions, the weakened power of unions

– increased numbers of poor and marginalized persons

– increased emphasis on "serv[ing] external market interests rather than on producing for the basic needs" of local populations[25]

– accelerating ecological damage

– increased social breakdown resulting from conditions of poverty and unemployment, manifest in "increasing alcoholism, suicides, family breakdown, vandalism, crime, racism, and street violence."[26]

---

20 Ibid., no. 23. For a similar analysis of the stages of capitalism, which draws upon insights from radical political economy, see Peter Henriot and Joe Holland, *Social Analysis: Linking Faith and Justice* (Maryknoll, NY: Orbis Books, 1983).

21 These structural features of capitalism are discussed in Canadian Conference of Catholic Bishops, "Ethical Reflections," especially no. 23-40.

22 Canadian Conference of Catholic Bishops, "Ethical Reflections," no. 24.

23 Ibid.

24 Ibid., no. 34.

25 Ibid., no. 35.

26 Ibid., no. 38.

The "basic social contradiction of our times," assert the Canadian bishops, "is the structural domination of capital and technology over people, over labour, over communities." "What is required," they argue, "is a radical inversion of these structural relationships."[27] Specifically, the Canadian bishops call for "an alternative economic vision" that would "place priority on serving the basic needs of all..., on the value of human labour and on an equitable distribution of wealth and power." Key components of this alternative economic model include:

> socially useful forms of production; labour-intensive industries; the use of appropriate forms of technology; self-reliant models of economic development; community ownership and control of industries; new forms of worker management and ownership; and greater use of renewable energy sources.[28]

Many of these suggested policies are similar to those contained in the papal encyclicals and in documents such as *Economic Justice for All*. The key difference, I would suggest, is that by engaging in deeper structural analysis than do the authors of these other CST documents the Canadian bishops highlight more adequately the radical nature of the break with the dynamics of contemporary global capitalism that is being called for and are therefore able to assess more realistically the obstacles to these changes that exist. They are therefore also better able to discern the crucial role that grassroots mobilization would have to play for such changes to be brought about, as will be discussed below.

WOMEN, DEVELOPMENT, AND CST

An additional area in which deeper structural analysis in CST is particularly needed concerns the impact of neoliberal forms of development upon women. CST expresses strong general concern for the rights of women.[29] At the same time, however, detailed attention to

---

27 Ibid., no. 42.

28 Episcopal Commission for Social Affairs, "Ethical Reflections on the Economic Crisis," in *Do Justice*, ed. E. F. Sheridan, 406-407.

29 It is important to note that CST contends that the rights of women must be interpreted in accord with women's "own nature." (GS 60) In particular, women must not be required to neglect their fundamental role as mothers. "The true advancement of women," Pope John Paul II argues, "requires that labor should be structured in such a way that women do not have to pay

the ways in which many women have been structurally discriminated against and disproportionately harmed by development and by neoliberal economic policies is often lacking. More attention, for example, to the ways in which structural adjustment policies have served to increase the workloads of women and have harmed the health and education prospects of women and girls in the Third World would strengthen CST. Discussion of the negative impacts of development upon rural women as highlighted by Vandana Shiva and other grassroots critics would also be a valuable addition to the analysis that CST provides.[30]

Increased participation by women in the process of formulating CST documents is also needed. In the case of papal encyclicals direct input from women has been very minimal, often nonexistent. It is again in the regional and national CST documents that greater attention to issues concerning women can be found. Most noteworthy are the reflections of the Latin American and Asian bishops. The final Puebla document, for example, has an important section devoted

---

for their advancement by abandoning what is specific to them and at the expense of the family, in which women as mothers have an irreplaceable role." (LE 19) While the emphases of CST upon family and upon family-friendly social policies are surely to be commended, the lack of attention in CST to the role of the father in child-raising tasks is at the same time a serious weakness. A more mutualist vision of shared parenthood would serve to strongly enhance CST.

30 See the discussion of the negative impacts of development and SAPs on women in chapters 2 and 5. At the same time, it should be noted that the effects of development on women are somewhat ambiguous. For example, while conventional development policies often serve to undermine women's economic security and lead to increased work burdens, the social disruption caused by development may provide women with opportunities to break out of traditional subordinate roles. New economic opportunities also may become available for some women. This is the case, for example, of jobs in export factories. While the pay in these factories is generally low and the working conditions very poor, these jobs nonetheless often provide women with a degree of independence that they formerly did not possess. What proponents of alternatives to conventional development argue is that there are ways by which the status of women can be improved that need not also involve the many negative features that accompany conventional development approaches.

to a discussion of the marginalization and exploitation of women.[31] Women, the bishops contend,

> have been pushed to the margins of society as the result of cultural atavisms—male predominance, unequal wages, deficient education, etc. This is manifest in their almost total absence from political, economic, and social life. To these are added new forms of marginalization in a hedonistic consumer society, which even go to the extreme of transforming the woman into an object of consumption.[32]

The Latin American bishops speak of women who live in poverty as being "doubly oppressed and marginalized."[33] The Santo Domingo documents emphasize that women "are frequently excluded, their dignity is imperiled, and they are often subject to violence." In response, the bishops call for "a greater solidarity between men and women... [and] the discovery that both find fulfillment in reciprocity."[34] The bishops highlight also the positive role played by women in struggles for social justice.[35]

The Asian bishops similarly reflect upon the violence and inequities that are faced by women, especially poor women. "Many are the injustices heaped upon them," the bishops declare, "because of the traditional societies that discriminate against them and because of the new economic and industrial situations."[36] The Asian bishops, like the Latin American bishops, also stress the positive contributions being made by women to the quest for social change. A further deepening of these reflections on both the problems and contributions of Third World women, particularly in the papal documents, would constitute an important addition to the CST tradition.

CST, MODERNIZATION, AND CULTURAL DIVERSITY

A third area in which CST could be strengthened concerns its views of "modernization." There exist, as we have seen, certain tensions be-

31 See Puebla, no. 834-849.

32 Puebla, no. 834.

33 Ibid., footnote accompanying no. 1135.

34 Santo Domingo, no. 106.

35 Puebla, no. 840.

36 See the section entitled "Laity and the Plight of Asian Women," in FABC, "The Vocation and Mission of the Laity in the Church and in the World of Asia," in *For All the Peoples of Asia*, ed. Rosales and Arevalo, 182-183.

tween CST's affirmation of modernization, which includes an emphasis on highly industrialized modes of production, and the call contained in CST to respect the values of traditional cultures.

In the documents of Pope John XXIII and Vatican II a very optimistic attitude toward "progress" and "development" is evident. Science and technology are viewed as having the potential to play a major role in solving humanity's problems, dependent only upon good will and a concern for the common good. "[A]dvances in science and technology and the prosperity resulting therefrom," states Pope John, "are truly to be counted as good things and regarded as signs of the progress of civilization." (MM 246) Poverty, as we have seen, Pope John traces mainly "to the fact that in these regions modern industrial techniques have only recently been introduced or have made less than satisfactory progress." (MM 68) Calling upon the Third World to abandon their "primitive and obsolete" economic methods (MM 154), Pope John XXIII calls for massive aid to "modernize" these societies. (MM 156, 163-165) Such aid for development the pope praises for "spreading, as it were, a wholesome civilizing influence." (MM 184) Clearly, development for Pope John seems to be largely synonymous with a certain type of westernization of Third World societies. Yet at the same time the pope warns about certain "grave dangers" that exist, particularly the undermining of praiseworthy traditional moral and spiritual values in the developing countries. (MM 176) He warns likewise against the richer nations imposing their "way of life" on the poorer nations. (MM 170)

In the Vatican II document *Gaudium et Spes* there is again a strong emphasis on progress and on development. "Technological progress," the bishops stress, "must be fostered." (GS 64) The bishops suggest that technical, cultural, and financial aid should be given "to nations striving for progress, enabling them to achieve economic growth expeditiously." (GS 86) Yet again there are warnings against destroying valuable aspects of Third World cultures. "Each branch of the human family," the bishops state, "possesses in itself and in its worthier traditions some part of the spiritual treasure entrusted by God to humanity." (GS 86) Nations "must beware of technical solutions...which offer men material advantages while militating against his spiritual nature." (GS 86)

Similar tensions between a highly westernized vision of progress and a call to respect valuable aspects of Third World cultures have continued to characterize more recent CST. Pope John Paul II, for example, highlights the importance of "scientific and technological progress" (SRS 29) and views technology transfer from the First World to the Third World as central to the process of development. He also persists in using the language of "economic backwardness" to describe the Third World. (SRS 12) Yet at the same time John Paul argues that "there must be complete respect for the identity of each people, with its own historical and cultural characteristics." (SRS 33) "Not even the need for development," John Paul states, "can be used for imposing on others one's own way of life." (SRS 32)

These affirmations of scientific/technological "progress" and simultaneous concerns that persons be able to retain cultural identity and preserve valuable cultural traits raise several important questions. First, it could be asked whether the generally positive view of progress and the positive view of the role of western science and technology in contributing to progress is justified. Much could be learned, I believe, from attending to some of the strong critiques presented by Vandana Shiva and other grassroots critics of development as highlighted in Chapter Five. Concerns with regard to the epistemological reductionism and violence inherent in the modern scientific method, the subordination of western science to capitalist interests, and the negative practical consequences that have accompanied attempts to bring westernized forms of progress to the Third World (the undermining of livelihoods of the rural poor, ecological destruction, cultural destruction, negative impacts on women, etc.) seem to have much merit. Even if the critics sometimes choose to focus almost exclusively on the negative and fail to give adequate attention to certain positive aspects of the changes that have taken place (e.g. increased life expectancy, decreased child mortality), the fact remains that there is much of a negative nature that does need to be taken into account.

Secondly, questions need to be raised as to whether it is possible to both adopt western forms of industrialization and modernization and simultaneously to preserve valuable aspects of traditional cultures such as a greater emphasis on community and spirituality as CST suggests. This approach presumes that these highlighted aspects of traditional cultures are easily separable from aspects such as economic organization. It also ignores the extent to which capitalist forms of modernization are in fact highly dependent upon the breakdown of communal social structures and the undermining of non-material values in favor of consumerist values. Those aspects of traditional cultures that CST would hope to preserve are viewed by many proponents of development as major obstacles to economic progress needing to be overcome.

If wholesale adoption of modern, western forms of technology and capitalist forms of economic and social organization are not a constructive approach for Third World nations and cultures to follow, however, what alternatives are possible? As we have seen, critics suggest the need for a selective appropriation of the technologies and values of modernity, emphasizing the importance of creating "alternative forms of modernity" that emerge from a rootedness in rather than a rejection of local cultures. These alternative forms of modernity would appreciate certain insights from modern science, for example, but would seek to do so in ways that avoid the *hubris* and reductionist ways of thinking that commonly have accompanied the application of science to public policy. Other ways of attaining insights into humanity and the rest of nature would continue to be valued. In the technological realm that which is newer, more industrial, or more chemicalized would not necessarily be assumed to be better. Technologies rather would be evaluated for their impacts on nature, labor, community, and culture. This approach both recognizes the inevitability and necessity of change, yet resists simply accepting the types of changes that are currently being promoted by outside forces and local elites pursuing their own political and economic interests.

The Ladakh Project, discussed briefly in Chapter Six, is one example of an organization that is seeking to resist conventional forms of development while working to foster alternatives that integrate the best of traditional culture with a selective appropriation of modern innovations. This organization, which has recently come to play an important role in shaping local governmental policy in the Indian state of Ladakh, endeavors to support technological innovations that are compatible with the positive features of Ladakhi culture. These have included, for example, solar heating and solar cooking to increase community self-reliance and decrease environmental damage, gravity-powered water pumps, improved traditional water mills, micro-hydro systems for domestic lighting, new innovations in organic farming practices, and others. At the same time the Ladakh Project works to educate Ladakhis about the problems of the western model of development, to counteract images from Hollywood movies and advertising, and to instill respect for traditional Ladakhi culture.

With regard to the technological innovations organized by the Ladakh Project, project founder Helena Norberg-Hodge states:

> All of these technological alternatives make sense economically, environmentally, and culturally. By encouraging a more human-scale and decentralized development pattern, they actively support traditional structures rather than destroying them. And they are not 'technologies for the poor,' suited only to the underprivileged. As we do our best to make clear, nonpolluting appropriate technologies based on renewable energy are *not* something second-rate, but highly effective and efficient solutions to the long-term needs of both developed and developing countries.[37]

Within CST there exist a variety of resources for adopting a more critical view toward conventional forms of "modernity" and "progress" and for moving further away from an equation of "development" with westernization. The notion of integral development clearly has strong potential in this regard, even if hitherto it has existed somewhat uneasily alongside affirmations of the need for First World-style industrialization. In his encyclical *Octogesima Adveniens* Pope Paul VI raised some important concerns regarding the notion of progress. Claiming that progress has become "an omnipresent ideology," Pope Paul argues that "a doubt arises today concerning both its value and its result." (OA 41) Pope Paul further warns against "sliding towards a new positivism: universalized technology as the dominant form of activity, as the overwhelming pattern of existence, even as a language, without the question of its meaning being really asked." (OA 29) Pope John Paul II echoes such concerns. While claiming that human technological achievements represent "authentic signs of man's greatness," John Paul argues that "this progress cannot fail to give rise to disquiet on many counts." In particular, he cites a breakdown of morality, lack of solidarity, ongoing exploitation of the poor, the dominance of consumerism, and increasing ecological destruction as evidence that much has gone awry with progress and development as conventionally understood.[38]

---

37 Helena Norberg-Hodge, *Ancient Futures: Learning from Ladakh* (San Francisco: Sierra Club Books, 1991), 173. Emphasis in original.

38 See Pope John Paul II, *Redemptor Hominis*, no. 15-16. With regard to technology, John Paul warns that "in some instances technology can cease to be man's ally and become almost his enemy, as when the mechanization of work 'supplants' him, taking away all personal satisfaction and the incentive to creativity and responsibility, when it deprives many workers of their

This critical analysis of westernized versions of progress has also been pursued in regional and national CST documents. The Latin American bishops, for example, warn of the dangers of "scientism" and "technocracy" and raise critical questions concerning modern views of reason.[39] "Postmodernity," the bishops state, "is the product of the failure of the reductionist pretensions of modern reason. It leads humankind to question some of the gains of modernity, such as trust in unlimited progress."[40] The Latin American bishops highlight many positive features of traditional cultures and are critical of the replacement of these values by problematic cultural features of modernity such as individualism and consumerism. They lament the fact that "values that are part of the rich, age-old tradition of our people are disregarded, marginalized, and even destroyed....Due to dominant influences from abroad or the alienating imitation of imported values and lifestyles, the traditional cultures of our countries have been distorted and attacked." Positively, the bishops highlight "the beginnings of a new valuation of our native cultures" and commend a "growing interest in autochthonous values and in respecting the originality of indigenous cultures and their communities."[41] "The indigenous cultures," the bishops state, "have undeniable values. They are the peoples' treasure. We commit ourselves to looking on them with sympathy and respect and to promoting them."[42]

The Asian bishops similarly raise many critical questions about modernity. "Modernization," the bishops state, "often leads to social and cultural dislocation. Traditional values and attitudes are called into question. Traditional symbols lose their power. The beneficiaries of modernization are too often infected with secularism, materialism and consumerism."[43]

---

previous employment or when, through exalting the machine, it reduces man to the status of its slave." (LE 5)

39 Puebla, no. 315. Also see no. 50.

40 Santo Domingo, no. 252.

41 Puebla, no. 52-53, 19. Such commitments are strongly reaffirmed and expanded upon at Santo Domingo. See, for example, Santo Domingo, no. 243-251. For the bishops' critique of central cultural features of modernity, see Puebla, no. 51-62.

42 Puebla, no. 1164.

43 FABC, "Journeying Together Toward the Third Millennium," 276.

A continued deepening of reflection upon cultural issues, including awareness of the need for the creation of alternative forms of modernity, is crucial to the future of CST. Also crucial is a clearer recognition that the concerns expressed in CST for the preservation of traditional cultural values imply the need for different approaches to industrialization than those that have been pursued in the First World.

CST AND ECOLOGY

Closely related to the topic of modernization and cultural preservation is the issue of ecology. The reflections of CST concerning ecological issues, as in the case of its broader reflections on modernization, contain both significant promise and significant ambiguities. This is yet another area in which CST could be enhanced through dialogue with grassroots critics of development.

The CST documents frequently highlight humanity's calling to have "dominion" over and to "subdue" creation. Pope John XXIII refers to humans as the "lord" of creation, called to rule over all of God's works. (PT 3) *Gaudium et Spes* speaks of humans as having been "appointed by [God] as master of all earthly creatures." (GS 12) "Man," the council states, has "received a mandate to subject to himself the earth and all that it contains." (GS 34) Being created in the image of God, asserts Pope John Paul II, involves in part "the mandate received from [the] creator to subdue, to dominate, the earth." (LE 4) Humans "must cooperate with others so that together all can dominate the earth." (CA 31) "Man," John Paul declares, citing *Gaudium et Spes* (no. 24), "is the only creature on earth that God willed for its own sake." (CA 53)

Along with this recurrent language of mastery and domination, however, CST has become increasingly sensitive to the need for humanity's dominion to be exercised in ways that recognize the importance of environmental factors. Ecological issues first entered CST as an important concern in the 1971 documents *Octogesima Adveniens* and *Justice in the World*. "Man is suddenly becoming aware," states Pope Paul VI in *Octogesima Adveniens*, "that by an ill-considered exploitation of nature he risks destroying it and becoming in his turn the victim of this degradation." (OA 21) *Justice in the World* strongly critiques the ecological impact of the world's richer nations: "[I]rreparable damage would be done to the essential elements of life on earth, such as air and water, if their high rates of consumption and pollution, which are constantly on the increase, were extended to the whole of mankind." (JW 11) The bishops emphasize the need for a simplification of lifestyles by the wealthy:

> It is impossible to see what right the richer nations have to keep up their claim to increase their own material demands, if the consequence is either that others remain in misery or that the danger of destroying the very physical foundations of life on earth is precipitated. Those who are already rich are bound to accept a less material way of life, with less waste, in order to avoid the destruction of the heritage which they are obliged by absolute justice to share with all other members of the human race. (JW 70)

Pope John Paul II further extended these ecological reflections, particularly in his encyclical *Sollicitudo Rei Socialis* and in his 1990 World Day of Peace Message, "The Ecological Crisis: A Common Responsibility." In these documents John Paul emphasizes "the need to respect the integrity and the cycles of nature" (SRS 26) and the importance of taking into account "the nature of each being and its mutual connection in an ordered system."[44] (SRS 34) He addresses the relationship between structural injustice and ecological damage, stressing the need for structural reforms to overcome poverty and the need for lifestyle simplification by the wealthy. (EC 11, 13) John Paul criticizes the "indiscriminate application of advances in science and technology" (EC 6) and argues that a major root of the ecological problem lies in an "unnatural and reductionist vision" according to which "the interests of production prevail over concern for the dignity of workers, while economic interests take priority over the good of individuals and even entire peoples." (EC 7) Such a reductionist vision, rooted in a flawed view of the human person, gives rise to serious ecological crises.

The global CST documents thus show evidence of growing and deepening environmental concern. Particularly valuable, I would argue, is the strong linkage made in CST between issues of ecology and structural injustice, as well as the perception that ecological problems are deeply rooted in a broader reductionist vision (similar to the claims

44 In *Centesimus Annus*, Pope John Paul II states: "Man thinks that he can make arbitrary use of the earth, subjecting it without restraint to his will, as though it did not have its own requisites and a prior God-given purpose.... Instead of carrying out his role as a cooperator with God in the work of creation, man sets himself up in place of God and thus ends up provoking a rebellion on the part of nature, which is more tyrannized than governed by him." (CA 37)

of Vandana Shiva) concerning the human person and nature and an overemphasis on the value of economic growth.

A key weakness of CST is that the papal tradition still provides relatively little recognition of the inherent value of non-human nature. Rather, nature continues to be viewed almost exclusively in instrumental terms. This instrumentality includes dimensions such as the aesthetic value of nature and not only its economic usefulness, but in all cases the value is judged in reference to humanity. The Second Vatican Council's assertion (reaffirmed by John Paul II) that humans are "the only creature on earth that God willed for its own sake" can be seen as particularly problematic. It is an assertion that is in tension with the biblical witness. In the Genesis creation story, for example, each part of creation is declared "good" even before humans are created. Similarly, there are numerous other biblical passages in which God is portrayed as taking delight in creation apart from any reference to humanity.[45] Humans clearly are perceived in the biblical tradition as having a special role within the created world. Such a strong devaluation of the rest of nature as is implied in the Vatican Council's statement, however, is not a necessary corollary of this affirmation of the significance of humanity.

It is again in the regional and national CST documents (e.g. those of the bishops of the United States, the Philippines, and the Asian and Latin American bishops' conferences) that deeper insights can be found. In these documents the links between the lifestyles of the wealthy, structural injustice, and ecological degradation are more deeply explored. Ecological concern is more fully developed as an integral component of the "common good."[46] Strong emphasis is also placed in these documents upon the importance of a more creation-centered spirituality. Creation is understood to have inherent value as a sacrament of divine presence. The Latin American bishops, for example,

45 For good discussions of ecological issues from Christian biblical and theological perspectives, see James Nash, *Loving Nature: Ecological Integrity and Christian Responsibility* (Nashville: Abingdon Press, 1991) and Larry Rasmussen, *Earth Community, Earth Ethics* (Maryknoll, NY: Orbis Books, 1997).

46 See, for example, the reflections by the U.S. bishops on the notion of the "planetary common good." *Renewing the Earth*, 5. Also see the Filipino bishops' pastoral letter *What is Happening to Our Beautiful Land?* This document can be found in *And God Saw That It Was Good*, ed. Christiansen and Grazer, 309-318.

stress the need to "cultivate a spirituality that can recover the sense of God that is ever present in nature." In the mystery of the incarnation, the bishops affirm, "Christ assumed all that is created."[47] The Asian bishops similarly describe creation as "the divine handiwork and the place of divine presence."[48] These documents emphasize that important insights can be learned from indigenous traditions of spirituality. "Believers of all faiths," the Asian bishops declare,

> have an urgent responsibility to open themselves once again to the voice of nature and its mystery, to return to their primordial attachment to and respect for nature, to grow in a creation-centered spirituality. Believers in any place are called to come together in silence and love before creation, to accept the God-given order and harmony of nature, to counteract the forces of exploitation and ruin.[49]

Perhaps the most impassioned CST document on ecology is that of the bishops of the Philippines. In their pastoral letter, "What is Happening to Our Beautiful Land?," the Filipino bishops highlight the urgency of ecological issues in their society. Their statement is worth quoting at length, both for its own sake and because similar conditions characterize many Third World countries:

> To put it simply: our country is in peril. All the living systems on land and in the seas around us are being ruthlessly exploited. The damage to date is extensive and, sad to say, is often irreversible. One does not need to be an expert to see what is happening and to be profoundly troubled by it. Within a few short years brown, eroded hills have replaced luxuriant forests in many parts of the country. We see dried up river beds where, not so long ago, streams flowed throughout the year. Farmers tell us that, because of erosion and chemical poisoning, the yield from the croplands has fallen substantially. Fishermen and experts on marine life have a similar message....The picture which is emerging in every province of the country is clear and bleak. The attack on the natural world which benefits very few Filipinos is rapidly whittling away at the very base of our living world and endangering its fruitfulness for future generations....

---

47 Santo Domingo, no. 169.

48 FABC, "Journeying Together Toward the Third Millennium," 278.

49 "Final Statement of the Twelfth Bishops' Institute for Interreligious Affairs on the Theology of Dialogue," in *For All the Peoples of Asia*, ed. Rosales and Arevalo, 331.

> We often use the word progress to describe what has taken place over the past few decades....But can we say that there is real progress? Who has benefited most and who has borne the real costs? The poor are as disadvantaged as ever and the natural world has been grievously wounded. We have stripped it bare, silenced its sounds and banished other creatures from the community of the living. Through our thoughtlessness and greed we have sinned against God and His creation....It is already late in the day and so much damage has been done. No one can pinpoint the precise moment when the damage becomes so irreversible that our living world will collapse. But we are rapidly heading in that direction.[50]

These reflections on current ecological crises, like the reflections on cultural preservation, highlight the need for a vastly different approach to technology and industrialization than that which has been pursued in the First World.[51] The willingness to learn from traditional techniques, particularly in the realm of agriculture, is important, as are new insights from the field of appropriate technology. A variety of concerns – cultural, ecological, and socio-economic – converge in the concept of appropriate technology. While papal documents have not reflected much upon this topic, regional/national CST documents have begun to do so. The Asian Catholic bishops, for example, express the socio-economic concerns well. They highlight the importance of "shaping an appropriate technology that prevents the concentration of power in the hands of a few, and supporting the use of technology in the service of labor and not the reverse. Such a model means developing small-scale technology that workers can own and control, at least as a cooperative."[52] The United States' bishops emphasize especially the ecological aspects of appropriate technology. "[B]y laboring to make human environments compatible with local ecology, by employing appropriate technology, and by carefully evaluating technological

50 Catholic Bishops of the Philippines, "What is Happening to Our Beautiful Land?, 309-310, 313-314.

51 For good discussions of technological choices, see Ian Barbour, *Ethics in an Age of Technology* (San Francisco: Harper San Francisco, 1993); Denis Goulet, *The Uncertain Promise: Value Conflicts in Technology Transfer*, rev. ed. (New York: New Horizons Press, 1989); Langdon Winner, *The Whale and the Reactor: A Search for Limits in an Age of High Technology* (Chicago: University of Chicago Press, 1986).

52 FABC, "The Vocation and Mission of the Laity," 189.

innovations as we adopt them," the bishops assert, "we exhibit respect for creation and reverence for the Creator."[53]

Increased attention to the issues of appropriate technology, to the ecological impacts of capitalism, and to the deeper changes in worldview that grassroots critics of development call for (e.g. an overcoming of "reductionism") would serve to further strengthen the ecological reflections of CST.

CST, GRASSROOTS MOVEMENTS, AND SOCIAL STRUGGLE

A common question that is presented to CST concerns how the CST documents envision the implementation of the reforms that they propose. The dominant approach of CST at the papal/conciliar level has been to appeal to persons in positions of economic and political power to heed the church's call to carry out the needed changes. Relatively little emphasis has been placed on active organization of the poor and on grassroots social struggle as the vehicle for implementing change. While there has been some consideration of the need for social struggle in recent documents of the universal magisterium (especially in *Justice in the World* and in some of the encyclicals of Pope John Paul II), the prevailing emphasis continues to be more on an organic, consensual model of social change.

Numerous critics argue that the relative lack of emphasis on grassroots mobilization has been a major weakness of CST, leaving CST with no viable implementation strategy.[54] These critics stress that issues of economic and political power must be directly confronted. The social forces that oppose the reforms suggested by CST must be clearly identified. At the same time, countervailing social forces must be fostered. Otherwise CST will be left simply making appeals that are destined to go unheeded.

A key point that is stressed by critics is that the universal solidarity that CST calls for requires first a preferential solidarity with the poor and oppressed that will involve social conflict. "Only when the historical conditions of justice have been created," argues Gregory Baum, "can solidarity become universal. Preferential solidarity is a first step

53 U.S. Conference of Catholic Bishops, *Renewing the Earth*, 5. Also see *The Harvest of Justice is Sown in Peace*, 10; Canadian Conference of Catholic Bishops, "Ethical Reflections," 406.

54 Critics who make this claim include persons such as Gregory Baum, Donal Dorr, Mary Hobgood, and Larry Rasmussen.

toward the unfolding of a truly universal solidarity."[55] Denis Goulet makes a similar claim. "Ironically," asserts Goulet, "genuine solidarity can be won only after much conflict, because worldwide community can be established only if the rules presently governing exchange and access to power are totally revised."[56]

Theologian Gregory Baum emphasizes that the forms of social struggle being advocated by liberation-oriented Christians should not be confused with Marxist notions of class struggle. He highlights several key differences:

– Christian struggle does not promote hatred or violence. Although some liberationists accept with regret the legitimacy of recourse to violence in extreme cases, the overwhelming preference of Christians is for nonviolent means of social change that respect the dignity of all persons.

– The goal of Christian liberationists is not class victory but is rather the fostering of solidarity, justice, reconciliation, and the common good.

– Persons of all classes are invited to join in the needed social struggle. Making a commitment to an "option for the poor" is an ethical choice. It is not a commitment that is predetermined by one's social class.[57]

In reflecting upon the topic of social struggle, I would suggest that much can be learned from the philosophy of conflict set forth and embodied by Mohandas Gandhi. In Gandhi's understanding, nonviolent struggle (*satyagraha*) is best conceived not as a struggle against other persons but rather as a way of creatively seeking to transform the complex patterns of relationships in a given situation so that new and more positive patterns can emerge. While injustice is to be resolutely opposed, the struggle is to be carried out in a way that seeks to avoid hatred and vengeance. Those persons undertaking the struggle are also to maintain a certain humility, aware that their own insight into truth is partial and must be open to revision. A good discussion of Gan-

55 Gregory Baum, *Compassion and Solidarity: The Church for Others* (New York: Paulist Press, 1990), 85.

56 Denis Goulet, *The Cruel Choice: A New Concept in the Theory of Development* (New York: Atheneum, 1971), 170.

57 For a more detailed discussion of the differences between a preferential option for the poor and class struggle, see Gregory Baum, *Theology and Society* (New York: Paulist, 1987), 32-47.

dhi's philosophy of conflict can be found in Joan Bondurant's classic work *Conquest of Violence: The Gandhian Philosophy of Conflict.* "The Gandhian contribution, more directly than any other effort in history," asserts Bondurant, "speaks to one of the most fundamental questions of mankind: how can conflict be conducted constructively?"[58] Gandhian ideas have influenced organizations engaged in nonviolent action in many parts of the Third World, including the network of *Servicio Paz y Justicia* groups that have played leading roles in nonviolent struggles against dictatorial governments and oppressive social structures throughout Latin America.[59] CST could learn much concerning the nature and importance of nonviolent struggle through enhanced dialogue with participants in these groups.

The importance of grassroots efforts and the need to understand social struggle as an integral part of the quest for the common good has been recognized in many of the documents of regional and national Catholic bishops' conferences. The Latin American bishops have pioneered such emphases. At the Medellín conference in 1968 the Latin American bishops emphasized the importance of the work of base communities, small farmers' organizations, labor unions, and other grassroots groups in struggling to counteract the forces that support unjust social structures. "[P]easants' and workers' unions," the bishops state, "should acquire sufficient strength and power." "It is necessary," they contend, "that small basic communities be developed in order to establish a balance with minority groups, which are the groups in power....The Church – the People of God – will lend its support to the downtrodden."[60] The bishops highlight in the Medellín documents the importance of "a dynamic action of awakening (*concientizacíon*) and organization of the popular sectors."[61] They commit the church "to encourage and favor the efforts of the people to create and develop

58 Joan Bondurant, *Conquest of Violence: The Gandhian Philosophy of Conflict,* rev. ed. (Berkeley, CA: University of California Press, 1971), xi.

59 For discussions of nonviolent struggles in Latin America, see Stephen Zunes, Lester Kurtz, and Sarah Beth Asher, eds., *Nonviolent Social Movements: A Geographical Perspective* (Malden, MA: Blackwell, 1999), part VI; Gerald Schlabach and Philip McManus, eds., *Relentless Persistence: Nonviolent Action in Latin America* (Philadelphia: New Society Publishers, 1991).

60 "Justice," no. 12, 20.

61 "Peace," no. 18.

their own grassroots organizations for the redress and consolidation of their rights and the search for true justice."[62] At the Latin American bishops' next continent-wide meetings in Puebla, Mexico in 1979 and Santo Domingo, Dominican Republic in 1992 these commitments were broadly reaffirmed.[63] These commitments are also at the heart of a recent 2003 document of the Latin American bishops' conference (CELAM) on globalization. "[W]e cannot," CELAM asserts,

> ignore or fail to recognize the value of the efforts by society's marginalized people to unite, demand their rights and acquire greater power by creating groups that defend these rights....As they prophetically question economic and political power structures, churches, especially the Catholic Church, contribute to this emergence of new civil society groups that confront large economic and political power groups in defense of weaker communities of various types.[64]

The Asian bishops similarly have highlighted the importance of grassroots movements for social change and the call of the church to support them. Among the signs of hope in Asia they include "movements for democracy, participation and human rights," "the women's movement," "ecological movements," "Basic Ecclesial Communities," "neighborhood groups," and similar grassroots organizations.[65] "We value the initiatives," the Asian bishops state, "of people who organize themselves into self-reliant, participative, self-determining peoples' groups. These will enable the poor to become aware of their situation, realize their dignity and their human equality...and give them an instrument with which they can secure what is their due."[66] The Asian bishops acknowledge that the struggle for justice and ecological concern will involve conflict. They assert that this conflict is both necessary and legitimate:

62 Ibid., no. 27.

63 See, for example, Puebla, no. 18, 96; Santo Domingo, no. 174-185.

64 CELAM, *Globalization and New Evangelization*, no. 117.

65 FABC, "Journeying Together Toward the Third Millennium," 277-278.

66 "Final Reflections of the 4th Bishops' Institute for Social Action," in *For All the Peoples of Asia*, ed. Rosales and Arevalo, 212-213. The bishops laud "all sort of initiatives of people, by people, for people. The growth of basic communities is the best illustration of this phenomenon." "Final Statement and Recommendations of the 5th Bishops' Institute for Social Action," in ibid., 219.

> Social action work often faces the reality of conflict. We want to stress two points: conflict is not necessarily violence (which needs another process of discernment), nor is it necessarily opposed to Christian charity. Secondly, conflict is often a necessary means to attain true dialogue with people in authority. The poor do not achieve this until they have shown that they are no longer servile and afraid. Dialogue of this type searches for the common good....[67]

The Asian bishops affirm the importance of endeavoring to maintain ties with and to influence persons in positions of economic and political power–"those [persons] who, being affluent, powerful, or educated, control the decision-making centers of society." The bishops also affirm, however, that the church's calling to foster justice may lead to serious tension with these persons. The option for the poor, the bishops state,

> may mean prophetically denouncing and opposing them [i.e. wealthy and powerful persons] if they refuse to share this concern [for the poor]; and this even at the cost of losing their aid and support. Thus, opting to be with the poor involves risk of conflict with vested interests or 'establishments,' religious, economic, social, political.[68]

"The Church's preferential love for the poor and her duty to raise her prophetic voice," the Asian bishops recently reaffirmed in their 1998 Synod of Bishops, "demand that she actively support and participate in the struggle of the poor for justice."[69]

Among First World bishops' conferences it is the Canadian bishops who have been in the forefront of those recognizing the need for grassroots action on behalf of social change. The Canadian bishops outline a 5-step pastoral methodology for social action. This noteworthy methodology consists of:

> (a) being present with and listening to the experiences of the poor, the marginalized, the oppressed in our society;

---

67 "Final Reflections of the 4th Bishops' Institute for Social Action," 213.

68 "Final Reflections of the 1st Bishops' Institute for Social Action," in *For All the Peoples of Asia*, ed. Rosales and Arevalo, 200.

69 "The Synod's Propositions," in *The Asian Synod: Texts and Commentaries*, ed. Peter Phan (Maryknoll, NY: Orbis, 2002), 159. Also see volumes 2 and 3 of *For All the Peoples of Asia*, which include Federation of Asian Bishops' Conferences documents for the years 1992-2001.

> (b) developing a critical analysis of the economic, political and social structures that cause human suffering;
>
> (c) making judgments in the light of Gospel principles and the social teachings of the Church concerning social values and priorities;
>
> (d) stimulating creative thought and action regarding alternative visions and models for social and economic development; and
>
> (e) *acting in solidarity with popular groups in their struggles* to transform economic, political and social structures that cause social and economic injustices.[70]

The Canadian bishops are well aware that many powerful social forces oppose the types of alternatives and transformations that they propose. "[A]ll too often," the bishops state, "the legitimate struggles of peoples to bring about these necessary changes are impeded by local governments and business elites, as well as by outside intervention of both governments and corporations."[71] The very capacity to envision alternatives is itself hindered by the realities of concentrated economic and social power. "The dominant forces of transnational capital and technology," the bishops lament, "largely dictate what is desirable and feasible, thereby limiting the capacities of nations and peoples to develop viable options. In addition, social imagination is further hampered by the kind of technological rationality that prevails in our culture today."[72]

What is urgently needed, the Canadian bishops suggest, is a broad-based, grassroots movement devoted to the struggle for building a new society based on social and economic justice.[73] Like the Latin American and the Asian bishops, the bishops of Canada acknowledge that concern for justice can give rise to legitimate forms of social conflict. "It

---

70 Canadian Conference of Catholic Bishops, "Ethical Reflections," no. 4. Emphasis added.

71 Bishop G. Emmett Carter, President of the Canadian Conference of Catholic Bishops, "To the Canadian Catholic Organization for Development and Peace," in *Do Justice*, ed. E.F. Sheridan, 324.

72 Canadian Conference of Catholic Bishops, "Ethical Reflections," no. 43.

73 Episcopal Commission for Social Affairs, "Supporting Labour Unions – A Christian Responsibility," in *Do Justice*, ed. E.F. Sheridan, 455. For additional discussions by the Canadian bishops of the importance of grassroots movements and "people power" see especially the following pages in *Do Justice*: 165-167, 175-177, 186-187, 311-312, 317-319.

is even acceptable," the bishops state, "that this new power [possessed by grassroots organizations] can lead to contestation and conflict."[74] The struggle for social justice, the bishops assert, "involves contention, conflict, and suffering....The prize is fullness of life."[75]

The Australian bishops emphasize many of the same themes as the Canadian bishops. They speak with enthusiasm of a "mighty web of action for justice," composed primarily of the activities of a multitude of grassroots organizations throughout the world. "God," the bishops declare, "has chosen the little and excluded ones to play the key role in the drama of humanity and to act as the central agents of the Kingdom."[76] The Australian bishops also acknowledge a role for conflict in the quest for justice, and suggest that even anger has its proper place:

> Appropriate anger, the kind experienced at unfair treatment or in relation to injustice, is not destructive or unchristian. It is an utterly necessary response, as Jesus demonstrates many times in the Gospels....Such anger is an expression of both love and justice, and, when well anchored in both, serves to energise those involved in difficult and prolonged struggles and to guard them against compromises that are not in the long-term interest of justice.[77]

The emphasis on struggle and conflict contained in the Latin American, Asian, Canadian and Australian bishops' documents stands in contrast with the stronger emphasis on consensual change that is present in most of the documents of the United States bishops.[78] In *Economic Justice for All*, for example, the U.S. bishops repeatedly as-

74 Episcopal Commission for Social Action, "Labour Day Message," in ibid., 177.

75 The Canadian Catholic Conference and the Canadian Council of Churches, "To the Special Senate Committee on Poverty," in ibid., 186.

76 Australian Catholic Bishops' Conference, "A New Beginning: Eradicating Poverty in Our World," 68. The bishops highlight the importance of "[t]he breaking through of poor people and the oppressed as visible, active, and organised actors in human history." Ibid., 87.

77 Ibid., 69.

78 A notable exception to the general downplaying of the importance of social struggle in the U.S bishops' documents are the documents issued by the bishops of the Appalachian region, "This Land is Home to Me: A Pastoral Letter on Powerlessness in Appalachia" (1975) and "At Home in the Web of Life: A Pastoral Message on Sustainable Communities" (1995).

sert that the notion of a preferential option for the poor should not be understood in conflictual or adversarial terms. "The 'option for the poor,'" they state, "is not an adversarial slogan that pits one group or class against another." (EJA 88) Elsewhere, they argue again that "this 'option for the poor' does not mean pitting one group against another, but rather, strengthening the whole community by assisting those who are most vulnerable." (Introduction to EJA, 16) The U.S. bishops consequently do not place major emphasis upon the need for grassroots movements committed to social struggle. Instead, they highlight primarily the need for widespread "partnership" and "cooperation" on behalf of the common good, terms which envision a much more harmonious and non-conflictual process of social change.

The papal documents, while recently acknowledging the legitimacy and importance of nonviolent social struggle, also have mainly emphasized a more consensual (and generally top-down) model of change. A more thorough and consistent emphasis on the need for grassroots mobilization and nonviolent social struggle, and a deeper awareness of the powerful forces that oppose social change would strengthen CST. Nonviolent social struggle, while having certain adversarial and conflictual dimensions, is not for this reason opposed to the common good. Rather, nonviolent struggle can and should be viewed as having an indispensable role to play in the quest for the common good. The challenge to Christians is not to avoid struggle and conflict, but instead is to learn how to engage in social struggle in loving and constructive ways.

THE CHURCH AND SOCIAL CHANGE

The preceding discussion of social struggle raises broader theological questions concerning the nature of the church and church-world relations. Some critics of CST claim that the organic social model inherited by the Catholic Church from the medieval period, with its ideal of a harmonious church-state-culture relationship, contrasts sharply with the biblical vision of the community of faith. They suggest too that the rather optimistic view of modern culture present in the documents of Pope John XXIII and in the Vatican II document *Gaudium et Spes* also fails to adequately reflect biblical insights. A more biblically-grounded understanding of church and world, these persons contend, would view Christian communities as generally existing in a state of tension with central aspects of surrounding cultures. Christians are to be salt and light for the world, living by and modeling for the world Gospel values such as nonviolence, servanthood, economic sharing, forgiveness, and commitment to justice. Because these values often contradict dominant cultural values, those Christians who seek to live faithfully can expect to generally be on the margins of society. They will be often misunderstood and even persecuted yet will at the same time contribute to the broader social good through their faithfulness and example.

One's understanding of the social location of the church influences greatly how one views the church as contributing to social change. An organic social model, for example, would emphasize especially the role of the church in educating and forming the consciences of the leaders of society. These leaders in turn are expected to implement the needed social reforms. An understanding of the church that acknowledges the church's more marginal or minority status, however, would envision differently the ways that the church could contribute to social change. An important proponent of the latter position is Christian ethicist John Howard Yoder. Numerous critics of the church-world understandings present in CST, such as Larry Rasmussen (whose views will be discussed below) have drawn upon Yoder's thought. It therefore seems helpful to briefly sketch Yoder's understanding of the relationship between church and society.

For John Yoder, the social mission of the church has three main components – pioneering creativity, direct action on behalf of justice, and prophetic critique.[79] The first and primary social task of the church is that of modeling the values of the Kingdom of God. Relying on God's grace, the church seeks to incarnate Gospel values in its own life and thereby to be "salt" and "light" for the world. Yoder especially highlights the call of the Christian community to develop and embody creative social alternatives: "It is the nature of the love of God not to let itself be limited by models or options or opportunities which are offered to it by a situation....Jesus would ask, 'How in this situation will the life-giving power of the Spirit reach beyond available models and options to do a new thing whose very newness will be a witness to divine presence?'"[80] Often this example of pioneering creativity on

79 This "three-fold social mission of the church" is my own summary/interpretation of Yoder's reflections as expressed in his books and articles.

80 John Howard Yoder, *The Original Revolution* (Scottdale, PA: Herald Press, 1972), 50. For Yoder's discussion of the modeling mission of the

the part of the church will provide inspiration for subsequent public policies or actions by other social groups.

In addition to pioneering creativity, Yoder highlights the importance of direct action in pursuit of social justice – "the creative construction of loving, nonviolent ways to undermine unjust institutions and to build healthy ones."[81] This can take various forms, including activities such as lobbying as well as grassroots activism and mobilization. Closely connected with this is the third primary social mission of the church, that of prophetic critique, the willingness to "speak truth to power" publicly and boldly when harm is being caused.[82]

A fundamental component of Yoder's social thought is his questioning of the assumption that the primary persons shaping history are those at the top of the social ladder.[83] In the political realm, for example, Yoder argues that leaders are generally constrained from doing significant good by the many deals and compromises that they have had to make to attain and retain their current status. The ruler, Yoder asserts, "is not at the place in society where the greatest contribution can be made."[84]

Yoder argues that the margins of society are in fact the locus of creativity and the site of authentic, constructive social change. "The marginal," Yoder asserts, "is not irrelevant. The creativity provoked or

---

church, see *Body Politics: Five Practices of the Christian Community Before the Watching World* (Nashville: Discipleship Resources Press, 1992). Also see the essays "Firstfruits: The Paradigmatic Public Role of God's People" and "The New Humanity as Pulpit and Paradigm," both in *For the Nations: Essays Public and Evangelical* (Grand Rapids: Eerdmans, 1997); "The Kingdom As Social Ethic," in *The Priestly Kingdom: Social Ethics as Gospel* (Notre Dame: University of Notre Dame Press, 1984).

81 John Howard Yoder, *The Royal Priesthood* (Grand Rapids: Eerdmans, 1994), 212-213.

82 "[T]he Christian community," Yoder argues, " is not only a model as community; it is a pastoral and prophetic resource to the person with responsibilities of office, precisely in order to keep the office from becoming autonomous as a source of moral guidance." *Royal Priesthood*, 186.

83 Yoder rejects "the assumption that historical movement is mostly the work of powerful people." "Ethics and Eschatology," *Ex Auditu: An International Journal of Theological Interpretation of Scripture* 6 (1990): 125.

84 Yoder, *Original Revolution*, 177-178. "There are," Yoder suggests, "other more useful ways to contribute to the course of society than attempting to rule." Ibid., 170.

enabled by that marginality is more relevant than is trying to fix the system on its own terms. It is on the margins that the search for alternatives prospers."[85] Yoder in his writings highlights the many ways that active, prophetic minorities have contributed throughout history to social change. These include initiatives such as the movement to abolish slavery, the civil rights movement, the labor movement, and the movement for women's rights.[86] In these cases it was grassroots action arising from the margins that reshaped the social and political context so that structural and legal reforms became possible that otherwise would have been impossible. "Progress in history," Yoder contends, "is borne by the underdogs."[87] A central social role of the church is to act in nonviolent solidarity with the underdogs and through its creative and prophetic actions to contribute to the broader social good.

Larry Rasmussen presents an analysis of the nature and role of the church very similar to that of John Yoder. Rasmussen examines and critiques CST in light of that vision. With regard to the major emphasis of the U.S. Catholic bishops upon non-confrontational attempts to foster cooperation on behalf of the common good, for example, Rasmussen asserts: "Both on theological grounds–the understanding of church–and on strategic ones...it is doubtful [that] the bishops should favor a church/world model that prefers partnership with power."[88] Efforts to effect change *primarily* by working within the prevailing options of given systems and by appeal to ruling elites, Rasmussen suggests, both undercuts the radicality of the Gospel and, pragmatically, will likely have a less constructive impact than would an approach based on seeking to demonstrate and promote more creative, far-reaching alternatives. "Concrete public witness, rather than efforts at moral consensus and reformist measures within established systems,"

85 John Howard Yoder, "Politics: Liberating Images of Christ," in *Imaging Christ: Politics, Art, Spirituality*, ed. Francis Eigo (Villanova, PA: Villanova University Press, 1991), 161.

86 See Yoder's essays "The Kingdom as Social Ethic," in *Priestly Kingdom;* "Christ, the Hope of the World," in *Royal Priesthood;* "The New Humanity as Pulpit and Paradigm, in *For the Nations*.

87 Yoder, *Royal Priesthood*, 137.

88 Larry Rasmussen, "The Morality of Power and the Power of Morality," in *Prophetic Visions and Economic Realities: Protestants, Jews, and Catholics Confront the Bishops' Letter on the Economy*, ed. Charles Strain (Grand Rapids, MI: Eerdmans, 1989), 142.

claims Rasmussen, "is the more catalytic service."[89] Using the language of "pioneering creativity" employed by Yoder, Rasmussen asserts:

> Two parabolic actions are vital: unrelenting criticism and pioneering creativity....Radical criticism would better expose and illumine the world of economic power. Pioneering experimentation would help shape Christian imagination and markedly aid public policy by demonstrating concrete possibilities. Both the wider world and the integrity of faith itself would be served.[90]

SOCIAL CRITICISM AND PIONEERING CREATIVITY:

HOW CHRISTIANS CAN CONSTRUCTIVELY ADDRESS ISSUES OF DEVELOPMENT AND GLOBALIZATION

One essential task of the Christian community with regard to development is to seek to move governmental policies in the direction of the alternatives outlined in the preceding chapter. Even Yoder and Rasmussen, despite their emphasis on avoiding Constantinian forms of "partnership with power," acknowledge an important role for these efforts. Where they and grassroots activists differ from persons holding to a more organic social model is in their understanding of the ways that attempts to influence policy can best be exercised. Yoder would highlight, for example, the priority of building grassroots movements and engaging in various forms of nonviolent action and prophetic critique as ways of seeking to influence policy (though the value of these actions is not limited to this) rather than relying primarily upon appeals to the good will of existing rulers.

Yoder and Rasmussen emphasize strongly that Christian communities must not wait for governments to act. Rather, they should take a leading role in working to establish at the grassroots level the kind of alternatives that they are suggesting that governments implement. Neither Yoder nor Rasmussen explicitly reflects upon what forms such pioneering creativity could take with regard to issues of development and globalization. Various possibilities, however, come to mind, most of which are equally applicable in both First World and Third World settings. A brief discussion of these suggested actions follows, drawn largely from the work of grassroots critics of development. In some cases the suggestions that will be highlighted are already con-

89 Ibid., 143.

90 Ibid., 145.

tained in CST documents. In other cases they provide possibilities for the further strengthening of CST.[91]

EDUCATION

Education on issues of peace, justice, and ecological concern should be an integral part of Christian educational ministries at all levels. This would include, of course, extensive formation in the biblical foundations of these concerns and in the principles of Catholic Social Teaching. It should also include some introduction to social analysis, exploring for example some of the causes of global poverty, hunger, and ecological degradation. One crucial part of this educational task is the provision of alternative sources of information. The major global media, controlled predominantly by large First World corporations, tend naturally to provide a portrait of the world that reflects the interests of these corporations and their advertisers. This is particularly the case with regard to issues such as economic globalization, development, and United States foreign policy.[92] Alternative channels of information are essential for the perspective of the world's poor majorities and grassroots organizations to be heard. Christians can play an important role in this task of information provision both through church-related media and through decisions to support other alternative media sources. Some especially valuable sources of information concerning development and globalization issues include the magazines *Third World Resurgence*, *The Ecologist*, and *Yes! A Journal of Positive Futures*. Good websites include those of the International Forum on Globalization, the Development Group for Alternative Policies, Corporate Watch, Public Citizen's Global Trade Watch, Global Exchange, the Institute for Food and Development Policy, Inter Press Service, Upside-Down World, and Third World Network.

LIFESTYLE CHOICES:

Simplification of lifestyle for wealthy Christians and a search for sufficiency rather than affluence on the part of all Christians has an

---

91 Further discussion of issues related to the implementation of CST can be found in John Sniegocki, "Implementing Catholic Social Teaching," in *Faith in Public Life*, ed. William Collinge, College Theology Society Annual Volume 53 (Maryknoll, NY: Orbis, 2008), 39-61.

92 For good discussions of media issues, see the writings of Robert McChesney, Ben Bagdikian, Noam Chomsky, and Edward Herman.

important role to play in the fostering of alternatives to conventional models of development/globalization. This emphasis on sufficiency would serve to counteract the pervasive idolatry of consumerism and would free time and resources for efforts to meet the basic needs of all. "Simplicity of life, deep faith and unfeigned love for all, especially the poor and outcast," says John Paul II, "are luminous signs of the Gospel in action."[93] Living simply would also play an important role in minimizing ecological harm. "Modern society," John Paul rightly asserts, "will find no solution to the ecological problem unless it takes a serious look at its lifestyle."[94]

Some particularly important lifestyle decisions concern transportation, housing, diet, and discretionary spending.[95] Seeking to minimize fossil fuel usage by using public transportation, bicycling, walking when possible, and using fuel efficient vehicles when driving are some ways of trying to embody concern for God's creation. These are also generally measures that can save money, which can be used to respond to some of our world's pressing needs. Similarly, living close to one's place of employment, living in the smallest size house that reasonably meets one's needs or living in community with others can minimize ecological impact and expenses. Practicing simplicity with regard to discretionary spending also is crucial, freeing up additional money (and possibly time) for constructive purposes.

Dietary choices are an especially important but often overlooked aspect of lifestyle. What we choose to eat has profound impacts on the environment, world hunger, our own health, and the well-being of animals. A recent United Nations study, for example, found that the livestock industry is responsible for the emission of more greenhouse gases than all forms of transportation (airplanes, cars, trucks,

---

93 John Paul II, *Ecclesia in Asia*, no. 34.

94 John Paul II, *The Ecological Crisis: A Common Responsibility*, no. 13.

95 Good books on lifestyle issues include Michael Schut, ed., *Simpler Living, Compassionate Life: A Christian Perspective* (Denver: Living the Good News, 1999); Janet Luhrs, *The Simple Living Guide* (Broadway Books, 1997); Alan Durning, *How Much is Enough? The Consumer Society and the Future of the Earth* (New York: W.W. Norton and Co., 1992); Arthur Simon, *How Much is Enough? Hungering for God in an Affluent Culture* (Grand Rapids, MI: Baker Books, 2003).

etc.) added together.[96] The meat industry is also a major contributor to water pollution, water shortages, deforestation, desertification, soil erosion, and a variety of other ecological problems.[97] In addition, modern methods of factory-farm meat production contribute to world hunger due to their inefficiency. It takes, for example, an average of approximately eight pounds of protein in the form of beans, grains, and other foods fed to animals to produce one pound of meat protein. The remaining 7/8 of the protein and many other nutrients are lost to human consumption. Much land in the Third World is used to grow export crops for First World livestock rather than being used to produce food for local consumption. A choice to become vegetarian or at least significantly reduce meat consumption would not in and of itself eliminate hunger (as issues of economic power and distribution also need to be addressed), but it is one necessary component in ensuring that the resources are available for all to be fed. Adoption of a more plant-based diet would also help to model Christian virtues of nonviolence and respect for creation and would withdraw support from the extremely inhumane practices that characterize modern factory-farm methods of meat production.[98] In making these and other lifestyle changes the aid of a supportive community is very important. The Christian churches should be a major source of "pioneering creativity" in this area.

---

96 United Nations Food and Agriculture Organization (FAO), Livestock's Long Shadow: Environmental Issues and Options (Rome: FAO, 2006); Dan Brook, "Another Inconvenient Truth: Meat is a Global Warming Issue," *E: The Environmental Magazine* 18, no. 4 (July/August 2007), <www.emagazine.com/view/?3312>.

97 Michael Jacobsen, *Six Arguments for a Greener Diet: How a More Plant-Based Diet Can Save Your Health and the Environment* (Washington, DC: Center for Science in the Public Interest, 2006); Jim Motavelli, "So You're an Environmentalist: Why Are You Still Eating Meat?" *E: The Environmental Magazine* 13, no. 1 (January/February 2002), <www.emagazine.com/view/?142>.

98 For good general discussions of vegetarianism and the implications of dietary choices for ecology, world hunger, health, and animals, see John Robbins, *The Food Revolution: How Your Diet Can Help Save Your Life and the World* (Berkeley, CA: Conari Press, 2001); Sally Kneidel and Sara Kate Kneidel, *Veggie Revolution: Smart Choices for a Healthy Body and a Healthy Planet* (Golden, CO: Fulcrum, 2005). Also see the website of the Christian Vegetarian Association at <www.christianveg.org>.

RESPONSIBLE PURCHASING

Through purchasing decisions (as well as investment decisions, to be discussed below) it is possible to seek to counter the forces of enclosure and marginalization that are highlighted by grassroots critics of development. Efforts to support small and medium-sized businesses and farms, locally-owned businesses, worker and consumer-owned cooperatives, fair trade organizations, ecologically sustainable production practices (e.g. organic agriculture) and similar enterprises all can make a valuable contribution to the quest for more just and ecologically sustainable economic alternatives. One especially helpful source of information on responsible purchasing is the website of the organization Coop America.[99]

RESPONSIBLE INVESTMENT

The institutional Roman Catholic church, like other ecclesial bodies and many individual Christians, is heavily invested in the stock of major transnational corporations. A transfer of a significant portion of these ecclesial and individual funds to more socially and ecologically constructive investment alternatives could play a crucial role in serving to foster the kinds of economic alternatives that CST calls for. These investment alternatives could include community development funds, microlending initiatives similar to the Grameen Bank, cooperative lending funds, public sector bonds that are used to fund valuable governmental programs and projects, and various other socially responsible options.[100]

ORGANIZING, ACTIVISM, AND AID PROVISION

Christians can also work for development alternatives by providing monetary donations to grassroots organizations throughout the world and by taking an active role in the formation and ongoing activities of these organizations. As highlighted above, grassroots organizations

---

99 See <www.coopamerica.org>. Excellent resources on this topic and other action ideas can also be found in Ellis Jones, Ross Haenfler, and Brett Johnson, *The Better World Handbook: Small Changes That Make a Big Difference* (Gabriola Island, BC, Canada: New Society Publishers, 2007).

100 For detailed discussion of alternative investment possibilities, see Susan Meeker-Lowry, *Invested in the Common Good* (Philadelphia: New Society Publishers, 1995). Also see <www.communityinvest.org>, <www.cooperativefund.org>, and <www.self-help.org>.

play crucial roles in a vast array of areas including the creation of economic alternatives, human rights, ecology, cultural preservation, and peacemaking.[101] The fostering of base Christian communities with a strong sense of social mission is an especially important way that the church can contribute to the strengthening of grassroots social movements.

DIRECT SERVICE/SOLIDARITY

Another way of contributing to the creation of a better world is through direct service to those in need. Such service can of course take many forms, both domestic and international.[102] This is an area in which many Christian churches have strong traditions. In performing service it is of course crucial to avoid paternalism and to recognize that the persons that one serves have much to share and offer. In reality it is often the persons who are "serving" who are more transformed by the experience than those being "served." Because the term "service" often does bear strong paternalistic connotations, it may be better to speak of experiences of "solidarity" rather than service. The language of solidarity embodies a more mutualist vision and highlights more clearly the recognition of interconnectedness that should characterize these actions. The language of solidarity also highlights the need for attention to issues of structural injustice. It is important not only to

---

101 There are many thousands of grassroots organizations doing inspiring work throughout the world. For a book that highlights a mother-daughter journey to visit some of these groups, see Frances Moore Lappé and Anna Lappé, *Hope's Edge* (New York: Tarcher/Putnam, 2003). Two organizations that provide financial assistance to grassroots efforts include Oxfam America, <www.oxfamamerica.org>, and the Small Planet Fund, <www.smallplanetfund.org>. For links to additional organizations, see <site.xavier.edu/sniegocj/resources.htm>.

102 An excellent resource for Christian faith-based service in the United States and internationally is the Catholic Network of Volunteer Service. CNVS publishes a free directory of service opportunities, with brief descriptions of over 200 faith-based volunteer programs. CNVS also maintains an extensive online volunteer database. See <www.cnvs.org/volunteers/response_directory.php>. An excellent book on international volunteer service is Joseph Collins, Stefano DeZerega, and Zahara Heckscher, *How to Live Your Dream of Volunteering Overseas* (New York: Penguin, 2002). A website connected with the book is <www.volunteeroverseas.org>.

take direct action to meet needs, but also to examine and respond to the structural realities that prevent needs from being met.

RESPONSIBLE PARENTING

One of the most important challenges facing parents is to find ways to encourage and support the moral formation of children. This is a particular challenge for Christian parents since so many of the dominant cultural values, such as consumerism and reliance on violence, tend to run sharply counter to the message of the Gospel. Seeking to model a simple lifestyle, respect for all persons, respect for creation, nonviolent methods of conflict resolution, and a commitment to prayer are a few ways that parents can provide a morally and spiritually enriching context for their children. Finding age-appropriate ways to expose children to realities of justice and injustice and involving children in projects of solidarity also are very important. Numerous helpful resources exist to aid parents in these vital tasks.[103]

APPLYING CST IN THE LIFE OF THE CHURCH

For the Christian community to truly be "leaven," "salt," and "light" for the world it must endeavor to put into practice in its internal life the values that it recommends to the broader society. As the world's Catholic bishops stated in *Justice for the World*, "While the Church is bound to give witness to justice, she recognizes that anyone who ventures to speak to people about justice must first be just in their eyes. Hence we must undertake an examination of the modes of acting and of the possessions and lifestyle found within the Church herself." (JW 40) The resurgence within the Catholic Church in recent years of more top-down, centralized, and secretive ecclesiastical practices, while the church at the same time recommends to the broader world the importance of grassroots participation, dialogue, and human rights, makes ongoing attention to these issues especially urgent. Also urgent, as the bishops highlight, is attention to lifestyles within the church, including those of bishops and other church leaders. These lifestyles need to be evaluated in light of an option for the poor and their ecological impact. There are numerous bishops who have set very inspiring examples of lifestyle simplification, such as Oscar Romero of El Salvador, Dom

103 A few good books include Susan Vogt, *Raising Kids Who Will Make a Difference* (Chicago: Loyola Press, 2002); Jan Johnson, *Growing Compassionate Kids* (Nashville: Upper Room Books, 2001).

Helder Camara of Brazil, and Kenneth Untener and Bernard Topel of the United States. Other church leaders could learn much from their witness. Similarly, there are many other examples of vowed religious and lay people who have taken seriously the Gospel call to simplicity, solidarity with the marginalized, and concern for creation and have allowed their lifestyles to be transformed as a result. It is this lived witness that will have the most catalytic impact on the world.

The examples given in the sections above represent but a few ways that positive contributions can be made to the quest for more just and ecologically sustainable societies. Many other opportunities exist. In this time of profound social, cultural, and ecological crisis throughout the world, the church is called to truly be a light to the nations. Responding to the needs of those who have been marginalized and harmed by conventional models of development and neoliberal globalization is one important way of being faithful to that call.

CONCLUDING REFLECTIONS

This book has explored the impact of conventional approaches to development and economic globalization in the Third World. While the past half century has witnessed certain positive changes, such as increased life expectancy and decreased child mortality, many very serious problems persist and often have been worsening. Widespread poverty and hunger remain, inequality has often increased, processes of enclosure have escalated, traditional cultures are being progressively undermined, consumerism has become the world's dominant religion, and ecological crises abound. New approaches to development are direly needed. The tradition of Catholic Social Teaching since the 1960s has reflected upon the problems of conventional development and has made numerous suggestions concerning alternative approaches. These reflections can make a very important contribution to contemporary development debates, particularly notions such as integral development, the universal purpose of created goods, the recognition of structural injustice, and the call to a preferential option for the poor. At the same time, as we have seen, there are several ways in which the framework for analysis and action provided by CST could be further strengthened. These include a deepened structural analysis of capitalism, increased attention to the impact of development and structural adjustment on women, deepened attention to cultural and ecological issues, and a heightened awareness of the need for grassroots movements as primary agents of social change. Some of these suggested enhancements have begun to be incorporated into CST, particularly at the national and regional levels. More participatory processes of formulating CST, including ongoing dialogue with development critics, could enable the analysis presented in CST to be further enriched. Insightful analysis, however, is of course not sufficient. The primary challenge is to begin to find concrete ways to more fully translate the principles of CST into practice in the lives of Catholic parishes and communities.

THEOLOGICAL EPILOGUE: THE PATH OF DISCIPLESHIP

The need for far-reaching personal and social transformation has been highlighted throughout this work. Changes in worldviews, lifestyles, and economic and social policy have been called for. These changes presuppose spiritual change, *metanoia,* a conversion from self-centeredness to solidarity and communion.

A sober analysis of existing obstacles to change is important. Foremost among these obstacles is the existence of concentrated economic and political power, power that will undoubtedly be deployed in attempts to prevent substantive change. This concentrated power includes the capacity to profoundly shape public opinion and to foster consumption-centered lifestyles, e.g. through control of the media and pervasive advertising. As the Appalachian bishops have stated : "[Capitalism] wants to teach people that happiness is what you buy...and that all of life is one big commodity market. It would be bad enough if the attack only tried to take the land, but it wants the soul, too."[104]

The realization that social change faces major obstacles is not a reason for despair or inaction. The call of the Christian community is to serve as a witness to alternative possibilities, seeking to live by Gospel values even in the midst of unfavorable and discouraging circumstances. It is certainly to be hoped that efforts on behalf of greater justice, solidarity, and ecological responsibility will succeed. Even if they do not, however, it is crucial to recognize that the very efforts themselves have enormous value. They are ways of witnessing to the love of God and to God's desire that justice and communion be present within creation. "Success, as the world determines it," the Catholic Worker movement wisely asserts, "is not the final criterion for judgment. The

104 Catholic Bishops of the Appalachian Region, "This Land is Home to Me," 493-494.

most important thing is the love of Jesus Christ and how to live His truth."[105]

Central to the possibility of Christian faithfulness is a deep rootedness in the practice of spiritual disciplines, the integration of contemplation and action. It is such an integration, for example, that sustained Dorothy Day, co-founder of the Catholic Worker movement, in her many years of faithful service. Numerous spiritual disciplines including daily mass, prayer, and regular silent retreats played central roles in Day's life. Speaking of the importance of the silent retreats, Day states: "It is not only for others that I must have these retreats. It is because I too am hungry and thirsty for the bread of the strong. I too must nourish myself to do the work I have undertaken. I too must drink at these good springs so that I may not be an empty cistern and unable to help others."[106] It is rootedness in these and other spiritual practices that can sustain us and enable us to continue to be faithful even amidst difficult circumstances.

Emphasizing the primacy of faithfulness does not, of course, imply that Christians are to be unconcerned with effectiveness. To stress faithfulness, John Yoder states, "does not mean that we don't care about mechanisms and social analysis, political analysis, and calculation of results." These all are important. Yet, says Yoder, this concern "is held within a wider trust."[107] This wider trust includes faith that through the Risen Christ the vanquishing of sorrow and evil has been assured. Christians are therefore empowered to act in hope and with joy, secure in the knowledge that God's love and mercy will finally prevail. "Hope," Richard Foster states, "has the final word....We [Christians] are to walk cheerfully over the face of the earth, conquering evil with

---

105 Catholic Worker, "The Aims and Means of the Catholic Worker Movement." See <www.catholicworker.org/aimsandmeanstext.cfm?Number=5>.

106 Dorothy Day, *The Long Loneliness* (New York: Harper and Row, 1981), 263. For several good books on spiritual practice and its connections with social and ecological action, see Ruben Habito, *Healing Breath: Zen for Christians and Buddhists in a Wounded World*, rev. ed. (Boston: Wisdom Publications, 2006); John Dear, *Living Peace: A Spirituality of Contemplation and Action* (New York: Doubleday, 2001). Thich Nhat Hanh, *The World We Have: A Buddhist Approach to Peace and Ecology* (Berkeley, CA: Parallax Press, 2008).

107 Yoder, *For the Nations*, 151.

good in the power of the Spirit."[108] Let us open ourselves to this challenging and life-giving task.

108 Richard Foster, *Freedom of Simplicity* (New York: Harper and Row, 1981), 164. Foster's statement echoes the famous saying of George Fox, one of the founders of Quakerism, who asserted that Christians are to "walk cheerfully over the face of the earth answering that of God in everyone."

BIBLIOGRAPHY

Adedji, Abedayo, ed. *Africa within the World: Beyond Dispossession and Dependence*. London: Zed Books, 1993.

Altieri, Miguel. *Genetic Engineering in Agriculture: The Myths, Environmental Risks, and Alternatives*. 2nd ed. Oakland, CA: Food First Books, 2004.

Alvares, Claude. *Science, Development, and Violence: The Revolt Against Modernity*. Oxford: Oxford University Press, 1992.

Amin, Samir. *Maldevelopment: Anatomy of a Global Failure*. London: Zed Books, 1990.

Appelbaum, Richard and William Robinson, eds. *Critical Globalization Studies*. New York: Routledge, 2005.

Athanasiou, Tom. *Divided Planet: The Ecology of Rich and Poor*. Boston: Little, Brown, and Co., 1996.

Baiman, Ron, Heather Bouchey, and Dawn Saunders, eds. *Political Economy and Contemporary Capitalism: Radical Perspectives on Economic Theory and Policy*. Armonk, NY: M.E. Sharpe, 2000.

Bales, Kevin. *Disposable People: New Slavery in the Global Economy*. Rev. ed. Berkeley: University of California Press, 2004.

Barbour, Ian. *Ethics in an Age of Technology*. San Francisco: Harper San Francisco, 1993.

Barone, Charles. *Radical Political Economy: A Concise Introduction*. Armonk, NY: M.E. Sharpe, 2004.

Batliwala, Srilatha and L. David Brown, eds. *Transnational Civil Society: An Introduction* Bloomfield, CT: Kumarian Press, 2006.

Barra, Ximena de la and Richard Dello Buono, *Latin America After the Neoliberal Debacle: Another Region is Possible*. Lanham, MD: Rowman & Littlefield, 2009.

Baum, Gregory, and Robert Ellsberg, eds. *The Logic of Solidarity: Commentaries on Pope John Paul II's Encyclical "On Social Concern."* Maryknoll, NY: Orbis Books, 1990.

Bello, Walden. *Deglobalization: Ideas for a New World Economy*. London: Zed Books, 2002.

———. *Dilemmas of Domination: The Unmaking of the American Empire* (New York: Metropolitan Books, 2005).

———. "The End of the Asian Miracle." *Nation* (January 12/19, 1998): 16-21.

Bello, Walden with Shea Cunningham and Bill Rau. *Dark Victory: The United States, Structural Adjustment, and Global Poverty*. Oakland: Institute for Food and Development Policy, 1994.

Bello, Walden, and Stephanie Rosenfeld. *Dragons in Distress: Asia's Miracle Economies in Crisis*. San Francisco: Institute for Food and Development Policy, 1990.

Black, Jan Knippers. *Inequity in the Global Village: Recycled Rhetoric and Disposable People*. West Hartford, CT: Kumarian Press, 1999.

Blum, William. *Killing Hope: U.S. Military and CIA Interventions Since WWII*. Rev. ed. Monroe, ME: Common Courage Press, 2004.

Bond, George. *Buddhism at Work: Community Development, Social Empowerment, and the Sarvodaya Movement*. Bloomfield, CT: Kumarian Press, 2004.

Bond, Patrick. *Against Global Apartheid: South Africa Meets the World Bank, IMF, and International Finance*. 2nd ed. London: Zed Books, 2003.

———. *Looting Africa: The Economics of Exploitation*. London: Zed Books, 2006.

Bondurant, Joan. *Conquest of Violence: The Gandhian Philosophy of Conflict*. Rev. ed. Berkeley: University of California Press, 1971.

Bowles, Samuel, and Herbert Gintis. *Democracy and Capitalism: Property, Community, and the Contradictions of Modern Social Thought*. New York: Basic Books, 1987.

Boyer, William. *Myth America: Democracy vs. Capitalism*. New York: Apex Press, 2003.

Brackley, Dean. "A Radical Ethos." *Horizons* 24, no. 1 (1997): 7-36.

Brecher, Jeremy, and Tim Costello. *Global Village or Global Pillage: Economic Reconstruction From the Bottom Up*. 2nd ed. Cambridge, MA: South End Press, 1998.

Buckland, Jerry. *Ploughing Up the Farm: Neoliberalism, Modern Technology, and the State of the World's Farmers*. London: Zed Books, 2004.

Buckman, Greg. *Global Trade: Past Mistakes, Future Choices*. London: Zed Books, 2005.

Catholic Bishops of Appalachia. *This Land is Home to Me: A Pastoral Letter on Powerlessness in Appalachia*. Webster Springs, WV: Catholic Committee of Appalachia, 1975.

———. *At Home in the Web of Life: A Pastoral Letter on Sustainable Communities in Appalachia.* Webster Springs, WV: Catholic Committee of Appalachia, 1995.

Catholic Bishops of the Philippines. "What is Happening to Our Beautiful Land?" In '*And God Saw That it Was Good': Catholic Theology and the Environment,* edited by Drew Christiansen and Walter Grazer. Washington, DC: U.S. Catholic Conference, 1996.

Caufield, Catherine. *Masters of Illusion: The World Bank and the Poverty of Nations.* New York: Henry Holt and Co., 1996.

Cavanagh, John and Jerry Mander, eds. *Alternatives to Economic Globalization: Another World is Possible.* 2nd ed. San Francisco: Berrett-Koehler, 2004.

Consejo Episcopal Latinoamericano (CELAM). *Globalization and New Evangelization in Latin America and the Caribbean.* Translated by Walter Blake. Bogota, Colombia: Publicaciones CELAM, 2003.

Chomsky, Noam. *Hegemony or Survival: America's Quest for Global Dominance.* New York: Metropolitan Books, 2003.

Chomsky, Noam, and Edward Herman. *Manufacturing Consent: The Political Economy of the Mass Media.* New York: Pantheon, 2002.

———. *The Washington Connection and Third World Fascism.* Boston: South End Press, 1979.

Christiansen, Drew, and Walter Grazer, eds. *And God Saw That it Was Good: Catholic Theology and the Environment.* Washington, DC: U.S. Catholic Conference, 1996.

Chua, Amy. *World On Fire: How Exporting Free Market Democracy Breeds Ethnic Hatred and Global Instability.* New York: Doubleday, 2003.

Collins, Joseph, Stefano DeZerega, and Zahara Heckscher. *How To Live Your Dream of Volunteering Overseas.* New York: Penguin, 2002.

Coote, Belinda. *The Trade Trap: Poverty and the Global Commodity Markets.* Oxford: Oxfam, 1992.

Cornia, Giovanni Andrea, ed. *Inequality, Growth, and Poverty in An Era of Liberalization and Globalization.* New York: Oxford University Press, 2004.

Davis, Mike. *Planet of Slums.* London: Verso, 2006.

Dear, John. *Living Peace: A Spirituality of Contemplation and Action.* New York: Doubleday, 2001.

Dorr, Donal. *Option for the Poor: A Hundred Years of Vatican Social Teaching.* Maryknoll, NY: Orbis, 1992.

Durning, Alan. "Action at the Grassroots." *Worldwatch Paper 88*. Washington, DC: Worldwatch Institute, 1989.

———. *How Much Is Enough? The Consumer Society and the Future of the Earth*. New York: W.W. Norton, 1992.

Eagleson, John, and Philip Scharper, eds. *Puebla and Beyond: Documentation and Commentary*. Maryknoll, NY: Orbis, 1979.

Eckstein, Susan, ed. *Power and Popular Protest: Latin American Social Movements*. Rev. ed. Berkeley: University of California Press, 2001.

Ecologist, The. *Whose Common Future? Reclaiming the Commons*. Philadelphia: New Society Publishers, 1993.

Edwards, Richard, Michael Reich, and Thomas Weisskopf, eds. *The Capitalist System*. Englewood Cliffs, NJ: Prentice-Hall, 1986.

Ekins, Paul. *A New World Order: Grassroots Movements for Global Change*. New York: Routledge, 1992.

Eitzen, D. Stanley and Kelly Eitzen Smith. *Experiencing Poverty: Voices from the Bottom*. Belmont, CA: Thomson Wadsworth, 2003.

Engler, Mark. *How to Rule the World: The Coming Battle Over the Global Economy*. New York: Nation Books, 2008.

Epstein, Gerald, Julie Graham, and Jessica Nembhard, eds. *Creating a New World Economy*. Philadelphia: Temple University Press, 1993.

Escobar, Arturo. *Encountering Development: The Making and Unmaking of the Third World*. Princeton: Princeton University Press, 1995.

Farmer, Paul. *Pathologies of Power: Health, Human Rights, and the New War on the Poor*. Berkeley: University of California Press, 2003.

Ferguson, James. *Global Shadows: Africa in the Neoliberal World Order*. Durham, NC: Duke University Press, 2006.

Food and Agriculture Organization (FAO). *Livestock's Long Shadow: Environmental Issues and Options*. Rome: FAO, 2006.

Fort, Meredith, Mary Anne Mercer, and Oscar Gish, eds. *Sickness and Wealth: The Corporate Assault on Global Health*. Cambridge, MA: South End Press, 2004.

Foster, John Bellamy. *Ecology against Capitalism*. New York: Monthly Review Press, 2002.

George, Susan. *The Debt Boomerang: How Third World Debt Harms us All*. Boulder: Westview Press, 1992.

———. *A Fate Worse Than Debt: The World Financial Crisis and the Poor*. Rev. Ed. New York: Grove Weidenfeld, 1990.

Glaeser, Bernhard. *Environment, Development, Agriculture*. Armonk, NY: M.E. Sharpe, 1995.

———, ed. *The Green Revolution Revisited: Critique and Alternatives*. London: Allen and Unwin, 1987.

Glennie, Jonathan. *The Trouble With Aid: Why Less Could Mean More for Africa*. London: Zed, 2008.

Goldman, Michael. *Imperial Nature: The World Bank and Struggles for Social Justice in the Age of Globalization*. New Haven, CT: Yale University Press, 2005.

Goulet, Denis. *Development Ethics: A Guide to Theory and Practice*. New York: Apex Press, 1995.

Grandin, Greg. *Empire's Workshop: Latin America, the United States, and the Rise of the New Imperialism*. New York: Metropolitan Books, 2006.

Green, Duncan. *Faces of Latin America*. 3rd ed. New York: Monthly Review Press, 2006.

———. *From Poverty to Power: How Active Citizens and Effective States Can Change the World*. Oxford: Oxfam International, 2008.

———. *Silent Revolution: The Rise and Crisis of Market Economics in Latin America*. 2nd ed. New York; Monthly Review Press, 2003.

Greider, William. *One World, Ready or Not: The Manic Logic of Global Capitalism*. New York: Simon and Schuster, 1997.

Gremillion, Joseph, ed. *The Gospel of Peace and Justice: Catholic Social Teaching Since Pope John*. Maryknoll, NY: Orbis, 1976.

Habito, Ruben. *Healing Breath: Zen for Christians and Buddhists in a Wounded World*. Rev. ed. Boston: Wisdom Publications, 2006.

Hahnel, Robin. *Economic Justice and Democracy*. New York: Routledge, 2005.

Harding, Sandra. *The Science Question in Feminism*. Ithaca, NY: Cornell University Press, 1986.

———. *Whose Science? Whose Knowledge? Thinking From Women's Lives*. Ithaca, NY: Cornell University Press, 1991.

Harris, Richard and Melinda Seid, eds. *Critical Perspectives on Globalization and Neoliberalism in the Developing Countries*. Boston: Brill, 2000.

Harrison, Paul. *Inside the Third World: The Anatomy of Poverty*. 3rd ed. New York: Penguin, 1993.

Harvey, David. *A Brief History of Neoliberalism*. New York: Oxford University Press, 2005.

Hennelly, Alfred, ed. *Santo Domingo and Beyond.* Maryknoll, NY: Orbis, 1993.

Henriot, Peter, and Joe Holland. *Social Analysis: Linking Faith and Justice.* Maryknoll, NY: Orbis, 1993.

Himes, Kenneth, ed. *Modern Catholic Social Teaching: Commentaries and Interpretations.* Washington, DC: Georgetown University Press, 2005.

Ho, Mae-Wan. *Genetic Engineering: Dream or Nightmare?* 2nd ed. New York: Continuum, 2000.

Hobgood, Mary. *Catholic Social Teaching and Economic Theory: Paradigms in Conflict.* Philadelphia: Temple University Press, 1991.

Hossay, Patrick. *Unsustainable: A Primer for Global Environmental and Social Justice.* London: Zed Books, 2006.

Hunt, Diana. *Economic Theories of Development: An Analysis of Competing Paradigms.* Savage, MD: Barnes and Noble, 1989.

Jacobsen, Michael. *Six Arguments for a Greener Diet: How a More Plant-Based Diet Could Save Your Health and the Environment.* Washington, DC: Center for Science in the Public Interest, 2006.

John XXIII, Pope. *Mater et Magistra.* Vatican, 1961.

———. *Pacem in Terris.* Vatican, 1963.

John Paul II, Pope. *Centesimus Annus.* Vatican, 1991.

———. *Laborem Exercens.* Vatican, 1981.

———. *Sollicitudo Rei Socialis.* Vatican, 1987.

Johnston, Josée, Michael Gismondi, and James Goodman, eds. *Nature's Revenge: Reclaiming Sustainability in an Age of Corporate Globalization.* Orchard Park, NY: Broadview Press, 2006.

Jones, Ellis, Ross Haenfler, and Brett Johnson. *The Better World Handbook: Small Changes that Make a Big Difference.* Rev. ed. Gabriola Island, BC: New Society Publishers, 2007.

Khor, Martin. *Rethinking Globalization: Critical Issues and Policy Choices.* London: Zed Books, 2001.

Kim, Jim Yong, Joyce Millen, Alec Irwin, and John Gershman, eds. *Dying for Growth: Economic Inequality and the Health of the Poor.* Monroe, ME: Common Courage Press, 2000.

Kinzer, Stephen. *Overthrow: America's Century of Regime Change from Hawaii to Iraq.* New York: Times Books, 2006.

Kivel, Paul. *You Call This a Democracy? Who Benefits, Who Pays, and Who Really Decides.* New York: Apex Press, 2004.

Kneidel, Sally and Sara Kate Kneidel. *Veggie Revolution: Smart Choices for a Healthy Body and a Healthy Planet*. Golden, CO: Fulcrum, 2005.

Korten, David. *Agenda for a New Economy: From Phantom Wealth to Real Wealth*. San Francisco: Berrett-Koehler, 2009.

———. *When Corporations Rule the World*. 2nd ed. San Francisco: Berrett-Koehler, 2001.

Kovel, Joel. *The Enemy of Nature: The End of Capitalism or the End of the World?* 2nd ed. London: Zed Books, 2007.

Kramer, Mark. *Dispossessed: Life in Our World's Urban Slums*. Maryknoll, NY: Orbis Books, 2006.

Krishna, Anirudh, Morman Uphoff, and Milton Esman, eds. *Reasons for Hope: Instructive Experiences in Rural Development*. West Hartford, CT: Kumarian Press, 1997.

Langer, Erick and Elena Muñoz, eds. *Contemporary Indigenous Movements in Latin America*. Wilmington, DE: SR Books, 2003.

Lappé, Frances Moore and Anna Lappé. *Hope's Edge*. New York: Jeremy P. Tarcher/Putnam, 2002.

Lappé, Frances Moore, Joseph Collins, and Peter Rosset. *World Hunger: Twelve Myths*. Rev. Ed. New York: Grove Press, 1998.

Leo XIII, Pope. *Rerum Novarum*. Vatican, 1891.

Lernoux, Penny. *Cry of the People: United States Involvement in the Rise of Fascism, Torture, and Murder and the Persecution of the Catholic Church in Latin America*. Garden City, NY: Doubleday, 1980.

Lines, Thomas. *Making Poverty: A History*. London: Zed Books, 2008.

Lippit, Victor, ed. *Radical Political Economy: Explorations in Alternative Economic Analysis*. Armonk, NY: M.E. Sharpe, 1996.

MacEwan, Arthur. *Neo-Liberalism or Democracy? Economic Strategy, Markets, and Alternatives for the 21st Century*. London: Zed Books, 1999.

Madeley, John. *Big Business, Poor Peoples: The Impact of Transnational Corporations on the World's Poor*. London: Zed Books, 1999.

———. *Food for All: The Need for a New Agriculture*. London: Zed Books, 2002.

———. *Hungry for Trade: How the Poor Pay for Free Trade*. London: Zed Books, 2000.

———. *A People's World: Alternatives to Economic Globalization*. London: Zed Books, 2003.

Mander, Jerry, and Edward Goldsmith, eds. *The Case Against the Global Economy – And for a Turn to the Local.* San Francisco: Sierra Club Books, 1996.

Marsden, Terry and Nicholas Parrott. *The Real Green Revolution: Organic and Agroecological Farming in the South.* London: Greenpeace Environmental Trust, 2002.

Mayo, Marjorie. *Global Citizens: Social Movements and the Challenge of Globalization.* London: Zed Books, 2005.

McCarthy, George, and Royal Rhodes. *Eclipse of Justice: Ethics, Economics, and the Lost Traditions of American Catholicism.* Maryknoll, NY: Orbis, 1992.

McManus, Philip, and Gerald Schlabach, eds. *Relentless Persistence: Nonviolent Action in Latin America.* Philadelphia: New Society Publishers, 1991.

Merchant, Carolyn. *The Death of Nature: Women, Ecology, and the Scientific Revolution.* New York: Harper and Row, 1980.

Mertes, Tom, ed. *A Movement of Movements: Is Another World Really Possible?* London: Verso, 2004.

Mich, Marvin Krier. *Catholic Social Teaching and Movements.* Mystic, CT: Twenty-Third Publications, 1998.

Millet, Damian and Eric Toussaint. *Who Owes Who? 50 Questions About World Debt.* Translated by Vicki Briault Manus. London: Zed Books, 2004.

Nandy, Ashis. "Cultural Frames for Social Transformation: A Credo." *Alternatives* 12 (1987): 125-152.

------, ed. *Science, Hegemony, and Violence: A Requiem for Modernity.* Tokyo: United Nations University, 1988.

Nelson-Pallmeyer, Jack. *School of Assassins: The Case for Closing the School of the Americas and for Fundamentally Changing U.S. Foreign Policy.* Maryknoll, NY: Orbis Books, 1997.

Nhat Hanh, Thich. *The World We Have: A Buddhist Approach to Peace and Ecology.* Berkeley, CA: Parallax Press, 2008.

Norberg-Hodge, Helena. *Ancient Futures: Learning From Ladakh.* San Francisco: Sierra Club Books, 1991.

Novak, Michael. *The Catholic Ethic and the Spirit of Capitalism.* New York: The Free Press, 1993.

———. *The Spirit of Democratic Capitalism.* New York: American Enterprise Institute, 1982.

O'Brien, David, and Thomas Shannon, eds. *Catholic Social Thought: The Documentary Heritage*. Maryknoll, NY: Orbis, 1992.

O'Connor, Martin, ed. *Is Capitalism Sustainable? Political Economy and the Politics of Ecology*. New York: Guilford Press, 1998.

Oman, Charles, and Ganeshan Wignaraja. *The Postwar Evolution of Development Thinking*. New York: St. Martin's Press, 1991.

Paul VI, Pope. *Octogesima Adveniens*. Vatican, 1971.

———. *Populorum Progressio*. Vatican, 1967.

Parenti, Michael. *Against Empire*. San Francisco: City Lights Books, 1995.

Peet, Richard. *Geography of Power: Making Global Economic Policy*. London: Zed Books, 2007.

Phan, Peter, ed. *The Asian Synod: Texts and Commentaries*. Maryknoll, NY: Orbis Books, 2002.

Pius XI, Pope. *Quadragesimo Anno*. Vatican, 1931.

Potter, George Ann. *Deeper Than Debt: Economic Globalisation and the Poor*. London: Latin American Bureau, 2000.

Pradervand, Pierre. *Listening to Africa: Developing Africa From the Grassroots*. New York: Praeger, 1989.

Queen, Christopher, and Sallie King, eds. *Engaged Buddhism: Buddhist Liberation Movements in Asia*. Albany: SUNY Press, 1996.

Rahnema, Majid, ed. *The Post-Development Reader*. London: Zed Books, 1997.

Rasmussen, Larry. "The Morality of Power and the Power of Morality." In *Prophetic Visions and Economic Realities: Protestants, Jews, and Catholics Confront the Bishops' Letter on the Economy*, edited by Charles Strain. Grand Rapids, MI: Eerdmans, 1989.

———. "The Public Vocation of an Eschatological Community." *Union Seminary Quarterly Review* 42, no. 4 (1988): 25-35.

Rau, Bill. *From Feast to Famine: Official Cures and Grassroots Remedies to Africa's Food Crisis*. London: Zed Books, 1991.

Rich, Bruce. *Mortgaging the Earth: The World Bank, Environmental Impoverishment, and the Crisis of Development*. Boston: Beacon Press, 1994.

Richards, Howard and Joanna Swanger. *The Dilemmas of Social Democracies: Overcoming Obstacles to a More Just World*. Lanham, MD: Lexington Books, 2006.

Riley, Maria, ed. *Trouble and Beauty: Women Encounter Catholic Social Teaching*. Washington, DC: Center of Concern, 1991.

Robbins, John. *The Food Revolution: How Your Diet Can Help Save Your Life and Our World*. Berkeley: Conari Press, 2001.

Romm, Joseph. *Hell and High Water: Global Warming – The Solution and the Politics – and What We Should Do*. New York: William Morrow, 2007.

Rosales, Gaudencio, and C.G. Arévalo, eds. *For All the Peoples of Asia: Federation of Asian Bishops' Conferences Documents From 1970 to 1991*. Maryknoll, NY: Orbis, 1992.

Ross, Andrew. *Low Pay, High Profile: The Global Push for Fair Labor*. New York: New Press, 2004.

Ross, Robert. *Slaves to Fashion: Poverty and Abuse in the New Sweatshops*. Ann Arbor: University of Michigan Press, 2004.

Rosset, Peter. *Food is Different: Why We Must Get the WTO Out of Agriculture*. London: Zed Books, 2006.

Sachs, Jeffrey. *The End of Poverty: Economic Possibilities for Our Time*. New York: Penguin Books, 2005.

Sachs, Wolfgang, ed. *The Development Dictionary: A Guide to Knowledge as Power*. London: Zed Books, 1992.

------, ed. *Global Ecology: Conflicts and Contradictions*. London: Zed Books, 1993.

Sachs, Wolfgang and Tilman Santarius, eds. *Fair Future: Limited Resources and Global Justice*. Translated by Patrick Camiller. London: Zed Books, 2007.

Schrijvers, Joke. *The Violence of 'Development'*. New Delhi: Kali for Women, 1993.

Schuck, Michael. *That They Be One: The Social Teaching of the Papal Encyclicals, 1740-1989*. Washington, DC: Georgetown University Press, 1991.

Schumacher, E.F. *Small is Beautiful: Economics as if People Mattered*. New York: Harper and Row, 1973.

Schut, Michael, ed. *Simpler Living, Compassionate Life: A Christian Perspective*. New York: Living the Good News, 1999.

Schwartz-Nobel, Loretta. *Growing Up Empty: The Hunger Epidemic in America*. New York: HarperCollins, 2002.

Seabrook, Jeremy. *Children of Other Worlds: Exploitation in the Global Market*. London: Pluto Press, 2001.

———. *In the Cities of the South: Scenes From a Developing World*. London: Verso, 1996.

———. *Pioneers of Change: Experiments in Creating a Humane Society*. London: Zed Books, 1993.

———. *Victims of Development: Resistance and Alternatives*. London: Verso, 1993.

Sheridan, E.F., ed. *Do Justice: The Social Teaching of the Canadian Catholic Bishops*. Toronto: Jesuit Centre for Social Faith and Justice, 1987.

Shiva, Vandana. *Biopiracy: The Plunder of Nature and Knowledge*. Boston: South End Press, 1997.

———. *Earth Democracy: Justice, Sustainability, and Peace*. Cambridge, MA: South End Press, 2005.

———. "Let us Survive: Women, Ecology, and Development." In *Women Healing Earth: Third World Women on Ecology, Feminism, and Religion*, edited by Rosemary Radford Ruether. Maryknoll, NY: Orbis, 1996.

———. *Monocultures of the Mind: Biodiversity, Biotechnology, and 'Scientific' Agriculture*. London: Zed Books, 1993.

———. "Reductionist Science as Epistemological Violence." In *Science, Hegemony, and Violence: A Requiem for Modernity*, edited by Ashis Nandy. Tokyo: United Nations University, 1988.

———. *Staying Alive: Women, Ecology, and Development*. London: Zed Books, 1989.

———. *Stolen Harvest: The Hijacking of the World's Food Supply*. Cambridge, MA: South End Press, 2000.

———. "The Violence of Reductionist Science." *Alternatives* 12 (1987): 243-261.

———. *The Violence of the Green Revolution*. London: Zed Books, 1991.

Shiva, Vandana, and Maria Mies. *Ecofeminism*. London: Zed Books, 1993.

Simon, Arthur. *How Much is Enough? Hungering for God in an Affluent Culture*. Grand Rapids, MI: Baker Books, 2003.

Sniegocki, John. "Catholic Social Teaching, Empire, and the Quest for Justice." *Journal for the Study of Peace and Conflict* (2006-2007): 70-81.

———. "Catholic Teaching on War, Peace, and Nonviolence Since Vatican II." In *Vatican II: Forty Years Later*, edited by William Madges. College Theology Society Annual Volume 51. Maryknoll, NY: Orbis Books, 2006. Pp. 224-244.

———. "The Catholic Worker and Socially Engaged Buddhism: A Dialogue." In *Dorothy Day and the Catholic Worker Movement: Centenary Es-*

says, edited by William Thorn, Phillip Runkel, and Susan Mountin (Milwaukee: Marquette University Press, 2001). Pp. 531-549.

———. "Christian Ethics and Global Injustice: The Case of Third World Debt." In *Reframing the Issues: Contemporary Essays in Peace Studies*, edited by Caroline Higgins. Richmond, IN: Earlham Press, 2004. Pp. 163-181.

———. "Creating a New Society: The Catholic Worker and the Community of the Ark." *Contemporary Justice Review* 8, no. 3 (2005): 295-306.

———. "Implementing Catholic Social Teaching." In *Faith in Public Life*, edited by William Collinge. College Theology Society Annual Volume 53. Maryknoll, NY: Orbis Books, 2008. Pp. 39-61.

———. "Neoliberal Globalization: Critiques and Alternatives." *Theological Studies* 69, no. 2 (2008): 321-339.

———. "The Social Ethics of Pope John Paul II: A Critique of Neoconservative Interpretations." *Horizons: The Journal of the College Theology Society* 33, no. 1 (2006): 7-32.

———. "The Social Teaching of Pope Benedict XVI: Clergy, Laity, and the Church's Mission for Justice." In *Catholic Identity and the Laity*, edited by Tim Muldoon. College Theology Society Annual Volume 54. Maryknoll, NY: Orbis Books, 2009. Pp. 120-133.

So, Alvin Y. *Social Change and Development: Modernization, Dependency, and World-Systems Theories*. Newbury Park, CA: Sage, 1990.

Sogge, David. *Give and Take: What's the Matter with Foreign Aid?* London: Zed Books, 2002.

Speth, James Gustave. *The Bridge at the Edge of the World: Capitalism, the Environment, and Crossing from Crisis to Sustainability*. New Haven, CT: Yale, 2008.

Stiglitz, Joseph. *Globalization and its Discontents*. New York: W.W. Norton, 2002.

———. *Making Globalization Work*. New York: W.W. Norton, 2006.

Structural Adjustment Participatory Review International Network (SAPRIN), *Structural Adjustment: The Policy Roots of Economic Crisis, Poverty, and Inequality*. London: Zed Books, 2004.

Synod of Bishops. *Justice in the World*. Vatican, 1971.

Thomas-Slayter, Barbara. *Southern Exposure: International Development and the Global South in the Twenty-First Century*. Bloomfield, CT: Kumarian Press, 2003.

United Nations Childrens Fund (UNICEF). *State of the World's Children.* New York: Oxford University Press. Published annually.

United Nations Development Programme. *Human Development Report.* New York: Oxford University Press. Published annually.

U.S. Catholic Bishops (National Conference of Catholic Bishops). *The Challenge of Peace: God's Promise and Our Response.* Washington, DC: U.S. Catholic Conference, 1983.

———. *Economic Justice for All: A Pastoral Letter on Catholic Social Teaching and the U.S. Economy.* Washington, DC: U.S. Catholic Conference, 1986.

———. *The Harvest of Justice is Sown in Peace.* Washington, DC: U.S. Catholic Conference, 1994.

———. *Renewing the Earth: An Invitation to Reflection and Action on Environment in Light of Catholic Social Teaching.* Washington, DC: U.S. Catholic Conference, 1991.

U.S. Department of Labor. *By the Sweat and Toil of Children.* 6 vol. Washington, DC: U.S. Department of Labor, 1994-2000.

Uvin, Peter. *Aiding Violence: The Development Enterprise in Rwanda.* West Hartford, CT: Kumarian Press, 1998.

Vandermeer, John and Ivette Perfecto. *Breakfast of Biodiversity: The Political Ecology of Rain Forest Destruction.* 2nd ed. Oakland, CA: Food First Books, 2005.

Verhelst, Thierry. *No Life Without Roots: Culture and Development.* London: Zed Books, 1990.

Wallach, Lori and Patrick Woodall. *Whose Trade Organization? A Comprehensive Guide to the WTO.* New York: New Press, 2004.

Wignaraja, Ponna, ed. *New Social Movements in the South: Empowering the People.* London: Zed Books, 1993.

Winner, Langdon. *The Whale and the Reactor: A Search for Limits in an Age of High Technology.* Chicago: University of Chicago Press, 1986.

World Development Movement. *Denying Democracy: How the IMF and World Bank Take Power from People.* London: World Development Movement, 2005.

Yates, Michael. *Naming the System: Inequality and Work in the Global Economy.* New York: Monthly Review Press, 2003.

Yoder, John Howard. *Body Politics: Five Practices of the Christian Community Before the Watching World.* Scottdale, PA: Herald Press, 2001.

———. *For the Nations: Essays Public and Evangelical.* Grand Rapids, MI: Eerdmans, 1997.

———. *The Original Revolution: Essays on Christian Pacifism.* Scottdale, PA: Herald Press, 1972.

———. *The Priestly Kingdom: Social Ethics as Gospel.* Notre Dame: University of Notre Dame Press, 1984.

———. *The Royal Priesthood: Essays Ecclesiological and Ecumenical.* Scottdale, PA: Herald Press, 1994.

Yunker, James. *Economic Justice: The Market Socialist Vision.* Lanham, MD: Rowman & Littlefield, 1997.

Zunes, Stephen. *Tinderbox: U.S. Foreign Policy and the Roots of Terrorism.* Monroe, ME: Common Courage Press, 2003.

INDEX

M

N

O

P

Q

R

S